I0892050

Lincoln Memorial University and the Shaping of Appalachia

Lincoln Memorial University and the Shaping of Appalachia

Earl J. Hess

THE UNIVERSITY OF TENNESSEE PRESS
KNOXVILLE

Copyright © 2011 by The University of Tennessee Press / Knoxville.
All Rights Reserved. Manufactured in the United States of America.
First Edition.

The paper in this book meets the requirements of American National Standards Institute / National Information Standards Organization specification Z39.48-1992 (Permanence of Paper). It contains 30 percent post-consumer waste and is certified by the Forest Stewardship Council.

Library of Congress Cataloging-in-Publication Data

Hess, Earl J.
Lincoln Memorial University and the shaping of Appalachia / Earl J. Hess. — 1st ed.
p. cm.
Includes bibliographical references and index.
ISBN-13: 978-1-57233-752-7 (hardcover: alk. paper)
ISBN-10: 1-57233-752-4 (hardcover: alk. paper)
1. Lincoln Memorial University—History.
2. Education, Higher—Appalachian Region—History.
I. Title.

LD3071.L72.H47 2011
378.768'944
2010045072

For Pratibha and Julie,
with love

Contents

Figures

Maps

Preface

Named as a living memorial to the sixteenth president, Lincoln Memorial University was planted in Cumberland Gap, Tennessee, an isolated, mountainous region. Its founding honored a "commission" Lincoln gave Maj. Gen. Oliver Otis Howard during their last meeting in 1863 to serve the needs of mountaineers who had remained loyal to the Union during the Civil War. The university also was created to serve the needs of Appalachian young people who could not take advantage of educational opportunities elsewhere at the turn of the twentieth century.

These original purposes have shaped much of the history and culture of the university. The money to found it came from outside Appalachia, a region still sunk in poverty and cultural isolation. In short, the idea of a college at Cumberland Gap had to be sold to potential donors in New York, Boston, Chicago, and a variety of smaller cities and towns across the north. The first wind-up in the pitch was Lincoln and the mountain loyalists of the Civil War; the second was to cash in on the current "discovery" of Appalachia as a place set apart, bypassed by modernization, and needing help to enable it to become part of the new America. The founders of the university argued that Appalachians were a worthy target of missionary work, as deserving as the huddled masses of immigrants from eastern Europe flocking to America. In fact, the mountaineers were more deserving than all, in the view of university founders, because they were of "pure" American stock.

An institution founded on an idea, Lincoln Memorial University has remained an independent college dedicated to elevating the condition of Appalachian youth through hard work as well as study. The founders, especially Howard, believed that the most important benefit of a college education was learning self-discipline, American values, and Christian piety. Lincoln Memorial University has been a seeder of change in its region of middle Appalachia, planting the elements of culture to grow in soil considered foreign to modern concepts, practices, and achievements in 1897. But the founders sought to sow a particular kind of seed. The university's effort to uplift mountain youth was an effort to teach them to become good laborers, good Americans, and reliable Christians rather than to produce radical thinkers or creative geniuses. Its mission also was to produce teachers who could expand educational opportunities in the primary and secondary schools of the region, tinged with a heavy dose of the "Lincoln spirit." Uplift involved transformation, because the founders considered many aspects of mountain life to be backward and degraded. They wanted to discard these unproductive elements of Appalachian culture and turn crude mountaineers into something like the kind of person one might have seen on farms, in factories, or on the streets of the Northeast and Midwest.

The history of Lincoln Memorial University is a history of struggle, as it was with most small colleges in the post–Civil War South. As a later president of the institution put it, the university was "sometimes painfully" independent. But that independence has been an important legacy of the school, exemplifying the mission of uplift that drove the university through many decades of trial until, in recent years, it has achieved a level of maturity, growth, and sustainability only dreamed of by those who chartered the institution. The school has endured even though the regional conditions of 1897 have changed dramatically. It has adapted itself to thrive in the twenty-first century. Despite this change, the university has maintained a remarkable faith in its original purpose and celebrates that purpose in its curriculum and in the values with which it approaches the important task of serving its constituents. Lincoln, and the values he represents in American life, have always been an integral part of the university's culture.

This book is not a traditional, internal history of Lincoln Memorial University. It seeks to illuminate a number of themes that distinguish the university's story and connect it to the larger world outside the narrow confines of the campus. The internal history obviously is connected to the external story, but it is not the main focus of this study.

Mountain Loyalists

Among the themes discussed here is that of mountain loyalty to the federal government during the Civil War. Lincoln's injunction to Howard to help the loyalists of Appalachia became a reality over thirty years later and remained a strong theme throughout much of the university's history. It particularly resonated during the era of Howard's involvement with the school, for the general had discovered firsthand how fervently the mountain loyalists displayed their devotion to the federal government and how much they had suffered for that devotion when his command was transferred to East Tennessee late in 1863.

DISADVANTAGED APPALACHIAN YOUTH

Another major theme of this book is Appalachia itself, and Lincoln Memorial University's role within its regional culture. Connecting the Lincoln example to the needs of the regional student population dominated thinking on campus for many decades as college administrators sought to shape Appalachian youth according to role models existing outside the mountains. Appalachia was a region bypassed by modernization, in the view of university founders, and their mission was to lift the people out of their backwardness and into the blessings bestowed by progress.

WORK PROGRAM

The founders hoped to help the backward student population, in part, through a program offering jobs on campus to young men and women of modest means so they could work their way through college. The work program helped to set Lincoln Memorial University apart from many other colleges, for it was carried on more extensively and for a longer time compared to similar programs at the rest of the nation's institutions of higher learning.

RACE

The university was created for a select group of white southerners, descendants of Unionists who played a highly visible role in the turmoil of the Civil War. University founders had no intent to discourage black aspirations; very few African Americans lived in the primary area of recruitment for the university, and state law mandated segregation in Tennessee colleges very soon after the founding. Yet university officials repeatedly explained to many potential donors, who assumed that any college named for the Great Emancipator was a black school, why that was not the case. How they explained it, and how the institution was integrated quietly many decades after its founding, are major themes in this story.

ABRAHAM LINCOLN

The university has made full use of Lincoln as an icon of its mission to uplift regional youth. The imagery of the sixteenth president was a potent weapon in fund raising, represented a glittering ideal in the minds of many students, and served as an example for many people who took the college's mission seriously.

When the university began to collect artifacts and documents associated with Lincoln, it also gained recognition as an important repository of "Lincolniana" within scholarly ranks. Lincoln imagery remains vibrant on the only college campus located in a former Confederate state to bear the Emancipator's name. The university is still a living monument to Lincoln, made so not only by the force of heritage but also by a serious-minded effort to retain the sixteenth president in the institution's mind and heart, not just on its letterhead stationery.

Modernization

Ironically, the university's aim to bring Appalachia out of its premodern stage occurred at a time when the definition of modernity was fast changing. The founders sought to bring mountain youth up to what was beginning to be an old standard by 1897, teaching basic concepts revolving around a good work ethic, consistent morals, and civic responsibility. Early teachers had scant training, often nothing beyond the bachelor's degree level, and taught across the disciplines, acting as house mothers and fathers for boarding students at the same time. By the 1920s, only two decades after the founding, modern standards had far outpaced the conditions at Lincoln Memorial University, forcing school leaders to undertake financially risky efforts to improve conditions in order to attain membership in the Southern Association for accreditation purposes. The stress and strain of doing so created the environment for a massive student strike that tore the campus apart in April 1930. Who had the right to decide what kind of uplift the university had as its goal, and how to achieve it, has always been a strain in the history of the institution.

These six themes serve as consistent strands in the university's story, and they connect its history with that of many other colleges, with the history of the nation from the Civil War to the modern era, and with the history of higher education in Appalachia. They are the backbone of Lincoln Memorial University's past and have had an important effect on its present.

In its origin, its mission, and its people, Lincoln Memorial University has a unique heritage; it is time the story was told to a wider audience than those who have visited the campus or those who have studied and worked there. It is an important story to tell, for it exemplifies many aspects of Appalachian life, southern life, and American life from the turn of the twentieth century to the turn of the new millennium.

Several figures associated with the story of Lincoln Memorial University sought but failed to write its history. Robert L. Kincaid, who graduated from the university in 1915 and went on to serve as a publicist, board member, executive vice president, and president of the institution, wanted to write the history of the university's first fifty years. For many reasons he failed to do so, yet Kincaid wrote the best short history of the university's founding, within a landmark study, *The Wilderness Road,* which he published in 1947. Charles F. Eager, the first financial officer of the university, had intended to write about the institution's founding before he passed away in 1922. Frederick B. Avery, one of the original founders, began to write a history of "the organization and progress of the University" in 1934, but he never completed the task. As a result, the first and only history of the school was Joseph Suppiger's *Phoenix of the Mountains: The Story of Lincoln Memorial University,* initially published in 1977. Written under the auspices of the university and published by the university, it takes the reader, with updated editions, to the start of the twenty-first century. Suppiger's is an internal, institutional history of the school, designed to tell its story in a relatively short, popular narrative.[1]

This book is different from Suppiger's earlier history in many ways, and I think it is different from many other institutional histories. It is based on wide-ranging research in a variety of archives across the country. Detailed information about fund-raising efforts can be found in the archives of the Carnegie Corporation of New York at Columbia University and in the Rockefeller Family Archives at Rockefeller University. The Benjamin Newton Duke Papers at Duke University, and the Henry Ford and Ford Family Papers at Dearborn, Michigan, also reveal a great deal about fund raising for the university. Oliver Otis Howard's important collection of personal papers is at Bowdoin College. Lincoln Memorial University's historic relationship with other colleges and universities is revealed in the archival holdings of Berea College and the University of Tennessee.

The bulk of vital information on the student strike of 1930 can be found only in archives. The American Association of University Professors Records at George Washington University is the repository of documents telling the story from the viewpoint of the strikers and affected faculty members, while the Frank A. Seiberling Papers at the Ohio Historical Society tell the story from the viewpoint of the administration. This complex, difficult subject cannot be understood without reference to a combined total of fifteen hundred pages of documents in both collections that bear on the strike.

Nevertheless, the primary source of information for this study remains the University Archives at Lincoln Memorial University. It is a rich collection, essentially complete for the time period from the school's founding in 1897 to the 1970s. The holdings drop off in that decade and plummet to almost nothing by the 1990s, rendering it difficult to obtain a deep, behind-the-scenes understanding of university history for the past forty years.

My association with Lincoln Memorial University as a professor of history has extended for more than twenty years. I occupy an endowed chair created by Ann McClelland Ropkey, whose marriage to university president Stewart W. McClelland in 1947 created something of a scandal on campus due to the difference in their ages and McCelland's sudden divorce of his first wife. McClelland, however, was a significant president in the long sweep of university history, as the pages of this book demonstrate. Like McClelland, I have seen Lincoln Memorial University go through bad as well as good times, and I have always been impressed by the ability of students, faculty, staff, and administrators to endure. The bedrock of what happens at the university is teaching and shaping lives; most people keep their focus on those basic, all-important goals regardless of the problems that typically affect independent colleges in a comparatively poor region.

Despite my long association with the university, this book is not an official history. It was important to me that it be a work of independent scholarship, allowing me the freedom to say what the sources seem to indicate ought to be said about the university's history. The evaluations and scholarly opinions expressed herein are solely my own.

A word or two about the university's location is in order. Because of the rural, relatively undeveloped nature of the region in 1897, the "nearest town" to Lincoln Memorial University tended to shift with time. The university began as an offshoot of the Harrow School in the village of Cumberland Gap. College classes started in late 1899 two miles away on the site of the demolished Four Seasons Hotel, partly within the boundary line of Harrogate, but Harrogate was a town in name rather than reality for some time to come. As a result, most people continued to refer to Cumberland Gap as the location of the new school well into the 1920s, even though some began to use Harrogate as the reference point as early as 1917. The decade of the 1930s saw the shift in focus to Harrogate, which ever since has been the "home town" of Lincoln Memorial University.

I owe a debt of gratitude to several helpful people, including archivist Michelle Ganz, for assiduously ferreting out sources and providing numerous scans of illustrations. Bobby Harber helped to make available the interesting diary and reminiscences of Opal Ann (McDowell) Surber, and Mrs. Surber graciously allowed me to use this material about the student strike. James W. Schenkenfelder did yeoman's work in conducting research on the strike in area newspapers, as well as on John Wesley Hill, the results of which he has made available to all who are interested. Kay Davis was instrumental in obtaining many remote sources through interlibrary loan, while Misty Alvaro did wonderful research for this project at the Ohio Historical Society. I am grateful to all archivists and librarians at the institutions listed in the bibliography but must specially thank Jennifer King at Special Collections, Georgetown University, and Kenneth Rose at the Rockefeller Archive Center, Rockefeller University, for their extra measure of aid in obtaining essential archival sources for this study. Lothair Vanoverbeke of Moorsele, Belgium, generously provided information on Pat Williams and his own efforts to memorialize Williams's death during World War II. Among the faculty and staff at Lincoln Memorial University, I owe thanks to Helen Bailey, Regina Burns, Carol Campbell, Charles Hubbard, Elizabeth Lamont, Bill Porter, Larry Thacker, and Michael Toomey. I also was pleased to make contact with Nancy Banks, daughter of Clay McCarroll, leader of the student strike of 1930. Thanks also to Scot Danforth, director of the University of Tennessee Press, for supporting publication of this book, and to Stan Ivester, managing editor of the press, for shepherding the project through production. I also wish to thank the freelance copyeditor, Karin Kaufman, and freelance cartographer Bill Nelson for their help.

Finally, my gratitude to my wife, Pratibha, for her love and support.

Chapter 1
A Larger Enterprise

They are loyal there, General; they are loyal.
—Abraham Lincoln, September 26, 1863

After enjoying lunch, four men moved onto the porch of the Harrow School in Cumberland Gap on June 18, 1896, to have a talk. Oliver Otis Howard had given a lecture on "Grant at Chattanooga" to the assembled students and faculty of the preparatory school that morning. He was visiting Cumberland Gap at the invitation of Arthur A. Myers, founder and director of the Harrow School, while on his way to Chattanooga. Howard's friend, Darwin R. James, accompanied the general and shared his deep interest in educating the mountaineers of southern Appalachia. The last of the quartet who assembled on the porch also shared that interest. Rev. Frederick B. Avery, like James, was a member of the Berea College Board of Trustees; he also knew that Myers had an ulterior motive in inviting Howard to the school.

Myers's agenda became clear during the course of the conversation on that porch. He wanted to enlarge the institution at Cumberland Gap, which already included 250 students in the primary and secondary grades since its establishment six years earlier. Myers hoped to create a university for these students and other young people in the region. He had his eye on nearby property but needed money, and he was aware of Howard's record as a supporter of education for African Americans and poor southern whites. Myers hoped to enlist the retired general in the effort to raise funds for his enterprise and pitched his best plea with Howard's stomach full, resting on a comfortable chair and under the shade of the wide, covered verandah.[1]

Two men who were not on the porch that day also played a role, either as active participant in what was to come or as a symbol of the new enterprise. Cyrus Kehr, a patent lawyer who lived in suburban Chicago, had already confided to Howard his idea that a university ought to be established to honor Abraham Lincoln. Kehr believed this would serve as a more fitting monument to the sixteenth president than any statue. Howard fully understood the president's concern for the welfare of those mountaineers who had remained loyal to the Union cause despite persecution at the hands of Confederate sympathizers. Howard also knew that several schools and colleges already existed with Lincoln's name, but he apparently had not yet thought of creating an institution to honor the president's memory.[2]

Kehr did not participate in the conversation on the Harrow School porch, but Howard carried the lawyer's idea in the back of his mind. The general also had his own, personal memories of Lincoln. The idea of a university near Cumberland Gap had its origins in many factors among several men; those factors came together that afternoon to inspire Howard to support a college named for Lincoln, serving the descendants of loyalists who had stood by the Union during the war, which had ended barely thirty years earlier.[3]

Abraham Lincoln

Lincoln had never visited the Cumberland Gap region or set foot on Tennessee soil. His grandfather and namesake moved a wife and five children from Virginia to Kentucky about 1782, probably along Daniel Boone's Wilderness Trace, which brought two hundred thousand other migrants through Cumberland Gap and to the fertile lands west of the mountains.[4]

The Civil War fixed the southern mountaineers firmly in Lincoln's mind. The majority of residents in East Tennessee retained their loyalty to the United States government, and they often resented the economic, political, and cultural dominance that wealthy plantation owners wielded in southern life. As a result, East Tennessee voted against secession on two occasions and petitioned Nashville for permission to separate from the rest of the state when the ordinance of secession was approved. Some residents of the eastern counties, mostly living in areas linked to the Deep South by railroads, supported Confederate hopes for independence. Claiborne County, the location of Cumberland Gap, had no railroad link with any region. Fewer than 25 percent of the voters in this rural, sparsely populated county supported ratification of the secession ordinance on June 8, 1861, even though several prominent area families actively aided the Rebel cause.[5]

The Confederate government reacted harshly when a group of East Tennessee loyalists burned several bridges along the railroad that connected Knoxville with Virginia and Georgia, a major link between the eastern and western parts of the Confederacy, in November 1861. Repression and military occupation followed, which led thousands of loyalists to abandon their homes and flee to

Union-held Kentucky or hide out in isolated mountain hollows. Effective lobbying by prominent East Tennesseans, such as Parson William G. Brownlow and U.S. Congressman Horace Maynard, brought the plight of these loyalists to the attention of all northerners. Andrew Johnson, who served as military governor of the state as soon as Federal troops entered Nashville, vehemently pushed for the redemption of his homeland in the mountains. "The oppressions & inhumanity daily inflicted are indescribable & must be redressed," Johnson wrote the president.[6]

Lincoln became desperate to help the mountaineers. He urged military commanders to restore United States authority by sending troops into East Tennessee. While every general understood the human dimension of this problem and sympathized with the loyalists, they also understood the difficulties of supplying large numbers of troops along the mountain roads that led to Knoxville. In a military sense, the true line of Union advance lay not through East Tennessee but along the rail lines linking Louisville with Nashville and Chattanooga, and the generals had to give priority to this route. "But my distress," Lincoln pleaded with them, "is that our friends in East Tennessee are being hanged and driven to despair."[7]

Not until the summer of 1863 did Federal commanders find enough troops to send a column into the heart of East Tennessee. They controlled the region around Knoxville for the rest of the war, giving the loyalists an opportunity to dominate the state government in Nashville for years to come. But the Civil War devastated East Tennessee. Average wealth dropped by more than a third in many counties, and blood feuds spurred killings for years to come. One of the few African Americans living near Cumberland Gap was murdered by a gang of white men late in the war years, and the perpetrators apparently were never brought to justice. Poverty and lingering bitterness were the chief legacies of the war for loyalists and their counterparts alike.[8]

Oliver Otis Howard

Oliver Otis Howard, a man of deep convictions, was nearing the end of a lifetime of service to his country, his religious beliefs, and several disadvantaged segments of the American people when he came to Cumberland Gap in 1896. Born on November 8, 1830, near Leeds, Maine, he attained a good education at Bowdoin College and intended "to excel as a literary man or in a profession." But Howard took advantage of an opportunity to enter West Point, a decision he recalled as "a turning point" in his life. He graduated in 1854 and married early the next year. Howard saw service at various posts before transfer to West Point as an instructor of mathematics. By 1860, with three children to care for, Howard's religious beliefs had become so strong that he contemplated resigning from the army and becoming an Episcopalian minister.[9]

Howard's mother had fostered his deep interest in religion, and nature endowed him with an impulsive, stubborn streak. While walking to school one cold winter morning, his friend dared him to slide across a ditch filled with frozen water. "As quick as thought I sprang forward and started to slide," he recalled. The ice broke and young "Ote," as he was called, sank to his neck. He made his way out and walked to school with clothes frozen to his body. "Indeed," Howard concluded, "all my life it has been hard for me to resist a challenge."[10]

Oliver Otis Howard in 1894, the year he retired from the army and two years before the meeting at Harrow School that resulted in the creation of Lincoln Memorial University. Oliver Otis Howard Papers, ALLM-LMU.

An activist spirit, allied with a self-assured judgment of right and wrong, shaped the contours of Howard's life. He adhered to the new Republican Party when it was created to oppose the spread of slavery in the western territories. Howard became aware of Lincoln's championship of the Republican cause by reading newspaper accounts of the Illinois lawyer's debates with Stephen Douglas in 1858.[11]

At the outbreak of the war, Howard became colonel of the Third Maine Infantry and took his regiment to Washington, D.C., camping at Meridian Hill, only a mile and a half from the White House. Lincoln often came out to see the troops drill. Howard tried to restrict liquor and swearing, urging his men to attend religious services. Many of the troops did not take well to him. One recruit thought the colonel "talked down to us . . . with the tone and manner of an itinerant preacher." Yet Howard viewed his role as that of a father to his men.[12]

Howard's first meeting with Lincoln was brief. The president called the colonel to his carriage one day during a review at Meridian Hill. Howard was nervous, but Lincoln put him at ease by saying, "I have enjoyed very much looking at your show, Colonel Howard." A serious illness, possibly cholera, afflicted Howard in late June, and he lay unconscious for a few days. Howard later discovered that Lincoln had visited his tent to inquire about him. The president's youngest son Tad told the guard at Howard's tent that his father feared for the colonel's life.[13]

Not long after recovering, Howard was part of a group of officers who met Lincoln at the White House. During the discussion, he made a suggestion that Secretary of State William H. Seward treated in a way that made Howard feel "very small and very young." Lincoln "looked at me with a curious smile, and greeted me, as I remember, with both hands extended. Whatever he did or said I do not distinctly recall, but I do remember that my heart went out to him with that loyalty and affection that made me his personal defender and friend from that day on." After participating in the first battle of Bull Run and subsequent promotion to brigadier general, Howard rebuked a group of spectators watching a review of the troops because of their ungenerous remarks about Lincoln's gangly appearance as the president rode a horse too small for his stature.[14]

Howard suffered the loss of his right arm because of a wound received at the battle of Fair Oaks on June 1, 1862. After only two months of recovery, he was back on duty commanding a division at Antietam. Howard vividly recalled Lincoln's visit to the Army of the Potomac at Harpers Ferry following the battle. Dispensing droll jokes, the president "humorously, and with seldom a smile on his sad face," made the rounds of various commands. Howard's division participated in costly attacks against the stone wall at the foot of Marye's Heights during the battle of Fredericksburg in December 1862, and he replaced a German American commander at the head of the mostly German Eleventh Corps four months later. Again Lincoln visited the army and spent some time at Howard's headquarters.[15]

The cordial relationship between the president and the young corps commander was tested in the wake of Union defeat at Chancellorsville. Howard's command held the right of Maj. Gen. Joseph Hooker's Army of the Potomac, but Hooker assumed that Gen. Robert E. Lee's Army of Northern Virginia was in retreat and Howard paid less attention than he should have to protecting his flank. Stonewall Jackson led a large proportion of Lee's available troops in a daring attack that rolled up Howard's command on the evening of May 2, 1863. Even though the Eleventh Corps regrouped and stopped the Confederate advance, Hooker never recovered the initiative and Chancellorsville resulted in a shocking defeat that depressed Union morale. Howard spent the rest of his life arguing that he had done all that was reasonable, but newspaper reports and private opinion continued to denigrate the Germans and their leader for losing the battle. Hooker asked Howard to visit Washington and smooth official feelings, and he met Lincoln on May 20. There was little need to worry, for Lincoln gave the young general another chance. Howard later heard that the president had said, "He is a good man. Let him alone; in time he will bring things straight." These words heartened Howard. "I reverenced him greatly," he wrote of his feelings for the president. "I loved him."[16]

As the superior officer on the field at Gettysburg, Howard took charge of the First and Eleventh Corps of the Army of the Potomac for a few hours on July 1, 1863. Although both corps suffered a severe defeat that day, he played a role in establishing a good defensive position south of town, which the army held firmly on July 2 and 3. Howard briefly met Lincoln on August 29, 1863, when the president advised him to return to duty in the field even though there was little prospect of immediate action in Virginia.[17]

Howard met Lincoln for the last time before moving his corps to Tennessee to relieve the Union army in Chattanooga following its defeat at Chickamauga. He visited the White House for two hours on September 26, longer than any previous meeting with the president. Lincoln spoke in a kind, familiar tone to his young protégé, offering information about the military situation and the mood of the people in East Tennessee. Guiding Howard to "a kind of music stand" with maps, Lincoln showed him one made by the U.S. Coast Survey that well depicted the region around Chattanooga. As Howard recalled the incident, the president pointed to Cumberland Gap and asked him if he could march his corps through it and on to Knoxville to secure the region. He then said, "with a singularly intense expression of face: 'They are loyal there, General; they are loyal.'" Lincoln then gave Howard the map because it had a secure backing well suited for use in the field and he had a duplicate copy of it on the stand. They parted with words that Howard always felt denoted a fatherly feeling on the part of the president toward him, but they never saw each other again.[18]

When Howard's command reached Bridgeport, Alabama, he caught his first glimpse of Appalachian life. "How poor and how ignorant all the people are," he scribbled in his notebook. The Eleventh Corps was not heavily engaged in the battle of Chattanooga in late November but participated in the march to lift the siege of Knoxville right after the engagement. Howard was amazed at the unselfish loyalty to the flag exhibited among civilians. "Women and children brought food and water" to the passing Federals, "and men took off their shoes to give them to the soldiers who had none." He now understood what Lincoln had meant by his impassioned statement during their last meeting.[19]

The Chattanooga campaign also gave Howard an opportunity to work with Maj. Gen. William T. Sherman, his most important patron during the latter years of the war. He became an instant friend and admirer of Sherman even though the older man's forceful personality was quite different from his own. Sherman admired Howard's dedication to duty and came to count on him to accomplish difficult tasks with minimal risk to his command. The successful relief of Knoxville sealed the mutual confidence and respect each man felt toward the other.[20]

Sherman put Howard in charge of the Fourth Corps of the Army of the Cumberland when the Eleventh Corps was merged into the Twentieth Corps under Hooker. Howard performed well during the Atlanta campaign as Sherman led an army group into Georgia, fighting and maneuvering the Confederates out of several fortified positions. The Confederates launched an attack that took the Army of the Tennessee by surprise on July 22 and resulted in the death of Maj. Gen. James B. McPherson, its commander. Everyone was surprised when Sherman named the outsider, Howard, as McPherson's successor. Maj. Gen. John A. Logan, who had led the army for the remainder of the battle on July 22, was deeply hurt, and Joseph Hooker, who ranked all of Sherman's subordinates, resigned because he had been bypassed for the command.[21]

Sherman justified his decision by portraying Howard as "a Christian, elegant gentleman, and conscientious soldier," a "man of mind and intellect." He admired Howard's strong religious feeling even if he did not share it to the same degree, and he was impressed that Howard continued to perform heavy duty in the field despite the loss of an arm. Moreover, Sherman needed someone with administrative ability to take care of his old command, the Department and Army of the Tennessee.[22]

Howard worked hard to prove himself. He conducted the battle of Ezra Church on July 28, 1864, with caution and skill, preparing for the Confederate attack just in time. Howard's men inflicted heavy losses while suffering comparatively few casualties of their own. Ezra Church set the pace for Howard's tenure as commander of the army; well-planned, cautious advances, winning positions with minimal loss of life, and working diligently to turn Sherman's plans into reality. Howard played a large role in the final battle of the Atlanta campaign, fought near Jonesboro in late August and early September, which led to the capture of the city and a major boost in Lincoln's flagging prospects for reelection to the presidency that fall.[23]

Howard commanded the Army of the Tennessee for the remainder of the war, conducting its march through Georgia in late 1864 and through the Carolinas in early 1865. His abilities as an army administrator were proven in campaigns in which planning, marching, and logistics counted for more than inspirational fighting. Howard remembered that Sherman "generously gave both confidence and scope to his officers," and this was exactly what he needed to mature as a commander.[24]

Howard always tried "to soften the asperities of war," as he put it. He attempted to curb excessive pillaging by his troops, reduce swearing in the ranks, and avoid fighting on Sundays. As Sherman once said, "Howard runs the religion of this army."[25]

"I cannot get over the effects of the death of Mr. Lincoln," Howard wrote home a few days after the president died from an assassin's bullet on April 15, 1865. He had "the same complete confidence in Mr. Lincoln that I would in my own father . . . knowing that he would sustain me in every right course." Before his death, Lincoln had expressed "a decided wish" that Howard become commissioner of the newly created Bureau of Refugees, Freedmen, and Abandoned Lands, designed to aid former slaves in their transition to freedom. When the thirty-four-year-old general received the news from Secretary of War Edwin M. Stanton on May 11, 1865, he accepted the appointment knowing the many problems involved in the job. "I hardly know whether to congratulate you or not," Sherman wrote him upon hearing the news, but, he continued, "I cannot imagine that matters that involve the future of 4,000,000 souls could be put in more charitable and more conscientious hands."[26]

With painfully inadequate funds, sometimes open hostility from President Andrew Johnson and many members of Congress, and growing resistance from white southerners, Howard struggled for nine years to offer a variety of aid to meet the many problems faced by black Americans. He succeeded fully in none of his endeavors, but he softened the transition to some degree. Howard relied heavily on army officers he had known during the war to act as his subordinates in the southern states. His views on African Americans were more advanced than most of his countrymen. He sought to encourage the distribution of white-owned land to blacks, an effort Johnson stopped, and appeared at times to advocate the social equality of the races. Picking his way through political minefields, he achieved some success in creating a bit of social justice for the disadvantaged.[27]

The Freedmen's Bureau made more progress in education than in other areas. Howard believed that formal training was the key to advancement for blacks as well as poor whites. He funneled bureau funds to many schools and was instrumental in founding Howard University in Washington, D.C. Chartered in 1867 as a college for African Americans, Howard initially refused when his cofounders insisted the university be named for him. He served as its president from 1867 to 1873. Many other black schools, including Lincoln University in Pennsylvania, Lincoln Institute in Missouri, Wayland Seminary in Washington, D.C., and Hampton Normal and Agricultural Institute in Virginia, received bureau funds. Howard encouraged "men and women who love to do good and repair some of the ills of our past national and social crimes" to support black institutions.[28]

Howard also supported schools that admitted the children of white loyalists in Appalachia. A New York philanthropist named Christopher R. Robert established such a school on Lookout Mountain at Chattanooga in 1866, and Howard offered Freedmen's Bureau money and interceded with Grant to publicize its efforts. He supported Berea College in Kentucky, which encouraged biracial education. In his 1907 autobiography Howard proudly listed twenty-six schools he had supported as commissioner of the Freedmen's Bureau and in later years.[29]

In his educational efforts for whites as well as blacks, Howard stressed "practical arts" rather than "theoretical knowledge." He liked the term "industrial" better than "manual" to describe what he had in mind, for it "embodies hands, feet, brains, and souls." Howard believed in moral education, or "instruction in the principles of honor," and was convinced that strong primary and secondary schools fostered the creation of colleges and universities.[30]

Howard's stewardship of the Freedmen's Bureau made him a visible political target. In order to embarrass President Grant's Republican administration, congressional Democrats instituted a House investigation of his activities in 1870. The report cleared Howard of personal wrongdoing, but the army conducted a court of inquiry into financial irregularities four years later. Grant appointed Sherman to head the inquiry, which concluded that Howard had no personal involvement in the mismanagement of funds. But the negative publicity created an impression that Howard was a poor administrator. Sherman privately tried to prevent Howard's appointment as West Point superintendent in 1880 because of this impression, and Joseph Hooker sarcastically told a newspaper reporter that if Howard "was not born in petticoats he ought to have been, and ought to wear them. . . . He could command a prayer meeting with a good deal more ability than he would an army." Howard, who had to endure a few private lawsuits as well, "gladly left Washington" when the bureau was discontinued in 1874.[31]

Two years before leaving Washington, Howard had accepted Grant's request to serve as a personal intermediary to negotiate peace with Cochise in Arizona. He impressed the Chiricahua Apache leader with his courage by entering Cochise's territory unarmed and without military escort. Howard took command of the Department of the Columbia at Portland, Oregon, in 1874; three years later, he was one of the major commanders in the Nez Perce War, accepting Chief Joseph's surrender just short of the Canadian border.[32]

Howard penned his first postwar recollection of the Great Emancipator in a short letter he wrote to Lincoln collector Osborn H. Oldroyd in 1882. He also remained a warm friend of Sherman. "In the past *you* have been very kind to me and mine," he wrote him in 1884. The Howard family sent birthday greetings to Sherman nearly every year, and when the hero of Atlanta died in 1891, Howard and former Maj. Gen. Henry W. Slocum took charge of the funeral arrangements.[33]

Not long after moving to Portland, in 1876, Howard began writing short pieces about his Civil War experiences for publication in newspapers and magazines. Soon after, he also began to deliver them in public lectures. The general became a popular speaker and devoted most of his time to lecturing after mandatory retirement from the army in 1894. His son Harry Stinson Howard, named for a beloved staff officer who eventually died of a wound received during the Atlanta campaign, served as his secretary, managing his speaking schedule and handling correspondence. "Grant and His Generals" was Howard's best lecture, filled with stories of personal interactions with the Union hero. He also sought to foster sectional reconciliation in his public appearances. The "intention in all my efforts is not to anger and separate, but to pacify and unite," he wrote in his autobiography.[34]

Howard's speaking career brought him to Cumberland Gap in 1896. When Myers learned from fellow missionary R. D. Hill of Williamsburg, Kentucky, that the general planned to travel through the region, he wrote to Harry and invited him to stop at the Gap. "We could rally a crowd and would do all we could to compensate him for the service," Myers assured him. Howard asked his son to make the arrangements and telegraph him the details, suggesting he give "Grant at Chattanooga" and share half the net proceeds with the Harrow School. Harry finalized the date as June 18, which forced Howard to cancel a visit to Williamsburg. Harry reminded his father that he was scheduled to meet the New York Commission on Monuments atop Lookout Mountain on June 20 to discuss placing a memorial to New York soldiers who fought there in 1863. Myers was very happy, assuring Harry that his wife and colleagues would "do our best and advertise at once thoroughly."[35]

Howard earned as much as $125 delivering lectures during his June speaking tour in 1896. To make room for Cumberland Gap in his schedule, he cancelled not only his visit to Williamsburg, Kentucky, but also his planned attendance at a convention in St. Louis. Howard's talk to the Harrow School people, plus interested citizens of the area, netted the general and Myers fifty-two dollars each.[36]

Darwin R. James

Darwin Rush James accompanied Howard on the June trip. Born in Massachusetts, the descendant of a family that moved to the Massachusetts Bay Colony in 1638, James amassed his wealth in the import business and became active in Republican causes in New York. He served in Congress in the early 1880s and became a trustee of Berea College in 1893.[37]

Arthur A. Myers

The man who brought Howard to Cumberland Gap had a long history of pioneering missionary work in Appalachia. Born on December 23, 1838, in Perry County, Pennsylvania, Myers's original name was Aaron Arthur, but he preferred Arthur Aaron. The family moved to LaSalle County, Illinois, in 1850. His Catholic father disinherited Myers because he converted to a Protestant faith, and the young man left the family home at age seventeen. While three of his brothers served in the Union army, Myers entered Hillsdale College in Michigan, in 1861, graduating and marrying Ellen M. Green, who had completed a short course of study there, in 1865. Born January 10, 1843, in Cherry Valley, Ohio, Ellen was a fit companion for Myers, who worked as a minister at Hillsdale for many years.[38]

Ellen and Arthur A. Myers, a short while before Howard's visit to Cumberland Gap. UA-LMU.

The revivals Myers orchestrated brought him to the attention of the faculty at Berea College, who invited him to engage in missionary work in southern Appalachia. He and Ellen arrived in November 1877 and created an impressive record. After several months of hard work organizing churches in the Kentucky mountains, the leaders of Berea College persuaded the American Missionary Association to offer Myers a salary to replace the fee they paid him for his work. The association continued to fund Myers's efforts for twenty-two years.[39]

Arthur and Ellen were Congregationalists, but their missionary efforts were nondenominational. They created an impression on residents of the Williamsburg area after moving there in 1881. Myers's nephew recalled his uncle as "a traveling evangelist" who "was a powerful preacher and really knew the Bible." He used a hand organ to accompany his services. Myers liked to boast that no weather conditions could stop his travels and that he never used an umbrella or a lantern. "There never was but *one* Reverant A. A. Myers," wrote an admirer. According to reports, a saloon keeper shot Myers from ambush because the minister worked strenuously for temperance. Myers carried the bullet in his body for the rest of his life. He reportedly founded forty-four churches and academies during the course of his thirty-three-year ministry to the mountains, most of them with Ellen's help, and served on the Berea College Board of Trustees from 1886 to 1892.[40]

Myers and his wife were part of a large movement to redeem mountain culture, which developed from about 1870 to the turn of the twentieth century. Many northerners "discovered" Appalachian as a region set apart, a peculiar place bypassed by modern development. Isolated by the mountains, Appalachians seemed a fit people for saving. They had to be integrated into the mainstream of American life to create a greater degree of unity and coherence in the modernization of the country. Religion was as good a place to start as any. Protestant missionaries such as Myers and his wife came south with the assumption that they understood Appalachian life and knew what needed to be done to make it better. They rarely took into account the views of the natives, unless those views coincided with their own, and they brought a zealotry to their work that brooked no opposition.[41]

More than most other observers, the missionaries viewed Appalachia as a cultural challenge to a modernizing America. The new president of Berea College, William Goodell Frost, played a pivotal role in bringing this new attitude to the consciousness of the nation after 1892. In fact, Frost coined the term "Appalachia" and helped fix America's gaze on the southern mountains as a problem waiting for the right kind of people who could solve it.[42]

Ellen Myers was shocked by many aspects of Appalachian life. In a talk she gave at the Woman's Meeting of the American Missionary Association in Brooklyn in 1883, she argued that poor whites in the mountains were as needy as blacks, Native Americans, and Chinese. But she found most white residents in the Kentucky hills to be "unstable, thriftless, improvident, and ignorant." Their housing was poor, their farming techniques outdated, their material possessions worn out, and their general health very low. "Morality and sobriety are hardly looked for, even among church members and ministers," while "Anti-Missionary Baptists" wasted hours in superficial discussions over Bible passages. "They do all they can to prejudice the people against our work," Ellen complained. "They call our religion railroad religion" because modern conveyances imported it from outside the mountains.[43]

The Myers worked furiously to reverse these conditions. Arthur preached 142 sermons in twelve months, attended more than fifty religious meetings conducted by other preachers, built a church, and tried to create a high school for local children. "We never worked harder and saw less result in the conversion of sinners than while in Kentucky," Ellen admitted, "and yet never felt more satisfied that we were where God wants us, and doing an important work. Unless these people have help they will prove a fretting leprosy in our nation," she warned her audience. Ellen placed her hope in members of the younger generation. "If it were not for them, we could not feel it right to stay among them."[44]

Cumberland Gap

Arthur and Ellen Myers moved to Cumberland Gap to participate in the explosive growth of that region by 1890. The gap was famous in the annals of late-eighteenth-century westward migration, but most migrants had bypassed the rugged terrain in the area, making it a large region of sparsely populated, undeveloped terrain. The gap was a deep cleavage in Cumberland Mountain, a high ridge that stretched for some forty miles from Virginia into Tennessee and soared about one thousand feet above the surrounding countryside. Two bowl-like depressions lay on each side of the gap, a small one on the Tennessee side

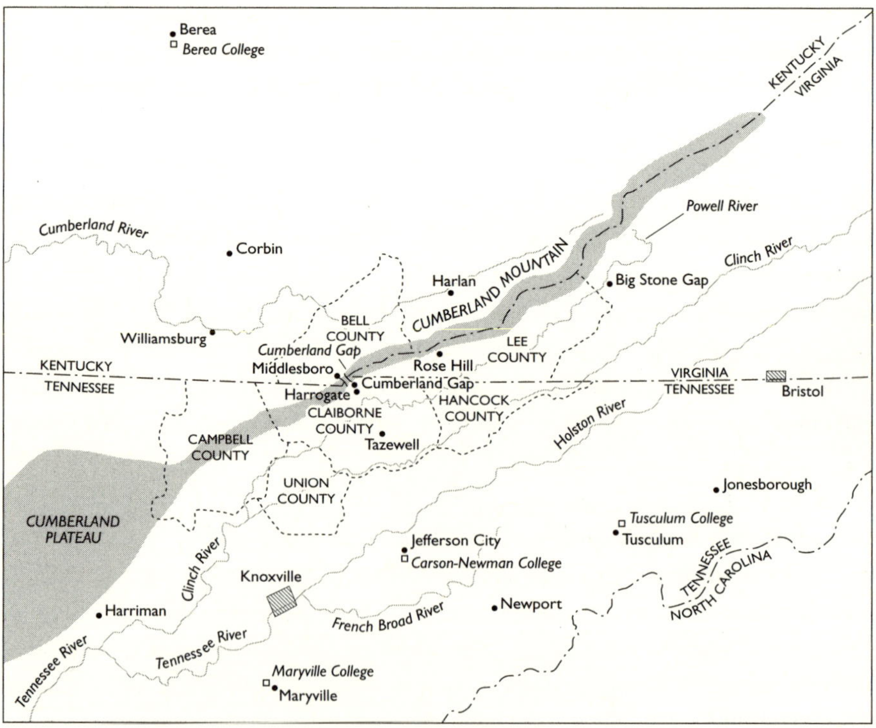

Tri-state area.

and a much larger one on the Kentucky side. The three state lines met on top of the mountain immediately south of the gap.[45]

The gap was heavily fortified when Federal troops held it from June to September 1862, and then again from September 1863 until the end of the war. After 1865 the lack of a railroad doomed the area to rural poverty until interest in its iron ore and coal deposits developed in the 1870s. Moreover, travel writers who rode through the region wrote popular articles about its natural beauty and industrial potential. Alexander Alan Arthur, a Scotsman who worked for timber interests in East Tennessee, was captivated by the area and spearheaded a transformation of the historic but isolated place. He enlisted the financial support of English investors and operated the American Association for them, purchasing thousands of acres around the gap, promoting the construction of a railroad linking it with North and South by 1889, and planting a new city in the large bowl on the Kentucky side of the gap to be called Middlesborough. Arthur, styled the "Duke of the Cumberlands," lived in the town he created, which was often called the Magic City. The village of Cumberland Gap grew up in the smaller bowl on the Tennessee side of the gap, while suburban communities with English names like Harrogate were also planted on the Tennessee side of the looming mountain.[46]

For three years, Middlesborough was an Appalachian version of a western boom town. Its explosive growth—five thousand people lived there only weeks after the first lot was sold in 1889—attracted investors who paid phenomenal sums to the American Association for land and lots. Three major fires, in April, May, and June 1890, failed to curtail the boom, until a worldwide depression, which began in England, dried up investment money and shook the confidence of Americans interested in the town. By 1893, when the depression hit the United States, all major businesses in Middlesborough had closed down, land values had dropped, and the Magic City had almost become a ghost town. Arthur lost his job with the American Association, which declared bankruptcy in 1893 only to reorganize in stable form the next year and continue to control most of the land in the area. Middlesborough survived the bust, recovering on the strength of the local coal industry, but the town officially dropped the "ugh" at the end of its name, becoming Middlesboro.[47]

The Four Seasons

Arthur and other entrepreneurs had not neglected the development of the Tennessee side of the mountain, and many of their properties became available at bargain prices after the bust. This offered Myers an opportunity to purchase

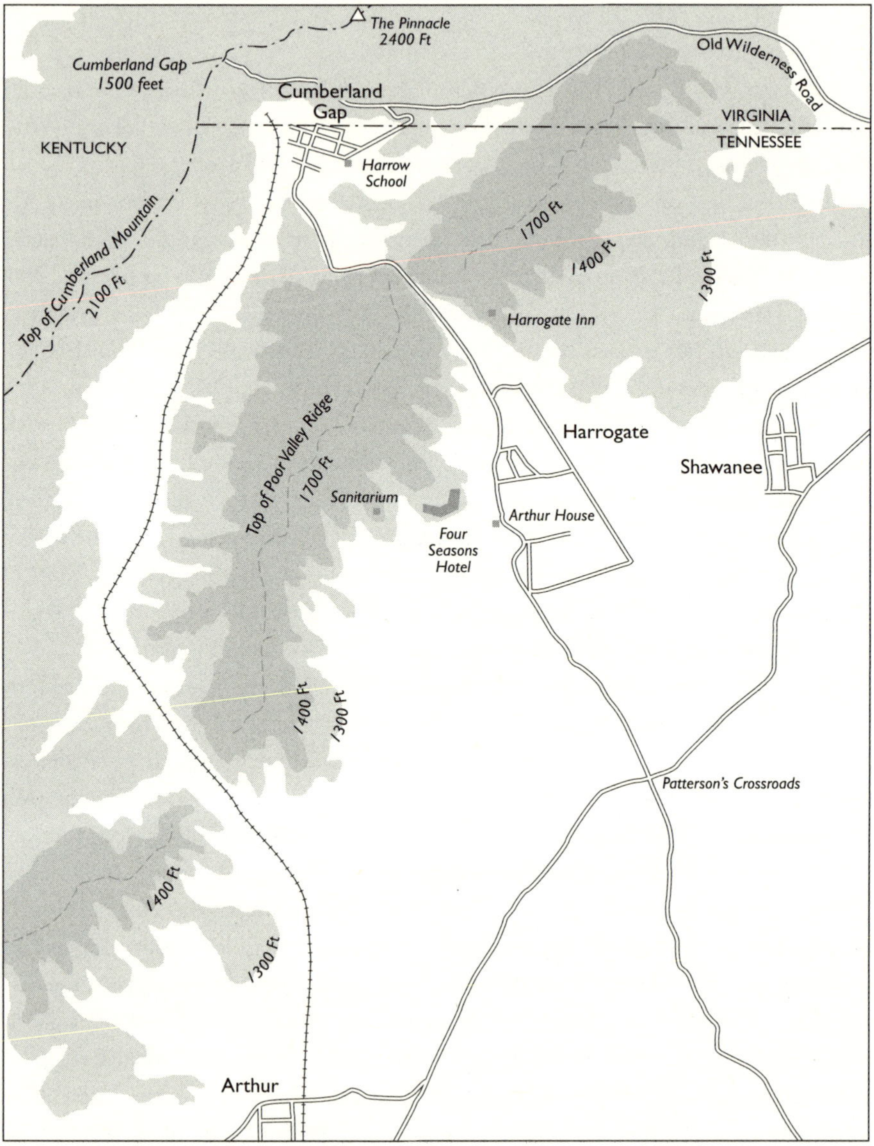

Cumberland Gap and vicinity, 1896.

Exterior of Four Seasons Hotel, 1892. Alexander A. Arthur Family Papers, UA-LMU.

land for his university, but only if he could find the right supporter. Arthur had built an ornate home in Harrogate, about two miles from the gap, where he lived much of the rest of his life. A northern investor named F. Randolph Curtis built Harrogate Inn on a southern spur of Poor Valley Ridge, a spiky line of hills that shadowed Cumberland Mountain on the Tennessee and Virginia side, separating the bowl from Harrogate. In 1890, the year Arthur and Ellen Myers came to Cumberland Gap, Arthur broached the idea of building a health resort to Dr. Allan McLane Hamilton (a specialist in nervous disorders and a grandson of Alexander Hamilton) and Dr. Holbrook Curtis (brother of F. Randolph Curtis). They raised more than one and a half million dollars, mostly from New York investors, and constructed a resort hotel called the Four Seasons on a hill just southeast of Poor Valley Ridge and adjacent to Harrogate. It was the centerpiece of an ambitious development named Cumberland Gap Park.[48]

The hotel site had once been part of the landholdings of Daniel Huff, who had owned forty slaves before the Civil War broke out. Huff constructed his house on a knoll about two miles south of Cumberland Gap. He died as the result of a buggy accident while descending Cumberland Mountain after dining with friends in the Confederate army at the gap in the fall of 1861. His house was caught in the crossfire during a skirmish when the Confederates recaptured Cumberland Gap in September 1862. Much of Huff's land later became part of

Interior of Four Seasons Hotel, 1892. Four Seasons Hotel Papers, UA-LMU.

Lincoln Memorial University's campus, as did that of James M. Patterson about a mile farther south. Originally from Pennsylvania, Patterson owned twenty-two slaves in 1860. His eldest son, Capt. Robert F. Patterson of Company C, Twenty-ninth Tennessee, had invited Huff to dine at the gap on the day of his death. Arthur built his private home, called Craig Neuk, on the site of Huff's house by 1892.[49]

The Four Seasons was a lavish building designed for wealthy visitors who wished to enjoy the comparatively mild summers of the mountains. Constructed of limestone and wood, with an outer coating of stucco, the hotel had three wings that crowned the flattened top of the hill, facing east, southeast, and northeast. It had seven hundred rooms arranged in four stories, with a tower 125 feet tall. The expansive grounds included driveways, six hundred acres of land, and a stable large enough for fifty horses. The owners spent thirty-five thousand dollars to purchase sterling silverware for their pampered guests.[50]

About a third of a mile south of the hotel, on a spur of Poor Valley Ridge, Hamilton constructed a large sanitarium capable of holding two hundred beds. No expense was spared on this building made of stone with a wooden roof, equipped with marble baths modeled after French, German, and Turkish spas. "There were hot vapor, medicated pine-needle, and sassafras baths," according to a later historian. "Mercurial, sulphur, and brine atomizations were provided. A Department of Massage and Gymnastics was installed." Hamilton's syndicate invested at least one hundred thousand dollars in the sanitarium, which was completed in the summer of 1892.[51]

The Four Seasons resort staged its grand opening in April 1892. The hotel flew both American and British flags as it hosted a two-week gala attended by the fashionable elite of the northeast. After that magnificent beginning, everything quickly went down hill. The depression hit, and the hotel had no more than about thirty guests at any one time. The splendor of the place still attracted visitors, even if most of the seven hundred rooms were empty. Ella M. Andrews, who later married a president of Lincoln Memorial University, remembered it as "a veritable fairy land," but none of the hopes of Hamilton and Curtis were realized. Creditors filed suit against at least eighty people who were investors in the hotel in 1895. Attila Cox, president of the Columbia Finance and Trust Company of Louisville, took possession of the property as a trustee. Columbia carried away its movable furnishings in thirty box cars and auctioned them at Louisville for a mere twenty thousand dollars. Then Cox sold the empty building to the Chicago Wrecking and Salvage Company for nine thousand dollars, and that company tore the place down, carting off the building material for resale in the summer of 1895. All that was left for Cox to dispose of were the grounds and the sanitarium, which reportedly had only one patient during its very short existence.[52]

The Harrow School

Arthur and Ellen Myers came to Cumberland Gap when the boom was soaring toward its peak in 1890. They told residents at a prayer meeting in a room over the local drug store, "We have been down in the mountains of Kentucky doing some missionary work . . . and we decided to come and see what the prospects are at Cumberland Gap." They built a church with minimal funds and Ellen began teaching primary classes in the basement until the school outgrew the

Harrow School. The wide porch is crowded with an audience for a band. UA-LMU.

confined space. When the Four Seasons held its gala opening in April 1892, Lady Julian Pauncefort, the wife of the English ambassador to the United States, was among the guests. She visited Myers and suggested he name his enterprise the Harrow School to honor the nearby town and the Harrow School in England, which had been founded in 1571 to provide free education for boys. Arthur and Ellen continued to charge tuition, but they positioned their school as a way "to pay our country's debt to these Highlanders of America by educating the children of the G. A. R. on slave soil."[53]

Myers expanded his education work by purchasing a half-finished hotel and casino located on the slope of the bowl at Cumberland Gap a few hundred yards from his church. He completed the structure and moved his students there in the fall of 1892. The Harrow School proved to be the most successful institution he ever created. Supported by the American Missionary Association, its Local Board consisted of Myers (as president), J. H. S. Morison, Robert F. Patterson, and Charles F. Eager, to name a few local leaders who also would strongly support his effort to establish a university. The school was coeducational and provided boarding for most of its students, the great majority of whom came from families in Claiborne County, Tennessee, and Lee County, Virginia. The school produced its first high school graduate in May 1894 and contained 111 children in the primary grades, 48 in the intermediate section, 34 in grammar classes, and 62 in the academic department in 1896. The academic students were studying to prepare for college work. The Harrow School laid down strict rules for its boarding students: no smoking, drinking, or chewing tobacco, and a strict curfew that began with study at 7:00 a.m. and ended with sleep at 10:00 p.m. Tuition was only a dollar a month, board was two dollars per week, and room rental not more than three dollars per year.[54]

Frederick B. Avery

Myers initially pinned his hope of expanding the Harrow School into a college on Frederick B. Avery. Born on June 7, 1854, in Cleveland, Ohio, Avery graduated with a law degree from Ohio State University in 1875 but went on to study for the ministry, with a degree from the Philadelphia Divinity School in 1880. He pastored several congregations but had settled at an Episcopalian church in Painesville, Ohio, by 1892. Avery became interested in educational work in the mountains through William Goodell Frost, who had met his father at a religious revival in Michigan in 1866. Frost paved the way for Avery to become a trustee of Berea College in 1894. Avery met Myers at a board meeting in Berea that year and found that Myers had fond memories of Avery's father when the older man had preached at Hillsdale College. Myers even claimed to have converted to his present calling because of that contact. Trusting "the pioneer prophet of the mountains," as Avery later described him, the Painesville minister accepted Myers's invitation to visit Cumberland Gap. Myers told Avery he had a network of fifteen "Log Cabin Schools" scattered through the mountains, with his headquarters at the Harrow School.[55]

Avery arrived at Cumberland Gap on July 3, 1895. He had a long talk with Ellen, a "wonderful woman" who told Avery "of their years of struggle, and her hope of establish [*sic*] a higher school of learning in the neighborhood of Cumberland Gap." Myers and Avery fished in nearby Yellow Creek and Powell River. The pair shared their catch with a woman living nearby, who cooked it for their lunch. During the meal, she questioned Myers about his plans and supported them by saying, "Weuns know that larnin' makes you." "That really thrilled me," Avery recalled thirty-eight years later. "It went to my heart, and ever since it has been my inspiration to do what little I could to 'Lend a hand.'" Thus Avery understood why Myers took him to see the empty building of the Four Seasons resort, very soon to be torn down. "This would make a grand school for our college," Myers told him. "We will have all this property some time, the Lord has caused this company to fail."[56]

The Porch at Harrow School

Avery was unable to raise funds to realize Myers's dream, which is why Howard and the others assembled on the porch at Harrow School on June 18, 1896. In fact, Howard would emerge as the most important of the founders of Lincoln Memorial University because he took on the task of raising large sums of money over a long time period. He kept the institution afloat during its first twelve years of existence. He also framed the appeal for Lincoln Memorial University, even though the idea to name it after Lincoln was Kehr's, and Myers already was promoting the Harrow School as a reward for the descendants of Civil War loyalists and the disadvantaged youth of Appalachia. Howard fervently believed in all these initiatives and became the chief spokesman for the institution and all it represented. Most people who became aware of Lincoln Memorial University outside Cumberland Gap learned of it from the retired general's many public lectures, the numerous letters he sent to individuals, the public fund-raising events he organized, and the newspaper and magazine articles he authored or caused to be written. The university became almost as much a monument to Howard's dedication as it became a memorial to the president he loved.

That this sixty-five-year-old retired general would take on such a responsibility was symptomatic of his commitment to a good cause. During the course of the conversation on the porch of the Harrow School, Myers told everyone that his school needed room for expansion. He told Howard that Daniel Kimball Pearsons had promised funds for this endeavor and that other Chicago-based philanthropists were interested as well. He needed Howard "to lend his name to the proposal," and the general gave it much thought, pacing back and forth along the porch floor.[57]

This meeting on the porch represented the birth of Lincoln Memorial University, but it is interesting that there is no clear evidence that two important points were raised in the discussion. First, it is unclear whether Myers actually proposed that the expansion include the creation of a college. Howard himself, ten years later, recalled only that Myers told him the Harrow School was in financial distress. "'What shall we do with our school?' was asked." Howard continued to pace and then "stopped suddenly and remarked: 'Friends, if you will make this school a larger enterprise I will take hold and do what I can.'" If Howard's memory was accurate, and it was supported by Harry S. Howard, who recalled his father's telling of the tale, then the retired general might have introduced the idea for creating a college at Cumberland Gap rather than merely expanding the existing offerings of Harrow School. There is no indication why Myers failed to introduce that idea himself, although his friends insisted that the minister intended to create a college even before he invited Howard to the Gap. The difficulty lies in the fact that, of the participants in the porch discussion, only Howard wrote his memories of the event. It is possible that he forgot exactly what was said by whom, or deliberately kept Myers out of the picture because of the troubled relationship the minister later developed with Howard and others associated with the university. Howard did not even mention Myers's name when detailing the discussion on the porch in two published accounts. Second, there is no conclusive evidence that anyone suggested naming the "larger enterprise" after Lincoln during the porch discussion. It is possible that Howard did not think of this until after the event, when he recalled Kehr's idea and told the Chicago lawyer what had happened at the Gap.[58]

Chapter 2
A Monument to Abraham Lincoln

Said University shall ever seek to make education possible to the children of the humble common people of America, among whom Abraham Lincoln was born, and whom he said God must love because he made so many of them.
—Charter, February 12, 1897

Howard stayed only one day and a night during his initial visit to Cumberland Gap, but Myers showed him enough of the area to demonstrate its potential. The Four Seasons property, especially the sanitarium, impressed Howard as "ready for school purposes." He left on June 19 for Chattanooga, but his thoughts turned to Cyrus Kehr and the Chicago lawyer's idea to name a school after Lincoln. Howard enlisted Kehr's aid in the enterprise at Cumberland Gap.[1]

Kehr was born in Goshen, Indiana, on March 30, 1856. His earliest known ancestor had immigrated from Rotterdam to Pennsylvania in 1733, but Kehr's father took the family to a farm near Sterling, Illinois, at the end of the Civil War. Kehr attended Cornell College at Mt. Vernon, Iowa, and Knox College in Galesburg, Illinois. He taught school, studied law, and practiced patent law in Chicago beginning in 1886, establishing his home in Lakeside, a suburb of the Windy City. Howard became acquainted with Kehr when he engaged the services of a Chicago lyceum bureau in the winter of 1894–95. Kehr had a hand in scheduling at least one of his lectures, "Grant at Chattanooga," delivered at Webster City, Iowa, on April 16, 1895.[2]

Kehr read about the southern Appalachians in a magazine article that year, and he soon learned that Congressman Walter Evans of Kentucky had introduced a bill to erect a monument to Lincoln "at some point in" that state, without specifying Appalachia. Kehr developed the idea that an educational institution would be a more fitting monument to the president and wrote to Evans with his proposal. The congressman never replied, but Kehr told Howard of his idea in February 1896. The general liked it but told Kehr he did not have time to support the project.[3]

Cyrus Kehr, Lincoln Memorial University's first president, 1897–99. UA-LMU.

The visit to Cumberland Gap opened the possibility of making Kehr's idea a reality. Howard recommended that Kehr make an early trip to the Gap and sent railroad passes so the lawyer could travel free of charge. He reached Cumberland Gap on July 20, 1896, finding that Myers "had already planned in detail what I had planned." He was impressed by the Four Seasons property, which consisted of nearly six hundred acres of land, the sanitarium building, many miles of macadamized driveways, and dozens of trees planted in a gardenlike manner. All that was left of the hotel, however, was the foundation. The Myers were encouraged to meet Kehr. Ellen suffered from poor health and Arthur seemed "old and needing help," so Kehr worked with the minister to secure the property at once. He went to Louisville and agreed on a sale price of thirteen thousand dollars with Attila Cox. Kehr telegraphed Myers the news, and the missionary brought five hundred dollars, Ellen's family inheritance, to use as a down payment. The first payment of fifty-five hundred dollars was to be made in five months, the rest divided into two payments one year and two years later. Kehr and Myers signed the contract on July 27, 1896. Scarcely a month after the meeting on the porch, the future campus of Lincoln Memorial University was secured.[4]

Taking advantage of the opportunity, Myers told Kehr of his plans to buy much more land in the area. He envisioned a total acquisition of some five thousand acres that would "make the University rich from the beginning," in Kehr's words. The Chicago lawyer believed Myers when the minister told him that he owned sixty-five acres of land on top of Cumberland Mountain plus forty-two acres in the saddle of the gap and several "small buildings from which he gets a considerable income." There is no evidence to substantiate these claims, however, and Myers's apparent poverty makes them hard to believe.[5]

Kehr was excited by everything he saw and everyone he met at Cumberland Gap. Myers assured him he could "secure a thousand pupils for the Academy" if he only had enlarged facilities, and that he could recruit at least one hundred college students immediately. One-fourth of them, according to Myers, were already taking college preparatory courses at the Harrow School. Myers and Kehr explored the area from July 21 to 25 and concocted plans to create a medical department based at the sanitarium. They anticipated that this would draw summer visitors for treatment, and the university facilities could be used to house them while students were on vacation. "My family has agreed to cut loose and make a home at the Gap," Kehr informed Howard, "and I hope to give the rest of my days to the work."[6]

Kehr naturally looked to Howard to play a major role in the university, but the general was noncommittal. "My trouble is that you make me take what I call the 'laboring oar,' in this new enterprise," he complained in September 1896. He was gearing up to campaign for Republican candidate William McKinley in the presidential campaign and suggested Kehr find someone else to serve as patron of the new school. Howard even thought someone other than a prominent Union general ought to serve as spokesman for this southern institution. He threw himself into presidential politics that fall, joining a group of aged Civil War veterans who stumped for McKinley. Because Howard had lost an arm and Dan Sickles a leg in the conflict, McKinley's opponents called them the "Wrecks of the Civil War," but the group helped secure Republican victory. Howard led a column of veterans who participated in McKinley's inaugural parade.[7]

Meanwhile, supporters of the new school decided that the current members of the Harrow School Board of Trustees would also serve as trustees of the university. Kehr could not decide when to move his family from their Chicago suburb to the mountains. Because there was no school yet, he could work as well in Illinois as at Cumberland Gap and therefore postponed the move indefinitely. Kehr took on the task of preparing all legal documents associated with the Four Seasons property.[8]

The name of the new institution was a point of some discussion. The founders favored Lincoln Memorial University as early as October 1896, but the administrators at Lincoln University, a historically black college in Pennsylvania, got wind of the enterprise and quietly informed Kehr that they objected to it. Kehr asked Howard's advice, and the general replied, "It is only necessary to have a name which will be clearly distinctive. If we name the institution The University of Abraham Lincoln, we shall have a noble name and one clearly distinctive." Kehr also considered forging a union between the new institution and two existing schools in East Tennessee, Washington College near Jonesborough and

Tusculum College at Tusculum. The proposal was to combine their resources and base all operations on the Four Seasons property. Both colleges had a classical curriculum, and making Lincoln Memorial University primarily an industrial college would balance all three out. Kehr visited both colleges and stirred up interest in the scheme, but it never went beyond a suggestion.[9]

In the end, Kehr focused on his original idea and inserted not only Lincoln's name but also the word "Memorial" to the institution's title when drafting the charter. He brought the document to Cumberland Gap on February 11, 1897, and a meeting of local board members officially signed it the next day, the eighty-eighth anniversary of Lincoln's birth. Howard was unable to attend the meeting. The document the founders signed on February 12 actually was an application to the state of Tennessee for a charter, but it included the full wording of the founding charter as well. As a nonresident of the state, Kehr could not sign the application, which specified that at least two-thirds of the members of the board would be members of Christian churches. Although Kehr had earlier referred to the "Board of Trustees," for some reason the term "Board of Directors" appeared in the charter application. Howard much preferred the word "Trustee," probably because it implied a more responsible relationship with the students and faculty than "Director." The Claiborne County registrar filed the charter application at his office on February 13 and sent it to Nashville. Secretary of State William S. Morgan affixed the seal of the state on February 17. Morgan sent the document to Cumberland Gap with a bill for three dollars, which was paid in early March.[10]

Given the desire to make the institution "an expression of renewed good will and fraternal feeling between the people of" the North and South, it was appropriate that not only Howard but also a former Confederate officer served on the Board of Directors. Robert F. Patterson, whose family farm lay just south of the Four Seasons property, had served as captain of Company C, Twenty-ninth Tennessee, enlisting at Cumberland Gap in August 1861. He was not reelected when the regiment reorganized under the auspices of the Confederate Conscription Act in April 1862. Patterson joined the staff of Brig. Gen. Seth M. Barton's Georgia brigade when the Confederates confronted Union forces holding Cumberland Gap in August and September 1862. Although serving as a volunteer aide, with no official position, Patterson remained with Barton throughout the rest of the war, surrendering to Ulysses S. Grant when the Vicksburg siege came to an end. When Barton was transferred to a command in Virginia, Patterson again surrendered to Grant at Appomattox. He studied law at Washington University in Lexington, Virginia, drawn there by the president, Robert E. Lee, and practiced law upon returning to the family farm near Cumberland Gap. Patterson was a member of the Local Board, lodged within the ranks of the Board of Directors, who were immediately available to handle day to day matters of the institution.[11]

The issue of sectional reconciliation, symbolized by Patterson's support of the enterprise, was important to Howard. While naming the sanitarium for university purposes, some founders suggested either Grant Hall or Lee Hall. "No, we want them joining hands," Howard replied. "Let us call it Grant-Lee Hall."[12]

The first meeting of the Board of Directors took place at Cumberland Gap on February 18, 1897. The members elected Kehr president to serve for three years. They also planned to create a new primary school, ranging from kindergarten to the eighth grade and named to honor Ellen Myers for more than twenty years of "self-sacrificing pioneer service in the founding of" educational institutions. The founders intended it to be the model of a modern school, but Ellen died on June 26, 1897, before it became a reality. She had developed "dropsical complications" from an operation to remove two ovarian tumors in the fall of 1895 and died in the Harrow School building. This was a hard blow from which Arthur never fully recovered. Myers also lost the financial support of the American Missionary Association soon after Ellen's death. Just when he reached the highest goal of his life's work, two essential supports were ripped from under him. He suffered an emotional decline that complicated the early years of the university. Ellen was buried in Cherry Valley Cemetery near Ashtabula, Ohio, where Arthur arranged for a "boulder of pink stone" to be shipped from Michigan to serve as her headstone.[13]

The property of the Harrow School, valued at forty thousand dollars, was transferred to the control of Lincoln Memorial University on December 13, 1897. Myers resigned as president of the Harrow School Board that day. Management of the Harrow facility, the yet unrealized Ellen M. Myers School, and the Four Seasons property was invested in the hands of the University Board of Directors on July 16, 1898. As yet there was nothing on the Four Seasons property to manage. The board had mandated that "collegiate schools or departments, also a University Library, Historical Museum, a Lincoln Collection and a Biological Park" should be created there "as fast as feasible," but this required a great deal of money. The board also decided to charge tuition and authorized the commissioning of paid fund-raisers to solicit donations. Kehr wanted the institution to be open to support from members of all religious denominations and to "be national in its character."[14]

The Board of Directors adopted a flag designed by Kehr. Horizontal blue and gray bars served as the background, and a yellow *L* lay in a circle of white on the left of the field. The letter stood for "Lincoln, Love, Loyalty, Liberty, and Labor." In adopting the flag, the board viewed it as "emblematic of the new fraternal relations between the North and the South. . . . In the founding of this University, the North and the south, the blue and the gray unite." The first promotional brochure, issued sometime before January 21, 1898, pushed the Lincoln connection, the needs of the "southern mountains," and the "fraternal feeling" between the two sections which had fought in the Civil War.[15]

Howard did not have a direct hand in the first meeting of the Board of Directors, although it is evident he was consulted on several issues. His chief work for the enterprise was in serving as a contact to potential donors in the northeast. When writing to John Wanamaker of Philadelphia, Howard offered him the opportunity to "control all matters in . . . shaping" the institution if Wanamaker would give five thousand dollars to help pay off the Four Seasons mortgage.[16]

Kehr repeatedly postponed moving his family because he could not find property in Tennessee that held the same equity (about twelve thousand dollars) as his Lakeside home. The first signs of discontent with Kehr began to appear in late 1897. Eugene P. Fairchild, an important fund-raiser for the university, found Kehr to be "really quite visionary" but admitted he "could not always rely upon his statements." Kehr sensed that the other founders were dissatisfied with his contribution and sought to keep Howard in his corner by reminding the general that he had originated the idea of founding a Lincoln university in the first place and that he had neglected his family's finances while devoting time to university work.[17]

Kehr also persuaded Howard to take a larger role in the enterprise. When the general reluctantly agreed to become managing director of Lincoln Memorial University in May 1898, he initiated a personal commitment to the institution that had been lacking beforehand. Howard requested that Kehr continue as president and assist his work, that Myers and Fairchild serve as financial agents for the university, and that the Local Board handle as much business as possible because he anticipated visiting Cumberland Gap only sporadically.[18]

Kehr issued the first presidential report of the university on May 24, 1898, although he had little progress to report. His salary was not set, and although allowed a stenographer, he was not authorized to pay her a salary. Kehr had spent more than $500 of his own funds on university expenses and managed to drum up $370 in donations. He presented a bill to the Board of Directors for the balance. Kehr also solicited the donation of six thousand books for a library. He was willing to resign as president as soon as the board created the position of managing director for Howard and suggested leaving the presidency vacant for the time. Kehr reported that "Lincoln Memorial University has not yet directly conducted any educational work." He also had not been able to set up the Ellen Myers School. The intention was to stop offering elementary-level education at the Harrow School, transferring those grades to the new institution while keeping the Harrow facility open to prepare students for college.[19]

Kehr reported that much of his time during the past year had been absorbed in dealing with the abstract of the Four Seasons property. He had made the first payment of twenty-five hundred dollars in cash on December 24, 1896, with five hundred dollars from Myers and the rest borrowed from one of Kehr's friends. Attilla Cox transferred the deed to Kehr and Myers at that time, but the two gave a trust deed to Cox as security for the rest of the payments and a trust deed to Kehr's friend for the two thousand dollars. In October 1897, Kehr created a second mortgage to secure a loan and pay off part of the debt, but he had to put together an abstract of the title according to laws in Illinois, which were stricter than in Tennessee. As there were no abstract companies in Claiborne County, Kehr decided to take on the "tedious and complicated task" himself. It took nine weeks, much of it at the law firm of Rogers and Davis in Knoxville, to compile an abstract six volumes long, filled with maps and plats. Kehr also negotiated the cancellation of many liens on the property, totaling about fifty thousand dollars, but two significant suits were still pending as of May 1898. Kehr did not intend to charge the university for compiling the abstract, although he estimated that appropriate charges would total $1,500, plus $500 for travel expenses. Jesse L. Rogers reviewed his work, certified the abstract, and later charged the university $250 for his fee and the use of his office.[20]

Kehr's contribution to Lincoln Memorial University had about run its course when he submitted the first presidential report. It was a substantial contribution, but Howard began to take more responsibility for the institution. Howard recommended the creation of three departments, the Normal to educate precollege students, the Collegiate to offer college-level courses, and the Industrial to provide manual training and put students to work in campus jobs.[21]

Howard put his efforts on hold when he agreed to lecture and distribute religious tracts for the Army and Navy Christian Commission at military camps during the Spanish-American War. The general traveled to Florida and reached

Santiago, Cuba, a few days after the city fell to American forces in July 1898. Howard was held up in quarantine at Tampa on his way back to the United States, delaying efforts to raise money for the next payment of the Four Seasons mortgage. Kehr also needed funds for operating expenses. Eugene P. Fairchild pointed out that raising money was more difficult because neither the American Missionary Association nor the Presbyterian Assembly were willing to help.[22]

Howard plunged ahead in August 1898 with a letter-writing blitz. Surely everyone would "be willing to give a little for the sake of Abraham Lincoln," he assured Kehr, and "for the sake of education; for the sake of industry; for the sake of humanity; for the sake of the Master and his cause, and for the sake of Kentucky Tennessee and the whole mountain region in the interest of God and of mankind." Roswell P. Flower, a wealthy philanthropist and Democratic politician in New York, was the first to respond with a check for one hundred dollars. Howard forwarded it to Charles F. Eager, board member and treasurer of the university, calling it "the first bird of the summer."[23]

Howard also negotiated with Attila Cox for more time to raise money for the next mortgage payment. Lincoln Memorial University "is alive and in earnest," he assured Cox. "The work it proposes is most important and at a remarkable center so that I am confident of success." Howard pointed to his previous record, having "been successful in the starting of a large number of institutions of learning and have not failed in any of them." He persuaded Cox to extend the deadline by several months.[24]

Howard issued a circular in October 1898 extolling the concept of a living memorial to the slain president. Lincoln Memorial University was "founded with the distinctive object in view of bringing young people to Christ, and at the same time afford thousands in the mountains the opportunities to better their condition by increasing their theoretic and practical knowledge." The general announced that he considered "this as the last call I shall make in the interest of a particular institution." Checks in the amount of up to twenty dollars began to pour in, from individuals, Sunday schools, and churches across the Midwest and Northeast. "May God bless and prosper the work of the school," wrote J. D. Gardiner as he forwarded a donation of $2.75 from a Congregational Sunday school in Kansas. "Fetch through the first payment and I haven't a doubt that the next and other payments will be met without any embarrassment," Howard assured Myers. "The Lord is strong and mighty."[25]

Howard was determined to pay off the Four Seasons mortgage and was upset that Eager diverted considerable funds he sent him into the monthly operating budget. Illness and emotional imbalance prevented Myers from raising much money for the new college. He was "very restless and uneasy," thought Eager, "and in that condition does many things that cause some friction here, in the management of the business." In contrast, Fairchild raised a number of small donations, many of them for the Harrow School rather than for the university. Attila Cox asked for something to be paid on the next mortgage installment in January 1899 and promised to offer another extension after that good faith effort. Fairchild joined with all other founders in urging everyone to dig deep. "Let's burn our bridges behind us," he wrote Eager, "and make a payment, and *trust* to the future." They managed to send more than three thousand dollars to Louisville the next month and received a favorable extension.[26]

The founders sought to add property to the university holdings early in 1899. The Four Seasons land was physically separated from the Harrow School lot, and Howard wanted a connection between them across privately owned land. He urged Eager to begin with a footpath, and he hoped the owners would allow the university a right of way across their ground or donate the land to the university. Fairchild urged the purchase of Alexander Arthur's house at Harrogate, which was adjacent to the Four Seasons ground. Howard also sent another one thousand dollars to Attila Cox in March, ahead of schedule for the next payment.[27]

The executive committee of the board discussed two plans for utilizing the nearly six hundred acres of farm land within the Four Seasons property. Their vision was to hire a farm manager who could supervise work by student laborers and to rent some of the pasturage to local farmers for cash. The money to pay a manager and develop the farm was not yet available, so Howard advised they use the only team of draft horses the university owned to grow vegetables for the boarding halls and rent the rest of the ground to area farmers. This was only a temporary plan, for the university was able to hire a manger within a few months. The farm became a major source of food and revenue for the struggling college.[28]

Howard tried to avoid negative publicity. When a potential donor from Boston visited Harrow School, she was "not favorably impressed." It is possible that the quality of food served at the boarding school was the problem; a month later, the teachers themselves complained of not only bad cooking but also meager servings and lack of variety. Howard naïvely asserted that "there was plenty of good food" when he last visited, and his answer to the problem was to encourage the faculty to pray and "co-operate with me in a Christian way to the last degree." A more effective remedy lay in the Local Board's decision to buy additional food and allow faculty to eat at separate tables from students.[29]

Howard's duties as managing director were confined to raising money, not running the school. He appointed Col. Henry H. Adams as his New York treasurer and the American Exchange National Bank as the New York depository for the funds he raised. This was necessary because the wealthy men and women he approached "seldom look beyond the city for anything." Myers spoke to Sunday schools and churches in New England during the spring of 1899, but his warmest pitch was for the Harrow School, the institution that was "always on his heart," rather than for the university. Fairchild helped Howard to create a new circular for distribution in New York, along with new letterhead stationery that listed influential men as supporters and included a picture of Grant-Lee Hall. Fairchild worked among Chicago philanthropists but reported that they were leery of giving money until the mortgage was paid.[30]

"In rain and in snow, evening and morning all the winter, I have carried this cause of the mountain boys from office to office, from man to man," Howard informed D. K. Pearsons. National awareness of Lincoln Memorial University soared when the general convinced the editor of the *Christian Herald* to run a story about it in early 1899.[31]

Despite his success at encouraging numerous small donations, Howard wanted to find a wealthy patron who could support the university over a long period of time. A lady who had promised to give one hundred thousand dollars backed out, and Pearsons, who had indicated that he would at least pay off the mortgage, also backed away.[32]

Howard approached Andrew Carnegie, hoping to begin a long association with the steel industrialist by asking for the donation of a library building. Carnegie was too busy to see Fairchild when the fund-raiser tried to visit him in 1899. When Howard and Charles E. Hall tried to see him, the Scottish-born millionaire was out of town. Howard wrote a letter to Carnegie, noting that most residents of the mountains were from Scotland and northern Ireland, "with a sprinkling of Huguenots and English proper." He suggested that, if Carnegie could commit large donations over time, Howard would do all the leg work and allow him to garner all the publicity. Carnegie did not respond to Howard's first salvo in a long battle to bestow Carnegie money on the institution. Howard also contacted Mr. and Mrs. Russell Sage to inform them of the enterprise at Cumberland Gap. Far less well known than Carnegie, the Sages were enormously wealthy and interested in worthy causes. Howard apparently had approached them earlier, for he now feared that "I have wearied you and perhaps worn out a good welcome," but he could not resist asking them for a donation of one thousand dollars.[33]

Howard was eager to begin raising money for the endowment as soon as the Four Seasons property was secure. He planned to make a "systematic effort . . . to bring the whole country to my aid" and pleaded with Eager to solicit money in the Gap region, urging him to remember "that every $5. and $10. is a God-send."[34]

Lincoln Universities

The leaders of Lincoln University near Philadelphia again protested the naming of the Cumberland Gap institution with an editorial in the February 1899 issue of their school newspaper, the *Lincoln University Herald.* "It will cause confusion and misapprehension, and be in some respects injurious to our institution," argued the editor, who claimed that Lincoln's name "rightfully belongs to us." Having begun in 1854 as the Ashmun Institute, a preparatory school for blacks, the school had converted into a college and changed its name to Lincoln University in 1866. Noting that the newest college to adopt Lincoln's name was located in a slave state, the editor suggested Howard should honor Washington, Jefferson, or even Lee instead.[35]

Howard wrote to the editor to express regret that he was upset. There could be no confusion in the public mind because the two institutions were so far apart, and the word "Memorial" would sufficiently distinguish the Cumberland Gap institution from all others. Given that a charter had already been issued, and thousands of dollars had been donated, he doubted that a change of name was feasible but promised to bring it to the board's attention. Howard had supported Lincoln University with Freedmen's Bureau funds. "My heart has always been with your University," he wrote, "and I would not have it injured in any possible way."[36]

Howard wanted to treat the problem gently, "for we don't want to be talked against while we are in our infancy!!" Eager did not see any need to change the name, and he argued that the Cumberland Gap institution could derive "great strenght [*sic*]" from it. The board discussed the issue on May 17, 1899, and agreed with Eager.[37]

A total of four colleges, including the one in Pennsylvania, had been named for Lincoln before 1897. The first was Lincoln College, located in Lincoln, Illinois, a railroad town that also had been named for the future president in 1853. The university was chartered on February 6, 1865, and ground was broken for the first building on Lincoln's fifty-sixth birthday. Lincoln Institute in Jefferson City, Missouri, had been created in 1866 with seed money donated by the soldiers of two black regiments raised in the state, the Sixty-second and Sixty-fifth

United States Colored Troops. Admitting only black students, the institute added college-level courses to its curriculum by 1877. An institution called Lincoln College had begun at Topeka, Kansas, in 1866, with enrollment open to all races. It changed its name to Washburn College two years later to honor a New England benefactor who contributed twenty-five thousand dollars.[38]

JOHN HALE LARRY

In January 1899, Howard asked the American Missionary Association to help him find "a large man—that is—one who is apt to teach as well as apt to preach and who will be big enough for President of the whole concern if we so desire." The association put him in touch with John Hale Larry, a minister in Providence, Rhode Island. Born on December 2, 1843, in South Windham, Maine, Larry had attended public schools and Gorham Academy before becoming a teacher in the Boston area. He had served as a private in the Eighth Massachusetts, a nine-month regiment raised in the fall of 1862, and had participated in one small skirmish near Washington, North Carolina, before the regiment mustered out in August 1863. Three months later, he joined a heavy artillery company and served as a lieutenant when it became Company H, Third Massachusetts Heavy Artillery. Larry helped to garrison forts protecting Boston Harbor and, later, the ring of earthen forts that protected Washington, D.C. His service record listed him as standing five feet nine inches tall, with blue eyes, and light hair.[39]

Larry became a high school principal in Weston, Massachusetts, before entering the ministry in 1873. He taught at Hampton Institute in Virginia and by 1888 was pastor of the Richmond Street Congregational Church in Providence. He and wife Mary had six children, although she passed away in January 1899, at exactly the time that Howard asked the American Missionary Association for help in locating someone to take charge of the university.[40]

In early May 1899, Larry visited Cumberland Gap, where he met Howard and the faculty of the Harrow School. Larry's daughter played the violin and school girls performed and recited in a competition on the importance of temperance. Howard, Larry, and the faculty rode from Cumberland Gap to Grant-Lee Hall on May 6, "with beauty & grandeur all around," as the general reported to his daughter Bessie. Larry was excited; he proposed that the school create a printing department to publish a university newspaper and train students for a printing career. This was a long-term interest; Larry had published a newspaper at the Massachusetts high school that he principled and had established a trade school in New Hampshire to teach printing. Only two weeks after returning to Providence, Larry decided to move to Tennessee. He requested a salary of $160 per month but understood that the university needed to create a fund to sustain its first salaried employee. Meanwhile, Eager wrote an article about the university for *Faith and Works,* a Christian newspaper Larry published in Providence. By June university stationery was listing Larry as assistant managing director.[41]

Myers endorsed him as the new president of Lincoln Memorial University and Howard eagerly supported the idea, but accumulating the funds to pay his salary delayed the move for months. His congregation protested the plan when word leaked out. "It is pleasant to be wanted," Larry admitted to Eager. Meanwhile, Larry created a new circular and mailed promotional literature. He had big plans for the school, predicting a thousand students in short order, and purchased with his own funds a set of new type for the publication he now began to call the *Herald.* "I want the L.M.U. to lead the schools of the nation" in its printing department, he proclaimed.[42]

The Decline of Cyrus Kehr

The rise of John Hale Larry hastened the fall of Cyrus Kehr, who continued to defend his slim record of accomplishment for the university. Kehr knew that Eager and other founders thought he was "not a safe man from the business stand-point, . . . that I might reach out in an impetuous way and undertake work beyond the ability of the treasury to pay." Kehr defended his actions in the acquisition of the Four Seasons property. "There was nothing to do but to take risk in that purchase and then use 'boom' methods to get the money for payment," he asserted. Kehr admitted that he had no experience in creating a college curriculum, demonstrating the need to find a replacement for him.[43]

Kehr's only effort to create a program of study involved approaching B. B. Herbert, author of a course on printing for correspondence schools, to garner his advice about instituting a printing department at Lincoln Memorial University. Herbert, who had created the National Editorial Association and published the *National Printer-Journalist,* was enthusiastic about helping the university, but Kehr set himself at odds with John Hale Larry because he did not inform the new man about his initiative. Kehr also planned an extension program for Lincoln Memorial University that would include traveling libraries. He shipped a box of books and an oil painting of Lincoln from his home in Illinois to be part of this program.[44]

Kehr continued to talk about moving his family to Tennessee and requested four hundred dollars for expenses plus a minimum of fifty dollars per month as a salary. Howard wanted someone to create academic departments to teach woodworking, metal working, printing, stenography, typing, and a variety of other practical arts, but he had little faith in Kehr's ability to do so. Howard relied on the Local Board to decide what to do with Kehr but could not promise to underwrite the expenses needed to move Kehr's family to Tennessee. After spending two weeks at Cumberland Gap in October 1899, Kehr despaired of ever finding a suitable home there and began to contemplate moving to Knoxville instead. He could commute to the university by train, a trip of two and a half hours in one direction. Kehr wanted to practice patent law in Knoxville "so as to earn my living independently of the University."[45]

Larry Takes Charge

Howard appointed Larry to take charge "of all matters touching the organization, development and management of the University" and authorized him to act as president until the board could officially appoint him to that position. Larry "cut the strings" that bound him to his congregation in Providence and prepared to move. He also printed a sample issue of the *Mountain Herald.* Larry wanted to live in the Alexander Arthur house or the Harrogate Inn, but if they were not available at an affordable price, he preferred to live in Grant-Lee Hall with his family. The building would also serve as a boarding hall for the first contingent of college students on the Four Seasons property. Investing his own money, Larry forwarded three hundred copies of the *Herald* to Cumberland Gap. He wanted to institute a policy of "military drill and discipline for the young men and careful domestic and hygienic training for the girls." Larry sought to "make cleanliness and promptness the leading features" of his regime. He expected each student to work at least four hours each day to instill a strong work ethic and save operating expenses for the institution. Larry looked to others to handle the classical curriculum, while personally managing the commercial and industrial training. He also expected to return up to one-third of his salary to the institution during the first few years of his tenure.[46]

The news that Kehr was working with B. B. Herbert to create a printing department unsettled Larry. He admitted that such news would have led him to curtail plans to move to Cumberland Gap if he had not already tendered his resignation at the church. "But I am in for it now," he told Eager, "and must solve all such problems with the aid of my common sense and the Lord's added wisdom." Howard made it clear that Kehr must act according to Larry's instructions, but the new man from Providence did not know what to make of the Chicago lawyer: "From the way you write and Gen. talks about Kehr, I think he must be an interesting character."[47]

Even after tendering his resignation in September 1899, Larry continued to linger in Providence for a month because the *Christian Herald*'s promise to fund a printing department did not materialize. When Myers told him that many publications bore the title *Mountain Herald,* Larry contemplated renaming his magazine the *Cumberland Gap Herald.*[48]

The Decline of Arthur A. Myers

With Larry on the ascendant and Kehr on the decline, Myers continued to be an erratic element among the founders. By the middle of 1899, he felt isolated from the rest. He suffered emotionally from Ellen's loss and physically from some unexplained illness that dogged his existence. He concentrated on new ventures that were only loosely tied to the original purpose of Lincoln Memorial University. He and Ellen had offered to put up parents of students when they brought their children to Harrow School, but now he no longer had a place to do so. Telling Howard that he was boarding at Harrogate Inn and had "no furniture and no income and a heavy daily expence," he wanted to rent a house but needed financial help. Myers also wanted to open a boarding school "for the very poor girls" but of course had no funds to do so.[49]

The local economy had not fully recovered from the crash of 1893, so property was easily available. Alexander Arthur had moved to New York and was willing to give up his house in Harrogate to help "satisfy his creditors." The house was sold at auction in the fall of 1898. By October 1899, Myers somehow had found two thousand dollars as a down payment for it and was attempting to acquire the Harrogate Inn as a school for girls. Howard assumed Myers would have difficulty paying off the mortgage on the Arthur house and that the university would probably be able to acquire it sometime in the future. Myers asked that the deed for the Arthur house be made out to himself, though he intended to transfer it to a "friend who will help us to make a social center of it for the good of all the interests of this country." Myers also acquired the Harrogate Inn for three thousand dollars in November 1899, making the deed to Isaac J. Lansing and Franklin Nettleton of Scranton, Pennsylvania, "as trustees for the Childrens

Institute for Childs Study at and about Cumberland Gap Tenn." The inn was converted into a boarding school for orphan girls, as Myers had intended, and named for Nettleton's daughter Grace, who had died at age twelve. Starting operations in October 1900, it filled an important need for many decades to come. As Howard predicted, the university later acquired the Arthur house and used it as a music conservatory. The university also operated the Grace Nettleton Home for Girls until 1904, and continued to play a role in it until the place closed in 1956. The home Myers created housed more than one thousand girls by that time.[50]

Kehr had lost his faith in Myers's judgment since their first meeting in 1896. "While all the people around Cumberland Gap regard Mr. Myers as unbalanced, he retains a remarkable shrewdness," he informed Howard. "He has a way of putting his exaggerated stories into convincing form." Myers had assured a woman in Middlesboro that he had given sixty thousand dollars of his own money to develop the university and had worked for the institution without a salary. Both points were untrue. Kehr was concerned that the "giving public know that Mr. Myers is incapacitated and that we are honestly trying to carry the work forward." When reports circulated that Myers was "secretly working to prevent Dr. Larry from coming to the Gap," Howard could only urge his colleagues to "keep Mr. Meyers friendly if you can. . . . Pacify him & make him love you if you can."[51]

Guy's Death and Lincoln Memorial University

In the middle of efforts to start course work on the Four Seasons property, Howard was hit by the worst tragedy of his life. His eldest son, Guy, was killed by guerrillas while serving in the Philippines on October 22, 1899. Guy had graduated from Yale University and had worked in the banking industry before asking his father to obtain a commission in the army. Through Sherman's help, Howard managed to secure his son a lieutenancy in the 12th U.S. Infantry, where Guy became an accomplished quartermaster through his own merits and rose to the rank of colonel. He married and had two children. While shipping supplies down the Rio Grande River, Filipino guerrillas opened fire on the steamer and a bullet penetrated Guy's right lung. "He sprang to his feet and cried: 'Whatever happens to me, keep the launch going,' then instantly fell and died." This is all Howard knew of his favorite son's death.[52]

"The blow upon a father is heavy indeed," Howard wrote to a consoling friend, "but it seems as though the mother's heart will never cease to bleed." Guy "was my strong helper: he was the critic I could trust; he was my hope for the future. I wanted him to outlive us & carry forward important work. Crowds & crowds of hopes were baffled & dashed to the ground in his death." Eager sent a condolence telegram, in the name of all directors, faculty, and friends at Cumberland Gap.[53]

Howard depended on his work as managing director to deal with grief. He had to go to Omaha to take charge of Guy's remains in late November, sending a representative to a planned meeting with John Jacob Astor about the school "in which my heart is absorbed." Before leaving, Howard also talked with *New York Tribune* correspondent Whitelaw Reid. He told Reid that Guy's last words were "burnt into my brain and affects my heart night and day." Howard derived courage to go on by remembering those words. He reminded Reid that the correspondent and he had endured Confederate artillery fire on Cemetery Hill at Gettysburg, and he linked that battle with the educational struggle into which he now put renewed energy: "We workers in the mountains centered at Cumberland Gap, Tenn., have a Gettysburg, a strategic point, to be held, and we want to plant veritable monuments there in the shape of education and all its accompaniments." The first priority was to pay off the thirty-three hundred dollars still owed on the mortgage, then create an endowment and further develop the property. Howard told Reid the story of Lincoln's last message to him in 1863, further linking the war with the enterprise at Cumberland Gap.[54]

Shift to Grant-Lee Hall

Two and a half years after the university's charter was issued, Henry H. Adams suggested it was time to move away from the Harrow School to escape the "friction" and "somewhat stultifying" influences there. "The University should be transferred to the Grant & Lee Hall, together with the pupils that desire to attend," Adams told Eager. Lack of funds had hampered the move longer than anyone had anticipated. Howard's efforts to create a proper road linking the Harrow School with Grant-Lee Hall in the summer of 1899, using student labor, contributed to the effort to physically create Lincoln Memorial University as a separate reality from the Harrow School. The university spent $150 on student labor for the roads as well as for working the farm that year.[55]

Larry's willingness to come to Cumberland Gap and take charge of the Four Seasons property was the key to setting up college course work. Before moving west, Larry quietly married Georgiana Fraser, who had been the business manager of *Faith and Works* for eight years. She was twenty years younger than Larry when the two repeated their vows on November 14, 1899. Larry wanted Eager to keep the news of their wedding quiet in Cumberland Gap, probably fearing the residents would misunderstand why the new president married his business manager less than a year after the death of his wife. The family established residence in Grant-Lee Hall later in November. Soon after, about twenty-five Harrow School pupils who had been taking college preparatory classes moved to Grant-Lee as well. All of them were boys. Almost three years following the founding of Lincoln Memorial University, the institution was finally in operation.[56]

"I have everybody in line but Mr. Myers," Larry assured Howard, "and he declares he is [in line too] and we get along like chums but the Lord only knows where he will make his influence known next. He cannot help being just what he is." Larry admitted that Myers "cannot be governed. You must 'yes, yes' along with him and while you work out your plan try to please him." At the same time Larry fully understood how important Myers had been in the creation of the university. "This school would never have existed but for his restless, erratic, scheming spirit," he reminded Howard.[57]

At the end of 1899, Howard submitted a yearly report of expenses incurred while working for the university. They included $306 for travel, $143 for postage, and $167 for secretarial wages. The total came to $703.50, but Howard asked for no compensation for his time or labor. He included a note for $350 that the institution had given him, which he now forgave, and a deed for 7.18 acres of land he had purchased at the entrance to the Four Seasons property. These contributions more than made up for the expenses he expected the university to pay him. Howard wanted to give fund-raisers up to 20 percent of the total they raised for the school, but he insisted that the board decide this question because he had been criticized in the past for his generosity in such matters. "I want an order like those of Sherman or Grant given to me of old," he lectured Eager, "one to be obeyed."[58]

The founders had nearly retired the debt on the Four Seasons property by the turn of the century. Eager paid off most of the first, large mortgage, contracted by Kehr and Myers in 1896, in four large payments throughout 1899. With 6 percent interest, this amounted to nearly $12,000. Eager paid off the second mortgage with $2,456 in March 1900. About $3,300 remained on the first mortgage. Out-of-pocket expenses soared in 1899 because of general expenses ($6,160.45) and the need to buy furniture for dorms and classrooms ($1,052.71), farm machinery and tools ($566.24), printing equipment for Larry ($1,392.20), and a telephone line ($89.62). The university's budget was still combined with that of the Harrow School; even though fund-raisers brought in $29,978.01 from July 16, 1898, to April 1, 1900, expenses exceeded income by $3,559.71. The development of the university proceeded at a cautious pace.[59]

CHAPTER 3
YOUNG LINCOLNS

What the L.M.U. is seeking to do, is to find the young Lincolns of this section and help them to help themselves. We are trying to found a school where one may earn to learn and learn to earn.

***—Mountain Herald,* December 1901**

John Hale Larry made a good impression as the first live-in president of Lincoln Memorial University. An early student recalled him as "a big man physically, and his manner was wonderfully genial, wonderfully kind, wonderfully lovable. He had a charming voice and a most alluring manner of speaking, so that his talks to the students always seemed to me models of the kind." Another student thought Larry was the only one at Cumberland Gap who had "pep and speed" and contrasted him with the local members of the board who were "distinctly Southern. Slow, dignified etc."[1]

Larry instituted a semi-military regime at Grant-Lee Hall. Henry H. Adams tried to secure some cadet rifles for the male students, and Larry issued cadet uniforms. Student W. C. Thompson was the bugler, blowing calls to wake up his colleagues and signal time to enter the dining room for breakfast. Daily drills took place in the evening after dinner, and the student officers of the day were responsible for making certain all students were in their rooms, then Thompson blew the signal for lights out at 10:00 p.m.[2]

The university continued to push the theme of rewarding mountain loyalty in its publications and boasted that, with three hundred students, it was forced "to refuse hundreds of applicants, for lack of funds and accommodations." About sixty of those students took college courses and lodged at Grant-Lee Hall by March 1900. The rest stayed at Harrow Hall and were in the primary and secondary grades. Larry described the discipline as "parental, firm but kind." He prohibited the use of tobacco, alcohol, firearms, and "improper language." Larry characterized the school as "Christian but non-sectarian," with the students attending church services, Sunday school, and "one prayer-meeting during the week." Six faculty members handled the needs of the college students; two of them held baccalaureate degrees, one was a minister, and the other three had completed no college degree. They taught across the disciplines, and two of them were close relatives of the president. John Dewitt Larry taught history, math, and military drill, with no college degree to his name, and his wife taught phonography and typewriting.[3]

The students in Grant-Lee Hall made do with one chair each, carrying it to the dining room and to class as needed. Everyone in the hall paid for his or her board; students averaged two dollars and teachers three dollars per week. Larry charged them "reasonable rates" for the food grown on the university farm, keeping accounts with Eager so that balances could be maintained on a monthly basis.[4]

Oliver Otis Howard visited campus once or twice a year and stayed in a room on the southern end of Grant-Lee overlooking the expansive valley of the Powell River. Larry often consulted with board member Robert F. Patterson at the latter's farm just south of the campus. One of Larry's sons recalled those meetings under the shade trees of Patterson's yard, when the two old veterans reminisced about the war while conducting school business.[5]

Lincoln Memorial University Board of Directors. *Left to right, first row:* Arthur A. Myers, Frederick B. Avery, Oliver Otis Howard, John Hale Larry (president 1899–1904), and Mr. Blanchard; *second row:* Edgar O. Achorn, Millard Overton, Charles F. Eager, Eugene P. Fairchild, Darwin R. James, and Robert F. Patterson. UA-LMU.

From the beginning, especially through Howard's influence, Lincoln Memorial University was a work-learn college. The board institutionalized the policy in March 1900. The concept of university-funded work for students began in the 1820s in Ohio, where a handful of colleges experimented with offering labor to students. It was not a success because most northern college students did not see the need to participate, but the work college ideal flourished among both white and black colleges and academies in the post–Civil War South due to war-induced poverty. It flourished not only because of poor students but also because of poor schools. Work-learn was a useful tool for those who wanted to acquire an education and those who wanted to provide it to them.[6]

At Lincoln Memorial University, students received seven cents per hour for manual labor and five or more cents extra if they brought some skills to the campus. Students were "paid" at the end of each week, but not in cash. An account was kept so the amount accumulated could be used to pay the student's board, room rent, and tuition. Depending on how many hours they worked and their pay rate, they either owed money to the school, received a small amount from it, or considered themselves even at the end of the school year. Larry encouraged applicants to specify what kind of work they were able to do.[7]

The students worked on essential jobs associated with running the school on a daily basis. Most of them labored on the university farm and in the kitchen and boarding hall. The university hired James H. Rector as farm manager early in 1903 and authorized him to grow as much food as possible to supply the boarding hall kitchens at Grant-Lee and Harrow School. Rector recalled that he started with virtually nothing and even had to wait three months before receiving part of his salary. He ran the farm "almost entirely with student help," with eventually sixty students under his charge. They were "largely from the country" and turned out to be "fine workers." Rector divided them into crews of eight to ten boys each, headed by a student foreman. "I made it my business to visit each squad at least twice before noon and twice in the afternoon," he remembered. During his many years with the university, Rector could recall only one student worker who "disobeyed my orders."[8]

Many students at Lincoln Memorial University deeply appreciated the opportunity for a college education. W. C. Thompson came to Cumberland Gap from Rose Hill, not far across the Virginia state line, in 1901. He had what he later called "an 'inferior complex' and it was at L.M.U. under the officers and teachers that I found myself[,] because we were just one big family." His university experience "was the breaking point in my life which meant success." He felt "a confidence that I could meet anyone in the world and feel perfectly at home and at ease."[9]

Berea College, Lincoln Memorial University, and Race

Significant connections with Berea College highlighted the early history of Lincoln Memorial University. Most of the founders had been associated with the Kentucky college as benefactors or board members. Eugene P. Fairchild's father had served as president of Berea, and he had been its chief fund-raiser for many years. The two institutions were only 120 miles apart, joined by a common interest in the education of mountain whites and a commitment to the ethics of the work-learn college. They were separated by competition for the same clientele and the thorny issue of multiracial education.[10]

Berea originated as an abolitionist school in pre–Civil War Kentucky, but the institution had not yet been established before the conflict forced its founders to flee. They returned and chartered a college in 1866, opening the doors to blacks as well as whites. Enrollments remained modest for nearly thirty years, and blacks outnumbered white students. Eugene P. Fairchild played a large role in inducing Frost to come to Berea as president in 1892, and the new man introduced new policies that propelled Berea into a more stable phase of its history. He was committed to biracial education but assumed the experiment would fail unless he increased white enrollment. Frost initiated a promotional campaign aimed at white mountain youths, even though Berea was located on the edge of the Kentucky Bluegrass region just west of the Appalachian highlands. He utilized many of the themes that Howard later employed for Lincoln Memorial University: sectional reconciliation, offering a hand up to deprived mountain youth, and stressing the work-learn opportunity. Frost was highly successful. In 1892, 184 blacks and 170 whites were enrolled at Berea; by 1903, the proportion had shifted to 157 blacks and 804 whites. Frost popularized the use of the word "Appalachia" to denote the mountain's subculture in 1895 and used the endorsement of former Union general Jacob D. Cox, who had campaigned in the mountains during the Civil War, to appeal to veterans for support.[11]

Frost became alarmed when many of his current and former supporters started the new enterprise at Cumberland Gap, using similar themes to appeal to the same student audience. Berea presidents had been using Lincoln's imagery for their promotional purposes as early as 1888, and Frost himself began to do so in 1896. Lincoln appeared on the letterhead stationery of Berea College three years later. The *Berea Quarterly* defined Lincoln as "sociologically, although not quite geographically, a mountain man" because his upbringing foreshadowed the kind of backwardness suffered by early-twentieth-century mountain whites. Eventually Berea came to use many icons of Appalachia, including Daniel Boone and Alvin York, in its promotional literature, diluting the commitment to Lincoln as the central feature of its mission.[12]

Frost worried that competition from Lincoln Memorial University would derail his strategy. He approached Howard with his concerns in December 1896, noting that black enrollment at Berea was not keeping pace with white recruitment. He warned Howard that if Lincoln Memorial University progressed, it would draw white students who might prefer an all-white school, thus undermining his effort to "clear the race prejudice out of Kentucky." Frost admitted that Berea could not "compete with a school of Northern methods and support which practically excludes the Negro."[13]

William E. Barton, a graduate of Berea and author of a popular book about Lincoln, also tried to wean Howard away from the Cumberland Gap enterprise. He told the general that Lincoln Memorial University had no chance because it "builds on a foundation of collapsed ambitions." Even if he was wrong, and it succeeded, that could only occur at the expense of Berea's effort to achieve racial justice. He also characterized Myers as noble, but "not always safe and prudent."[14]

Howard ignored these warnings and continued to garner donations for the Cumberland Gap college. Frost became desperate to stop the enterprise after Larry established operations at Grant-Lee Hall. He warned Howard on May 5, 1900, that the general's continued support of Lincoln Memorial University could destroy Berea. "The labors of an entire generation would be ruthlessly undone," he wrote, "and the advanced position which Berea has occupied would be rendered practically untenable." The only solution, Frost believed, was for Lincoln Memorial University to recruit black as well as white students. He admitted that very few African Americans lived within its region, but Frost called on Howard to emulate the example of Berea and Maryville College, the most prominent Tennessee school that allowed biracial education. Frost also complained of Eugene P. Fairchild, who had left Berea because of personal and policy differences with his administration. Frost believed Fairchild was spreading negative publicity about his college and shifting potential donors from Berea to Lincoln Memorial University.[15]

Howard was stunned by Frost's attack. He refrained from replying until the Board of Directors met on May 15, 1900. After careful consideration, the entire board addressed a response to Frost, expressing surprise and grief at the tone of his letter. The board wished to avoid controversy with Berea in any way, yet it fully asserted its right to shape university policy without interference from outside agents. The board wished Berea success in its plan, and by implication it requested a similar respect for its own endeavor.[16]

Fairchild was stung by Frost's accusations and wrote an open letter to everyone at Berea College, and its potential donors, disclaiming any ill will toward its mission. He admitted that he could not "endorse methods used by Pres. Frost in his efforts to secure money and students," but he also made it clear that Berea had no right to claim a monopoly on serving mountain youth. Privately Fairchild deplored the suspicions Frost and Barton created among potential donors to Lincoln Memorial University, but he was ready to work harder to overcome those prejudices. Fairchild's fears were not ungrounded. Cyrus Kehr noted with frustration that Berea secured a donation of fifty thousand dollars from D. K. Pearsons, which he thought should have gone to Lincoln Memorial University, in 1899. Because Pearsons had expressed distrust of Fairchild, Howard assumed Frost had poisoned the donor's mind against the Cumberland Gap school. Howard had also written an endorsement for Berea that Frost used to secure a donation of one thousand dollars from Henry Villard in 1899. "Yes, and it prevented Mr. Villard from giving me a thousand for the University," the general complained.[17]

Ironically, Berea's biracial mission came to a crashing halt soon after the exchange of views in 1900. Kentucky legislator Carl Day sponsored a bill outlawing multiracial education in the state. Frost argued against it, but the state legislature passed the Day Bill on January 12, 1904. Berea created an all-black school, the Lincoln Institute, near Louisville, which offered only secondary-level courses. No black students were allowed on the Berea campus. Biracial education came to an end in Tennessee even before that time. The Tennessee legislature passed a bill banning it in 1901. Maryville College, which had quietly allowed African Americans, Native Americans, and whites to attend classes for many decades, was the chief target of this legislation.[18]

The founders of Lincoln Memorial University never intended to deliberately exclude blacks. Their enterprise originated from a desire to offer poor mountain whites, the descendants of loyalists in the Civil War, the opportunity to better their lives. There were so few African Americans living within the recruiting field around Cumberland Gap that they were ignored by the founders.[19] Moreover,

Howard's credentials as a supporter of black education had been well established long before he took part in the creation of Lincoln Memorial University. Booker T. Washington honored him in a speech at the Waldorf Astoria in New York on November 8, 1900. "Howard is a name that the Negro keeps tenderly folded in his bosom by the side of that of Garrison, Phillips, Lincoln and Grant. The Negro is not and will never prove himself ungrateful for what you did," he told the general.[20]

If any hint of racism existed in the origin of Lincoln Memorial University, it derived from the circumstances of its founding and was inadvertent rather than intentional, extremely mild rather than blatant and aggressive. The founders sought to target mountain whites not out of racial prejudice but because they thought here was a large and deserving population not yet served by educational opportunities. In a real sense, this was indicative of a general shift in philanthropy following the demise of Radical Reconstruction in the 1870s, the restoration of white conservative political power in the South, and the onset of segregation and denial of black voting opportunities in the 1890s. The tide of charitable work had shifted away from southern blacks to white Appalachians, a population almost as poor and disadvantaged in some ways as former slaves. Lincoln Memorial University's mission represented the wave of the future in southern education, while Berea's mission was doomed to fail. The Lincoln image could be as powerful an incentive to ambitious mountain whites as it was to aspiring blacks.[21]

Howard

Just as he tried to avoid controversy with Berea, Howard felt disturbed any time negative publicity arose concerning Lincoln Memorial University. When a student at Harrow Hall cut down a few "shade trees" and vandalized other property, the incident escalated until Larry expelled seventeen pupils. "I am working too hard and spending too much to permit difficulties to arise in Cumberland Gap," Howard informed Eager. He would have preferred the president consult with the parents to settle things peacefully. Harrow Hall was crowded and the facility was showing wear and tear. Nevertheless, Howard had a grand time when he visited in April 1902. Larry took him on a tour of "typical ridge country, rough enough in all conscience where log tenements and such mountain folk abounded. We met with politeness everywhere." That night Howard dined at Eager's house in Cumberland Gap, where "a regular mountain preacher" offered prayer. "His voice would have reached at least a mile if there were no obstructions," Howard reported.[22]

Howard had little patience with those who criticized the school's use of the word "university," arguing that the educational system around Cumberland Gap was in such an infant state that it was forced to include all grades. As soon as the local public and secondary schools matured, he could "abolish the lower grades" and keep several college departments to justify the meaning of "university." In reality, no one held a monopoly on defining what that word meant. Educators had been using it since the 1850s; while some used it to identify an institution that offered graduate degrees, others thought scholarly research was the main difference between a university and a college. Still others thought it denoted an institution that embraced diverse disciplines and a modern curriculum based on the sciences rather than a classical course of study. Howard and others dismissed the fact that their institution did not fit any of these models of a university and continued to use the term as significant of their hopes for the institution.[23]

Howard's greatest success lay in publicizing Lincoln Memorial University to the world outside Cumberland Gap. He was its most effective spokesman because of his background and stature, his personal connection with Lincoln, and his sincere desire to make the institution a success. "I am so anxious to present the case of these mountain people," he wrote in a widely read article titled "The Folk of the Cumberland Gap." In this article, and many others, Howard retold the story of his last meeting with Lincoln. He argued that the mountain youth were hungry for learning but the university could accommodate only a limited number. Howard continued to give lectures on his Civil War experiences, which often were slanted toward the story of the mountain loyalists and ended with a plea for the Cumberland Gap school. He gave a talk in Newark on "A Group of Schools for Boys & Girls of the Mts.—a Lincoln Memorial."[24]

Howard's persistent approaches to Andrew Carnegie convinced the industrialist to pay off the remaining debt on the Four Seasons property, which amounted to twenty-three hundred dollars. Howard next asked Carnegie for a large sum to expand the school and make it something like the University of Chicago or Stanford University. He promised Carnegie that it would take far less money to do this at Cumberland Gap than John D. Rockefeller spent at Chicago or Leland Stanford spent in California, arguing that an endowment of half a million dollars would go farther in the mountains than two million dollars in a large city. Carnegie, however, did not respond.[25]

ARchives C69 P7 L3

Gen. O. O. Howard, *Managing Director,*
Col. Henry H. Adams, *Treasurer,* No. 177 Broadway, New York.
E. P. Fairchild, *Financial Secretary,*

The Trustees' Executive Committee of New York.
Gen. O. O. Howard,
Col. Henry H. Adams,
Dr. W. C. Gray,
Rev. Newell Dwight Hillis, D. D.,
Hon. Darwin R. James,
Hon. Levi P. Morton.
Rev. A. A. Myers, Financial Secretary. Cumberland Gap, Tenn.
John Hale Larry, Acting Pres't. Cumberland Gap, Tenn.

Lincoln Memorial University
Cumberland Gap, Tenn.

A MONUMENT TO ABRAHAM LINCOLN

OFFICE OF MANAGING DIRECTOR,
150 NASSAU STREET,
NEW YORK CITY.

Advisory Board:
J. Edward Simmons, Pres. Fourth Nat. Bank, N. Y.
Frederick D. Tappen, Pres. Gall'n Nat. Bank, New York City.
William Sherer, Gen'l Manager N. Y. Clearing House.
Hon. Darwin R. James, Pres. N. Y. Board of Trade.
Maj.-Gen. Oliver O. Howard, U. S. Army (Retired).
Col. Henry H. Adams, 177 Broadway, New York.
Hon. Wm. Brookfield, 220 Broadway, New York.
Hon. S. S Blanchard. 177 State Street. Boston, Mass.

Jan. 11th, 1901.

Dear Mr. Eager:

The "Mail & Express" has promised to put in a good article about our celebration of Lincoln's Birthday and in connection with it a discription of our work at the University itself. They want, however, some pictures of buildings on and near our establishment. A picture of Cumberland Gap itself, that is of the Mountain and the village together has been very effective. Send as many photographs as you can scrape up and we will make choice. Grant-Lee Hall, Harrow School building must be included. The Grace Nettleton Home is a good picture. Please do not delay this as the paper wants the pictures immediately. "The barn and buildings about it ~~is a~~ are nice things to exhibit industry. See how quickly you can do this for us.(?) We hope that you have old photographs enough - eight or ten will be sufficient,-so as not to delay to get new ones.

Very truly yours,

O. O. Howard

Ansd. 1-14-01.

Oliver Otis Howard letter, showing type of letterhead used by the managing director, 1901. UA-LMU.

Howard again approached Mr. and Mrs. Russell Sage of New York, forwarding the glowing testimony of Tazewell attorney Herman Y. Hughes, who extolled the value of the university. The lawyer, who acted as legal counsel for the institution, noted that the "very spirit of industry . . . pervaded" Grant-Lee Hall. Larry ran the school like "a well-regulated family. It had a homelike feeling," and all the students seemed to possess "the correct idea of the dignity of labor." Still, the Sages failed to send a large donation.[26]

Howard often was frustrated by his dealings with wealthy benefactors. If they could not fulfill their "subscriptions" (promised donations), he allowed them to pay 6 percent interest on the amount each year to create something like a small endowment. "Men of wealth say '*no*' to me often on the ground that my acquaintance is so large that I will certainly succeed without their sacrifice," he complained. He had heard that D. K. Pearsons had promised Lincoln Memorial University fifty thousand dollars, but all the visits and importunities Howard offered never wrenched it from his purse. Financier J. P. Morgan seemed disposed, but he too never sent a check. Many people promised large sums, but only if Howard could secure even larger sums from others, evidently wishing to bet on a winning horse. Through it all, Howard kept his sense of humor. While visiting New York, he informed his daughter Bessie that someone they both knew failed to see him. "I guess he was afraid I would tell about the L.M.U."[27]

Howard connected his university work with his desire to promote sectional reconciliation. He often told the story of naming Grant-Lee Hall and pointed out that Captain Patterson, a Rebel, was active on the local board. "I want a circular such as would please both Union and Confederate soldiers as soon as possible," he wrote Eager. Howard attended the large gathering of blue and gray veterans on the battlefield of Peachtree Creek, north of Atlanta, on July 20, 1900. He related touching incidents of the war that reflected the common soldiers' regard for their enemy. Howard also spoke of former Confederate general John B. Gordon, who stopped briefly at Cumberland Gap on his way to a speaking engagement in Knoxville when Howard was in town for commencement. The former Union general saluted Lee's trusted lieutenant and said, "Gordon, we tried to whip you once." Gordon replied, "Well, you succeeded mighty well, but we are now all under the one flag." The story never failed to bring cheers from every gathering, and Frederick Avery remembered it for thirty years after he witnessed the meeting of the two generals. Gordon strove, like Howard, to heal the sectional wounds without relinquishing pride in what the Confederate soldier had tried to accomplish, giving his lecture on the "Last Days of the Confederacy" hundreds of times.[28]

Two years after the Peachtree Creek reunion, Howard attended the dedication of a monument to Confederate general William H. T. Walker, who had been killed in the battle of Atlanta on July 22, 1864. "I have spent a great deal of my time in the south," Howard told an Atlanta newspaper, "and I think I understand the southern people and the problems which confront them." He felt that former Confederates realized how earnest he was "to sow the seeds of education, and help build up the places laid waste by war." Reporters argued that Howard's presence at the Walker monument ceremony showed "that all sectional strife is ended, and that we are now united as one people."[29]

The general continued to be a staunch Republican, campaigning for McKinley in the fall of 1900. With Dan Sickles he led "the escort from the White House to the Capitol" in the president's second inaugural parade. As part of his effort to promote sectional reconciliation, Howard fondly described how West Point Superintendent Robert E. Lee came to his bedside to cheer him up when he was "extremely ill" as a cadet before the war and noted that he "followed General Grant, the great commander," during the conflict.[30]

Mark Twain and Lincoln Memorial University

Sectional reconciliation intertwined with the university's image most prominently when Howard planned an elaborate dinner to celebrate Lincoln's birthday and raise money for the school. He chose two former Confederates, both of whom expressed an admiration for Lincoln. Mark Twain, who had served briefly in a pro-Confederate home guard organization in Missouri, was happy to preside at the Lincoln dinner scheduled for the evening of February 12, 1901, but he worried that an article he had written for the *North American Review* might upset Howard. Twain severely criticized McKinley's policy in the Philippines, establishing the Missouri-born writer as one of the chief spokesman of the anti-imperialist cause in America. Twain courteously offered Howard the opportunity to "disinvite me if you find you don't want a person of my stripe," after the general had a chance to read the article. A little more than a year following Guy's death on Luzon, Howard was sensitive to criticism of the country's course in the Philippines. His fourth son, John Howard, was currently serving one of three tours of duty in the Philippines as major of the Forty-eighth U.S. Infantry. But Howard assured Twain that the article would not cause any trouble. He even invited the president, although McKinley declined. "Let us not part till our present agreement is fulfilled," Howard wrote Twain, "and then as your heart is patriotic, *I* shall not banish *you!!*"[31]

While Twain would serve as master of ceremonies, Sam Watterson would give the main address at the Carnegie Hall event. Born to a Tennessee congressman in Washington, D.C., Watterson had served as an aid to several Confederate generals during the war and edited a pro-Confederate newspaper for a time at Chattanooga. Watterson founded and edited the *Louisville Courier Journal* after the conflict and garnered fame and influence through his editorials. He took the lecture circuit in the 1890s, giving a popular and admiring talk about Lincoln that symbolized the healing of sectional wounds. Eugene P. Fairchild had tried to engage Watterson to give his Lincoln speech at Carnegie Hall in 1900, but the editor could not find room in his busy schedule. Howard secured Watterson's commitment in 1901. The idea that two former Confederates should celebrate Lincoln's birthday in New York was compelling. "Think of it," commented Twain to a friend, "two old rebels functioning there—I as President, and Watterson as Orator of the Day! Things have changed somewhat in these 40 years, thank God."[32]

Howard pushed for as much publicity as possible. He printed a special letterhead stationary emblazoned with the message "Lincoln's Birthday Celebration for the Benefit of the Lincoln Memorial University." The *New York Times* gave a promotional plug for the event while the *New York Tribune* ran a long story in its *Illustrated Supplement* that included Howard's lengthy plea for the school and its students. The *Supplement* article carried photographs of the buildings and the people at Lincoln Memorial University. Howard also gathered photographs for a long story in the *New York Mail and Express Illustrated Saturday Magazine.* Seats at the dinner cost one or two dollars, and Howard made it clear that the funds raised would support the daily running expenses of the school. He added that virtually all students worked on campus to pay their way, and the university was "mainly for white boys and girls of the mountains."[33]

Despite the effort expended on the biggest public event in the university's history to date, Howard doubted the prospects of raising more than a modest sum. Even so, the event could not fail to raise public awareness of the university and its mission. In fact, he sold enough tickets by January 31 to cover expenses. Twain requested "good seats" for his wife and two daughters.[34]

A bust of Lincoln, draped with an American flag, formed the centerpiece of the platform decor at Carnegie Hall on the evening of February 11, 1901. The entertainment featured music by the Fifth U.S. Artillery Band and the People's Choral Union of New York, prayer by a local minister, and the recital of a poem, "High Tide at Gettysburg." Twain introduced Watterson with witty remarks about his own and the speaker's war service, coupled with serious consideration of

Lincoln's legacy, and ended the celebration by reading a letter sent by McKinley that praised Lincoln. Former Union general Nelson A. Miles and former Confederate general Joseph Wheeler were among the platform guests.[35]

The event was a resounding success. "Our family have been talking about you all the morning," Howard wrote Twain the next day. "You & your revered 'confederate' did us wonderful service." John Hale Larry was effusive in his praise of Howard's efforts when the proceeds began to roll into Cumberland Gap. "I think likely that Mr. Myers will make some folks think that he did it all," he snidely told Eager. A similar effort was launched the next year in Boston, which included Civil War–era luminaries such as Dan Sickles, Joseph Wheeler, Julia Ward Howe, and Edward Everett Hale, but it failed to garner the attention that Twain and Watterson brought to the proceedings at Carnegie Hall.[36]

SEARCHING FOR THE BIG DONOR

Howard continued to look for the grand donor who could solve the university's financial problems in one stroke and persisted in approaching John D. Rockefeller. A month before the Lincoln celebration in New York, he asked Rockefeller for only seven hundred dollars to help the university meet its "running expenses." The oil industrialist agreed, but his secretary laid down some conditions upon forwarding the check. Frederick T. Gates made it clear that Rockefeller did not intend to become a patron of the institution and wanted to remain anonymous, requesting that he simply be listed in the records as "A friend." Rockefeller made the contribution in recognition of Howard's service to the country.[37]

Rockefeller's personal fortune was estimated at $900 million in 1901, and he had allocated $500 million of it for charity during his lifetime. His donations to the University of Chicago amounted to $35 million. While Baptist causes were closest to his heart, Rockefeller was willing to consider other institutions, but he began to rely heavily on Gates to manage much of his business affairs by the time Lincoln Memorial University had been founded.[38] Rockefeller created the General Education Board in 1902 and funded it with $183 million for disbursement to worthy educational causes. Gates and Dr. Wallace Buttrick ran the General Education Board for twenty years. The two were linked by a common background in the Baptist ministry, having both studied at the Rochester Theological Seminary in New York state. Gates, in fact, had initially secured Rockefeller's commitment to the University of Chicago. Gates and Buttrick agreed on what kind of school deserved the board's support.[39]

Unfortunately for Howard, he would have to work primarily through Gates and Buttrick rather than through Rockefeller to seek aid, and neither man regarded Lincoln Memorial University well. The aged general tried time and time again, urging a donation of fifteen thousand dollars to seed the creation of an endowment. When his appeals failed, Howard asked for up to four thousand dollars to help meet monthly expenses. Gates informed Rockefeller that he had declined Howard's plea several times. Buttrick and other members of the General Education Board had talked with the general and concluded "that his work does not merit attention." Rockefeller conceded, even though he regarded Howard highly.[40]

The general achieved a significant victory when he secured money to build a dorm for women, the first new construction on the Four Seasons property. Samuel P. Avery, an art dealer in New York city who had made his money by introducing the work of many European artists to America, had established the Avery Architectural Library at Columbia College in honor of his son, who had passed away in 1890. He and his wife read an article John Hale Larry wrote for the *Christian Herald* and became interested in Lincoln Memorial University. They donated six thousand dollars to finance the construction of what came to be known as Avery Hall in 1902.[41]

The new building went up with the labor of many university students. Gideon T. Spencer, who had helped construct the Four Seasons Hotel, supervised the student labor force as it raised the new building on part of the northern foundation of the old structure. He established a sawmill nearby to produce lumber and a brick kiln on the other side of the construction site. Student W. C. Thompson was involved in almost every phase of the construction, "from excavation to making the bricks, hauling the sand, snaking the logs, hauling the logs to the mill, and finally when the sawyer became ill with some epidemic that struck [Grant-Lee] Hall, I took over as sawyer and finished the job sawing lumber." The building not only contained dormitory rooms for girls but also held the small library and was the venue for chapel services. Sometime later, a one-story wing was added as a dining hall, which later was converted into a chemistry lab. Although the Averys provided the bulk of its construction cost, Howard had to drum up small donations at least until the end of 1903 to finish the building.[42]

Searching for the Right Man

Larry worked at Cumberland Gap little more than a year before his colleagues saw disturbing signs that he was not the right man to run the university. Howard thought that the only real problems lay in what he called "home scandals." Larry seemed to needlessly antagonize people, leading to their "disposition . . . to slander him, to fight him, or to antagonize him." He also worried about Larry's "prejudice against our 'village branch,'" the Harrow School. Larry tended to blame Myers for many of his troubles; he accused the minister of poisoning the views of Cumberland Gap residents against him. Moreover, Larry apparently covered up some sort of improper relation between his son Ralph and a young woman. Howard learned that the president also had "intervened to prevent one of his young lady students from corresponding with a desperado, and that the desperado is determined to drive him away."[43]

Charles Eager thought the problems stemmed from Larry's personality. The president needed "an entirely different spirit from what he has had" and told Howard "what we need is the *right man*." Many students came to dislike him, despite his initial good impression. "He was a little domineering and did not fit in very well," recalled Robert W. Barnett. "He referred to the Southern people as 'fools'" and "would berate them sometimes for eating 'hog meat.'" The story of his second marriage, so soon after his first wife had died, was repeated on campus to his detriment. Howard acknowledged Larry's success in setting up the first college operation on the Four Seasons property and urged him and his wife to forget about trying to raise funds and simply concentrate on university operations.[44]

The crisis came to a head in April 1901, when the citizens of Cumberland Gap petitioned the board to replace Larry with Myers. Howard was not pleased. "As he cannot write a single sentence correctly and as he seems to be almost completely without education himself in books, and as his reputation is not now unsullied, I do not see how worthy citizens can ask such a thing." The managing director now was convinced that Myers intended to ruin Larry. The problem worsened Howard's sciatica, which was beginning to affect his ability to walk, yet he began to think of replacing Larry as soon as possible. He asked Eager if a southern man could be found "big enough for President."[45]

The most important item on the agenda of the next board meeting, on May 22, 1901, was finding someone to replace Howard as managing director. The general's health was such that he wanted relief. The board agreed that Frederick B.

Avery would be a good choice, and the Ohio minister consented to serve as managing director on May 29. His first act was to suggest inserting the word "living" before the phrase "monument to Abraham Lincoln" on the letterhead stationery. Ironically, Larry had proposed that Avery be appointed president rather than managing director; apparently he was tired of fighting with Myers, but the board believed Howard needed relief more than Larry.[46]

Avery's short experience as managing director was filled with trouble, despite his genuine desire to help the institution. He and Fairchild organized a fund-raising event at Tremont Temple in Boston for the next year, and the pair traveled to Ohio, New York, and Buffalo to solicit donations. But the needs were pressing; Eager reported in early 1902 that the teachers had not been paid for two months because the university spent up to seven hundred dollars more each month than it received. Avery's constitution broke down. "Being of a sensitive nature," as Edgar Achorn put it, Avery found the life of a door to door solicitor "arduous and obnoxious." He had difficulty eating and sleeping and became "a fit subject for a hospital." Rumors of the fighting between Myers and Larry and prospects of bankruptcy worsened his state of mind, and Avery resigned as managing director in March 1902.[47]

Howard resumed his duties after less than a year. By now Larry's stock had sunk so low that the board was eager to replace him. Achorn, a Boston lawyer who had graduated from Bowdoin College in 1881, had hoped that Avery could have restrained the president, but that proved impossible. Achorn acknowledged that Larry was "a Christian gentleman and that he means all right," but he was not suited to be president.[48]

William L. Stooksbury emerged as a viable candidate to replace Larry. Born near Loyston, only about forty miles south of Cumberland Gap in Union County, Tennessee, he had the advantage of being a local man. The son of a Baptist minister, Stooksbury had taught in the rural schools for a time before earning his bachelor's degree at Ulysses S. Grant Memorial University, in Athens, Tennessee. Stooksbury became the protégé of the most influential man at the Athens institution, John F Spence, whose service as a chaplain in the Forty-eighth Ohio during the Civil War had led him to make his home in the postwar South. Spence created the American Temperance University at Harriman, Tennessee, and Stooksbury pursued postgraduate studies there and at the University of Chicago. He was very interested in becoming president of Lincoln Memorial University in the spring of 1902 but did not receive an offer before accepting an appointment to teach natural sciences at the Virginia Institute in Bristol.[49]

Larry continued to run Lincoln Memorial University during the next two years, but Stooksbury maintained his interest in the Cumberland Gap institution. He thought that "with the proper management," it "would make wonderful success." He admired its emphasis on "practical education" and its location in a region not yet served by a local college. He married teacher Ella Jamison in 1903, and the pair became a dynamic professional couple. When the board once again became interested in him, Stooksbury explained his qualifications to Herman Hughes. Noting that he had visited universities in eight nations during a three month tour of Europe, Stooksbury asserted, "I feel that I know every stone the teacher must turn to succeed." While he had little experience at soliciting funds, he had great success at recruiting students for American Temperance University and Carson-Newman College in Jefferson City, Tennessee. The board offered him the presidency, and Stooksbury accepted on May 20, 1904.[50]

Stooksbury came with the highest recommendations. Spence called him "*pure gold*," noting that he was the best of about one hundred teachers Spence had worked with over the course of thirty years in higher education. The former army chaplain wrote so glowingly "because of my interest in the poor mt boys" and "because I believe in Stooksbury." The Tennessee preacher's son took the reins from Larry on June 1.[51]

Larry's short, troubled time at Cumberland Gap led to an important accomplishment, the beginning of college operations that were physically separate from the crowded atmosphere at Harrow Hall. The semi-military regime he had instituted quietly disappeared well before he left the university. Larry had right motives, assuring Andrew Carnegie that "the feeling against [blacks] is bitter" in the region. "But the youth who come into this institution are taught that the negro is one of God's children and should always be treated with kindly consideration. Such education of the mountaineers will help to solve the problem of the South." He took time to write a letter to Alexander Arthur, praising him for spurring the development of the Cumberland Gap area. Designed to lift the Scotsman's spirits, Larry wrote, "I often think of the brilliant brain that planned so much and have great respect for it."[52]

Yet Larry's parting was anything but cordial. He insisted on taking several volumes of an encyclopedia that he had ordered and paid for with university funds, which caused some heated words between himself and the board members. "I feel satisfied that we did a great work in deposing Larry," Achorn concluded. Booker T. Washington, who knew Larry while a student at Hampton Institute, told Achorn that "he never believed Larry would be a success" at Cumberland

Gap. Larry moved to Big Stone Gap, Virginia, to serve as founder and president of the unsuccessful Highland Technical Institute for a couple of years. He applied for a war-related pension in 1906, listing his occupation as "missionary on my own charges." At five feet ten inches tall, and 250 pounds, Larry based his application on "obesity, poor circulation etc." and received the pension. He later pastored Edgewood Congregational Church in Providence before retiring in 1917. In poor health, the first on-site president of Lincoln Memorial University died on August 17, 1919.[53]

Exit Cyrus Kehr

Cyrus Kehr drifted away from the University during Larry's presidency, and his educational co-workers were ready to part with him. "The more I have to do with the man," wrote Herman Hughes, "the more thoroughly I become impressed with his total inability to do anything right, however amiable his disposition or intentions may be." Kehr presented a bill to cover his expenses while engaged in university work in May 1900. The board formed a committee to investigate, but Myers influenced it to take the position that Kehr was never meant to receive a salary and had contributed nothing to the university that justified recovery of expenses. Sympathetic board members asked Howard to verify Kehr's contributions, but the general could think of nothing beyond the fact that Kehr had written some letters soliciting funds. Other than Myers, everyone wanted to be fair with Kehr, but beyond playing a key role in naming the university and purchasing the Four Seasons property, he had done little for the school. His failure to move to Cumberland Gap and set up the college curriculum was a disappointment to everyone.[54]

Kehr was essentially an urban man with a progressive spirit. His attempt to become an absentee president, after moving his family to Knoxville in 1899, did not work out. He practiced patent law in Knoxville for more than twenty years. A parcel of land he owned south of the Tennessee River, and adjacent to land owned by the University of Tennessee, led to efforts to coordinate the care of this ground with the state's flagship university. Kehr was interested in establishing a bird sanctuary, but only if all hunting of birds was prohibited. He also disliked the growing practice of fox hunting among the affluent population of Knoxville. Kehr moved to Washington, D.C., in 1920, where he continued to practice patent law. He developed another passion, studying scientific methods of urban and state planning. Kehr authored a number of books on the subject, the best known of which was *A Nation Plan,* published in 1926, in which he advocated a comprehensive system of modern highways to accommodate the explosive growth of the automobile industry. A Congregationalist and Republican, Kehr died in Washington at age eighty-five on July 14, 1941.[55]

Exit Arthur A. Myers

John Hale Larry's antagonist, Arthur A. Myers, also left the scene during his presidency. Dissatisfaction with Myers's unpredictable nature had been brewing for many years. Howard noted that he "sometimes gives permission to do a thing or desires to do it, expresses his desire and then forgets." The general tried hard to be patient, always hoping that the errant missionary could be brought back into the fold, but Myers lost touch with the spirit of the institution he helped to found. The untimely passing of his wife Ellen greatly affected his emotional health. Ellen's nephew, Ernest G. Dodge, noted, "She had a strong influence over him, and was always a sort of 'balance wheel' to assist him in directing his powerful and restless energies into wise and fruitful channels." Myers also felt alienated by what he viewed as the intrusion of Howard and other northerners into his enterprise. He told James H. Rector that "he was the real founder of the school" and felt "disturbed and shaken over the fact that they were gradually crowding him out." Instead of cooperating with the northerners to build what he had started, Myers tried to establish yet more institutions by purchasing the Harrogate Inn and the Arthur house, neither of which was initially part of the university operation. In fact, Howard suspected that Myers used money the minister had collected for university purposes to make his down payment on the Arthur home without telling the donor. Shady deals seem to have been part of Myers's modus operandi, but he pursued them in his genuine desire to help people.[56]

Myers also suffered from poor health, recuperating at the home of a friend in Clifton Springs, New York, in 1901. He resigned from the Board of Directors as a result, much to the relief of John Hale Larry, but continued to spread negative publicity about the president. Larry wondered "how such a crazy man as Mr. Myers is can so hoodoo so many people. Sometimes it seems to me as though some strange spell rests there and keeps everybody in a continual stew." The situation became so bad that Howard bluntly asked Myers to explain his "avowed dislike to some members of our Board, whom you once loved." Howard appealed to Ellen's spirit, pointing out that she would not have approved of his spiteful talk. The general even hinted that Myers might be trying to ruin the university "to force us to sell, and that you may buy everything in at a small valuation, and set up an institution more after your own heart." Myers responded with protestations of his loyalty to the school, leaving Howard perplexed as to his motives. "Probably it is to get back again where he can raise money and have control," he concluded.[57]

Eugene Fairchild treated Myers more sympathetically than most of the group. He talked with the erratic minister but could never get to the bottom of his troublesome behavior. Fairchild cautioned Eager to remember that the Cumberland Gap citizens knew him well and probably discounted much of what he told them. "He is in deep water and it should, of course, be kept in mind the good he has done, and his wife," he wrote. Fairchild urged that everyone "be as considerate as we can with Mr. M. and remember that since his wife's death he has had no one to guide or shield him."[58]

The Arthur house, ca. 1899–1904. *Left to right, first row:* Robert F. Patterson, Arthur A. Myers, Oliver Otis Howard, Mr. Blanchard, and Darwin R. James; *second row:* John Hale Larry, Millard Overton, Charles F. Eager, Eugene P. Fairchild, Edgar O. Achorn, and Frederick B. Avery. UA-LMU.

Howard may have come close to the truth when he told Eager that Myers probably did not like the treasurer because of "your having fifty dollars a month and he nothing." Myers lived a hand-to-mouth existence. He claimed that the university owed him a thousand dollars, a claim his colleagues took seriously, but they were reluctant to authorize him to raise the funds for himself, given the irregularities that attended his financial endeavors. As farm manager Rector put it, "Myers was a good money getter but a careless man about looking after business affairs."[59]

In the end, Myers left an ambivalent legacy with the institution he helped to create. A good planter of seeds, he did not have the temper to nurture an institution to maturity. Although he had founded forty-four schools and churches, only the Harrow School grew into a large success, and Lincoln Memorial University grew out of it. He maintained a sense of humble dignity, professing continued support for the institution in his correspondence, but did many things that could only hurt the school behind the scenes, and for reasons that are difficult to pin down.[60]

Myers served as president of the Industrial Girls' Home and School in Cumberland Gap, more popularly known as the Grace Nettleton Home, for some years after severing his relations with Lincoln Memorial University. He married Grace Funk, whom he met at an evangelist meeting in May 1903. The couple lived in the Arthur house while James Rector and his wife rented a cottage on the Arthur house site and provided the Myers their meals. Grace published a book, *Them Missionary Women,* in 1911, but barely mentioned her husband in it. She died about 1921, and Arthur appeared one last time on the campus of Lincoln Memorial University to accept an honorary doctoral degree in 1923. A year later, on May 5, 1924, Myers died in Jackson, Michigan.[61]

CHAPTER 4
STOOKSBURY'S SCHOOL

I haven't much chance to go to school here I'm eager for an education and have troubled about an education a great deal.
—Ola Good, of Difficult, Tennessee, April 19, 1909

I hope to emerge from the drowsiness of ignorance, and awake in the glories of an education.
—Grover Day, of Sand Lick, West Virginia, January 19, 1909

The idea of Lincoln Memorial University is to teach young men and women not only *to know* but *to do* things.
—William L. Stooksbury, undated

The new president took charge of Lincoln Memorial University on June 1, 1904, and began a period of consolidation and expansion. William L. Stooksbury had solid academic credentials and was "full of youth and energy," as Howard put it. A visitor to the campus described Stooksbury as "tall, lean, steely of frame, humorous of mouth, unafraid of eye." To Jesse H. Moore, who began a long teaching career at Lincoln Memorial University in 1905, the new president "was a positive man, quick in his decisions, keen in insight, and prompt to act." Moore particularly admired Stooksbury's ability to inspire and discipline the students. He ran a tight ship and constantly had his eye on future growth and development.[1]

By the fall of 1904, Stooksbury reported an increase in enrollment, even though he did not hesitate to expel students for just cause. The faculty, with Stooksbury's blessing, warned several students, on October 24, that they faced expulsion for bad behavior. Four days later, two other pupils who were considered "guilty of conduct unbecoming students of the university" were expelled by a unanimous vote of the faculty.[2]

Stooksbury retained the basic organization of the school, which Howard himself had established. The Industrial Department managed the student work assignments and contained some programs in business training and basket and mattress making, but the department never emerged as a degree-granting element

William L. Stooksbury, university president, 1904–10. UA-LMU.

on campus. The Normal Department was the most important, training teachers for the local elementary and secondary schools. About fifty students from this department went out every year to teach for short terms in the local institutions, coming back to take more courses until they completed their bachelor's degrees. The Collegiate Department offered the traditional curriculum, with required courses in history, English, and languages, all designed to prepare the student for further study elsewhere. The Musical and Commercial Departments were yet in their infancy. Lincoln Memorial University was "co-educational, non-sectional, non-sectarian, but Christian," as Stooksbury carefully pointed out.[3]

The majority of students continued to be in the primary and secondary levels at Harrow Hall rather than taking classes on the Four Seasons property. Stooksbury worried about how "to separate the college from the grades" but considered it possible at some point in the near future. In the meanwhile, he supervised the students with a benign authoritarianism. Stooksbury forbade the use of tobacco, liquor, and "profane language." "Laziness and deception will not be tolerated for a single day in this institution," he proclaimed in the catalog. "We do not wish to aid in any way those who are ungrateful, and most surely we do not wish to educate them at the expense of benevolent friends." Stooksbury warned anyone who was "out to beat his way" through college that Lincoln Memorial University was not the place to do so.[4]

Stooksbury assured parents that their sons "will not learn to be drunkards, card-players or gamblers," and that their daughters "will not be buggy driving at night, nor attend the dance hall nor the euchre party." The president wanted Lincoln Memorial University to "throw around its students the strong arm of

Picnic at the Pinnacle, atop Cumberland Mountain, 1906. UA-LMU.

moral and religious life." Girls were not permitted to spend the night off campus, but they could visit relatives who lived nearby on Saturdays. Stooksbury refused when a father asked permission for his daughter to break this rule because "sometimes undesirable young men would insist on paying attentions to the young ladies" if they stayed in town. "I take it for granted," Stooksbury wrote the parent, "that you expect us as teachers and managers of the school to look after the girls in every respect as a parent would." Stooksbury conducted roll call at breakfast and dinner to ensure that students were not absent without permission.[5]

By 1905, the university's eight faculty members could not boast a single doctoral degree, but two held master's diplomas and four held bachelor's degrees. Two of the faculty members had not yet earned any college degree. Apparently only four of the eight taught classes in the Collegiate Department, in English, history, math, applied science, Latin, and Greek. The normal teaching load was eight classes per day, for a salary amounting to seventy dollars per month. Professors were expected to pay up to ten dollars per month for room and board and provide their own bed linen, pillow, and towels.[6]

The academic work was demanding. Jesse H. Moore, who grew up in Civil War North Carolina as a Quaker, placed his invalid wife in the Hospital for the

Insane at Knoxville and sent his young daughter to a boarding school, then moved into a ground floor room in Grant-Lee Hall in 1905. Stooksbury expected him to teach Greek and Latin and supervise the boys during the evening. "I gave myself without reserve to my work," he recalled. Moore was already fifty years old when he joined the faculty, and his health worsened under the strain. He had no relief, day or night, and developed digestive troubles in the spring of 1909. Stooksbury allowed him to move out of Grant-Lee Hall into a private room, where he quickly recovered his health.[7]

The university began to confer bachelor's degrees in 1906. George W. Morton became not only the first graduate but also the only member of the graduating class that year, when 125 students were enrolled in college courses. Morton was a thirty-five-year-old native of Campbell County, Tennessee, the only one of eleven children born to his carpenter father who attended college. Because he had considerable experience as a teacher, and was much older than his fellow students, Stooksbury asked Morton to teach math and supervise residents in Grant-Lee Hall even before he graduated. The latter duty consisted mostly of watching a particular window to prevent boys from leaving after curfew. Morton went on to teach math and serve as an administrator in several public school districts near Knoxville and retired in 1945. He was feted for the rest of his life as the first graduate of Lincoln Memorial University, a fame he took in good-natured stride. The university did not graduate anyone in 1907, 1908, or 1910, and it conferred but one degree in 1909. The graduating class of 1911 consisted of six people.[8]

The most important work Stooksbury accomplished while president was to increase the size of the student body. He knew how to advertise and appeal, and he was diligent in his efforts to respond quickly and in an encouraging manner to letters of inquiry. Many young people wrote to express their desire for an education and for the opportunity to work their way through the curriculum. "I am a poor girl," wrote Lizzie Garrett of Pennington Gap, Virginia, "my mother is dead and my Father is getting old I want to try to get education if I can I hope you will try to help me all you can." Garrett assured the president she was willing to work. "I hope you will let me in just as cheap as you possible can." Even prospects in New York City read about the university in newspaper stories planted by Howard and other promoters. Sam Suntotsky, a young Russian immigrant to America, informed the university that he was penniless but eager to learn. "This is my only one wish I don't want nothing in my life but only education," he wrote. Suntotsky understood that the university had been created to honor Lincoln and give a boost to poverty-stricken youth, but Alexander Gambol of Cedartown,

The university's baseball team, early twentieth century. UA-LMU.

Georgia, did not seem to realize those basic points. He innocently addressed his letter of inquiry to "Mr lincoln."[9]

Usually letter writers wanted to learn the financial details of attending the university. As Ray Dills of Norton, Virginia, rather impatiently put it three days before the fall session began, "I want Come there and go to School ans. this letter at once and Send me terms." Stooksbury explained the arrangements to everyone; with charges for room rent and board, tuition, and incidental fees, the entire cost amounted to $125 per year. If the student could work, Stooksbury only required that he or she make a down payment at the start of the term with the intention of paying off the rest through their wages. The institution accepted barter when necessary, although this does not appear to have been common. Boarding clubs in the two dorms helped to reduce the cost of food a bit, and Stooksbury was willing to tailor courses of study to meet the legitimate needs of students who demonstrated the ability to accelerate their academic work.[10]

Lincoln Memorial University offered a limited number of scholarships to deserving students, but they were "in the nature of loans" and never more than fifty dollars each. The recipient had to sign a note promising to repay the loan, but Stooksbury assured everyone he had no intention of legally pursuing students who defaulted. The scholarships were available to men and women alike, and the funds came from donations. Stooksbury encouraged selected students to write letters to prospective donors. As Carr Butcher put it, "What I want, is for you, Dear Mrs. Upham, to get me a scholarship in Lincoln Memorial University, where I have gone to school for the past two years." Whether Butcher was successful is not known, but Erskine H. Cox of Boston visited the campus in 1905 and was so impressed that he continued to fund the Mary F. Cox scholarship, although he believed the students "did not get enough to eat."[11]

Parents wanted to know that they were sending their sons and daughters to the right kind of school. Mrs. John Engle of Blowing Rock, North Carolina, assured Stooksbury, "I am sending you a good boy no bad habits and I do hope and pray he will not be" corrupted. She was "so glad you say you will look after him." Sarah Frost Hill contemplated sending her son and daughter, and she assured Stooksbury, "My heart & best wishes is with you & I only wish the whole world could realize the good work being done there. . . . May God bless beautiful, beautiful. L.M.U."[12]

Student Labor

Stooksbury was a strong advocate of the work-learn concept. "What we need in Appalachian America is an institution whose object is to teach young men and young women that labor is ennobling and not degrading," he declared. If more "young women of the country understood domestic science as we teach it, there would be less stomach troubles and less family rows and fewer divorces and a less number of men remaining away from home at night at the clubs."[13]

Students received seven to nine cents per hour, more for skilled labor and for managing other student workers. The money was applied to the student's account with a reckoning at the end of the academic year. By comparison, farm laborers across the South received on average 84 cents per day, without board, in 1909. Farm laborers across the United States received on average $1.30 per day without board that year. The rate of student labor was only a little below the southern average.[14]

Female students cleaned rooms, halls, and dining rooms, served food, washed dishes, and filled oil lamps. Male students tended the livestock on the university farm, milked cows, and constructed buildings. When O. B. Stark sent his son Howard to Lincoln Memorial University, Stooksbury assured him that "besides his literary work, he has taken up plumbing." The class schedule began at 7:15 a.m. and lasted until noon. After lunch, classes resumed at 1:15 and ended at 3:30. Students could plan to take all their classes in the morning and work all afternoon. A time book for the week ending October 26, 1907, indicated that twenty-eight students worked on the farm, from five to fifty-nine hours each, at a rate of five to ten cents per hour. Most of the students worked four to ten hours per day, six days that week, but seven worked only on Saturday and four worked on Friday and Saturday. The twenty-eight students earned credit in their accounts that ranged from 40 cents to $5.90.[15]

The students helped to cultivate at least two hundred acres of the six-hundred-acre Four Seasons property. Stooksbury reported the harvesting of five hundred bushels of Irish potatoes, three hundred bushels of sweet potatoes, and enough tomatoes to supply both the boys and girls dorms in the fall of 1909. The farm also produced cabbage, turnips, strawberries, and raspberries. The university slaughtered a cow each week, and sometimes a pig, to feed the dormitory residents, and a herd of eighteen dairy cows supplied milk to the students. Lincoln Memorial University also employed pupils in a small gristmill for grinding corn, a planing mill to finish lumber, and a blacksmith shop.[16]

Stooksbury and Students

True to the promise of his earlier career, Stooksbury fostered a large increase in the student population. He paid a fee amounting to 10 percent of the student's tuition and fees to a few recruiting agents and waived tuition and fees for any male students who intended to become ministers. More than 425 students were enrolled in all programs and grades by May 1905, and 570 were enrolled by the fall of 1907. Stooksbury noted that the university produced 65 teachers the next year, estimating that they instructed 3,250 area pupils. He assured friends of the university that some dorm rooms were packed with 3 and 4 students, and he had to turn away from 75 to 300 interested people each year.[17]

Yet Stooksbury did not coddle students in order to retain them. "I am sorry that Edyth was not thoughtful enough to be careful of her conduct while here in school," he wrote the girl's father when sending her home. Given her lack of maturity, "we would not like to assume any responsibility for her any longer at the present." Isaac Hopkins of Pineville, Kentucky, received some blunt news when Stooksbury wrote of his son Fred, "He does not appreciate kind treatment." Stooksbury intended to send him home if he did not improve his behavior. "In my opinion, there is just one kind of school for him, and that is the State reform school." Howard Stark, the plumber, did "not apply himself" to his studies and insisted on using tobacco in violation of university rules. Stooksbury intended to expel him if he did not improve quickly. A boy from Harlan, Kentucky, became so drunk on campus that he had to be carried to a house in Cumberland Gap to sober up. Stooksbury expelled him and two other young men for the same reason, although he caved in when the Harlan student's father begged a second chance for his son.[18]

Stooksbury invested a great deal of patience in the case of Jerome Stevens of Clearwater, Minnesota. Stevens rebelled and left campus for a job in Cumberland Gap. Stooksbury had a talk with him one day but found the young man "quite impudent," displaying no real desire to return. "I told him to go back to his job at the Gap," Stooksbury informed Jerome's father, "and when he felt like making a man of himself, to come back and I would be more than glad to do whatever I could for him." Stooksbury conveyed this message to Jerome, challenging him to show that he was ready "to apply yourself both to labor and to books, that you are willing to take suggestions from those under whom you work, that you are willing to get down to business and not be running about over the country from pillar to post." Jerome took the president at his word; he signed a pledge promising "to do my best to conform to all requirements, both as a laborer and student, while in Lincoln Memorial University."[19]

Sometimes there was nothing Stooksbury could do but rely on the local law authorities. When a young man from Rose Hill, Virginia, came onto campus one night and drunkenly displayed a revolver in the dorm, the president called on the deputy sheriff of Claiborne County to arrest him. The man, however, escaped from the jail later that night. Stooksbury offered a ten-dollar reward for his capture, although it is unclear if the man was caught.[20]

Southern Issues

Many interested friends of the university wondered why more donations did not come from southern supporters. S. A. Lewis, the secretary of the university, cautioned a woman in Missouri not to be misled by the Lincoln name when she asked that question. He assured her that most of the teachers and students were southerners and more of them were descended from Confederate veterans than from Union soldiers. Lewis assured the prospective donor, "We believe that the war is over and, all things considered, think that matters have been settled for the best; hence it is unnecessary to stir up bitter feelings."[21]

When support came from the South, it often came from Union veterans who lived there. F. H. Earle ended his Union army service by deciding to live and work in Mississippi. He supported his grown daughter, a widow with a child, as she attended school at Lincoln Memorial University. "I voted for Lincoln in the field," Earle wrote to Lewis. "I know the work Gen'l Howard is doing."[22]

Howard appreciated support such as this, but he worried that so little help came from true southerners. He hoped that Stooksbury could serve as a conduit, given his southern background, and rejected the notion once advanced by Larry that the name of Lincoln served as a barrier to larger donations from southerners. Howard argued that "even the conservative Democrats now acknowledge that Lincoln is next to Washington, if not even in advance of him, in his greatness of soul and in his wonderful capacity." When Eager suggested tapping into southern regard for Jefferson Davis, Howard bluntly told him, "I couldn't get a hundred dollars outside of Davis' personal friends, and I do not know any of them. . . . Lee is popular and Stonewall Jackson is popular, but Jefferson Davis has not really touched the popular heart, north or south."[23]

When contacting prospective donors in the South, Howard emphasized the "decidedly Christian" nature of Lincoln Memorial University. He also hoped to solicit more money from an entirely opposite direction, his "Jewish friends" in the northeastern cities, but was unsuccessful in that endeavor. Frederick B. Avery also pointed out that the nonsectarian nature of the institution hurt its chances of gaining support from established churches, which preferred to promote denominational schools.[24]

The university's most prominent southerner, Robert Patterson, continued to serve on what now was called the Executive Committee of the Board of Directors. Stooksbury invited him to give an address on the Great Emancipator to commemorate the gift of a Lincoln bust by J. Ackerman Coles of New York city on February 12, 1908. It was the first Lincoln statue to appear on the campus. Patterson's address was short on facts and displayed little true understanding of Lincoln's role in American history; but he spoke in rhetorical flourishes about the important theme of sectional unity. Patterson admitted that he embraced the image of Lincoln because, as a strict Calvinist, his mother had taught him to accept God's will. Since the South had been defeated, despite all its efforts, Patterson accepted Lincoln as an agent of divine destiny. Patterson wrote another essay about Lee, filled with similar rhetorical flourishes about the South's greatest war hero.[25]

Race

Racial concerns remained the chief southern issue associated with Lincoln Memorial University. Stooksbury continued the policy of the founders to encourage white students to enter the university. "The whole scheme of instruction," wrote a visitor named Clarence Ludlow Brownell, of Dayton, Ohio, "is planned especially to meet the requirements of the . . . white population in the region of Cumberland Gap." Many people continued to assume, however, that a university named for Lincoln in a southern state was a black institution. John F. Spence reported the accusations of a man in Florida who claimed that Lincoln Memorial University was "made up of children & Niggers." When the *Christian Work and Evangelist* of New York city printed a story about the university in December 1908, the editor mistakenly called it a school for "young colored people." S. A. Lewis remonstrated with the magazine, saying it had done "us A GREAT INJUSTICE, especially among our southern patrons." Lewis assured the editor that blacks had never attended classes. "This is strictly a school for the white people of these mountainous parts of the states around us, and no negroes are admitted." Lewis believed that this printed misstatement "would do us more damage than ten thousand dollars would do us good."[26]

The touchy issue of race was of importance to more than just southerners. When D. D. Walker of Santa Barbara, California, was asked to serve among the vice-presidents of the Lincoln Endowment Fund campaign in 1909, he admitted that he had never heard of Lincoln Memorial University. "If colored children are admitted to the University I desire that you erase my name as one of the Vice Presidents. If only white children are admitted," he was willing to donate one hundred dollars. Robert Lee Dunn, the New York–based professional fund-raiser who managed the Endowment campaign, assured Walker that "this school in the southern mountains is *strictly* for *white* children."[27] The "strictly white" nature of Lincoln Memorial University not only emanated from the original mission of the school but also had been mandated by the state of Tennessee, which had prohibited interracial education on the college level in 1901. There is no evidence that African Americans wished to study at Cumberland Gap or inquired about terms to do so.

Racism was a deeply entrenched element of American culture during the first decade of the twentieth century, but it was not always expressed in aggressive, exclusionary terms. In 1905, for example, Stooksbury published a short article, "The Race that Will Predominate," in a Christian magazine called the *Treasury* in which he predicted that the Anglo-Saxon "race" was destined to win the global competition for the world's diminishing resources because it represented the ideal of civil liberty and "a pure spiritual Christianity."[28] The kind of racism Stooksbury enunciated was benign, aimed at extolling the virtues of a particular brand of ethnicity rather than suppressing the rights and privileges of another race. It had a Darwinian flavor, in that Stooksbury envisioned global competition with the most competitive race predominating. In this, however, Stooksbury differed from Howard, who continued to argue that teaching young Appalachians to respect the rights "of their black brothers and sisters" was "a right purpose" that the world desperately needed.[29]

In another vein of thought, Stooksbury expressed an attitude typical of many mountaineers when he characterized the poor white trash of the southern lowlands as a "worthless, shiftless class that live[d] in the midst of slavery, owning neither land nor slaves." He distinguished them from the "typical mountaineer . . . with all the pride and self respect which belongs to a landholder." In denigrating the legacy of slavery, Stooksbury ignored the fate of blacks, who were most affected by the institution of slavery. Indifference rather than racism accounts for the lack of attention paid to African American issues by the university. Howard never insisted on imposing a black agenda for the college, content to make Lincoln Memorial University a school for the descendants of mountain white loyalists.[30]

Ironically, the Lincoln image Stooksbury used to interest mountain whites in the university had a naturally compelling appeal to blacks all across the South. As Booker T. Washington put it during the centennial of Lincoln's birthday, his race could best honor the Great Emancipator "by putting into daily practice the lessons of his own life." Every African American ought to "resolve from this day forward that we shall lead sober, industrious, frugal, moral lives, and that while being ambitious we shall at the same time be patient, law-abiding and self-controlled as Lincoln was." A similar message served as Lincoln Memorial University's appeal to the white men and women of Appalachia. Few people other than Howard dared to admit that the plight of mountain whites was similar to that of former slaves. The old commissioner of the Freedmen's Bureau often remarked that he was trying to accomplish something for whites at Lincoln Memorial University that Washington had already accomplished for blacks at Tuskegee Institute in Alabama.[31]

"University"

Representatives of the school continued to defend their use of the word "University" in connection with the Cumberland Gap enterprise. Howard explained to a potential donor in Atlanta that he considered the word to signify "a union of departments." He supported the board in thinking the word suited the institution's goals if not its current condition. In the eyes of some conservatives, the word connoted "unchristian and unpatriotic teachings"; in short, a university operated a modern, secular curriculum. W. S. Witham was unwilling to give money but endorsed the use of the word in connection with "the name of that great man, Mr. Lincoln." The pragmatic Stooksbury thought "much valuable time is being lost by quibbling over the word 'University.'" He wanted to focus on the work, not the name, and would have been happy with "institution or some other good word."[32]

Presidential Power Struggle

Stooksbury's health began to suffer because of overwork. He submitted his resignation in April 1906, but Howard deferred its acceptance until he could find some way to ease the president's burden. Spence told Fairchild that Stooksbury had experienced the same problem in a previous appointment.[33]

Howard decided to appoint Rev. R. A. Beard of Cambridge, Massachusetts, as chancellor of Lincoln Memorial University to share the workload with both Stooksbury and himself. Beard asked William Goodell Frost's opinion of the prospect at Cumberland Gap and received a stunning reply. Frost denigrated Lincoln Memorial University as an enterprise "conceived in other than the spirit of wisdom and benevolence, partly as a money-making scheme of real estate men in that town to retrieve the fortunes of the place, and partly as spite work—to use the common phrase—by E. P. Fairchild when he was dismissed from his position at Berea." Frost noted that none of the faculty were well trained and accused Fairchild of manipulating one president after another out of office. He also argued that Howard's fame allowed the university a kind of "pathetic interest" that drew only minimal donations. Frost relayed the comment of a religious leader in New York that Howard was "not qualified to administer the affairs of a kindergarten!"[34]

To his credit, Beard continued to be interested in the university despite Frost's opinion. He visited Cumberland Gap in May 1906 and worked out the details with all concerned. The position of chancellor had been noted in the charter, but its exact duties had not been enunciated. The board promised to do so, but Beard realized that virtually all duties were already performed by Howard as managing director or by Stooksbury as president. Nevertheless, it was agreed that Stooksbury should list Beard as chancellor in the next catalog. Beard, however, was surprised to find that his name appeared only as a member of a committee that he had never agreed to serve on when the catalog appeared in July. He realized that Stooksbury meant to sabotage his appointment and began to back away from the job.[35]

Howard was upset, for he hoped that Beard would relieve himself and Stooksbury of much labor. In fact, Howard wanted him to direct Stooksbury's work. He called a special meeting of the board and pleaded with Beard to "do what you can to relieve my great care." While some members of the board understood Beard's position, the body called on him to reconsider his resignation as chancellor. Beard decided to bow out with grace, and Howard was left to continue his demanding duties as the chief fund-raiser. Fairchild incorrectly assumed that Beard could not get along with Howard, for "the Gen has been a commander so long he has not yet learned to gracefully work in a subordinate position."[36]

In fact, the true cause of the Beard fiasco was Stooksbury. The president quietly refused to subordinate himself to this stranger from Massachusetts. In August, after taking a vacation, Stooksbury felt fine. At the next board meeting in May 1907, he argued against a change in the administrative structure, proposed by Edgar O. Achorn, which would have separated the office of president from the board. "Now, if the President of the Institution is not a man of sufficient strength, and his ideas of school work are not of sufficient importance to have a voice in some way in the general government and management of the entire Institution, he is not fit to be President of the institution." Stooksbury's argument had an effect. He was listed as ex-officio president of the Board of Directors and of the Executive Committee in the next catalog, replacing Howard in both positions.[37]

Harrow Hall

The university lost the building that was "the real birthplace of L.M.U." when Harrow Hall burned in mid-February 1907. The monetary loss was twenty thousand dollars. While Howard was sorry to learn the news, he saw the fire as an opportunity to separate the grades from the college work at the Four Seasons property. He suggested the residents of Cumberland Gap rebuild the school and operate it as a public institution. The university had three insurance policies on Harrow Hall, issued by three different companies in New York, St. Louis, and Columbus, Georgia. Charles Eager represented all three companies, but Tennessee law prohibited insuring a building for more than three-fourths of its value. Howard had begun a campaign to raise money for the construction of a multipurpose building on the Four Seasons campus and had already gathered more than four thousand dollars in pledges, but he was not interested in replacing Harrow Hall.[38]

Local residents devised a plan to build a new public school under village auspices. Lincoln Memorial University provided one thousand dollars, from the five thousand dollars it collected from the insurance companies, to help Cumberland Gap construct a small building for the elementary grades. It would be called the Ellen Myers School, putting into effect a dream that the Board of Directors had initiated ten years earlier to honor Ellen's role in local education. The community added more than four thousand dollars to the university's contribution and constructed a small, two-story building in Harrogate, opposite the entrance to the Four Seasons campus. The new building also hosted Sunday school classes and community events. Lincoln Memorial University provided the teachers and paid the school's expenses until 1930, when financial difficulties forced it to bow out and allow the county to carry the entire fiscal burden. Ellen Myers School remained, however, a significant training facility for teacher education students at the university. The secondary grades were shifted to an academy operated by Lincoln Memorial University, using the facilities on the Four Seasons property, soon after Harrow Hall burned down. It seems as if the graded students mingled with the college students in the classroom and the dormitories for many years to come, further obscuring the legitimacy of the collegiate departments in the minds of some donors.[39]

Medical Training

Lincoln Memorial University involved itself in medical training when the Tennessee Medical College approached Howard with a proposal for articulation. Founded in 1889 to train both doctors and nurses, financial difficulties stemming from the burning of its main building, a drop in enrollment, and construction of a private hospital to serve student training led the institution to seek an alliance with a liberal arts college in the area. Its directors initially approached Maryville College in Blount County, which offered only a loan of twenty-five thousand dollars. This did not satisfy directors of the medical school, because they wanted an academic link to an existing university as well as operating funds. They suggested a union that would allow themselves to be called the Medical Department of Lincoln Memorial University in July 1905. The Knoxville school would retain its faculty and dean but would exchange some directors from both boards. There would be no transfer of ownership, and the university would not be responsible for the medical school's debts. Stooksbury thought his university had little to lose and supported the union.[40]

But the Tennessee Medical College again approached Howard with a proposal to sell half its property to Lincoln Memorial University as a way to generate more operating funds in 1906. Daunted by the problems of maintaining a facility sixty miles away when he still owed money on the Arthur house property and had trouble meeting the monthly operating expenses at Cumberland Gap, Howard declined. Instead the university extended a loan of five thousand dollars to the medical college at 4 percent interest and accepted a second mortgage from the medical school as security. The first mortgage of twenty-five thousand dollars had been held by Maryville College since 1904. Lincoln Memorial University continued its articulation agreement with an option to purchase the Tennessee Medical College and its hospital. The Knoxville facility continued to be known as the Medical Department of Lincoln Memorial University, and brochures touted it as "one of the handsomest and best equipped hospitals south of the Ohio River."[41]

AUDITORIUM

Enough money was available for the construction of another new structure on the Four Seasons property by 1909, an auditorium large enough for assemblies and religious services. It was placed on the east side of the leveled hill top, over the foundation of another wing of the old hotel building. Quite possibly Howard used the nearly five thousand dollars he had solicited for a main building on campus for this purpose. Because it was used most frequently for daily chapel services and Sunday school classes, residents of the campus called it the "Tabernacle." Cheaply constructed with benches to accommodate six hundred people, it served its purpose until 1924.[42]

Stooksbury and Fund Raising

Stooksbury became more involved in fund raising after he became presiding officer of the Board of Directors in 1907, probably as a way to ease some of the burden from Howard's shoulders. A local lawyer named J. Frank White promised the president to push a bill in the legislature "asking the state for a donation to Lincoln Memorial University," but nothing came of the effort. In the centennial year of Lincoln's birth, Stooksbury promoted a plan to create a large memorial building on campus "in which every state in the Union may be represented by a part of the main building peculiar to that state." He hoped to provide space for any foreign nation to construct a building that would be "fitting as a monument and suitable for school purposes." The plan involved creating a new Board of Trustees (rather than Board of Directors) for this project, consisting of members of every state in the nation and appointed by the national government or state governments. Stooksbury urged East Tennessee's representative in the U.S. Congress to help in getting an appropriation of one million dollars to start this grandiose scheme. Of course, nothing ever came of it.[43]

When he contacted individual donors, Stooksbury stressed the explosive growth of the student body during his years as president, pleading that he had to turn away deserving students because of lack of space and a shortage of scholarships and jobs to offer them. "I have been overrun" by applications from prospective students, he wrote to one potential friend of the university. Stooksbury also pushed for funds to construct a second boys' dormitory to alleviate the problem. He warned that anyone turned away "must remain out of school, ignorant, in the common herd, rather than educate themselves and march in the front ranks of progressive men and women." To further promote the image that Lincoln Memorial University was a seeder of progress in its corner of Appalachia, Stooksbury noted that a well-graded, macadamized road had recently been cut across Cumberland Mountain through the saddle of Cumberland Gap to link the Tennessee villages with Middlesboro, and that a "new County road" stretched from Harrogate to Tazewell, the Claiborne County seat.[44]

As a student of Appalachian culture, Stooksbury became interested in the efforts of some institutions to preserve elements of mountain life. The "indigenous crafts tradition," which had begun at Berea under Frost, aimed at developing an appreciation of folk crafts as a money-generating endeavor. The crafts were made along modern business lines rather than traditional folkways; by creating a "factory" of sorts, institutions could standardize production and sales. Stooksbury was eager to establish a broom factory at Lincoln Memorial University as a way to create more campus jobs for students. He began to plant broom corn on the farm but needed funds to purchase machinery and prepare a building. He hoped to employ up to thirty students in making the brooms and at least one student in traveling the road to sell them.[45]

Stooksbury also became interested in the work of Emma Bell Miles, a Chattanooga-based writer and artist. He read her *Spirit of the Mountains,* a candid but sympathetic look at mountain culture published in 1905, with its loving depiction of Appalachian life, and was moved by it. Stooksbury encouraged Miles to come to Lincoln Memorial University, where he offered her husband a job as a gardener and rented one of the cottages to her family. Miles moved to Cumberland Gap by March 27, 1910, and stayed until June 22, soaking in the mountain atmosphere. She often took her small children for walks to the Arthur house and saw the passage of Halley's Comet in late May. Her journal is filled with artist impressions of nature and topography, but Miles also was taken by the sight of student laborers harvesting wheat in June. "After the reaper comes the sun-bronzed, blue-shirted University boys, by two and three, eating grains of wheat with their hollowed hands," she wrote. "One stops to talk, in his pleasant voice laughing and showing his strong, even teeth. He tells me how to cook fresh wheat." Although Stooksbury had hoped that Miles would be inspired to write or paint at Cumberland Gap, her brief stay at the university produced no lasting works of art.[46]

Chapter 5
Howard's Monument

Our little part is to plant that institution in the mountains, an institution of an industrial character which shall be an object lesson for others; which shall enable those who have no helper to get a practical education; which shall bring enlightenment and privilege to those who, like Lincoln, have had to carry loads too heavy for childhood and youth.
—Oliver Otis Howard, undated

I have devoted myself night and day to the building up of a central institution (Lincoln's Memorial University) near that Cumberland Gap, which in [*sic*] intended to be not only a great help to the mountain youth, but a veritable monument to him whom I have served and loved these many years, Abraham Lincoln.
—Oliver Otis Howard, 1908

The problems and prospects of Lincoln Memorial University dominated the last years of Oliver Otis Howard's life, even though advancing age led to periodic health problems that burdened his efforts to raise money for the institution. The only college that had enlisted more of his time and energy had been Howard University. The aging general's role as managing director and his large friendship for Lincoln Memorial University made him the chief founder and sage counselor whose advice was indispensable for the survival of the school.

Howard continued to raise awareness of the university in magazine and newspaper articles. In "Lincoln's Monument in the Mountains," published in a 1905 issue of the *National Magazine,* he contrasted the living monument to Lincoln at Cumberland Gap with monuments made of stone and described the backward nature of Appalachian life. Howard wrote of his personal love for Lincoln and the awakening of his love for the mountain Unionists during the war. The article included several photographs of buildings on campus, emphasizing the modern educational facilities already existing there. Howard reported his satisfaction at watching a professor teach a young lady who had charge of eighty-three pupils in a regional school. She soaked up all the knowledge possible while at Lincoln Memorial University before returning to her log cabin school for the fall term, intending to return for more classes during the next summer break. Howard also proudly reported that Stooksbury and his wife made a point of eating their meals with the students to maintain close touch with their needs.[1]

In "Personal Recollections of Abraham Lincoln," Howard asserted that his last visit with the president had inspired him to seed educational institutions for blacks as well as whites across the South. "I have devoted myself night and day to the building up of a central institution (Lincoln's Memorial University)" in order to open doors for the mountain youth and create "a veritable monument to him whom I have served and loved these many years," he wrote. J. T. Turner of Iowa City, Iowa, initially learned of Lincoln Memorial University by reading this article and decided to bequeath one thousand dollars in "a perpetual Schollarship" because he felt that Howard's "great work for Lincolns Memorial University is a very worthy & useful one."[2]

Howard continued to mix talks on his Civil War experiences with pleas for the university. He also appeared before the Republican Club in New York to celebrate Lincoln's birthday in 1907 and reported that "we had bold speaking before an audience of at least 1500 in behalf of the L.M.U., and I think I will gather fruitage from my effort." He promoted the university while speaking at a variety of churches. Howard pushed the university's cause before a chapter of the Daughters of the Revolution at Poughkeepsie, New York, and convinced the members to create a scholarship for deserving students.[3]

Howard's lecture, titled "Abraham Lincoln: 'What would he have us do,'" repeated the story of his last meeting with the president and asserted that Lincoln would have wanted everyone to love each other. "They are left behind," Howard asserted of the mountaineers, "they, his own people among whom he was born and whom he loved." In the mountains, "where girls are wedded from twelve to fifteen years of age, and boys grow up without being able to write their names," Howard promoted the creation of an institution to help "those who, like Lincoln, have had to carry loads too heavy for childhood and youth." The general related touching stories of real students who came to Lincoln Memorial University with nothing in their pockets. "I'll stay with you six years if you'll give me a chance!" he recalled one sixteen-year-old boy saying. Howard also described meeting a girl who lived with her parents and two sisters in a two-room log house near Cumberland Gap. The girl was very proud of never having missed a lesson during her stay at the university. "I love the school and I am going to bring my two sisters next term if we can work our way."[4]

Howard and Edgar O. Achorn arranged a public debate between selected university students and pupils at Newton High School, Newton, Massachusetts, in May 1905. They planned the event to demonstrate the mountain students' "ability to cope with our New England youth, and show how worthy they are of all the contributions which the Eastern people have made and are making to their intellectual and industrial up-building." Howard wanted to avoid any controversial topics, such as race, so the subject to be debated was "Is classical education course an essential part of a college curriculum?"[5]

Howard encouraged Stooksbury to become more active in public relations. "My great object is to place you in close relationship with our Northern givers." He wanted the president to give talks on Lincoln and tell stories of the mountain youth that would interest people in their welfare. He also encouraged Stooksbury to write letters soliciting support from potential donors but gently told the president that he ought to buy a typewriter: "It is not that I object to your good plain hand-writing but for those busy men a good neat type-written letter is the best. I ask for a neat letter because that has a great effect with men whose full sympathy we want." Howard also wrote letters to Bowdoin alumni, family friends, and in-laws. Edwin Ray Smith, who had married Howard's niece, agreed to fund a scholarship through donations provided by his Sunday school class, but a large portion of all donations went to pay monthly expenses at Cumberland Gap.[6]

Howard attended almost every annual meeting of the Board of Directors, as well as every commencement. On at least three occasions he also rode horseback through the area, making twenty miles a day during his week-long outings, to better understand and appreciate the people his university served. Even when he stayed at Grant-Lee Hall, he often rode around the university farm although well past seventy years of age. He endeared himself with many students by treating them as nephews and nieces. One young lady, who was named Howard, forever remembered that the general "claimed kin with her" and asked that she walk beside him during a commencement ceremony.[7]

"Mine has been a busy life," Howard admitted in his autobiography, even making a plea for the university in the pages of the two-volume book that he began writing in 1896, the same year in which he was introduced to the Cumberland Gap region. Lincoln Memorial University was "a decided labor of love" for the general, and the "continued success of this enterprise as a last work of an active life I greatly desire and earnestly pray for."[8]

Next to Howard, Eugene P. Fairchild was the university's most important fund-raiser. He worked quietly among the lesser donors, securing pledges of fifty to one hundred dollars, which added up to thousands over the course of many years. Fairchild earned a percentage of the donations as his fee. He knew

The south end of Grant-Lee Hall, before December 1909. UA-LMU.

his business well, lecturing Stooksbury that businessmen valued "*promptness* and *accuracy,* and the up to date circular or booklet will *always pay.*" He wanted to have storage space in New York so he would not have to rely on packages from Cumberland Gap every time he needed promotional literature, but that was not possible. Rev. John A. Cass was another financial agent of the university. He collected $260 and some books for the library in January 1907. Charles Eager advanced some cash on his fees and urged him in future to hold out part of the donations for his immediate use until the accounts could be balanced.[9]

Fairchild respected and valued Howard, but he also gave signs that he resented serving under the general's shadow. He criticized Howard's personal approach to the task, saying that the *Century* article "in general makes *too little* of the *work* and *location* of the University, and too much of the personal *wishes* of an *individual.*" Frederick Chamberlin, a friend of Howard's, attempted "to raise $100,000 for the university, on the strength of Gen. Howard's golden wedding anniversary." That event took place on February 14, 1905, with a reception in New York attended by thirty-four relatives and friends. All of the guests wrote their names in the family Bible, which had been a wedding gift from Lizzie's mother. Presumably, Howard's thirteen grandchildren were also in attendance.

But, Fairchild noted, Chamberlin "did not secure any thing." He thought Lincoln Memorial University should more heavily stress the central location of Cumberland Gap within southern Appalachia and try to take advantage of the centennial of Lincoln's birthday. "A monument to Gen. Howard must come later," Fairchild told Stooksbury. He also felt Myers was unjustly ignored in all the publicity and Myers's friends were bypassed as potential donors. "It is not the Gen. we love less," Fairchild assured Stooksbury, "but the institution more."[10]

Howard and the Big Donor

Fairchild, however, could not match Howard's ability to publicize the university among the nation's industrial elite or its political leadership. This was Howard's most unique contribution to Lincoln Memorial University, and it was the key to the institution's financial survival. Howard pursued this endeavor in the same way he attacked all tasks throughout his distinguished career: he made it a personal mission. The general used references to God, the venerated Lincoln, and the disadvantaged common man in every utterance or publication about the school. Howard championed the cause of Lincoln Memorial University with a persistency that impressed most people on the receiving end of his pleas—and annoyed a few of them as well. Even those potential donors who grew tired of Howard's crusade admired him for his selfless dedication.

Howard created a relationship with Theodore Roosevelt in an effort to enlist the president's aid. He campaigned for the team of McKinley and Roosevelt in the 1900 election and attended Memorial Day ceremonies at Gettysburg with Roosevelt on May 30, 1904, only days after attending commencement at Lincoln Memorial University. Howard campaigned for Roosevelt in 1904, enduring an "arduous" speaking tour of Illinois, Minnesota, and Colorado. He hoped the president would preside at a February 1905 meeting in New York to celebrate Lincoln's birthday: "If he will be present we will have a crowded house and I am in hopes to net very much for the University by that occasion." Howard felt that Roosevelt was "very much a friend of our University and I think our boys will like his tremendous vigor and energy if not altogether his politics." In the latter comment, Howard referred to Roosevelt's evolving commitment to Progressive reform efforts, which included a certain degree of government regulation of business.[11]

But Roosevelt was forced to disappoint Howard. The Republican Club Dinner was scheduled for the same night that Howard planned to host his Lincoln

Memorial University dinner in New York, February 13, 1905, and Roosevelt could not refuse to preside at the party function. The president invited Howard to attend the dinner as well, and he promised to speak a few words about the university, so Howard agreed.[12]

The dinner was a gala affair, celebrating Roosevelt's election to the presidency the previous November. It was held at the Waldorf Astoria, and Howard occupied a chair next to the president. Howard told him what Lincoln Memorial University was trying to do, pouring his heart into the telling as Roosevelt jotted some notes on the back of two menu cards. Roosevelt referred to the cards as he spoke a few words about Howard's beloved enterprise, accurately telling of the general's final interview with Lincoln and the needs of the residents around Cumberland Gap. "This monument (already 8 years old) is grander than stone or bronze & must commend itself to all," Roosevelt concluded.[13]

Less than a month after the Republican Club Dinner, Howard commanded the Civil War veterans who participated in Roosevelt's inaugural parade. Howard also tried to get a consulship for his younger brother Charles by interceding on Roosevelt's behalf, but he mostly asked favors of the president only for Lincoln Memorial University. In October 1908, a few months before leaving the White House, Roosevelt wrote an endorsement for Howard's use: "There could be no finer memorial to Lincoln than this university, placed just where you have built it." The quote was widely used on university stationary and promotional literature. Howard continued to support Republican causes, campaigning for William Howard Taft in 1908.[14]

While eminent statesmen contributed publicity, Howard targeted wealthy industrialists and philanthropists to secure a large donation that could serve the long-term financial needs of the university. Fairchild heard that Mrs. Russell Sage had sixty million dollars to give and was swamped with thirty-five hundred appeals. Her brother promised to tell her of the university's effort to raise seventy thousand dollars for a new administrative building in 1907. When Howard contacted Mrs. Sage directly, he assured her that the "students are flowing in upon us in great numbers," but she did not respond.[15]

Rockefeller and the General Education Board

Howard continued to pursue John D. Rockefeller, assuring him in March 1905 that the university was doing well but needed money to expand. Expected donations often did not materialize, he told Rockefeller, who forwarded the request to Frederick T. Gates with an endorsement that read, "If you could conscientiously recommend doing something for this work of the old gentleman, I should be glad. He is a good friend of ours, and I appreciate good and true friends who are not afraid to speak out."[16]

Howard had already written to Gates in December 1904, sending promotional literature written by Stooksbury in hopes of gaining support from the General Education Board. Gates replied to Rockefeller's request with blunt language, assuring him that Howard had appealed many times to the board and that he and Buttrick did not think Lincoln Memorial University was a good investment: "It is, of course, not a fraud nor a fake, but Mr. Buttrick thinks there are great numbers of schools, even schools for poor whites, in the mountains of Tennessee and Kentucky, where a gift from you would be more usefully employed than with General Howard's school."[17]

Gates also argued that Howard was not a true friend of Rockefeller, "except for revenue. I have known of no good words of his that have not been accompanied . . . in the same breath, with a request for a contribution. The pertinacity with which he has pressed his claims upon this office, month after month and year after year, in the face of denials, decisive though always courteous, . . . his resentfulness when denied impossible interviews for himself or his friends, his imperious demands for explanations of declinations," all contributed to a general weariness among the board members toward his cause. Howard had also tried to influence board decisions through editorial opinion in New York newspapers and had written directly to Rockefeller, ignoring repeated notices that he should only consult the board to apply for Rockefeller money. "He is leaping over all the barriers which you have erected for self protection and for the prevention of the waste and misuse of your benevolent funds," Gates noted. "This is not courteous or friendly." Gates was afraid that Rockefeller would never be rid of Howard if he gave a sizable amount to the university and was convinced that Howard was engaged in a desperate gamble because his methods were alienating other wealthy patrons. Gates admitted that Howard's long record of public service was impressive, and "I am willing to attribute what I blame him for above, more to the decay of his powers than to anything else."[18]

Rockefeller hesitated to approve a donation, given these circumstances, but Howard nearly won him over the next month with further appeals. The industrialist was inclined to give Lincoln Memorial University twenty-five hundred dollars to help with monthly expenses at Cumberland Gap, but not if it would encourage the general to ignore procedure. "I feel that you really want to give to General Howard," Gates responded, "and it will be a self denial to you not to do it, and for your sake, I wish I knew just how it could be wisely done." But Gates again explained to his boss that Howard's methods of bypassing the board could easily be copied by others, thus burdening Rockefeller with personal requests. Buttrick was adamant about Lincoln Memorial University, and Gates suggested that Rockefeller write Howard personally and tell him why he could not donate any funds. "The fact is that the General has not the smallest claim. His school has only lately begun," and Rockefeller had no hand in its origin or funding to date. The industrialist finally conceded, believing it was better to have a staff member spell out exactly what should be said so he could write to the general.[19]

Like a bull dog, Howard would not give up. He and Fairchild met Buttrick in October 1905 but gained no ground. Stooksbury took up the cause, telling Gates that he was "the son of a Baptist minister" in order to push a soft spot in Rockefeller's heart. He also assured Gates that 75 percent of his students were Baptists who could not attend a Baptist school, but these pleas fell on deaf ears.[20]

Howard mounted another push early in 1909, admitting that he could not understand why Rockefeller had yet failed to make a large donation. He assured him that at one point he had approached the members of the Baptist Missionary Board in New York about adopting the university, but they declined. Howard now felt it was a fortunate move, for the nondenominational nature of the institution suited its purpose, but he also stressed the strong Baptist connections of the university to interest Rockefeller. Howard noted that he received no salary for his work and often paid traveling expenses out of his own pocket. He also praised Rockefeller's financial success, insisting that "your business methods were as high-toned and unselfish as those of any other business man." Howard asked Rockefeller not to refer his plea to the board, as "for some reasons unknown to me they will not help me." A few days later, the general received a polite reply from Rockefeller's son, who told him that his father was out of town. Despite the general's plea, his request was referred to Gates and Buttrick.[21]

Howard's dogged efforts to secure Rockefeller money foundered on the General Education Board's opinion that Lincoln Memorial University was not a worthy object of charity. Buttrick indirectly spelled out his reasons in a book detailing the activities of the board up to 1915. Rockefeller had charged the board with helping to shape a comprehensive, national system of education in 1902, so Buttrick studied about seven hundred American colleges and universities. Many "were hardly more than secondary schools, not always good secondary schools at that." Buttrick thought that few of them tried "such work as they were equipped to do," and most of the institutions seemed to need financial help. He detected "laws of college growth," noting that up to half the students were drawn from a radius of fifty miles from campus, while up to 90 percent were drawn from a radius of one hundred miles.[22]

Even so, many colleges were so close to each other that they competed for the same students. Buttrick thought Tennessee had too many colleges, twenty-nine of them, for its population of 2.1 million people, and he identified only five of those institutions as deserving of board support. Two of the five were located in the mountainous eastern part of the state, Maryville College and the University of Chattanooga. Maryville College enrolled only 203 students by 1915, and it had a substantial endowment of more than three hundred thousand dollars; fifty thousand dollars of that endowment had been contributed by the board in 1907. In comparison, Lincoln Memorial University had more than double the students and less than one- third the endowment.[23]

Buttrick, with Gates's approval, took the position that only those institutions which were already successful deserved support. He also believed that institutions which were true colleges or universities, rather than a mix of elementary, secondary, and college-level instruction, should be favored. Buttrick seemed to feel that only the strong, secure institutions deserved to survive. By all standards of measurement adopted by the board, Lincoln Memorial University was out of the running for support. Stooksbury understood that Buttrick was "prejudiced against our work" and accurately concluded, "I doubt very seriously if that board ever does anything for Lincoln Memorial University."[24]

Carnegie

Andrew Carnegie also had created a corporate entity, the Carnegie Corporation of New York, to distribute his philanthropic funds. Unlike Rockefeller, he personally retained control of that entity. This is a major reason why Howard was able to secure large amounts of Carnegie money. His personal approach worked well with the Scots industrialist, and it would have worked equally well with Rockefeller if Gates and Buttrick had not controlled the General Education Board.

Howard began proposing a library building for the university and for use by area communities early in 1903. He estimated that about one hundred readers lived at Cumberland Gap, with fifty at Shawanee and thirty at Arthur, and an additional two hundred at Tazewell, the Claiborne County seat. Lincoln Memorial

University filed a formal application in March 1903. Delays and problems ensued, dragging the process out through 1904 and the early part of 1905. The twenty thousand volumes promised the school did not seem enough to justify a separate building to the corporation. Howard complicated the situation by proposing the volumes be held in a library room within a multipurpose building costing sixty thousand dollars, three times the normal cost of a Carnegie library. He also reported that Stooksbury wanted to build inexpensive lodgings just off campus to rent to families of students. James Bertram, Carnegie's secretary, informed Howard that if "we did not know you the correspondence would be at once dropped," because of these complications.[25]

When pressed to the wall, Howard listed the priorities for Carnegie on April 4, 1905. A multipurpose building topped the list. It would accommodate classes, chapel services, and the library and cost an estimated sixty thousand dollars. Howard placed Stooksbury's rental cottages, at a cost of seventy-five hundred dollars, second on the list, with an increase of the endowment to the tune of one hundred thousand dollars as the third item. "We think it better that we should give up asking for a library building at present," he assured Bertram, but Howard was working at cross-purposes with other friends of the university. Darwin R. James and others wrote to Carnegie on April 11, asking for a library building. The Scotsman decided to ignore Howard and take up James's initiative, offering twenty thousand dollars if the university could raise an equivalent amount as an endowment to maintain the building. Howard quickly rounded up pledges from thirteen friends to cover the challenge, and Bertram authorized the first installment of funds released to Lincoln Memorial University on June 19, 1905.[26]

The addition of the second new building on the Four Seasons property was a major triumph for Howard and James. It was constructed in the Italianate Georgian architectural style similar to many of the other 1,689 Carnegie libraries built in the United States from 1889 to 1930. By late August 1906, the frame was up and the roof affixed, and finishing work proceeded inside. At this point, Howard began asking Carnegie once again for a multipurpose building to be placed on the east side of the quadrangle atop the flattened hill, opposite the new library, but Carnegie did not respond. In April 1907, Howard persuaded him to donate thirty-five hundred dollars to help the university meet an operating deficit caused by a decline in donations. Financial agent John A. Cass solicited a number of books for the new library, including copies of Carnegie's own publications.[27]

Stooksbury became active in pushing for more Carnegie money when he visited the industrialist in November 1907. The president noted that the univer-

Group in front of Carnegie Library, soon after its construction in 1906. UA-LMU.

sity had an endowment of $60,000, but it needed $200,000 to free Howard of the need to solicit funds for running expenses. James Bertram reported to Carnegie that his corporation had already given $33,500 to Lincoln Memorial University, and the industrialist declined any more donations for the time being. Howard weighed in with another request in April 1908, citing a further decline in donations due to a downturn in the national economy and the need to pipe water from a cave in Cumberland Mountain to the campus. "I hope you will not let him forget us," Howard wrote Bertram, but Carnegie again declined further contributions.[28]

Lincoln Centennial Endowment

Howard turned his attention to a massive fund-raising effort, the largest yet for the university, as the centennial year of Lincoln's birth approached. The editor of the *New York Globe* had suggested he mount a campaign to create a large endowment by banking on this noteworthy date as early as 1905. Howard suggested it to the Board of Directors in their May 1908 meeting, with the goal of raising half a million dollars for the school. The campaign was in full swing before the end of the year, bolstered by contributions from well-known figures. Howard himself pledged three thousand dollars, and former Union general Grenville M. Dodge contributed the same amount. Most other pledges were one thousand dollars or less, and Howard encouraged many people to "send a small check."[29]

The drive involved another Lincoln birthday celebration at New York's Metropolitan Opera House. Howard invited Mark Twain to preside, hoping to recapture the excitement of the Lincoln Day festivities of 1901. He also hoped to publicize a statement by Twain, suggesting the writer endorse the university as "the most fitting memorial to Lincoln, serving as it does to uplift his very own people." Howard noted that he was "still young at seventy-nine" and poked gentle fun at Twain's Confederate background—"Never mind if you did fight on the *other side.*"[30]

Twain gladly submitted an endorsement while declining to preside at the meeting. "But I am older than people think," he playfully told Howard, "nearly twice as old as I used to be," and he did not circulate much anymore. "You ought not to say sarcastic things about my 'fighting on the other side,'" Twain continued. "General Grant did not act like that. General Grant paid me compliments. . . . He said if all the Confederate soldiers had followed my example & adopted my military arts he could never have caught enough of them in a bunch to inconvenience the Rebellion. General Grant was a fair man & recognized my worth; but you are prejudiced, & you have hurt my feelings. But I have an affection for you, anyway."[31]

Howard enjoyed the playful language, assuring Twain that he would never hurt "a confederate's feelings. I did love them & do love their descendants & am trying so hard to show my love by my works, that I ache inside & out." Howard then invited Carnegie to preside, but the Scotsman also declined. Howard persuaded Gen. Benjamin F. Tracy to take charge of the affair. Tracy had won a Medal of Honor for bravery at the battle of the Wilderness and had served as secretary of the navy.[32]

The proceedings, on the afternoon of February 9, 1909, had a decidedly military flair. Maj. Gen. Leonard Wood, commander of the Department of the East, was on the platform with his entire staff, and uniformed privates served as ushers. The platform guests included many well-known Civil War veterans, including Horace Porter (who had served on Grant's staff), former Confederate general Roger A. Pryor, Union veteran Thomas H. Hubbard of Maine (a friend of Howard's), and former Union general Alexander S. Webb. The New York Symphony Orchestra played several pieces, including Tchaikovsky's *Marche*

Slav and a piece by Liszt. There was a reading of the Gettysburg Address and a speech by Ida Tarbell, one of the major Lincoln biographers of the day. Howard included his own remarks, titled "Lincoln Stories," and the ceremony ended with a rendition of "The Star-Spangled Banner." Money raised by selling tickets, amounting to $6,446, was earmarked for the Centennial Endowment.[33]

After the first flush of success, the endowment fund totaled $125,000 by April 1909, when Stooksbury and Howard mounted another push to entice Carnegie into the fold. The president suggested the industrialist add $200,000 to the fund to honor Howard. Carnegie was moved by the appeal, calling Howard a "dear old Saint." He was strongly inclined "to make the gift as a tribute to him" but made the mistake of asking Buttrick if Rockefeller's General Education Board would like to join him. Buttrick arranged to see Carnegie on April 22. The next day, Bertram sent a note to Howard informing him that Carnegie declined to help.[34]

Howard continued to seek Carnegie's aid in August 1909, in addition to once again writing John D. Rockefeller, but both avenues were closed to the university. Stooksbury joined the letter-writing campaign, noting that "the rush of progress and development in the South is sweeping almost entirely around the thousands of white people in the mountains of the five Southern states." The president estimated that more than one thousand individuals had contributed to Lincoln Memorial University since its inception in 1896, and he hoped that "tens of thousands" more would add to the Centennial Endowment. He wanted to double the size of the student body with the estimated twenty-five thousand dollars that the new endowment would generate in interest payments.[35]

Howard entrusted the Centennial Endowment campaign to a professional fund-raising firm, Robert Lee Dun and Company of New York. Dun used promotional literature that identified mountain youth as "*representative types of stalwart and worthy American stock*," eager for "the Lincoln gospel of duty and of sacrifice." A postcard titled "Will You Help Me?" displayed the photograph of a barefoot boy from Hell's Fork, Kentucky, with an appealing, good-natured grin. "I want to go to Lincoln Memorial University at Cumberland Gap, but they are teaching 640 Children now and haven't room or money for more," the boy says.[36]

Howard rounded up endorsements from many well-known figures in public life. "Of course you can count on me to be your first subscriber, if you so desire," wrote President William Howard Taft. And Vice-President James S. Sherman agreed to be honorary vice-president of the Endowment Association. Former president Teddy Roosevelt and Ulysses S. Grant's son, Gen. Frederick D. Grant,

"Will You Help Me?" A postcard to raise money for the Lincoln Centennial Endowment campaign in 1909. UA-LMU.

added their endorsements, many of which were printed on the Endowment Association's letterhead along with photographs of buildings on campus and quotes by Lincoln. Newspapers in Boston, Baltimore, Philadelphia, and New York carried stories of Howard's efforts. The *New York Herald* printed a large spread in its magazine section on September 12, replete with eight photographs of the university. The accompanying article was written by someone who had visited the campus and emphasized the university's efforts to offer struggling students a chance to make something of themselves.[37]

The Endowment Campaign was the culmination of Howard's effort to publicize the university and raise money for its development. By mid-1909, he had increased the size of Lincoln Memorial University's endowment by more than 60 percent as a result of the campaign and had increased it 300 percent over the course of the past three years.[38]

End of a Long Life

But Howard was unable to raise the campaign's goal of half a million dollars. By the fall of 1909, it became apparent that the momentum had ended and the endowment still stood at about $125,000. Howard agreed to a grueling schedule of appearances in October, planning ten talks in Pennsylvania, Detroit, and

London, Ontario. His engagement book also listed several planned appearances in November, December, and January. A New York newspaper reported early in October that the general looked "feeble," prompting Howard to write the editor that it mattered little how he looked, only that people help in the "wonderful work yet to do to get our great monument of Abraham Lincoln thoroughly completed. . . . It is my last work, I have no doubt, and I need all the vigor the newspapers can give me."[39]

Howard slightly changed his version of the last meeting with Lincoln to give a stronger emphasis to the president's message: "General, if you come out of this horror and misery alive, and I pray to God that you may, I want you to do something for those mountain people who have been shut out of the world all these years. I know them. If I live I will do all I can to aid, and between us perhaps we can do the justice they deserve. Please remember this, and if God is good to us we may be able to speak of this later." His embellishment cannot be taken literally; prior to the fall of 1909, he had only indicated that Lincoln had said, "They are loyal." This change in the story was the sincere effort of an aging missionary to preach the Lincoln gospel with greater force as he weakened in the harness.[40]

Howard gave his talk, "Lincoln and Great Loving Kindness," at London on October 24, returning to his home in Burlington, Vermont, much fatigued. He continued to work in a downtown office fitted up for his use but began to feel chest pains at the start of the day on October 26. Nevertheless, Howard went to his office to work on an article titled "Changes in Warfare in the Last Fifty Years," but Harry insisted he consult a doctor. The physician ordered him home to rest; sometime during the course of the day, Howard wrote his last letter relating to university business, telling Stooksbury that he would send two thousand dollars to Cumberland Gap to help with the expenses of the Medical Department. Howard tried to relax in his upstairs room that evening. When Harry's wife, Sue, who was a physician, took some food to him, the two sat on his bed for a time. Howard suddenly was seized and fell against her. Harry ran up and tried to resuscitate his father, but the old general passed away in peace. His heart gave out as he had predicted. "Someday, it will just stop," he had told Harry, "and I will be on the other shore."[41]

Howard's funeral service was accompanied by black troops from the Tenth U.S. Cavalry, stationed at nearby Fort Ethan Allen, a post his son Guy had planned and laid out many years before. He was buried in Lakeview Cemetery, overlooking the waters of Lake Champlain. Congress awarded a pension to Howard's widow, who had suffered ill health since Guy's death. By 1909, she needed almost constant nursing care.[42]

Howard's death shook Lincoln Memorial University to its foundation. As Howard's biographer has aptly put it, the general's help "was probably indispensable to the success of the undertaking." The university "was truly a labor of love" for him, and the institution became "not only a memorial to Lincoln, it is a living monument to the one-armed soldier."[43] "We are all very sad at the university now," wrote Stooksbury's secretary. Frederick B. Avery thought the loss was "irreparable," that everyone associated with the school had lost "a loyal sympathizing friend." Edgar O. Achorn worried about the students. "How much General Howard loved them and to what extent he wrought for their welfare they will probably never fully realize," he wrote.[44]

Stooksbury assumed the burden of carrying on without "our General Howard." For a moment, he and the Board of Directors wondered if a reevaluation of the university's organization and "scope of work" was in order. No one of Howard's stature seemed ready to replace him, so the post of managing director was dropped. Stooksbury asked the president of the University of Tennessee in Knoxville for advice about the kind of educational work done at Cumberland Gap, but he retained the university's mission intact.[45]

A memorial service at Lincoln Memorial University honored Howard on his birthday, November 8, 1909, and Achorn gave the address. An 1881 graduate of Bowdoin College, Achorn had worked with Howard for the past ten years and had taken "eminent satisfaction in 'serving on his staff,' as we were wont to put it." Achorn thought the most fundamental way to understand the general was to realize that he "had an old fashioned New England religion" and "voiced it constantly in addresses." Howard's consistent message was "loving kindness." Achorn found him "a man of very strong impulses," "influenced more by instinct and intuition than by reason or logic." He "was keenly sensitive to criticism and depressing influences." Often in meetings of the Board of Directors, Howard stopped and implored everyone around the table, "I want you all to support me, pray for me, and I will get the money." He traveled as cheaply as he could while on university business. The general was driven by a demand "that every individual, however humble and of whatever color, should have an opportunity to make the most of himself."[46]

After Howard

Thomas H. Hubbard agreed to replace Howard as president of the "Lincoln University Endowment Association," as the organization sometimes was incorrectly labeled. Hubbard, a Bowdoin graduate, had served as a regimental and brigade commander during the Civil War. Stooksbury encouraged everyone associated with the effort to "build a monument not only to Lincoln, but General Howard as well." New promotional literature emphasized the general's role to capitalize on public sympathy in the wake of his death. It also emphasized that the students were "*white* Americans, of the finest pioneer stock," so donors would not mistake Lincoln Memorial University for a black institution. The promotional literature and letters called on the image of not only Lincoln but also of Daniel Webster, Henry Clay, Ulysses S. Grant, and James A. Garfield, and noted that Andrew Carnegie was a major donor.[47]

While still mourning Howard's loss, the university was forced to endure another hard blow. Jesse H. Moore was walking along a nearby ridge on the afternoon of December 14, 1909, when he heard boys yelling as they ran across campus. He then saw that smoke was rising from the roof of Grant-Lee Hall. The boys tried to throw buckets of water on the blaze and pull personal belongings from its reach, but the building went up in flames as the wooden roof collapsed. Almost everything in the building was lost. Eighty students, two professors, and the housekeeper's family were suddenly homeless.[48]

A student living on the upper floor had forgotten to close his stove properly, causing a fire that spread quickly to the combustible roof. Most of the students had only the clothes they wore while working on campus. Stooksbury, who also lived in the building, lost virtually all his possessions except the typewriter that Howard had convinced him to purchase several years before. The university's publication, the *Mountain Herald,* was printed in the basement; its equipment and most copies of the back issues were destroyed. Urgent appeals went out for donations of anything useful, including small stoves, lamps, beds, and chairs. When a box of donated clothes arrived, Stooksbury gave an old clergyman's coat to one student, who "seemed to be well pleased" with it.[49]

The university had experienced a shortage of dormitory space for some time already; now the problem was far worse. The faculty gathered in an emergency meeting and arranged to move the male students into the second and third floors of Avery Hall. Some of the sixty girls were moved to the first floor, while others moved to the second and third floors of the Arthur house, now called the

Conservatory of Music. The crowded conditions in Avery Hall led to the first instance of a coeducational dormitory at Lincoln Memorial University. "Some of the girls went wild with excitement" at this turn of events. Male teachers boarded with the boys on the upper floors, and female teachers on the first floor with the girls, to keep order. The remaining girls were moved out of Avery Hall by the end of the spring of 1910. They also evacuated the Conservatory when Norton Hall was constructed for them in 1912.[50]

Stooksbury was in New York trying to drum up funds for operating expenses when a telegram brought news of the fire. It "very much upset me," he noted, and it forced him to return much earlier than planned, missing a meeting of the Governing Board of the Endowment Association.[51]

The insurance coverage on Grant-Lee could not fund the construction of a new building. The insurers were unwilling to take a large risk on the structure because of its wooden roof, and state law prevented the university from insuring it for more than three-fourths of its estimated value of twenty-five thousand dollars. As a result, Lincoln Memorial University received only eleven thousand dollars for the loss and had paid a "very high rate" for the premiums as well. Stooksbury made sure that all other buildings on campus were covered as fully as possible by existing insurance contracts—fifteen thousand dollars each for Avery Hall and the Carnegie library, and ten thousand dollars for the Conservatory of Music.[52]

Stooksbury estimated that a new dormitory would cost at least fifty thousand dollars. By using as much student labor as possible, he hoped to begin construction as soon as he accumulated thirty thousand dollars. The new building was designed to house 150 students, plus rooms for maintenance staff, with a full dining room and kitchen. He injected a tone of desperation in fund-raising efforts, arguing that the institution might collapse if a new dormitory was not operational by the fall term. A number of students had already decided to leave the university rather than put up with the crowded conditions in Avery Hall and the Conservatory. Those who remained were "VERY LOYAL," as Stooksbury put it, and more applications continued to pour in.[53]

By late January 1910, the president had gathered thirteen thousand dollars in cash and pledges. But the first flush of donations began to dry up the next month and Stooksbury became frustrated. He noted that many "colored schools all over the South are being helped, but the sturdy mountain boys and girls, with practically no assets, are supposed to work out their own salvation with fear and trembling." Noting that students were "packed in the rooms like sardines, three and four in a room," Stooksbury forwarded a petition signed by 180 people to Andrew Carnegie, pleading for help to construct a new building. Carnegie initially declined to contribute but changed his mind a few weeks later and pledged five hundred dollars. An article in the *Christian Herald* elicited only "small contributions" from a number of different states. Stooksbury noted that very little money came from the local area, a consistent theme in the fund-raising history of Lincoln Memorial University.[54]

By April 1910, there was little more than $14,000 available, including the insurance claim of $11,000. Stooksbury himself had contributed $100 to the effort, and the university garnered $193.29 by selling scrap iron from the ruins of the burned structure. The university had raised a total of $37,000 the previous year but had to pay a 10 percent fee to its financial agents to accomplish that goal, leaving a bit over $33,000. Stooksbury had already "borrowed" $7,000 of that sum to pay debts, and the rest was needed for operating expenses because the endowment was still not large enough to cover them. For the same reason, Stooksbury could not spend $16,000 that the university held in its New York city bank account at the end of the year, and he had to collect $17,000 in pledges.[55]

Moreover, the university had taken the controversial step of purchasing the Tennessee Medical College in May 1909. The resulting debt totaled fifty thousand dollars, a huge financial drain. The early twentieth century witnessed tremendous changes in medical education, demanding improved facilities and highly credentialed faculty. The university did not have the financial resources to modernize its Medical Department. Stooksbury also heard reports that potential donors were reluctant to give because they thought ownership of the medical college was a financial mistake. With more than forty-one thousand dollars of the debt still unpaid, the Medical Department had "become a mill-stone about the neck of Lincoln Memorial University to sink it sooner or later," as Stooksbury put it.[56]

By the spring of 1910, the university had to decide whether the Medical Department or a new dormitory was more important. Initially, everyone agreed that the dormitory took precedence. The Board of Directors tried to find a purchaser for the Tennessee Medical College but failed. Faced with multiple demands for cash at the Knoxville facility, the board decided to divert money slated for the dormitory to the Medical Department. It reasoned that funds to build the new dormitory could be raised through other means. Stooksbury dug in his heels, begrudging any diversion of finances toward the Knoxville institution as long as his students were crowded into makeshift quarters at Cumberland Gap. Ironically, the eighty faculty members of the Medical Department complained that they received far too little support from the parent organization. As Achorn correctly saw it, neither group was able to understand the other group's problem.[57]

Stooksbury could not accept the board's decision and resigned in the early summer of 1910. He gave an interview to the *Knoxville Sentinel* in which he frankly told the world why he resigned, but he also promoted Lincoln Memorial University by noting the progress which had taken place during the past six years. Stooksbury had developed a more pronounced course of college-level instruction, with four years devoted to collegiate training and three years to secondary-level instruction in the academy. Student enrollment more than doubled during the six years, but tuition accounted for no more than one-third of the funds needed to operate the school. The rest had to come from donations.[58]

A new president had been in the wings for some time before Stooksbury took his leave. George Allen Hubbell had been born in Springfield, Ohio, on August 15, 1862, about the time his father briefly served in the Thirty-second Ohio. He earned his bachelor's and master's degrees at Antioch College and completed a doctorate at Columbia in 1902. Hubbell taught for many years at Erasmus Hall High School in Brooklyn, Berea College, and Transylvania University and had worked briefly for the Russell Sage Foundation. Described by colleagues as "wise in counsel, sound in judgment, and enthusiastic in work," Hubbell possessed "an easy, forceful, and entertaining" style of instruction and was "independent in thought and method." He also was an accomplished writer, having published five books. They included texts for geography courses, books on the Bible and childhood, and a biography of the educator Horace Mann.[59]

Hubbell was serving as president of Highland College in Williamsburg, Kentucky, when the American Missionary Association decided to curtail its support of that institution in July 1907 and transfer its assets to a local Baptist Institute. Hubbell and several faculty members were out of employment, but there seemed little prospect at that time of moving to Lincoln Memorial University. The next year, Hubbell married Ella M. Andrews of Frankfort, Michigan. Andrews had served as dean of women at Highland College but moved to Lincoln Memorial University to teach History and English. Hubbell was interested in the work at Cumberland Gap and contacted Stooksbury in the fall of 1909 with ideas about how to develop it. The president was so preoccupied with his many problems that he failed to respond until months later. The exchange of ideas apparently continued off and on until Hubbell created a relationship that enabled him to succeed Stooksbury in July 1910.[60]

"This is largely a mission work," Stooksbury informed a prospective faculty member a few months before he left Lincoln Memorial University, "and we need . . . those with a missionary spirit to teach. Our institution is not a charitable institution, but it is a school where a great deal of philanthropic work ought to be done." After six years of arduous labor, Stooksbury had masterminded a huge increase in the student body, improved the curricular offerings, presided over the construction of a new library building, established an executive leadership that survived the loss of Howard's commanding presence, and become a fairly effective fund-raiser in his own right. His impact on the institution was enormous.[61]

After leaving Cumberland Gap, Stooksbury moved to Los Angeles, where he became involved in the real estate business. Sometime later he moved to Knoxville and engaged in the furniture business. Stooksbury served as superintendent of Knox County Schools from 1917 to 1923, then he organized the Knoxville Business College and served as its president for fifteen years. When his hometown of Loyston was to be inundated following construction of Norris Dam, Stooksbury gave it a farewell speech before a gathering of residents. Shortly before he died on April 28, 1939, Stooksbury purchased a tombstone and had a full list of the jobs he held chiseled on it. When asked why, he said it was to give accurate information to his old students who happened to pass by. He was buried in Greenwood Cemetery in Knoxville.[62]

Chapter 6
Modernization

It is no small thing that honor, and truth, and patriotism are taught here; . . . it is no small thing that . . . these students . . . go out imbued with the spirit and teachings of Abraham Lincoln.

—George A. Hubbell, 1919

It is the kind of school Lincoln would have chosen to attend. The boys here are his kind of boys. . . . And there is nothing in the way of sacrifice too great for them to endure for the sake of an education.

—John Wesley Hill, undated

Survivals of primitive America, . . . a race of purest American stock. . . . It is the race left stranded on the rocky, inhospitable hillsides of the Appalachians in the westward march of American civilization.

—John Hays Hammond, 1926

George A. Hubbell took the helm at Lincoln Memorial University on July 1, 1910. "I have a genuine interest in that great retarded region," he informed the Board of Directors. "The interest of the institution will be continually on my mind and heart." Hubbell impressed many observers over the course of his twelve years as president. "He loved young people and drew them to him by his warm and friendly personality," recalled Robert L. Kincaid, who met him immediately after arriving on campus as a student in 1912. The president was "kind-hearted, unselfish, and devoted."[1]

Years later Kincaid aptly characterized the state of the university as "poorly equipped, heavily in debt, and little more than a 'barefoot college'" when Hubbell took over. "Less than a dozen students had graduated with degrees, and courses covered the whole range of academy and college subjects. The students were of all ages, and some had been at the institution since the first classwork started in 1899." Hubbell was disturbed that there was not a clearer distinction between the secondary and college curriculum. He organized eight committees to assume responsibility for operating the school, all reporting directly to the president. He

George A. Hubbell, university president, 1910–22. UA-LMU.

abandoned percentage grades and substituted letter grades for course work in 1912, and he introduced elective courses to free up the overly rigid baccalaureate program. Hubbell later experimented with a master of arts degree but soon gave it up because of inadequate faculty. The president continued to support the "industrial features" of Lincoln Memorial University, if for no other reason than to maintain the work-learn system already in place, but he also improved the liberal arts curriculum as much as possible.[2]

Hubbell continued the Lincoln Centennial Endowment campaign, but an official of Lincoln University in Pennsylvania again expressed alarm that the Tennessee school had appropriated the Great Emancipator's name for the purpose of white education. The professional fund-raising agency handling the campaign had mistakenly printed circulars and pledge blanks that omitted the word "Memorial" from the name of the university, causing much confusion among potential donors to both institutions.[3]

Everyone felt that the cheaply constructed "chapel," the latest addition to the campus, was ill suited to its purpose. Kincaid recalled it as a "big rambling tin-sheeted temporary structure with a sawdust floor and long, hard benches." It seemed a more appropriate venue for a camp meeting than the affairs of a respectable college. Hubbell mounted an effort to fund the construction of an administrative building with an auditorium and classrooms, to be named after Howard. Thomas Hubbard donated the initial $1,000. A flurry of letters to Carnegie followed, but the retired industrialist noted that he had already given more than $36,500 and declined to give more.[4]

Even if they could not raise funds to erect Howard Auditorium, university officials honored the general with a celebration of his birthday on November 8,

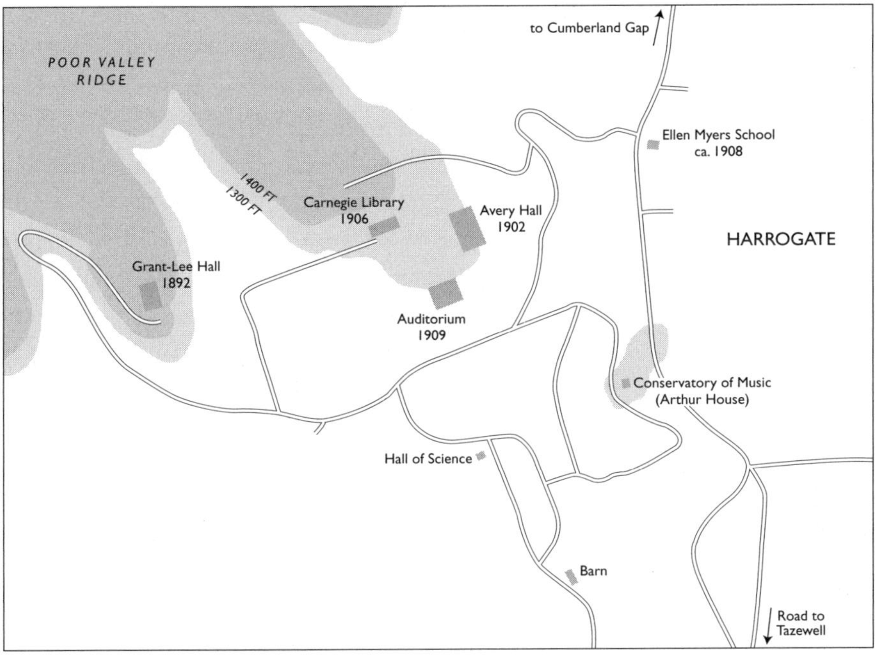

Lincoln Memorial University campus, 1910.

1912. The band and a male quartet provided music while several of the older faculty and staff members remembered Howard in talks delivered in the chapel. Knoxvillian Lawrence Tyson, who had been a cadet when Howard was superintendent at West Point, could not attend the ceremony but praised the general as "a Christian soldier and gentleman in every respect." Five years later, the university invited Stooksbury to give the main address at another celebration of Howard's birthday. Stooksbury retold the story of Lincoln's last interview with Howard and called the general "the most unselfish man I ever met." On one occasion, Howard pulled a small U.S. flag from his pocket and said, "Stooksbury, I want to know what the flag means to you? To me it is the ensign of the republic, to which I would gladly give my life." Efforts to erect a building to honor the general continued into the early 1920s, but they failed to elicit enough money.[5]

Hubbell was aware of Lincoln's significance in university affairs. He tried to support Osborn H. Oldroyd, a Union veteran who superintended the Lincoln family home in Springfield, Illinois, for many years. When Oldroyd attempted to move his private collection of Lincoln memorabilia to Washington, Hubbell searched for ways to help him fund the transfer so that the precious artifacts would not be lost.[6]

The president spearheaded efforts to rebuild Grant-Lee Hall by recruiting donations of labor and material from local residents. The cornerstone was laid on May 6, 1914, as a movie camera filmed the ceremony. It was the first time a motion picture was made on campus, thanks to a Lincoln impersonator named Benjamin C. Chapin, who also recited the Gettysburg Address. Participants placed copies of the *Mountain Herald,* the university catalog, the commencement program for 1914, the announcement of Howard's death, and the university charter inside the cornerstone, alongside a 1913 Lincoln penny. The building progressed slowly due to scarcity of resources, and it was rebuilt with a streamlined architectural plan to save costs and avoid expensive, combustible features such as the wooden roof and water tower. When completed in the fall of 1917, it housed one hundred male students.[7]

At about the same time that Grant-Lee was rising from the ruins, Lincoln Memorial University divested itself of the Medical Department. Since the university had purchased the Knoxville facility in 1909, it had constructed a medical laboratory building with fifteen thousand dollars that had been donated for that

Rebuilding Grant-Lee Hall, about 1914. UA-LMU.

purpose. It also had spent forty thousand dollars in improvements but had not been able to pay off the fifty-thousand-dollar purchase price. The Lincoln Memorial University Hospital, with sixty-five beds, operated at only half capacity, and the School of Nursing, with thirty-three students, had an operating deficit of seven thousand dollars. Eugene P. Fairchild asked Carnegie to pay off the debt, but the Scotsman declined.[8]

The American Medical Association refused to accredit the Medical Department because much-needed improvements in the property and its equipment had not been made. As a result, graduates could only be examined for medical licenses in the state of Tennessee. The university's Board of Directors finally agreed to sell the Medical Department in May 1914, and the last classes ended the following month. A number of students who had not yet finished their course of study transferred to the University of Tennessee's College of Medicine in Memphis. Twelve of them graduated in 1915, fourteen in 1916, and four the following year; all of them received diplomas from Lincoln Memorial University as the result of an articulation agreement. This collaborative venture led the American Medical Association to increase Lincoln Memorial University's rating from C to B. The city-owned Knoxville General Hospital purchased the School of Nursing and the Lincoln Memorial University Hospital in December 1917. It took another quarter of a century for the Cumberland Gap college to pay off all debts associated with its foray into the field of medical education.[9]

As Lincoln Memorial University's graduates began to seek further opportunities for study, many larger, more prestigious institutions began to wonder if they should take their credits seriously. Robert Kincaid sparked the first such inquiry. He had been born in straightened circumstances in rural northwest Georgia but displayed a talent for writing and a keen interest in journalism. Having completed his bachelor's degree at Lincoln Memorial University in 1915, Hubbell advised him to go to the School of Journalism at the University of Missouri. The dean of faculty at Missouri, however, relied on the University of Tennessee to evaluate the quality of educational work done at Cumberland Gap, since he had no information on the mountain school. President Brown Ayres replied, "We look upon the Lincoln Memorial University as about the grade of a junior college." His policy was to place a graduate of Lincoln Memorial University at junior level in the University of Tennessee. This was a fair assessment of the work done at Cumberland Gap. Kincaid entered the university in 1912 with three years of high school credit; he thus had to take some secondary-level courses, but he still managed to finish his baccalaureate course work in only three years. Lincoln

Memorial University's curriculum was not as rigorous as that of the University of Tennessee at this time.[10]

Fund Raising

In May 1915, Frank A. Seiberling visited Lincoln Memorial University to attend its largest commencement exercise thus far. He liked what he saw and accepted an invitation to join the Board of Directors. Born in 1859 near Akron, Ohio, he attended Heidelberg College and later drove Goodyear Tire and Rubber Company to a position of prominence in the tire industry.[11]

Seiberling initiated a new era by creating an activist group of directors who applied their business skills to raising funds for the university. He replaced Hubbell as the presiding officer of the board in 1917. Beginning in 1922, a year after Seiberling left Goodyear to create Seiberling Rubber Company in Akron, the university president was no longer a member of the board. In 1915 Seiberling financed the construction of a creamery and a barn for stock and dairy cows and purchased a herd of Holstein and Aberdeen-Angus cattle. He funded the construction of a new barn five years later when the first one burned. By 1930, the rubber magnate had reportedly donated $250,000 to the university.[12]

Hubbell published a publicity booklet, *The Living Memorial to Lincoln,* in which he defended the use of the term "university": "As a child takes a name that befits it not as a baby but as a man, so does this little groping college with its grammar

Entrance to Lincoln Memorial University, about 1925. Norton Hall (1912) is in the distance, and the road to Tazewell, with Harrogate town buildings nearby, is on the left. UA-LMU.

grade students, its high school students and its handful of collegiate students . . . , naming not its present but its destiny." The booklet included many photographs of students working on campus. It contained the first publicity photographs of a new stone gateway at the main entrance to the university, funded by the graduating class of 1915, as well as views of primitive dorms constructed to accommodate the many young people wishing to study. Excerpts from plaintive letters written by students filled several pages. "It is a real college," the booklet assured everyone. "It gives bona fide degrees which all American colleges recognize as the awards of genuine college work." A long article, essentially lifted from the pages of the booklet, appeared in *Collier's* magazine in February 1916.[13]

Seiberling was responsible for recruiting John Wesley Hill as chancellor of Lincoln Memorial University in 1916. Born in Kalida, Ohio, in 1863, Hill earned his baccalaureate degree at Ohio Northern University, his D.D. degree from Boston Theological Seminary, and his LL.D. degree from Upper Iowa University. He worked as a Methodist minister in Washington state, Utah, Montana, Ohio, and Pennsylvania. Hill campaigned for his friend William McKinley in 1896 and served as chaplain of the Pennsylvania Senate in 1900.[14]

Intensely ambitious, Hill was a master orator who could appeal to the masses with pungent phrases and overly simplified concepts. He often sought grandstand opportunities to obtain publicity in the press. On one occasion, he condemned President Benjamin Harrison's stand on prohibition at a rally in Orange, Massachusetts, which ended with Hill being escorted from the hall by a deputy sheriff for his own protection. Hill became pastor of the Metropolitan Temple in New York and gave a series of well-received sermons in London in 1909, which greatly boosted his career as a public speaker. He agreed to serve as president of an ambitious project called the International Forum, which hoped to sponsor symposia on world peace beginning in 1912. It involved massive fund raising and the operation of a twenty-five-acre conference center at Tangier, Long Island. Even the fact that a woman filed a breach of promise suit against Hill failed to sully his reputation as a combination booster, man of God, and friend of the rich and influential.[15]

Hill's job as chancellor restricted him, according to university bylaws, to raising money for the institution. Hill's first assignment was to revitalize the endowment campaign and raise a million dollars, and he spurred a marked increase in promotional literature for the school. A brochure, *Lincoln Memorial University,* proclaimed the institution to be the "embodiment of wholesome ideals; a training place for character and power; a school community permeated by ambition, high resolves and earnest purpose; a group of growing Americans over whom broods the spirit of Lincoln."[16]

Another brochure, *The Story of Lincoln Memorial University,* was published by Chapple Press in Boston, which published the *National Magazine.* "It is the most serious university I have ever known," Hill proclaimed in the brochure. There was "more work and more accomplishment per minute and per term than anywhere else." A photograph caption indicated that more than 95 percent of the students worked their way through school.[17]

Seiberling and Hill masterminded the most impressive event thus far to raise public awareness of Lincoln Memorial University, a symposium to celebrate Lincoln's birthday and the twentieth anniversary of the university. It was to be held on the campus itself, despite the primitive physical plant. The symposium was the brainchild of editor Joe Mitchell Chapple of the *National Magazine,* who visited the university at the suggestion of Robert Todd Lincoln, the slain president's only surviving son. Chapple joined the Board of Directors and told Hill of his idea to hold a meeting on campus. Seiberling agreed to pay the costs and Hill rounded up the speakers. Robert L. Kincaid, who became university correspondent after spending only one term at the University of Missouri because of financial difficulties, was deeply involved in preparations. Chartered trains brought one hundred invited guests to Cumberland Gap from Chicago and New York. The railroad placed a new sidetrack at Harrogate to park sleeping cars, as there was limited hotel space in the area. Robert Todd Lincoln and James Bertram, Carnegie's private secretary, declined invitations to attend.[18]

An impressive list of congressmen, governors, university presidents, military officers, and national, state, and local officials participated in the Lincoln Birthday Celebration held in the flimsy auditorium on February 10–12, 1917. More than eighty speakers held forth, including Hubbell, Hill, and Seiberling. Kincaid was asked to speak on "Lincoln Memorial of the Future," and half a dozen students spoke about "what Lincoln Memorial means to me." One hundred students formed a chorus to entertain the guests, supplemented by a band from Knoxville.[19]

The event took place when Germany's submarine war against shipping in the North Atlantic reached a crisis point, endangering American neutrality in World War I. Many of the speeches had a strongly patriotic flair, proffering support for President Woodrow Wilson if the country went to war. Chapple had a brilliant idea. He scribbled a resolution on a small piece of paper and thrust it into Kincaid's hands, telling him to go out when the current speaker had finished and read it to the assemblage. It stated that the young men of Lincoln Memorial University pledged their readiness to join the military in case of war. "I read it over hurriedly and saw the implications of it," Kincaid recalled years later. "It was not my business to present the resolution, but I obeyed Mr. Chapple." The crowd went wild with excitement, and newspapers across the country reported the incident. It caught the mood of the country and proved to be a brilliant piece of grandstanding.[20]

University officials announced at the Lincoln Birthday Celebration the start of a campaign to raise one million dollars for the endowment. A booklet publicizing the celebration and containing the resolution Chapple had cooked up for Kincaid was widely distributed. The booklet also carried a foreword by Hill proclaiming that the university "teaches not only the arts and sciences but the fundamentals of character, and the necessary elements of liberty and self-government. . . . It is a veritable bulwark of American patriotism." Hill positioned the university as a place that opened "the door of opportunity" for mountain youth. He also played loose with the facts when stating that Lincoln "was mountain-born within a few miles of the location of the university."[21]

The Lincoln Birthday Celebration drew more national publicity for the university than any previous event. Hubbell sought advice about the best way to use the million dollars to modernize Lincoln Memorial University, academically as well as physically. He approached John C. Campbell during a conference held in Knoxville. Born in Indiana in 1867, Campbell had attended Williams College and Andover Theological Seminary. He had taught in public schools in Wisconsin and principled academies in Alabama and Tennessee, as well as serving as president of Piedmont College in Demorest, Georgia. Campbell and his second wife, Olive Dame Campbell, thoroughly studied Appalachian society and its educational needs. John became the driving force of the Southern Highland Division, a component of the Russell Sage Foundation, in 1912. He was critical of much educational work being done in the mountains because it tried to standardize Appalachia as another part of mainstream American culture rather than make it a better-functioning version of its distinctive self.[22]

Campbell and his wife had visited Lincoln Memorial University in November 1908 while touring Appalachian schools. They were enchanted by the view from Cumberland Mountain and spent most of one day on campus. Stooksbury was away in New York, but his wife entertained the couple, taking them to a mid-afternoon chapel service. "They make a great feature of the music here," Olive recorded in her diary, and "wish to attract students from all South: evidently are bent on a big thing, though have developed little so far industrially." She had a long conversation with Mrs. Stooksbury about health problems among the mountaineers but came away thinking that no one at the university "had a vital interest or hold on the mountain situation." Olive referred to the institution as Lincoln Memorial School rather than University, because she and John thought many institutions in Appalachia used the words "university" and "college" too loosely. John worried that too many colleges failed "to adapt education to the mountain environment."[23]

Lincoln Memorial University seemed to be an example of such an institution, according to the Campbells. John responded to Hubbell's plea for advice by arguing the president should completely alter the school's mission. He suggested renaming it the Lincoln Memorial Folk School. Campbell hoped to transform the university into the pilot institution of his scheme to introduce the Danish folk school tradition to America. This tradition had begun after Denmark had lost the important province of Schleswig-Holstein during a short border war with Prussia in 1864. The country's agriculture and economy declined, and its national pride suffered a severe blow. The folk school model deemphasized book learning and focused on oral training; it included lessons in Danish myths, language, geography, and history. The curriculum also included up-to-date scientific methods of agriculture. By working on both cultural and selected scientific fronts, the Danish folk school model of primary and secondary education helped rejuvenate impoverished areas of the country within a few decades and helped restore national pride. The Campbells became the chief advocates of this model in America by about 1914, but they could not find a practical way to implement it. Yet they were convinced the model held promise for progress in Appalachia, stimulating competitiveness with the outside world while teaching young Appalachians to be proud of their distinctive heritage.[24]

"The mountains do not need more colleges," Campbell told Hubbell. The state and the region desperately wanted more and better secondary schools, those which "will face squarely mountain problems." Rather than college work, Campbell urged Hubbell to implement the folk school ideal and transform Lincoln Memorial University into a secondary school. Lincoln's name would be just as powerful an inducement for that endeavor as for a university. Hubbell, however, did not respond to this well meaning suggestion. No one at Cumberland Gap had any interest in shifting the emphasis of the institution toward a concept transplanted from Denmark. Only a handful of schools attempted to implement Campbell's idea. He passed away three years after corresponding with

Hubbell, the same year that a Danish model school opened at Berea College, and Olive created the John C. Campbell Folk School at Brasstown, North Carolina, in 1926. In fact, the Highlander Folk School at Monteagle, Tennessee, which opened in 1933, was somewhat modeled on the Danish example.[25]

WORLD WAR I

Soon after the Lincoln Birthday Celebration, the nation entered World War I with widespread enthusiasm. The day after Congress declared war, Chancellor Hill sent a message to Wilson offering "a regiment of sturdy mountaineers to be known as the Lincoln Sharpshooters." Hill participated in a massive celebration in New York city on July 4, 1917, delivering eight speeches at different locations, one of them on the "Spirit of Lincoln in Arms."[26]

The war, as Kincaid put it, had a "sudden and drastic" effect on the campus. More than two hundred male students volunteered for service, leaving mostly female students on campus. About half of the faculty and staff members also entered the military. Kincaid became a soldier and taught typing and other clerical skills to hundreds of army clerks. When Hubbell held chapel service to start the fall term in 1917, he read a letter by a former student who was then serving in the Ambulance Corps. The recruit assured his former classmates that "by fighting the nation's battles they will be fighting for L.M.U."[27]

Worried because 40 percent of male college students were going to war, many academic administrators urged Wilson to do something before the current generation suffered from a lack of trained professionals. The president created the Student Army Training Corps (SATC). After Congress approved it in August 1918, the program offered young males the opportunity to continue studying and receive military training at the same time. At least 525 colleges, including Lincoln Memorial University, took part in the program. More than 140,000 men continued to study after being sworn into military service and prepared for officer training. The number of males who enrolled in colleges and universities increased as a result.[28]

SATC officials set up a unit of more than ninety men at Lincoln Memorial University on October 1, 1918, taking over Grant-Lee Hall and imposing a semi-military regime for the whole campus. "At first the adaptation of civil and military ideas was just a little difficult," Hubbell reported, but everyone worked to smooth out the rough edges. Jesse Moore thought otherwise. "They called it education," he recalled years later, "but it was a farce. There was nothing substantial in it. . . . The roughness tolerated and encouraged among the boys was something fearful in its effects. It tended to dissipate all discipline in the school." The SATC experience was a short one, ending on December 10, 1918, a month after guns fell silent on the western front.[29]

The Red scare that followed the war energized John Wesley Hill. In a speech to the alumni at the Massachusetts Institute of Technology, he spoke of the contest "between 100-per cent. Americanism and the yellow-backed, cowardly attempt to undermine it." Hill suggested that all Communists be put on "a ship of stone, with sails of lead, the wrath of God for a gale, and Hell for the nearest port!" He approached Carnegie in 1919 with a scheme for a "Patriotic, Educational Extension Bureau," the aim of which was to "LINCOLNIZE AMERICA." Hill planned to send out speakers and distribute literature, because he was convinced that "popular patriotic education is the only antidote for evils born of ignorance and unrest. Neglecting this, we imperil our free institutions." But Hill tied this endeavor to the continuing effort to raise a million dollars for the endowment. Whether Hill was serious about creating a university speaking bureau is uncertain, but Carnegie and his gift-giving corporation were not interested.[30]

The endowment campaign languished in the postwar period, in part because a serious recession hit the country. Hubbell asked if the university's Knoxville-based efforts to raise money would embarrass the University of Tennessee, but its president assured Hubbell that his institution was more than happy to see the smaller colleges place themselves on a firmer footing. In the final analysis, the campaign brought in about half its target amount to Lincoln Memorial University over the course of several years.[31]

STUDENTS

Even after the reconstruction of Grant-Lee Hall, boys continued to stay at Avery Hall. "It smelled of strong disinfectants," recalled Robert Kincaid nearly forty years after he lived there. "The floors were greasy with oil. The doors were scarred and whittled for various kinds of locks. Plaster would fall off, sometimes in the middle of the night, awakening sleepers. Wash rooms and showers were antiquated. Radiators would bang with throbbing steam." The oil lamps were replaced by electric lights in 1914, and Hubbell organized a celebration of the event with speeches and recitations. One light was allowed per dorm room. The student residents moved out and administrative offices, classrooms, and science labs were moved into Avery Hall in 1921.[32]

Welcoming sign, about 1925. The stone gateposts were donated by the graduating class of 1915, and the white LMU letters were donated by the graduating class of 1924. UA-LMU.

The university increased student pay to twenty cents per hour by the early 1920s. In 1925, that was nearly equal to the average wage paid to agricultural workers in the South, but Knoxville newspapers carried ads from several employers promising twice as much, even for black workers.[33]

John R. Bumgarner was a sixteen-year-old boy fresh out of high school in the summer of 1928 and eager to make some money. He traveled with an uncle by car to Flint, Michigan, hoping to find a summer job in the General Motors plant, but the competition was too stiff. His uncle mentioned that a family member had attended Lincoln Memorial University, so Bumgarner made his way to Cumberland Gap and applied for admission. He was put to work for the summer, mostly in the limestone quarry that had recently been opened on the farm to sell gravel to the state's highway department. "We were charged 50 cents per day for food, and $5 per month for our room," Bumgarner recalled, but he accumulated a ninety-dollar credit in his account before the fall term began. Another student, Roland D. Carter, recalled working on the farm during the afternoon, after taking classes in the morning, and earning thirty cents over and above the cost of his meals for that day.[34]

Most students continued to come from the surrounding counties, where subsistence living was the norm. Claiborne County was still a rural area where tobacco was "the only cash crop of importance" and constituted the "major source of income on 10 per cent of the farms," according to a promotional booklet published in 1946. Three-fourths of all farmers in the county grew tobacco, and the average farm size was only forty-nine acres in 1935. The population of Claiborne County was 24,313 in 1930, and it increased by a mere 401 people during the next ten years. Only 573 African Americans lived in Claiborne County in 1930, a year in which the census indicated that the population density was 52 people per square mile, 11 fewer than the state average.[35]

Of 324 students in academic year 1916–17, 56 percent were from Tennessee, and only 12 percent each were from Virginia and Kentucky. The rest came from a mixture of states in the South and Midwest, with two from Cuba and one from Spain. A variety of Protestant denominations were represented, but 32 percent were Baptist and 22 percent Methodist, and only five students were Catholic. Twenty-nine percent of the students earned literally all the funds needed to put themselves through school, and 42 percent earned a portion of that amount. Only 14 percent did not work at all to pay their school expenses.[36]

Whether the credits earned at Lincoln Memorial University would be accepted at other schools continued to plague the students. When three graduates of the university applied to enter the University of Kentucky in 1921, intending to take advantage of the state and federally funded Smith-Hughes program to train agricultural teachers in the public schools, the Kentucky school wanted to know if the University of Tennessee considered Lincoln Memorial University's agricultural instruction to be at the level of a senior college. Tennessee's president, H. A. Morgan, noted that although the Cumberland Gap school was "doing very creditable work for mountain boys," it did not have a strong program in agriculture and the University of Tennessee did not accept all of its courses as equivalent to its own. Morgan promised to send a representative to Cumberland Gap to investigate so he could report on exactly which credits deserved to be accepted as equivalent to courses taught at the University of Tennessee and, by inference, the University of Kentucky.[37]

Despite the problems it encountered in modernizing its curriculum, Lincoln Memorial University continued to expand its student body. By 1921, 723 students were attending the Cumberland Gap institution, but only 129 of them were college students working toward a baccalaureate degree. The rest were taking classes in the Commercial Department, in the Ellen Myers School, or in the Lincoln Memorial Academy. Despite this, Hubbell experimented with many new programs. In addition to its degrees issued to doctors and nurses when the Medical Department was operating, Hubbell offered degrees to lawyers from 1919 to 1921 and to engineers from 1919 to 1926. He also created the Opportunity School in the 1920s as an outreach project for community people "to make up course work missed in their public school education." And Hubbell hired the university's first full-time librarian, Iris Grannis, who was married to science teacher Frank C. Grannis.[38]

Hubbell

George A. Hubbell left a significant legacy to Lincoln Memorial University. He acquired the Grace Nettleton Home in 1917, which had been created by Myers and housed in the old Harrogate Inn half a mile from campus. Hubbell maintained a separate endowment for its maintenance. Emily Winters of Springfield, Massachusetts, a former governess in Teddy Roosevelt's family, ran the institution for many years. Hubbell also saw the construction of several new buildings, including Norton Hall in 1912 (financed by the Norton sisters of Norwich, Connecticut, through Eugene P. Fairchild), which served as the new girl's dormitory; the president's house in 1913 (financed by Mrs. W. W. Smith of Poughkeepsie,

New York, wife of a founder of Smith Brothers Cough Drops); Blue Bird's Nest in 1920 (named by the students); and the DAR Hall in 1920 (financed by the Tennessee Chapter of the Daughters of the American Revolution), which served as the boys' dormitory for the academy.[39]

These buildings lasted, but most of Hubbell's programs of study fell by the wayside because of limited resources. A case in point was Hubbell's grandiose plan to create a department of American history. He promoted it to the Executive Committee of the Board of Directors by noting that the "university is a living memorial to one of the great characters American history has produced." Hubbell proposed a new building to house the department, with endowed professorships and a separate library and museum building. He estimated that a new endowment of three hundred thousand dollars would be adequate to maintain such an establishment but had no idea how to find such a large sum of money in 1922.[40]

As the university neared its twenty-fifth anniversary, the Pyramid Film Company of Dayton, Ohio, made a movie on campus in April and May 1922. Originally called "Taking Up Where Honest Abe Left Off," its final title was *The Spirit of Lincoln.* H. E. Hollister, the president of Pyramid, directed the film. Pyramid was not a major producer, but had released eight movies from 1915 to 1918. This film depicted the story of two mountain youth who come to Lincoln Memorial University for an education, using students, staff, and local residents as actors. Seiberling showed the film to friends in his Akron home and then planned to show it elsewhere for promotional purposes.[41]

Hubbell also announced an effort to increase the university's endowment by $2 million and created an alumni association to help in the cause. But then he suddenly offered his resignation as president in May 1922, when the endowment was at $750,000. His ambitious projects, often implemented with little regard to finding adequate funds, had created several opponents on the board. Hubbell felt it was time to leave. Jesse Moore, the oldest professor on campus, was not sorry to see him go. Moore lamented Hubbell's lax attitude toward student discipline, noting that he "often erred on the side of mercy," but he also pinpointed the reason for Hubbell's leaving: "His enthusiasm amounted to rashness. His hope seemed to be unbounded. He solicited funds and secured some but borrowed more." While the "students loved him," the president racked up a debt of about thirty thousand dollars for each year he was in office, according to Moore.[42]

For George and Ella Hubbell, it had been "twelve difficult but very rewarding years" as presidential couple. But for Robert L. Kincaid, Hubbell's resignation "was a depressing day." On confiding to his mentor, Hubbell told him, "Robert, I do not worry about the future of LMU. It will not swing far out of its course in any change in administration." Only "a few months" later, Kincaid also resigned and moved to Middlesboro to work on the local newspaper. He soon took ownership of the *Middlesboro Daily News,* becoming editor and publisher for many years to come.[43]

The rest of Hubbell's life was filled with disappointment and failure. He moved to Asheville, North Carolina, where he tried to create Asheville College but was foiled by lack of funds. He then moved to Cleveland, Tennessee, to create a new college, but he "suffered a physical collapse" and moved back to Asheville. Kincaid met him again in 1932, after Hubbell had recovered. The former president walked into Kincaid's Middlesboro office looking disheveled and tired. Kincaid pried the story out of him; Hubbell was penniless and hitchhiking to a brother's home in Ohio, having slept the night before under a tree in Lee County, Virginia. Kincaid took him to a restaurant for lunch, then to his house for much-needed sleep. After a warm bath, a new set of clothes turned Hubbell into his old, charming self before he continued his journey. Not long after that unusual episode, Hubbell became an invalid and rapidly declined, spending the last eight years of his life in bed. Kincaid visited him in Asheville several times, where Hubbell often talked as if the two were still working together at Cumberland Gap. In his more lucid moments, Hubbell implored Kincaid to look after the students. He died on September 28, 1943.[44]

Robert Orville Matthews

The presidency was vacant during the academic year 1922–23, until Robert Orville Matthews was hired. Born in 1880, he earned his undergraduate degree at Syracuse University and was a pastor in Iowa and Ohio. Matthews also was a missionary to lumberjacks in the Pacific Northwest, where his work supposedly inspired Ralph Connor's novel *The Sky Pilot.* He worked for the American Red Cross during World War I and served on the federal Prohibition Commission before his appointment at the university.[45]

The Matthews presidency saw the creation of a more systematic effort to cash in on popular interest in Appalachian crafts. While the university had produced mountain products such as brooms since the Stooksbury years, it had not invested much in the effort. The Board of Directors voted on February 12, 1923 "to provide practical training" in what the university called "Domestic Arts and

Fireside Industries." The program also would create on-campus jobs for girls who needed to work their way through college. The national Nancy Hanks Memorial Association sponsored the creation of Nancy Hanks Clubs in local communities to memorialize the mother of Abraham Lincoln. The women of Harrogate started one such club and worked to raise money for the university department. Although "several thousand dollars" flowed in during the next two years, the university was never able to fulfill its goal of building a log cabin to house the department. Student workers labored on traditional equipment throughout the 1920s and sold a variety of items from table mats to magazine holders, at prices that ranged from fifty cents to thirty dollars.[46]

A typhoid epidemic hit the campus beginning February 3, 1924, affecting both the girls' and boys' dormitories. A number of doctors were in attendance, and state officials investigated, declaring the milk and water supply clear and assuming a human carrier, perhaps in one of the kitchens, caused the problem. Several dozen people came down with the disease, and seven of them died.[47]

Hill's publicity campaign continued apace, with a major article in *Pictorial Review* in 1923 that was mostly lifted from Richard Lloyd Jones's 1916 article in *Collier's* (the Jones article, in turn, had been taken from *The Living Memorial to Lincoln*). In 1926 the Sunday edition of the *New York Times* also carried a major piece on the university. Written by John Hays Hammond, who was listed as vice-president of the university but really was an outside fund-raiser and publicist, it mimicked Hill's article by describing the students as "a race of purest American stock."[48] Another friend of the institution, John L. Dickson, authored a booklet in 1928 that extolled the university as a place spreading "the gospel of self-control, the gospel of clear thinking and clean living, the gospel of honest toil and neighborliness." Hill's photograph covered an entire page of this booklet. The ultimate goal was to raise five million dollars for the endowment, new scholarships, and new buildings.[49]

Hill solicited endorsements from politicians of the 1920s to use in his promotional campaign. President Warren G. Harding wrote a short appeal, using language already employed in the university's promotional literature. Harding elaborated on the themes Hill and others had used in their writings when he gave an address at the Lincoln Celebration held in Washington on February 12, 1923. After he passed away later that year, the new president, Calvin Coolidge, also contributed an endorsement of the university's mission.[50]

Hill liked to use photographs of typical mountain youth in his promotional efforts. He also began to publish a string of books and pamphlets about Lincoln to raise awareness of the university and create a reputation for himself as a scholar of sorts. They included *If Lincoln Were Here* (1925) and *Lincoln the Inspired Leader;* the latter was a speech delivered at the unveiling of a statue called *Lincoln the Debater* in Freeport, Illinois, in 1929. Hill's most widely read book, *Abraham Lincoln: Man of God,* initially published in 1920, was reprinted by G. P. Putnam's Sons seven times during the next seven years. Hill stated that he "consciously used few" sources in writing this book, allowing it to grow "out of travel, observation and interviews with the late Robert T. Lincoln and others who knew Lincoln." Hill inscribed the copy he gave to the university with the words, "To posterity who will probably be interested in knowing what sort of ancestor opened the way for them."[51]

Robert Matthews left the presidency in the spring of 1927 under mysterious circumstances, giving rise to rumors that are still not clarified. It was widely believed that John Wesley Hill fired him, although proof has never surfaced. Rumor further had it that he had some sort of liaison with Iris Grannis, and Matthews was known to have admitted to some students that he had been "unwise." Jesse Moore admired Matthews as "a man of liberal culture and of strong character" but admitted he had no experience or aptitude for teaching or running a college. Moore thought it was "soon evident that he did not fully understand his work." Matthews went on to become vice-president of Air Way Electrical Corporation in Toledo, Ohio, until he died in 1934.[52]

Hill served as acting president of Lincoln Memorial University from the spring of 1927 until the end of 1928, continuing to harvest large donations as the nation's economy boomed. But not everyone was swayed by his powers. Frederick P. Keppel, president of the Carnegie Corporation of New York, frankly told an interested party that "Lincoln Memorial University had no standards and no position as shown from memberships" in major accrediting agencies. Keppel also thought the school "had been much handicapped by the prominence of John Wesley Hill" among its fund-raisers.[53]

One of Hill's biggest successes as financial agent of the university was to ensure the money needed for a new multipurpose building, fulfilling one of Howard's dreams. The ramshackle auditorium burned down in 1924, and the university courted both Henry Ford and Benjamin N. Duke for money. Dean of Faculty Charles D. Lewis, business manager C. P. Williams, and science professor Frank C. Grannis visited Ford at his Michigan home in late 1926 and were pleased to learn that both Ford and his wife were keenly interested in mountain culture. The Fords visited Cumberland Gap in the spring of 1927 and agreed to

The "Tabernacle," the ramshackle auditorium constructed in 1909 and used as a chapel burned early in 1924. As the handwritten caption of this snapshot indicates, the fire cleared the way for a large, multipurpose building as a replacement. Tex Turner Papers, UA-LMU.

purchase the Overton farm adjacent to the campus for forty thousand dollars and deed it to the university. Ford also inquired about the quality of clay outcroppings in the area, as he contemplated a brick-making facility for the school. His staff also investigated improved machinery for making brooms to enhance the university's crafts industry, centered in the Nancy Hanks Memorial Association.[54]

Everyone hoped Ford would also help finance the new auditorium, and the school submitted a massive proposal, replete with technical specifications, that had been drawn up for the building in 1925. Hill personally solicited a pledge of one hundred thousand dollars from cigarette magnate Benjamin N. Duke, contingent on whether an additional one hundred thousand dollars for the building could be found. So far the university had seventy-five thousand dollars available to contribute to the project.[55]

Hill was very proud of his "catch" when he secured Duke's pledge, after consoling the ailing millionaire and inveigling his pitch among prayers for his recovery. He was so delighted that he contracted with sculptor Cartaino S. Paolo for a bust of Duke to be put on display in the new building. Born in Palermo, Sicily, Paolo had a modestly successful career in the United States, where his realistic style earned him many commissions for public statues and monuments. Paolo liked Lincoln and therefore was willing to charge Hill only fifteen hundred dollars for the Duke bust rather than his normal fee of thirty-five hundred dollars.

While working with him, Duke came to like Paolo and offered to do something for him. The Sicilian modestly declined anything for himself, but suggested he give more to the university, which Duke agreed to do. Paolo assumed that Hill would be grateful, but instead the chancellor became very cold toward the sculptor. When Duke's daughter asked for a duplicate of her father's bust to be placed in her home, Hill offered the sculptor only one-third his asking price of three thousand dollars for the duplicate but promised to give him an honorary degree. Paolo never received the degree, admitting of Hill years later, "I am still puzzled about his character. I tried my best in many ways to understand and please him, but I never got there."[56]

In the end, Ford chose not to partner with Duke in financing the auditorium, contenting himself with the deed of land on which he wanted the university to grow food for the dormitories. The automobile king also suggested it could be used to pasture sheep. The multipurpose building, which became the main administrative edifice on campus, was constructed where the old auditorium had stood on the south side of the quadrangle. The cornerstone of the Duke Hall of Citizenship was erected on May 30, 1927, honoring the man who donated $159, 550 to Lincoln Memorial University from 1925 to 1928. The university also awarded Duke an honorary doctor of humane letters degree.[57]

Duke Hall of Citizenship. The cornerstone was laid in May 1927, and the building, funded by Benjamin N. Duke, was completed the next year. The south wing of the Four Seasons Hotel stood on this spot from 1892 to 1895, and a chapel-auditorium was here from 1909 until 1924. Earl J. Hess.

THE NEED TO MODERNIZE

Higher education changed rapidly in America after World War I. Student enrollment increased about 25 percent in the 1920s, yet more than half of all colleges and universities were small institutions similar to Lincoln Memorial University. As a result of that increase, the "first era of mass higher education" dawned in the United States. Observers noted that the war had produced a heightened respect for "experts" in all fields, and surveys indicated that two out of three undergraduates wanted to study "a specific occupation or profession." Administrators deemphasized the older liberal arts curriculum in favor of vocational or professional curricula. The more progressive institutions recognized that modernization demanded faculty members who had the most advanced training in doctoral programs at respected institutions.[58]

At Lincoln Memorial University, Hubbell had tried to create new programs in the professions but did not have the resources to maintain them. Moreover, the power equation on campus had shifted away from the president into the hands of businessmen and boosters who had nothing to do with teaching and did not live in the South. Several members of the board were stamped in the Seiberling mold. William E. Schenck of Madison, New Jersey, held advanced degrees from Cornell University, had worked as a lawyer for the state of New York, and served as general counsel for the United States Guarantee Company at the time of his association with the university. Wade H. Cooper of Washington, D.C., originally from Nashville, was a lawyer and banking executive. Wade H. Ellis of Washington, D.C., originally from Kentucky, had served as attorney general of Ohio and had been an assistant to the U.S. attorney general. Ferdinand W. LaFrentz of New York, born on an island in the Baltic Sea, came to the United States at age fourteen. Based on a three-month course of study in a Chicago business college, his only formal education in this country, LaFrentz rose from the position of bookkeeper to running the American Surety Company. Before that success, he had lived for some time in the West, where he worked as a lawyer and served one term in the U.S. House of Representatives from Wyoming. Based on that experience, he wrote a volume of poetry called *Cowboy Stuff* and donated all the royalties to Lincoln Memorial University after it was published in 1928. The money funded a new dormitory, LaFrentz-Poole Hall, after the family names of his mother and his wife.[59]

It became apparent to everyone, educator, businessman, and booster alike, that the key to further success was accreditation by a major organization. While

Lincoln Memorial University already was accredited by local agencies, only the Southern Association carried enough weight to allow the university's credits to be recognized without question outside Tennessee. It was not easy to achieve recognition by the association, however. Berea College worked for it from 1906 to 1926. That institution's primary problem was the small size of its college enrollment and "insufficient separation" of the college-level curriculum and faculty from that of the secondary-level offerings. Lincoln Memorial University applied for recognition in November 1926 but failed. A second application the following November achieved a small victory. While the association did not grant full membership, it offered a "non-member relationship" that allowed graduates of the university to teach at secondary schools which were accredited by the association.[60]

As the university moved closer toward the goal of accreditation, John Wesley Hill began to interfere with its administration. As acting president, he fired the popular dean of faculty, Charles D. Lewis, along with two department heads, on April 8, 1928. The reasons, as with Matthews's case, remain obscure. Business manager C. P. Williams accused Lewis of trying to create "a sort of student government" and attempting to create ill feeling toward Hill among the faculty. Hill insisted that faculty contracts contain a clause giving the president complete power to terminate employment "for causes deemed sufficient." When Lewis appealed to the American Association of University Professors, which had been created only thirteen years earlier to serve the interests of faculty, the AAUP declined to interfere because Lincoln Memorial University was not on the organization's list of accredited institutions. Lewis and the two department heads left, and at least five other faculty members resigned in protest and fear.[61]

On June 4, 1928, in the wake of the Lewis incident, the Board of Directors voted to use interest income from half a million dollars in the endowment "to meet the standards of the Southern Association of colleges." Nothing less than a major, expensive push was on to achieve recognition later that year. Much of that money had to be expended in larger salaries to attract faculty members with advanced degrees. But as Hill had already demonstrated, the new faculty had to live and work within an increasingly hostile environment, subject to the desires of an acting president who was not an educator and did not live or work on the campus. The number of faculty members holding terminal degrees had slowly increased before Hill had become involved in campus affairs. In the academic year 1915–16, only two of thirteen college faculty held a master's degree, eight held a bachelor's degree, and three held no college degree at all. In the academic year 1920–21, three of eighteen faculty held the doctor of philosophy degree, three held a master's degree, seven held a bachelor's degree, and five held no degree at all.[62]

The university applied for admission to the Southern Association for the third time on October 1, 1928. Ezra L. Gillis, registrar of the University of Kentucky, examined campus facilities on November 10. He was impressed by the progress made since his visit the previous year, except that the university had a wretched chemistry lab. Basing his evaluation on the standards of his own university, Gillis would have recommended in 1927 that Lincoln Memorial University graduates were equivalent only to juniors at the University of Kentucky. Now, in 1928, he was willing to argue that they deserved to enter the larger university's graduate program.[63]

But the association decided not to admit Lincoln Memorial University that year. W. D. Hooper of the University of Georgia, who chaired the association's commission that processed applications, told the new dean of faculty, Hervin U. Roop, that the association had always been concerned about "the constant change in personnel" at Lincoln Memorial University. Hooper asked Roop "why there was not some resident responsible head . . . who could formulate a permanent policy" at the school. Roop used that information to persuade Hill to name him president of Lincoln Memorial University. Hooper was offended at this blatant bit of careerism but decided to give Roop an opportunity to prove himself.[64]

Born in Highspire, Pennsylvania, on November 16, 1869, Hervin Ulysses Roop graduated from Lebanon Valley College and earned several advanced degrees after studying at Yale University and the University of Chicago. He became a minister and public school educator in several states and served as president of Lebanon Valley College, Eastern College, and York College before working as a faculty member at Wheaton College. A prolific author, Roop wrote ten textbooks in psychology, ethics, and logic.[65]

Although his resume seemed impressive, Roop's career was checkered with controversy. He had secured funds from Andrew Carnegie for a new library building for Lebanon Valley College, but on December 24, 1904, before it could be constructed, fire destroyed the college's multipurpose building. Roop hastily scribbled a request for $125,000 to Carnegie, which the industrialist thought a bit disgraceful. "This is a very poorly written note—don't speak well for the College," he complained. Eventually Roop prevailed on Carnegie to pledge fifty thousand dollars to rebuild the structure, but then he lost control of the situation by authorizing a massive building program designed to separate the various functions of the building into other, new structures. In the end, Roop initiated the construction of at least four buildings and the purchase of six acres of land to allow for expansion, totaling nearly two hundred thousand dollars in expenses. Although he had done this without consulting Carnegie, Roop continued to beg the industrialist for more money. After donating seventy thousand dollars, Carnegie declined to give more. Roop resigned "in disgrace" on January 1, 1906, after nearly wrecking his alma mater.[66]

Hill apparently was unaware of this incident when he hired Roop to serve as dean of faculty and head of the Department of Philosophy and Sociology in the fall term of 1928. Roop was a blatantly religious, deeply conservative individual, which probably was all that Hill wanted. He served as president of the American Association of Conservative Colleges and had given a speech at its ninth annual convention in Atlanta the previous fall titled "The Issue of Modernism." Published in the first volume of the *Christian Fundamentalist,* the speech lambasted the teaching of "modern" ideas such as Darwin's theory of evolution as weakening the moral faith of college students. "Suicide is lacking in colleges where Christianity is the dominant factor," he asserted. Atheistic doctrines create "a moral and spiritual Bolshevik, a menace to society," and Roop was convinced that colleges needed "more educated *Christian* leaders—leaders shot through with the mind, spirit and plain teachings of Jesus the Christ."[67]

Roop's religion was nothing less than reactionary, and his attitude toward education tended to be old fashioned. Nevertheless, the university entered 1929 with high hopes for accreditation in the near future. Hooper, who took a personal interest in the future of the school, agreed to give the commencement address that spring. With Hill's blessing and the board's credit, Roop launched a huge expansion of the curriculum and faculty in 1929. He created new schools of Business Administration, Engineering, Forestry, Agriculture, Music, Physical Education, and Home Economics. The university vigorously sought more money to pay increased faculty salaries. The Board of Directors accepted a report in June 1929 that the budget deficit the next academic year would soar to at least ninety thousand dollars.[68]

The university catalog charted the increase in faculty members and their credentials. While college faculty had numbered fifteen or sixteen per year for a long time, in the fall of 1929, the total amounted to twenty-six. Eleven of those individuals held a doctoral degree, ten held a master's degree, and five held a bachelor's degree. Possessors of doctoral degrees had earned them at the

University of Missouri, American University, Harvard, Columbia, the University of Chicago, the University of Colorado, the University of London, and the University of Edinburgh. This was the largest accumulation of well-trained college professionals on campus thus far in the university's history.[69]

John Wesley Hill maintained a grueling pace in his fund-raising efforts, giving speeches and networking with as many influential men as possible. His health suffered, resulting in a nervous condition, and Hill spent some time at the Battle Creek Sanitarium, in Battle Creek, Michigan. "I am anxious to see you all," he wrote to Iris Grannis while awaiting release from the sanitarium. "There is some thing very magnetic in LMU." His efforts were netting an average of forty-four thousand dollars each year by the late 1920s.[70]

But Hill and Roop created a climate on campus that was ill suited to the workings of a modern institution. Clifford P. Lyons, a young teacher at Berea's academy, was lured to Lincoln Memorial University by a great many promises that proved to be false when he arrived with his new bride in the fall of 1928. University officials suddenly realized that Lyons did not have the required number of education credits on his transcript to head the academy, so they offered an uncomfortable arrangement whereby Lyons's wife ran the academy and taught classes and Lyons coached athletic teams, oversaw the dorms, took more classes, and even taught some education courses himself. But the couple received only one salary. Roop did not want Lyons to head the academy, even after he had earned the credentials to do so, because the young man was too outspoken in his views.[71]

Lyons was interested in the university's mission, but he became disillusioned after investigating its programs for mountain youth. He found the Grace Nettleton Home was divorced from the life of the institution, and Hubbell's Opportunity School seemed to have but a dozen students who lived a short distance from campus. Lyons could find no information on the academy students at all. In fact, there was "constant talk" of discontinuing the academy for financial reasons, but Roop and Hill wanted to retain those programs for publicity purposes. Lyons thought the college students at Lincoln Memorial University were tired of the many references to "mountain youth." It was "a joke among" them, he asserted, and even the faculty made light of the concept in their meetings. "In other words," Lyons concluded, "the institution gets all of its publicity, raises its money on a false basis."[72]

Lyons was severely critical of Roop and Hill. The former was untrustworthy and the latter had a bad reputation. Colleagues at Berea had told Lyons not to trust Hill, and he regretted the year he spent at Cumberland Gap before beginning graduate work. "In his visits to the school his cheap dramatics, his endless Jesus talk and sanctity were but cloaks to the most callous personality I know," Lyons frankly informed a confidant. "He does not find it the least incongruous to pray for someone he has just stabbed in the back." Hill enjoyed telling everyone "how he has persuaded people to give large sums of money to the school—how he prayed with Duke, . . . and laughs over it all." Lyons reported that Hill once confided to someone that he learned how to be a successful fund-raiser after he had become the victim of a confidence man. Lyons felt that Hill's dream was to leave "a great monument to himself in the beautiful foothills of the Cumberlands—a monument to himself and Lincoln."[73]

Hill certainly saw Lincoln Memorial University as a way to work out his own ambition as a fund-raiser, connecting it with the image of Lincoln that he single-mindedly cultivated in his promotional literature for the school. Iris Grannis had greatly improved the library holdings to meet Southern Association standards, as well as working on university publicity, but she also cooperated closely with Hill to shape the Lincoln image. When Grannis reported that some of the new faculty members thought the library's Lincoln holdings should be deemphasized, Hill retorted that if any teachers favored eliminating Lincoln from the library, "*they* should be eliminated." Grannis thought Lloyd Lewis's *Myths After Lincoln* "a most amazing book," but it also was "perfectly terrible in places." She concluded, "It cannot be read on our campus." Grannis also was deeply concerned about the lack of accreditation, for several students she had taken under her wing were unable to enter graduate schools at other universities. "We cannot expect our diplomas to be recognized until we get into the Southern Association," Hill wrote her in August 1929. "I hope it will come this fall, but we may be kept another year or two on the waiting list."[74]

CHAPTER 7
STRIKE

The protest of the fresh uncompromised idealism of youth against an administration which does not measure up to their expectations. This idealism of the student body is one of the finest assets of Lincoln Memorial and should not be crushed in an effort to impose discipline.
—Hazel Fulton, April 16, 1930

There was but one feeling,—namely, that rebellion must be stamped completely out of the minds of faculty and students without regard to consequences.
—Frank A. Seiberling, April 8, 1930

I just hear that *Hell is poppin*—at LMU. The Bolshevists are desperate!
—John Wesley Hill, April 9, 1930

Early on the afternoon of April 10, 1930, a group of twenty-five students hauled down the flag from its staff on the quadrangle and carried it into the office of acting president J. H. S. Morison. He was not in at that moment, but the group presented the colors to his secretary. "This flag is a symbol of justice and freedom," said Clay McCarroll, president of the senior class, "and we don't want it to float over the campus of a university where those qualities have ceased to exist."[1]

This extraordinary act of defiance occurred during a massive student strike that took place at Lincoln Memorial University. Triggered by the arbitrary firing of three teachers and one staff member, the strike involved almost all of the four hundred college students and nearly wrecked the university. There were many underlying causes that had been germinating for years, hidden by a façade of peace and cooperation within the context of an increasingly oppressive atmosphere created by the unscrupulous actions of Hervin U. Roop and the domineering presence of John Wesley Hill. Progressive-minded teachers and students reacted against that climate when the university's effort to achieve recognition by the Southern Association failed and Roop, with Hill's approval, exacted revenge against people who had earned a place on his blacklist. The student strike was an explosion of anger and frustration, encouraged by a small group of well-meaning faculty members, that tested the moral fiber and mission-driven aspirations of Lincoln Memorial University. The Lincoln ideals that inspired so many at the Cumberland Gap institution seemed to be at stake, but who had the right to define and interpret those ideals was at issue.

In the bright fall of 1929, when everyone expected the Southern Association to admit the university at its December meeting, no one could have predicted the student unrest to come. Iris Grannis prepared the library for inspection and used the mailing list of the *Mountain Herald* to publicize the school among southern educators. Ezra Gillis returned for another visit as the association's inspector on November 14. He spent a great deal of time sitting in on classes conducted by the new faculty and found the physical plant adequate. The "efficiency of the instruction and the scientific spirit seemed to be satisfactory, at least I went away with a favorable impression," he wrote. Gillis thought the chemistry and biology labs met association standards, and he reported that the academy and college were sufficiently separated to satisfy the association.[2]

The university probably would have been admitted in December 1929 except for an unforeseen problem. Some faculty members noticed a number of fictitious degrees attached to Roop's name and that of several other teachers as they perused the new college catalog. When they informed the association, W. D. Hooper was shocked. He immediately dropped the university's application. "All that the Commission demands is that an institution should live strictly up to its many obligations, and be scrupulously honest in its public statements," he explained.[3]

FALLOUT

Hill was sick with anger and frustration when he learned the news. "It is simply outrageous that we are left out," he fumed at Roop. "It takes the nerve out of me and leaves me greatly embarrassed as I had told a number of our friends that we would be admitted this year." Roop either did not know the real reason for the university's failure or he tried to hide it from the domineering chancellor. "Only God & the Com. Knew whether we would be admitted," he informed Hill. Roop blamed Registrar Maude Smith for a misstatement to Gillis regarding university policy on admitting freshmen with fewer than the required number of high school credits, and he noted that several faculty members still possessed no graduate degrees. Apparently members of the association's commission also had made reference to their distrust of John Wesley Hill, and Roop tried to tell the chancellor that he defended him, implying this also contributed to the decision not to admit the university.[4]

In late January 1930, Hooper informed Frank A. Seiberling, president of the Board of Directors, why the association could not recognize the university. Seiberling regarded Roop as "a terrible misfit" and authorized Hill to deal with the problem. The chancellor went to Lincoln Memorial University on February 22 to consult a committee of nine faculty members, all of whom demanded Roop's dismissal and the enactment of reforms in campus administration. Hill assured the nine that Roop would leave. The committee also suggested that one of their number, Merlin G. Miller, serve as dean of faculty during the interim between presidents. Hill agreed and met with the group again on February 23, informing them that Roop also was suffering from a cancerous condition of the lip.[5]

Miller now emerged as a major player in the strike story. Born in December 1898, he had joined the university in the fall of 1928 with an undergraduate degree from Mount Morris College and a master's degree from the University of Chicago, where his thesis dealt with the political aspects of the Whiskey Rebellion on the Pennsylvania frontier in 1794. He had several years of experience teaching

Class of 1930 (*left panel*). This panoramic photograph was taken in February or March 1930, a short time before the onset of the student strike. Avery Hall is in the background, and staff and faculty members are standing in the front row. Bessie B. Huntzinger, preceptress of Norton Hall, is fifth from right. UA-LMU.

in the high schools of Iowa before pursuing his graduate training, and he headed the Department of History at Lincoln Memorial University.[6]

Roop remained in office for another month following the February 22–23 meetings, as Miller prepared a thirty-eight-page proposal for reorganizing the administration of the university and dealing with the problem of gaining recognition by the Southern Association. He presented this document to Hill when the chancellor returned to campus on March 18. Hill and Seiberling liked the proposal, especially Miller's recommendation that the university divorce itself from the academy. This move was delayed, however, by Claiborne County's laxness in setting up a high school for the academy students to attend. Hill also announced that a new dean, to fill in until the next president could be found, would be elected by a vote of all the faculty members. That election took place on March 20, but many staff members as well as academy teachers attended and cast ballots to elect Henry Artis Miley, Roop's hand-picked successor, instead

Class of 1930 (*center panel*). Duke Hall is in the background, and controversial university president Hervin U. Roop (December 1928–March 1930) is in the center. Foreign language professor Madame Frances Eppinger is on Roop's left, sociologist Clifford G. Thompson (a staunch supporter of the administration) is the fourth person on Roop's left, and speech professor Earl Hobson Smith (who remained aloof from the controversy) is on Thompson's left. Historian Merlin G. Miller, an outspoken critic of the administration, is on the far right of Roop. UA-LMU.

of Miller. Miley, who had arrived at Lincoln Memorial University the previous fall to teach chemistry, had completed his doctoral degree at the University of Colorado in 1929. The balloting was followed by several prayers and religious hymns, and then Hill announced that Roop would not be fired after all but would be granted a leave of absence for a "few weeks." The chancellor then called for the resignations of any faculty members who did not agree with the proceedings that evening.[7]

Hill remained on campus until March 22. Four days later, letters of dismissal were delivered to three faculty members and the registrar just before Roop left campus on his sick leave. The letters were dated March 22, and rumor had it that Hill had dictated them before he left Cumberland Gap. In addition to Maude Smith, Elliott Van Nostrand Diller in psychology, Alfred R. W. deJonge in foreign languages, and Elizabeth Harris in foreign languages were notified that their yearly contracts would not be renewed at the end of the current term. The letters

Class of 1930 (*right panel*). DAR Hall, the dorm for boys of the Lincoln Memorial Academy, is in the background. Foreign language professor Lucia Danforth, a critic of Roop and the administration, is on the far right; philosopher Elliott Van Nostrand Diller, the chief target of Roop and John Wesley Hill, is second from right; foreign language professor Alfred Robert Willy deJonge, another target, is third from right; Greek and Latin professor Elizabeth Harris, who also was fired, is sixth from right; and popular coach Joe Alexander, who remained aloof from the controversy, is second from left. UA-LMU .

contained a reference to a hated clause in the university's faculty contracts allowing the president to fire anyone for "cause deemed sufficient."[8]

Roop's action triggered student unrest, but rumors that Hill had engineered the firings were exaggerated. It is true that both Roop and Hill disliked Diller, but Hill apparently had nothing to do with the firing of the other three people. Hill allowed Roop to leave the university on a sick leave to save what was left of the president's reputation and cooperated with him in electing Miley rather than Miller as dean. The chancellor tried to smooth the transition from Roop to another academic leader, although he used heavy-handed methods to place the young and compliant Miley in a position of temporary authority.

Diller was one of the most popular professors on campus, with a bachelor's degree from Williams College in 1926 and a master's degree from Columbia University in 1928. He was finishing his second year at the school but had agreed to work for one of those years without a salary after Hill complained of the institution's straitened circumstances. Diller taught for room and board and postponed his marriage a few months until his second-year salary made it possible. Students liked his personality and admired his training at famous northeastern schools. The graduating class of 1929 voted Diller not only its favorite teacher but also the university's most inspiring professor. But Diller ran afoul of Roop's jealousy. The president required his textbook on psychology to be used for all classes, and Diller could not hide his disgust with it. He refused to use the book and complained that a more up-to-date text was not available. Some of the more conservative faculty considered Diller a "random talker" who espoused unwholesome ideas, while the brighter students idolized him as a free spirit who offered a breath of fresh air on a campus that often seemed stultified.[9]

As far as Hill was concerned, Diller was "a constitutional recalcitrant" who was "as full of fustian doctrines as he is of cunning." The chancellor considered him nothing less than a Bolshevik espousing "philosophic and economic heresies." This view was reinforced by Business Manager C. P. Williams, who thought not only Diller but also a couple of other faculty members were teaching "communistic ideas." Roop, according to Williams, was "not strong enough to handle the situation and stop these things in time." Based solely on Hill's reports, Seiberling agreed that Diller was a bad man to have on campus. Even though Hill advised Roop to get rid of Diller, he was disgusted with the president's invocation of the hated clause in the contract that allowed the university to fire any employee at will. "I had no idea that you were so tactless," Hill informed Roop when he learned how the four had been fired, "or I certainly would have indicated the sort of notice to be served." Hill viewed Roop's action as a mean-spirited effort to throw his weight around just before leaving the university and deeply regretted the way in which the president had released the four.[10]

The other three who had been fired all had trouble with Roop, but not with Hill. Alfred Robert Willy deJonge had been born in Brussels in 1884 and had studied at the University of Berlin and the Sorbonne in Paris, migrating to England and then to the United States in 1909. He completed his doctoral training at Columbia University and published a book, *Gottfried Kinkel as Political and Social Thinker,* in 1926. Hill was particularly proud that he had convinced deJonge to join the faculty, at the impressive salary of three thousand dollars, in the fall of 1929. But deJonge ran afoul of Roop when he realized that another foreign language professor, Madame Frances Eppinger, was inflating the grades she gave to students in her German classes. He tried to administer the exams in those classes himself to correct the problem. Eppinger appealed to Roop, who sided with her. DeJonge offered his resignation in February 1930, but Hill convinced him to remain. The students generally did not like deJonge; he openly criticized conditions on campus, denigrated the backwardness of Appalachia, and was outspoken in his efforts to impose more rigorous standards. He represented a problem inherent in building a faculty by recruiting sophisticated, urban-oriented professionals to an area that was still relatively undeveloped.[11]

Latin teacher Elizabeth Harris had joined Lincoln Memorial University in the fall of 1928 to replace Jesse H. Moore when the old professor retired. With both undergraduate and master's degrees from Vanderbilt University, she was only twenty-four years old and considered very attractive. Her presence created jealousies and rumors that had nothing to do with her professional activities or her unassuming and innocent personality. The isolated, tightly knit community on campus bred stories, especially that Harris and T. Edward Terrill, the head of the English Department, were an item because Terrill took her home after evening meetings at Lucia Danforth's house in Cumberland Gap. Those meetings took place so that faculty members from other departments, who were teaching English classes in addition to their regular course work, could coordinate their activities. The preceptress of Norton Hall, Mrs. Bessie B. Huntzinger, apparently was jealous of Harris because no one paid attention to her daughter Mary. None of these issues seem to have involved Roop, except that he probably saw Harris as a dangerously alluring female who inspired intrigue.[12]

Maude Smith's downfall lay in her refusal to misrepresent the university's admission policies to Ezra Gillis. Foreign language professor Lucia Danforth testified that she overheard Roop pressure Smith to lie to Gillis, but the registrar bravely refused.[13]

FIRST STRIKE

News of the firings spread rapidly and led to a large student meeting in Duke Hall on the evening of March 27. Diller's firing, in particular, upset everyone. The invocation of the "cause deemed sufficient" language infuriated many students as well. A recent graduate of the university put it succinctly when she complained that "the administration is dismissing teachers who have the highest academic standing and who if permitted to remain . . . would contribute largely to L.M.U.'s admittance into the southern association." Before the assembled throng, senior class president Clay McCarroll read Roop's letter of dismissal to Diller, and the fired faculty member read a letter he wrote to Seiberling explaining his plight. At least nine faculty members, including Miller and Terrill, promised to support the students in whatever action they took. The crowd debated a motion to boycott all classes in exchange for an investigation of campus affairs, and a "*very large majority*" approved. The faculty who attended the meeting urged the students "to refrain from dating and to behave in a manner becoming ladies and gentlemen" during the strike.[14]

Clay McCarroll emerged as the driving force behind the student strike. Born in Texas on October 6, 1908, he had attended the Knox County Industrial School in Knoxville, Tennessee, and graduated from Knoxville High School. The twenty-one-year-old senior had nearly finished work on his degree in philosophy.[15]

Clay McCarroll, president of the senior class of 1930 and leader of the student strike, 1930. UA-LMU.

The students put their resolution into effect on Friday, March 28. Only a handful of them ignored the boycott and attended morning chapel exercise or classes, and a holiday atmosphere prevailed on campus. Opal Ann McDowell, who lived off campus, went to Miller's history class that day and recalled that Miller threatened the few students who attended with a poor grade if they did not support the boycott. McDowell was disappointed in a teacher she had formerly admired. "I was there for an education," she stated nearly eighty years later, "not for a strike."[16]

Another meeting took place in Duke Hall immediately after lunch time. McCarroll told the assembled throng that Harry E. Bullock, the chairman of the Executive Committee of the board, might help the students. Born in Whitley County, Kentucky, Bullock had attended Williamsburg Academy in Williamsburg, Kentucky, when George Hubbell's wife had been assistant principal there. He later attended Lincoln Memorial University as a student in the days of John Hale Larry. Bullock went to Brown University to earn a degree in metallurgical engineering and became a successful businessman in coal and farming. He lived in Lexington, Kentucky. Mrs. Hubbell remembered him as "a man of deep sympathies."[17]

Bullock called a meeting of the Executive Committee at the Cumberland Hotel in Middlesboro on March 29. The group, which included J. H. S. Morison and C. P. Williams, approved a resolution calling on the students to hold their strike in abeyance until the full board could meet to consider their grievances. The resolution characterized Roop's firing as "arbitrary and unreasonable" and called for measures to ensure "that justice may be done all parties concerned."[18] The students hailed Bullock's work as a victory and called off their strike. Meanwhile, Seiberling arranged an emergency meeting of the entire Board of Directors for April 6. Thirteen faculty members wrote a petition, and 287 students signed a separate petition, to be presented at that meeting.[19]

The board met at the Willard Hotel in Washington, D.C., with Bullock and most of the Executive Committee in attendance, but the result of the meeting surprised the students and their faculty supporters. A number of members were absent, including Frederick B. Avery and Reese Patterson, son of Robert Patterson, but their proxy votes were empowered to a number of board members who did attend. Although the petitions and messages from concerned faculty and striking students were read aloud, no discussion of them took place. The board members, most of whom were businessmen, lawyers, and government officials who lived outside Appalachia, ignored Bullock's initiative and decided to strong-arm the strikers in order to impose campus law and order. Gen. Frank T. Hines, veteran of the Spanish-American War and World War I and the current head of the Bureau of Veterans Affairs, made a motion to elect Morison as temporary president until the board could find a permanent replacement for Roop. Hines further moved that the board vote a resolution of confidence in Hill's "wonderful and efficient services to the University." Both votes were unanimous because Bullock gave up his effort to help the students as a lost cause. The board was determined, in the words of Arthur L. Garford, that "rebellion in whatever form cannot be allowed to flourish in an institution established as a living memorial to Abraham Lincoln."[20]

Morison also forgot his earlier support for Bullock's initiative. He rushed back to Cumberland Gap with his mission clearly spelled out: "Rebellion must be stamped completely out of the minds of faculty and students without regard to consequences," as Seiberling put it. James Henderson Stuart Morison, born on September 12, 1864, was the son of a doctor in the region of Cumberland Gap. He had earned bachelor's and master's degrees from the University of Tennessee and his law degree from the National University in Washington. Morison practiced in Tazewell before serving as a county and circuit judge and taught a class on citizenship at Lincoln Memorial University by 1928.[21]

Relatively isolated at his office in Washington, D.C., Hill knew details of the campus trouble only through reports, some of which implicated Iris Grannis in the rebellion. Grannis tried to explain her innocence. "The past ten days have been terrible," she wrote Hill on April 5. "I have aged ten years or more and shall never be the same again. Secret meetings, protests, strikes and one disgraceful thing after another. It doesn't seem possible that the school can survive and I think it is not so much a matter of 'walking the plank' or 'swimming out' but of sinking with the ship." Grannis blamed both Roop (who was "a great failure") and "certain teachers who have failed to adjust themselves to the objectives and purposes of the University." The school had acquired a reputation as a place where "teachers do not get a square deal," and all hope of recognition by the Southern Association seemed lost.[22]

Hill was disappointed that Grannis's reputation was tainted by the strike, but he did nothing to retain her services for the university. He also was sorry to see deJonge leave, for he considered the Belgian to be "one of the most valuable acquisitions to Lincoln Memorial" because of his advanced degrees from prominent universities. Hill informed Elizabeth Harris that her firing upset him but there was nothing he could do about it.[23]

Second Strike

Morison called a campus meeting on the night of April 8 to announce that he had taken charge of the university. He also pleaded for everyone's cooperation. It was obvious that Morison had no intention of discussing strikers' demands, so the students held their third meeting on April 9. This time they met in the "bowl," a wide and shallow drainage feature down the east side of the flattened hill that held the quadrangle. The class of 1924 had financed the placement of large white *LMU* letters on the upper slope of the hollow. The letters were prominent from the main road that linked Cumberland Gap with Tazewell. McCarroll and his associate, Ernest W. Fields, addressed the crowd, and Miller also spoke. The meeting ended with a resolve to resume the strike.[24]

Most students remained loyal to the cause, but Opal Ann McDowell was one of only five pupils who came to Miller's history class. Miller "was so mad at us," she wrote in her diary. "He is somewhat of a leader of the strike." The students also sent a telegram to Governor Henry H. Horton of Tennessee, asking for a state investigation of the situation at Lincoln Memorial University.[25]

A great deal happened on Thursday, April 10. Only 102 students out of 400 attended morning chapel, and McCarroll and 25 others hauled down the American flag early that afternoon. Not long after that event, McCarroll told yet another meeting of the students that Morison had threatened to expel him if he did not give up the cause. When they learned that Morison refused to allow reporter John T. Moutoux of the *Knoxville News-Sentinel* to take photographs on

The Bowl. The students met several times in the wide, shallow ravine on the east side of the main hill at Lincoln Memorial University, near the white LMU letters. The president's house was constructed in 1913. Poor Valley Ridge is in the distance. Earl J. Hess.

campus, they assembled in the bowl so he could take pictures from the shoulder of the highway. Morison called in reinforcements in the form of twenty deputy sheriffs. They were "the toughest gangsters I have ever seen (even in the slums of New York)," according to deJonge. The students were frightened and sent another telegram to Governor Horton, reporting that "rough appearing deputy sheriffs are threatening us and carrying on a campaign of terrorism in the name of law and order." The governor, however, replied that he could not interfere. "We will stay out until they are reinstated and the trustees get rid of Hill," McCarroll defiantly told the newspapers.[26]

Only a handful of students opposed McCarroll's course of action. Several of them told reporters that most of the students had no idea what they were striking for, and many took advantage of the turmoil to have a vacation. But most of McCarroll's fellow scholars continued to support the cause by boycotting classes. When Opal McDowell went to school on April 11, she "found strike still on and came back" home.[27]

Concerned faculty members struck back as best they could. Miller tried to find a solution to the trouble by negotiating with Morison about inviting educators from other institutions to help plan a strategy for securing accreditation. Morison, however, refused to consider reinstating the fired personnel, even though Miller told him it would improve the university's standing with the Southern Association. Diller and deJonge attempted to interest the federal government in the case. They informed a U.S. postal inspector in Knoxville of Roop's distribution of university literature containing false statements about the advanced degrees he and others held. They considered this a violation of federal law and hoped the government would move toward prosecution, but that never happened. Elizabeth Harris defended herself to the press. She admitted to advising some of the better students to transfer to Vanderbilt or the University of North Carolina. "Anybody else, with a conscience, would have done the same," she said.[28]

On the night of April 11, another student meeting in Duke Hall hammered out a set of four demands, formalizing strike objectives for the first time. The students demanded reinstatement of dismissed personnel, an investigation by outside educators, revision of outdated social regulations for female students who lived on campus, and clear limits placed on the authority of the chancellor.[29]

The next day, Morison listened to the demands and rejected them. He had no authority to reinstate the personnel and was unwilling to invite outsiders to snoop into university affairs. On the social regulations, he flippantly commented,

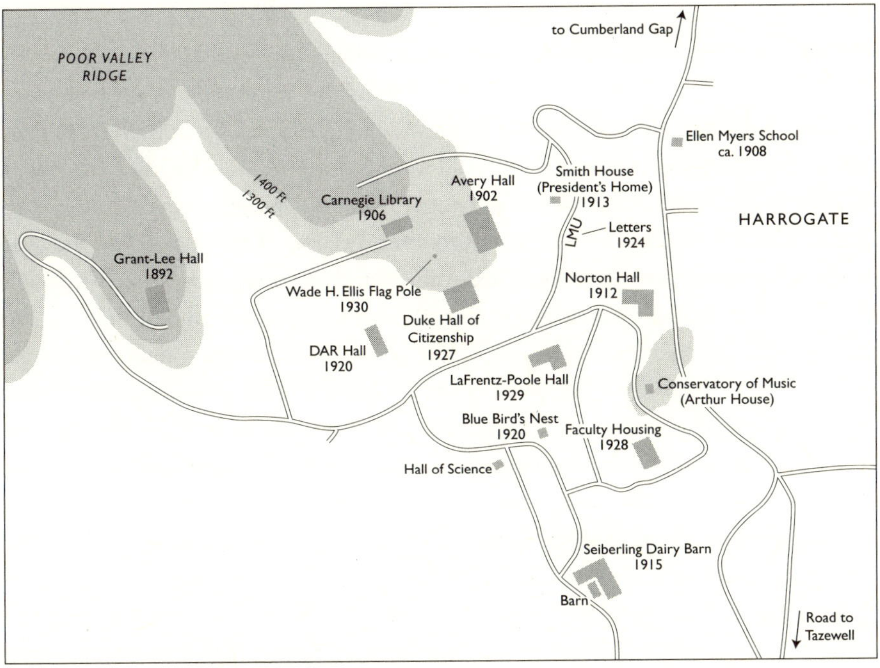

Lincoln Memorial University campus, 1930.

"I guess if the boys and girls need more time in which to do their courting, they ought to have it." Morison refused to take up the issue of limiting anyone's authority until the strike was over. The students were crestfallen but they resolved to continue the strike.[30]

Morison now took the offensive to break what had become a stalemate between irreconcilable forces. He called the student leaders "Bolshevists" and blamed McCarroll as "chiefly responsible for this whole affair." Morison expelled McCarroll and Fields on April 12. The two students refused to honor the expulsion, so H. K. Ryder, a deputy sheriff and employee of the university, swore a warrant for their arrest. Friends warned McCarroll that deputies were headed for his dorm room on the evening of April 12, so he hid in the wardrobe. McCarroll's roommate, Elmer H. Heaberlin, refused to disclose his whereabouts, but Ryder looked into the wardrobe and found him. Fields was released on his own recognizance, but McCarroll's bond was initially set at five hundred dollars, and tripled at the request of W. I.

Davis, an attorney for the university. Several faculty members, including Miller and deJonge, paid the bond, and a hearing was scheduled for April 19.[31]

When Davis announced that he would seek an injunction to stop student meetings on campus, the strikers walked two and a half miles to a friendly farmer across the state line in Virginia to hold a rally on April 12. Another front was opened in the strike when Mrs. Huntzinger tried to force the female students to stay inside Norton Hall all day except to attend classes. For three hours the girls stood at the windows shouting, "We want out," and then they walked through the door in a large group at 10:00 a.m. Reporter Moutoux argued that the social rules for female residents were "now stricter than at most denominational colleges." J. R. Ketron of Tazewell, a lawyer for the university, pointed out that the social regulations for the college girls were the same as that for the academy students. They included a limit of only one date per week, on Sunday afternoons, and no walking out after dark except with a chaperone.[32]

Morison also struck at the faculty. He had already determined to get Diller off campus even before his contract ran out, and now he targeted Miller as a troublemaker. On April 12, he informed the two that their employment was immediately terminated because of "activities in connection with the pending strike among the students." A bit later Miller also was told he had only five days to vacate his faculty lodgings, and he and his wife were enjoined not to attend any meetings. Morison told a newspaperman that "wholesale suspension" of students was the only way to end the strike. "I will just send them all home and let their parents tend to them," he said.[33]

The strikers received their first help from outside the university when John R. Neal came from Knoxville to aid the dismissed faculty members and the two students who had been arrested. Inevitably drawn to controversy, Neal had been the chief defense lawyer for John T. Scopes in the famous "monkey trial" at Dayton, Tennessee, five years earlier. Two years before that, Neal had lost his faculty position in the law school at the University of Tennessee because of persistent failures to hold classes regularly, grade tests promptly, and perform a number of administrative tasks assigned him. Several other faculty members were fired at the same time in what became famous as the "Slaughter of the PhDs." He established and operated a law school of his own in Knoxville that survived for many decades despite the fact that it was never accredited by a major agency.[34]

Neal counseled McCarroll, who rallied another meeting of the students in the bowl on April 14, attended by about thirty parents as well. The group read chapters from the Bible and sang "Onward Christian Soldiers." Chancellor John H.

Williams at Tazewell issued a temporary injunction against campus meetings that day and later modified it to allow dismissed faculty and McCarroll to retain access to their housing and other buildings on campus. Probably due to Neal's coaching, McCarroll knew that Tennessee law allowed evicted tenants five days to prepare for a hearing and an additional six days to move if the eviction was upheld. Neal characterized the university's employment arrangements with its faculty as "collegiate yellow dog contracts" and telegraphed several members of the board to inform them that "a reign of terrorism exists at the institution." Fewer than fifty students attended college classes on April 14.[35]

Elmer Heaberlin was elected McCarroll's replacement as strike leader, but the injunction barred further student meetings. Morison also decided to fire deJonge before his contract expired and force him and his wife to vacate their quarters. Chancellor Williams made the temporary injunction against further strikes permanent on April 16, even though his Tazewell courtroom was packed with anxious students who hoped he would see things their way. Williams, however, continued to allow the affected students and faculty to use campus facilities. Several university alumni who lived in Knoxville voiced support for the strikers as students sent pleas to board members for help, but Harry Bullock was powerless to do anything. In fact, he was under a cloud as far as Seiberling and Hill were concerned for what they viewed as his weak-willed stance in the crisis. Everyone else on the board toed the Seiberling-Hill line and refused aid to the strikers. As Seiberling put it, Hill's fund-raising efforts had been based on the idea that the university's Lincoln ideals were untainted by foreign doctrines such as socialism and bolshevism. It was tragic, he thought, "to have these boys strike at the hand that has fed them."[36]

Signs that the strike was weakening became apparent by April 18, when a number of faculty members submitted their resignations to escape the difficult conditions on campus. They were "scared to death," as deJonge told a reporter. Morison also expelled or enjoined twenty-four students, all of them male. He suspended and sent home ten female students as well. The executive committee of the alumni association, headed by Robert L. Kincaid, issued a statement deploring the strike as the wrong way to address student concerns. Observers estimated that about one hundred college students had gone home, and about one hundred others were attending classes. The rest, about half the college population, remained on campus but continued to boycott their studies.[37]

On May 19, Morison shocked everyone when he reported that three sticks of dynamite, one with a partially burned fuse, had been found in Duke Hall the previous day. They had been hidden under the organ. "I believe it was a bluff," he told the newspapers. "I have no fear for my life."[38]

The public relations war spread to many parts of the country, with newspapers in New York, Saint Paul, and Washington, D.C., reporting the strike objectively. The only newspaper that stridently supported the students was the *Knoxville News-Sentinel,* although the *Knoxville Journal* sometimes sided with the strikers as well. The local paper, Kincaid's *Middlesboro Daily News,* mixed objective coverage of the strike with strongly pro-administration editorials.[39]

Hill was a master of spin strategy. He was a partner in a Washington, D.C., public relations firm as well as director of public relations for the American Iron and Steel Institute. Hill prevailed on university board member Ira E. Bennett, longtime editor of the *Washington Post,* to print an editorial about the strike on April 20. "University Bolshevism" was the title of the piece. Bennett cheered the administration's efforts: "No greater perversion of education can be imagined than the teaching of bolshevism in a university that bears the name of the great empancipator [*sic*]." Bennett spread Hill's version of the strike story nationwide, accusing one faculty member of teaching red ideology and noting that the dynamite indicated "a few deluded youngsters . . . were willing to destroy the university" in the name of a hated philosophy. "The trustees of Lincoln Memorial have set an example worthy of emulation by all American colleges in which the hideous specter of communism shows itself."[40]

The *Knoxville News-Sentinel,* on the other hand, allowed students and faculty many opportunities to tell their stories. Harris argued that the strike resulted from "a long accretion of abuses—persistent repression, arrant injustice, and other medieval modes of administration." Diller noted that the campus had suffered from "years of vacillating and inconsistent policies and capricious legislation," while deJonge thought the administration never had "a correct conception of the position of faculty members." Miller pinpointed the yellow dog contract and Hill as the chief problems: "For many years he has made his periodic visits to the campus the occasion for display of summary action, he has mercilessly berated professors, both men and women, and has dismissed without cause teachers for whom he had formed any dislike on any trivial ground." DeJonge and Miller argued that the students were treated like children and their hard work often went for naught because the university could not gain admission to the Southern Association. The editors of the *Knoxville News-Sentinel* thought the strikers had "a truer sense of Lincolnian ideals of justice, democracy and the worth of the individual than the administration which was charged with the responsibility for inculcating them." The *New Republic* also sided with the strikers, calling them "naïve, idealistic, simple" fighters for "academic freedom."[41]

Their Day in Court

Newspaper and magazine support availed McCarroll and Fields little when they attended their hearing at the Claiborne County Court House on April 19. Chancellor Williams presided as hundreds of students applauded and laughed "when they thought the occasion warranted it." Because university lawyers could not produce evidence that either student had used profane language or incited a riot, John R. Neal suggested those two charges be dropped. Although the university agreed, it continued to press the basic charge of creating a disturbance on educational grounds. Prosecution witnesses included Mrs. Huntzinger, who cried that the university "has almost gone to pieces." Student Paris Houston, a strong supporter of the university, testified that the strike made it difficult to attend classes and concentrate on studies. The head of the campus dairy complained that he spent so much time serving as a special deputy that his work suffered.[42]

J. R. Ketron of Tazewell was the chief attorney for Lincoln Memorial University at the hearing. He had been born near Cumberland Gap and had attended American Temperance University at Harriman, Tennessee. Hill had given him an honorary doctorate of laws two years earlier. When Ketron called McCarroll to the stand, the lawyer asked him if he had not demoralized the university by his actions, and the young student replied, "It was already demoralized before we got hold of it." Ketron posed several questions so quickly that McCarroll asked him to slow down, saying, "I'm not a Socrates." Ketron good-naturedly replied, "No, but you're a Demosthenes all right." Everyone, including McCarroll, laughed at the banter.[43]

Ironically, one of the defense attorneys, John P. Davis, was an uncle of one of the prosecution lawyers, W. I. Davis. Born in Kansas, John Davis moved to Tazewell at age eight with his family. He had served in county and state government and was an assistant U.S. attorney general in the Taft administration. His nephew, W. I. Davis, had graduated from Lincoln Memorial University just two years earlier and vigorously defended his alma mater. "There never were two men who walked into this court house with more violent Bolshevik ideas than these two," he said of McCarroll and Fields. "They care no more for this court than Russians do for the Savior." By the end of the hearing, however, nothing was resolved. Both sides had used the occasion as a grandstand to publicize their views, but the university hesitated to press the issue further for the time-being.[44]

H. Robinson Shipherd

Perhaps one reason the university hesitated was because a new president arrived on the day of the hearing. Raised on Long Island, Henry Robinson Shipherd had written a Harvard dissertation on the texts of Shakespeare's *Richard III* and *King Lear,* following that with books and pamphlets on *Play-Publishing in Elizabethan Times,* and *The Fine Art of Writing, for Those Who Teach It.* Shipherd had taught at Boston University and the University of Cincinnati after serving as educational director of the Eightieth Division in World War I. He had nearly been hired as Lincoln Memorial University president to succeed Matthews in 1927, but a misunderstanding regarding salary caused that deal to fall through.[45]

H. Robinson Shipherd, university president, April 1930 to May 1931. UA-LMU.

News of the strike brought Shipherd forward once again. He called Hill to express interest in running the institution, and a quick round of interviews led to his appointment. Shipherd traveled to Cumberland Gap, and Morison introduced him to the faculty on the night of April 19. The new president told everyone, "I am not afraid of the situation at Lincoln Memorial University. I expect to try to pick up the threads. I believe in justice to all." Yet he also told them that any "conspiracy on the part of teachers with students to rebel is traitorous." Shipherd gave a formal address to the campus community on April 20. After a benediction, organ playing, and singing, he pledged himself to "make Lincoln Memorial University not a curse, but a blessing."[46]

Clay McCarroll was ready to cave in. He secretly met with the new president on the night of April 19 and told him, in Shipherd's words, that the strikers "had been fools, and had made a great mistake." Shipherd felt sorry for them and blamed a handful of disgruntled faculty members for egging them on. McCarroll called off the strike on April 20, but the president allowed him to address the students while they ate dinner. The senior class leader put on a brave front, announcing that the strikers had won and should now go back to their studies. Hill considered this "a foolish gesture" on Shipherd's part, but it allowed McCarroll to bow out with some degree of grace.[47]

It did not take long for the students and faculty to lose faith in Shipherd, for he refused "to allow Lincoln Memorial University to be Leninized." Shipherd also told the newspapers that expelled students could be reinstated "if they show a convincing penitence and change of heart." He sought to use the public press to his advantage, stating that the University of Tennessee had offered to provide instructors to replace departing faculty members free of charge for the rest of the current term. Shipherd inflamed opinion by publicly insulting students he identified as troublemakers.[48]

The new president also dismissed more faculty members. When Daniel F. Higgins, who had arrived at Lincoln Memorial University in the fall of 1929 to teach geology and biology, became seriously ill part way through the academic year, his wife Ethel took over his classes. Ethel also taught a German class that deJonge refused to handle. Daniel was hospitalized in Knoxville and passed away on March 21, 1930. After burying him in Illinois, and with two daughters to take care of, Ethel threw herself into teaching her husband's classes. She was promised a full-time appointment the following academic year, but Shipherd abruptly refused to give her the job. Ethel blamed Dean Miley, who had been jealous of Daniel's popularity with the science students. He apparently told Shipherd that Ethel had urged on the strikers. While Ethel had sympathized with the students' demands, at the time she was "too sad and worried to take an active part in the strike."[49]

Shipherd's dismissal of Higgins was tied to the firing of Miss Davis, director of the Nancy Hanks Department. She supported the committee of nine faculty members and shared Higgins's apartment after Daniel passed away, which further tainted the reputation of both ladies. Hill approved of Davis's dismissal even though her father was a close family friend. "I do not sacrifice the effiency [*sic*] of any department in the University to gratify even a member of my own family," he wrote to Shipherd.[50]

Frank Grannis also became the victim of Shipherd's axe. He received a letter of dismissal while on leave of absence to complete his doctoral degree at Yale University. Shipherd told him that Morison had dismissed Iris, and he assumed there would be no reason for Frank to return. Both Frank and Iris had campus reputations for flirting, and Shipherd referred to "moral reasons" in explaining to the Southern Association why he released Frank.[51]

Morison's use of the law had turned the tide in the struggle for control at Lincoln Memorial University. As Iris Grannis put it, he was "fighting the situation with the weapons he knows best—the law and courts." Shipherd followed through with efforts to impose order on the administration's terms. More students voluntarily went home, but estimates of how many departed ranged from Shipherd's 66 to McCarroll's 250. More faculty members resigned as well, until nearly one-third of them were counted among those who were dismissed or had voluntarily resigned. With the exception of these significant losses, conditions were nearly back to normal on campus by April 21.[52]

Also on that day, a grand jury in Tazewell prepared to take up the case against McCarroll and Fields but dropped charges when no prosecution witnesses appeared to testify. Ketron and W. I. Davis told John P. Davis that the university had no intention of pursuing further legal action now that the strike was ending. A year and a half later, the Claiborne County Court House burned to the ground, destroying the court records associated with the case. The county had refused to renovate the building, which had been constructed in 1867 to replace the original structure burned during the Civil War, even though it was widely considered to be a firetrap. Three days after the university dropped its charges against McCarroll and Fields, local authorities dropped their investigation of the dynamite incident in Duke Hall after having found no evidence to identify the culprits. The second strike had lasted twelve days, from April 9 to 20, exactly the duration of Morison's acting presidency.[53]

The directors were greatly relieved when the crisis came to an end. Hill claimed he received "a steady batch of congratulatory letters from men in high places, all of whom are with us in our stand for the right." He urged Shipherd to be lenient with the students but suggested they publicly recant their actions before the campus community at chapel services and give full information about the complicity of faculty members who were "guilty of fomenting all the trouble."[54]

Hill also tried to repair the university's reputation. He sent reprints of the *Washington Post* editorial to friends of the institution and proclaimed to Louis A. Warren of the Lincoln National Life Insurance Company in Fort Wayne, Indiana, that the "late unpleasantness" was over: "A Young Professor down there began unloading intellectual commodities incongruous with the trade mark of Lincoln. I have always insisted that obnoxious seed would not be permitted to take root on our Campus." The professor, Elliott Van Nostrand Diller, "was engaged in a sort of Socialistic shadow dance in his Class Room, while on the Campus he was quietly diffusing a radical spirit." When the students rose to protest his firing, the administration put down the rebellion. "Order prevails upon our Campus," Hill told Seiberling, "and Lincoln Memorial continues its educational program along distinctly American lines, free from revolutionary influences within, and the machinations of red flag sympathizers without."[55]

The university lost many good professors because of the oppressive atmosphere that Hill had helped create. Lucia Danforth was a popular and dedicated teacher of foreign languages who deeply loved the university and the Appalachian area. Born in 1865, she had earned her bachelor's and master's degrees at Carleton College and her Ph.D. from Illinois Wesleyan. Danforth taught at Carleton before moving to Lincoln Memorial University in 1917. She built a log house in Cumberland Gap and maintained high academic standards. When Hill decided that it would help his fund-raising efforts to change the name of Harrogate to Lincoln, he relied on former postmaster James H. Rector to convince the U.S. Postal Service in Washington to do so without consulting the residents of the village in February 1930. Many people, including Morison, raised such a strong protest that the Postal Service changed the name back to Harrogate. Hill wanted to fire Danforth for adding her name to the protest, but deJonge interceded and Hill allowed her to stay as long as she behaved herself in the future.[56]

Danforth felt humiliated by these conditions. She also was appalled by Roop's conduct and upset by the many misstatements and lies she detected in Shipherd's public announcements. Ironically, Roop had written an article for the January 1931 issue of *Education* in which he argued that teaching Christian faith was the most important goal of an educator. "The last five years have been horrible beyond description when touched by Hill, Roop and Shipherd," Danforth complained. "I stayed as long as I thought any honest teacher could for I love the place beyond words to express, but you can not trust one word—oath or not—of John Wesley Hill." She thought Roop was "the least dangerous of the three for his lies are so apparent."[57]

American Association of University Professors

The American Association of University Professors became a beacon of hope for disgruntled faculty members as they sought ways to find help outside the university. Four concerned faculty members, none of whom were directly targeted by the administration, telephoned the association's treasurer and executive secretary, Joseph Mayer, a professor at Tufts University, to introduce him to the problem on April 13, then followed up with a letter later that day. The AAUP's response was to publicize the crisis in their *Bulletin* to warn their members about considering employment at Cumberland Gap. When Miller also contacted the organization, General Secretary H. W. Tyler cautioned him that he could not offer a quick fix to complicated problems. Typically, the AAUP helped prevent a recurrence of injustice rather than correct an ongoing problem. Mayer contacted W. D. Hooper of the Southern Association, who frankly told him that "the people in charge" at LMU "haven't the remotest idea of what a college is, or of the treatment which should be accorded members of the faculty."[58]

Miller and Diller met key players of the association in Washington on April 26. Miller impressed everyone with his sincerity, and the organization telegraphed Shipherd that it intended to mount a formal investigation. The president requested a conference of his own; he and Hill met five members of the association in Washington on April 30. Board member Wade H. Cooper hosted the luncheon meeting at the Willard Hotel. It "was certainly a most unusual" event, for association personnel had never before consulted the administration at an early stage of its investigation. They were aware of the *Washington Post* editorial and questioned Hill and Shipherd, who had to admit that there was no real evidence of Bolshevism on campus. While the two wanted "to be let alone," they agreed to publicly invite the investigation as a show of good faith.[59]

The association officials came away from the meeting on April 30 with a negative opinion of Hill, believing him "as crooked as they can be made," a "wily old bird" who was "clever enough to cover up any tracks." The officials gathered opinions from newspaper reporters and the staff at the Carnegie Foundation for the Advancement of Teaching that confirmed their opinion of Hill. "Something is very rotten at Lincoln Memorial University," they concluded. S. A. Mitchell of the McCormick Observatory at the University of Virginia, chairman of Committee A on Academic Freedom and Tenure, also dug up information about Roop. During the former president's time as an educator in Virginia, apparently, twenty thousand dollars in his charge "was never accounted for."[60]

Mitchell selected a three-man special committee to visit Lincoln Memorial University and file a report. James Samuel Guy, a long-serving chemistry professor at Emory University, Albert George Adam Balz, a Cartesian philosopher at the University of Virginia, and S. Gale Lowrie, a political scientist at the University of Cincinnati, served on the committee. Hill suspected the committee members had "something up their sleeves" as he prepared for the visit. Joseph Mayer tried to invite Roop to meet with the committee at Cumberland Gap, but the former president begged off because his father had passed away a few days before the scheduled visit. Roop had every incentive to avoid the meeting at any rate. While conferring with Hill on May 6, he tried to shift blame for the strike to the controversy over the firing of Dean Lewis three years earlier. Meanwhile, Mayer charged Guy, Balz, and Lowrie to investigate "the situation in a broad way."[61]

The visit on May 17 was unpleasant for everyone involved. Shipherd, in particular, was offended. He thought the committee took on the role of "an inquisitorial prosecution and conviction" rather than trying to conduct a fact-finding mission. The committee members allotted only two hours for hearing witnesses. They called only Morison and Hill but refused to hear sociologist Clifford Thompson, who was a supporter of the administration. Committee members interrupted the testimony with accusatory comments and expressed sympathy with the strikers. Guy told university officials that the report would be unfavorable and asked if Danforth could be reinstated. When Morison displayed the burnt stick of dynamic found in Duke Hall, the committee members suggested it could have been planted by loyal students or professors to discredit the strikers. Balz reported that he tried hard to pin Hill down on some key issues, but the chancellor "jumped from one position to the other until he had a heart attack and the committee went on to other matters." Hill felt he had been "subjected to a sort of third degree process," but Balz concluded he was "slippery as an eel" and "utterly unfit to occupy a position of authority in an educational institution." Even as they lunched in the president's house, the committee members were formulating a conclusion that not only Hill but also Shipherd was a major stumbling block to improvement of conditions at Lincoln Memorial University.[62]

The special committee convinced the association that Hill and Shipherd had to leave. After receiving a preliminary report, Mitchell was appalled at "all of the rascality that has gone on there in the name of education and alas! In the name of religion." Harry Bullock quietly wrote to Balz to express his opinion that

Hill should be separated from the university, but he was unwilling to confront the powerful chancellor. For his part, Hill swore "to stand by until the storm is spent."[63]

Soon after the committee visit, Lincoln Memorial University prepared for its next commencement. Board member Wade H. Ellis donated three hundred dollars for the purchase of a new flag pole to symbolize the university's commitment to American ideals. Although Hill's wife suffered, her "nerves are shot through as a result of the trouble through which we have passed," she planned to accompany her husband to Cumberland Gap. The new flag pole was dedicated on Sunday afternoon, June 1. Two days later, forty-one students graduated, but the line included none of the seniors who had been expelled by Morison.[64]

Conclusion

The student strike of 1930 represented, among other things, a clash of cultures. A handful of worldly professors had invaded the insular world of Appalachia to inspire some bright students. Much of this new awakening involved a desire to attend top-ranked schools outside the region and a reaction against the repressive mode of administration imposed on the university by Roop and Hill. Hill overstepped his constituted authority by interfering with educational policies and personnel on campus. As the AAUP realized, the chancellor did not have the training, the patience, or the good sense to create sound educational policies. He seemed myopically focused on shaping the campus environment in ways that would help him raise money.

While Hill received the lion's share of criticism, Roop deserved a great deal more blame than he received. Danforth called him "a constitutional, ingrained, inveterate liar," while Clifford Lyons remembered that "faculty meetings were devastating affairs because of his ruthless, tactless methods." The president started the trouble by lying about his degrees and then exacted a bit of vengeance by gracelessly firing four people. Afterward, he escaped from Cumberland Gap to avoid the fall out from his actions. Morison made the situation worse through his heavy-handed methods of imposing order, but he managed to break the strike. Shipherd followed through with Morison's work, even though his background was much closer to that of the fired professors than to Morison's or Hill's. More important, Shipherd wrecked any chance of gaining the good will of students and faculty through his alliance with the administration.[65]

The inflammatory charge of bolshevism stemmed from Hill's ultraconservative reaction to Diller's teaching. There is no evidence that Diller, or anyone else on campus, was a Communist, or pretended to teach communism, but the charge came to be a handy tool for the conservatives. They used it widely after the dynamite incident in Duke Hall, even though no hint has ever surfaced to explain who might have planted that explosive. For members of the AAUP, the use of such inflamed rhetoric in relation to the strike garnered nothing but contempt.

The trouble was a college-level affair; the Lincoln Memorial Academy and the Ellen Myers School had no part in it. Moreover, it was purely an academic strike, with students boycotting classes rather than their jobs. While Miller and Diller tried to argue that they did not instigate the strike, both men spoke to nearly every meeting from the start. They probably did not encourage the students to take action, but they certainly provided inspiration and guidance. Miller and Diller were players in the strike, not bystanders.[66]

For the students, faculty, and staff who remained, the strike became a taboo subject. When subsequent graduating classes wrote their histories, they contained no mention of the tempestuous spring of 1930. The official historian of the university made one brief mention of the strike in his book. Jesse H. Moore remembered the trouble in his unpublished memoirs but denigrated the strike leaders as those "who knew more of the workings of labor unions than of colleges." He deplored the fact that the striking students "roamed over the neighborhood at will" instead of working in the classroom. A student, who had graduated four years before the trouble, branded the strikers as misguided and noted that many of them came back to receive their degrees "and have made good in their work." But Grace Moore, who was not related to teacher Jesse Moore, remembered the strike differently after looking through old clippings seventy years later, when she was ninety-one years old: "I recall the event as a *fun thing*—no classes to attend."[67]

Chapter 8
Crisis and Survival

This institution has only just got its neck out of a noose that came mighty close to complete strangulation. A little more, and there wouldn't have been anything left.
—H. Robinson Shipherd, July 23, 1930

The depression has reduced our resources to a hand to hand fight to provide food, fuel, books, work, scholarships and instructors.
—John Wesley Hill, February 12, 1933

In no place have I ever heard so much nasty gossip and scandle [*sic*]. The entire college campus seems to be alive with it.
—J. Samuel Guy, July 21, 1930

President H. Robinson Shipherd issued his annual report to the Board of Directors at its meeting on June 2, 1930, characterizing the strike as "a carefully organized conspiracy of teachers, who for reasons more or less selfish exploited the enthusiastic idealism which is conspicuous in this student body." The breaking of the strike purged the campus "organism of poisonous bacilli which had been too long accumulating," preserving "the fundamental principles of academic law and order." Clearly the victors in this struggle were going to write the history of the event. The president also reported that the university spent $415 in dealing with the strike. A total of 155 college students, about one-third the enrollment, withdrew because of the turmoil. As a result only half as many students graduated in 1931 as in 1930.[1]

The board voted to drop the Lincoln Memorial Academy and its support for the Ellen Myers School. Shipherd fully approved, noting that the county was capable of supporting public schools and that the continuance of both institutions had been a sore spot in efforts to achieve accreditation. Ironically, there is no indication in Ezra Gillis's reports that this was so. Berea College retained its academy, making it the largest component of the college well into the 1940s. The Southern Association had no difficulty with colleges that maintained primary or secondary schools, as long as adequate and separate facilities and teachers were used for each component. Lincoln Memorial University dropped its associated schools primarily to save money.[2]

One of Shipherd's first tasks was to find replacements for dismissed and resigned faculty members. Determined to secure the best teachers, he traveled that summer to Harvard and Columbia to interview junior faculty and recent graduates. For the time, John Wesley Hill supported this effort as part of the continuing move to gain accreditation. Shipherd found men and women "with the right biological background, the right training, the right experience, the right interest, and the right family." Eleven of the university's twenty-four faculty members were brand new in the fall of 1930. One-third of the faculty, old and new, held a Ph.D., nearly one-third held a master's degree, and almost all the rest held a bachelor's degree. One among the twenty-four had earned no more than an associate degree from a junior college.[3]

The university's finances became more troubled as the Great Depression deepened. The hiring of new faculty and the construction of additional faculty housing contributed to a large budget deficit. The withdrawal of one-third of the students also hurt the institution financially. Lincoln Memorial University suffered a loss of more than eighty-six thousand dollars in the academic year 1928–29, and of more than forty-nine thousand dollars during 1929–30. At Shipherd's insistence, C. P. Williams worked out a budget to enable the university to meet Southern Association standards, but Hill argued it could no longer afford to do so. There was no immediate prospect of association acknowledgment; "we are bleeding white without the slightest chance of realizing our ambition," he wrote. The board agreed that retrenchment was the only course of action. The executive committee, under Morison's guidance, took the lead in cutting teacher salaries by 25 percent as well as slashing administrative costs. Robert L. Kincaid, who joined the board at the June 1930 meeting as a reward for supporting the administration during the strike, played a large role in the retrenchment process. He admired Shipherd's academic goals but thought the new president had no idea of "the handicaps which face us financially." Shipherd quickly learned and pitched in to do what he could. After making cuts in all departments and administrative units, he announced to Hill that the budget had been reduced by about seventy thousand dollars.[4]

Initially, Shipherd and Hill had a cozy relationship. Hill addressed his letters to Shipherd "Dear nephew," while the president called Hill "Santa Claus." But Hill soon detected signs that Shipherd was not the right man to lead the uni-

John Wesley Hill at the White House, 1930, leading a delegation to present a set of Lincoln's works to President Herbert Hoover on July 30. *Left to right, front row:* Wade H. Ellis, John Wesley Hill (chancellor, 1916–36), Frank T. Hines, and Paris T. Houston (member of the graduating class of 1930 and staunch supporter of the administration); *second row:* Wade H. Cooper. UA-LMU.

versity. The president had a habit of writing candid letters to board members, spelling out the troubles he faced. Hill wanted to control information received by the board, while confiding only in Seiberling, and felt Shipherd's letters would "greatly retard my financial Program among a few particularly sensitive Members of the Board." Hill cautioned Shipherd that "it is better to keep ones dirty linen in the back yard, than to display it conspicuously" and pointed out that "begging is a poor business just now." He concluded that he had a president with "no idea of finance" and it seemed difficult to even "knock an idea into Shipherd's head." The president more fully understood the situation when Williams told him in August 1930 that the university's bank account contained only fifty-eight dollars.[5]

American Association of University Professors

The administration still had to deal with the American Association of University Professors, for that organization delayed issuing the report of its special committee for months in order to pressure the university into improving conditions to avoid negative publicity. Hill considered association officials to be little more than an "aggregation of pin heads," yet he tried to work with these "academic asses" to convince them not to publish the report or to tone down its content. "I have worked too hard & my love is too great for L.M.U. to stand by & see it hurt," he wrote. "I am nothing; The cause is *everything*."[6]

Association officials believed they could best serve Lincoln Memorial University by convincing its board to fire both Hill and Shipherd. Wade Cooper persuaded them to limit their objective to simply clipping Hill's wings a bit, for he was too valuable an asset as a fund-raiser to be divorced entirely from the university. Shipherd, on the other hand, had no strong supporter and was vulnerable.[7]

The association planned a meeting with selected board members, excluding Hill and Shipherd, to enlighten them on conditions at the university and urge them to work on improvements. As H. W. Tyler put it, such a course would have "a certain incidental advantage to the good name of Abraham Lincoln." Seiberling, Ellis, Cooper, Hines, and Bennett met with association officers at the Willard Hotel in Washington, on the hot day of July 31, 1930. They talked for three hours, broke for lunch, and resumed discussions until six o'clock. Mitchell read the report of the special committee which had visited Lincoln Memorial University on May 17, revealing many details about campus operations that were unknown to the board. The officials then recommended reinstating dismissed students, giving dismissed faculty members a fair hearing, eliminating the yellow-dog clause from faculty contracts, releasing Shipherd, and restricting Hill to fund raising.[8]

The board members agreed to implement all recommendations except the firing of Shipherd, which did not seem necessary at the time. But they agreed to reconsider this point after the association offered to compile a list of reasons for firing the president. Mitchell thought the meeting was "the finest piece of constructive work" undertaken by the AAUP, and Hill and Shipherd were relieved that the association agreed to hold its report for a while to allow the board time to move forward on reforms.[9]

When Hill realized that J. Samuel Guy was determined to unseat Shipherd, he quietly worked with the chemist to pile up evidence against his president. Guy's reasons for targeting Shipherd related to the arbitrary manner in which he exercised the powers of the presidency and his "unfounded charges of Communism, Leninism." He had already received letters from individuals at the University of Tennessee disproving that any offer to provide teachers free of charge had ever been made to Lincoln Memorial University. Shipherd had misinterpreted a rumor to that effect, making it public without verifying the truth.[10]

Hill began to call Shipherd the "crazy man at Lincoln Memorial" because he continued writing directly to board members asking for money. Shipherd also continued to plan massive expansion of the educational program at Harrogate with little regard to finances, "counting money by the square-mile & spending it like a drunken sailor," as Hill put it. The Harvard man seemed to be "a hopeless *egomaniac*," a "sort of irresponsible jackass, reduced to the caliber of a Billy goat." Hill compiled his own list of reasons to fire Shipherd, which included using curse words while speaking to the Rotary and Kiwanis clubs in Middlesboro, failing to produce a proper college catalog, lowering dorm and cottage rents on campus, using his own composition book as a textbook without going through the proper selection process, and publicly taking credit for accomplishments achieved by others on campus. With Guy's help, Hill also found out that Shipherd possibly had an affair with a female student who worked for him while he was a professor at Boston University. By October 1930, Hill was so desperate to fire Shipherd that he threatened to resign as chancellor if it was not done. Seiberling agreed, but he counseled that a better course of action would be to simply not renew the president's one-year contract.[11]

The Southern Association

Unaware of these machinations, Shipherd made strenuous efforts to pull the university into the Southern Association at any cost. W. D. Hooper frankly told him that, in the wake of the student strike, it would be impossible to consider accreditation. For their part, Hill and Seiberling were now disillusioned about association membership and lukewarm about any efforts to achieve it.[12]

In October 1930, the board informed Shipherd that his contract would not be renewed when it expired in May 1931. Nevertheless, he tried to find out why Lincoln Memorial University had failed to gain accreditation. He consulted local supporters of the school and attended an association meeting in Atlanta. Hooper assured him that his greatest concern was instability in the administration, the constant turnover of presidents and deans. Shipherd returned to Harrogate and wrote Seiberling that the association wanted to see "that arbitrary, non-resident control of educational affairs" had ceased. "Lincoln Memorial University has a black eye, which must have raw meat applied to it until it recovers its normal condition." This was a direct threat to Hill's role in university affairs, and when Seiberling shared the letter with other board members, nearly everyone was shocked. Even sympathizers such as Wade Cooper regretted Shipherd's bluntness and use of inflammatory language, convinced that both would make it impossible for Hill to garner funds for the school. Hill saw Shipherd's attendance at the Atlanta meeting as a desperate attempt to save his job, but in the eyes of board members, the president's usefulness to Lincoln Memorial University had ended after only six months. Meanwhile, the financial condition continued to worsen. By early 1931, the Executive Committee recommended the release of some teachers to save money.[13]

The AAUP Report

Shipherd's dismissal was an encouraging sign that the board took the AAUP recommendations seriously, but association officials also wanted to publish their report as an act of justice for the students and dismissed faculty members. The question then became how long, detailed, and negative it should be. Guy was primarily responsible for writing the initial draft, and he blasted the university administration; in fact, John M. Maguire thought the draft came "near enough to defamatory for the opinion of a tort lawyer to have value." Mitchell and Balz toned it down and redirected much of the emphasis until it was ready to be circulated among the members of Committee A, which dealt with issues of tenure, in mid-December 1930.[14]

During the review process, McGuire thoroughly revised the draft and Mitchell agreed that a much shorter, less pungent version of the report should be published. Mitchell was ambivalent about McGuire's product, while the members of the special committee were thoroughly displeased with it. Yet association officials decided to publish it anyway, given that so much time had passed since the investigation and no one seemed able to agree on what the report should look like.[15]

Hill and Shipherd tried, with scant success, to soften the report. Hill sought to defend himself against charges of arbitrary meddling with university affairs, but association officials refused to publish the evidence he submitted. They agreed, however, to show him the page proofs of the report before it went to press. Shipherd submitted a five-page defense of himself, insisting vainly that it also be published.[16]

When the report appeared in the May 1931 issue of the *Bulletin,* it was only four pages long and contained a summary of the special committee's findings. It identified the basic problem as "autocratic power directed by unsound educational conceptions." Hill was identified as the chief problem, with Shipherd coming in for nearly as much blame. The report included information about the form of faculty contract Lincoln Memorial University employed. It also explained how the association had met board members to spur reforms on campus. Although less than Guy and others had wanted, and much more than Hill and Shipherd had wanted, the report struck the right balance for most people who read it. Hooper thought it was very effective and hoped substantial changes at Lincoln Memorial University would result. The student strike had occurred when the number of incidents investigated by Committee A increased by 50 percent in one year because of Depression-related problems in the United States. The association had never actively negotiated with a university administration to effect change in policies, although its officers fully recognized that only time could tell if this experiment would have lasting effect at Harrogate.[17]

Dismissed Faculty

The dismissed faculty members relied on the American Association of University Professors to gain a measure of justice with Lincoln Memorial University. Joseph Mayer wrote a "clearance statement" for Merlin G. Miller to use, testifying to the organization's opinion that he had conducted himself in a professional manner during the strike. Miller tried to work through Wade Cooper to obtain a hearing for the dismissed teachers, threatening legal action as a result of the "utterly un-American and dishonest situation" at the university. He hoped that the board would clean house by dismissing Hill.[18]

Mayer offered to serve as an ombudsman for the dismissed professors, and Cooper recommended that the board grant them a hearing. Miller filed a list of grievances, including his financial losses. He had filed a legal suit against the university, now stalled, and he wanted compensation for loss of salary and for selling his possessions at less than their value while moving away from Harrogate. He already had a new appointment at Emporia State University in Kansas, but his losses amounted to $2,708. Miller's children were "emotionally hurt" by living "through a reign of terror" that probably "damaged their character," he noted, and he asked that the board apologize for his dismissal. Elliott Van Nostrand Diller estimated his losses at $3,281 but was willing to accept only part of that amount.[19]

The board had no intention of granting a hearing to the professors. Seiberling considered Miller to be "a wild-eyed, half-crazy individual" who sought to destroy the university by ruining Hill. Most board members deferred to his judgment. By November 1930 the dismissed professors decided to hire a lawyer. Charles V. Imlay met with officials of the AAUP to gather all the information he could, and finally he was able to meet representatives of Lincoln Memorial University on April 27, 1931. The university insisted that all the professors act as a unit in presenting their demands. To Miller, it looked as if the board had no intention of treating them fairly. Diller, who had left campus "practically at the point of a gun," also decided to give up all efforts to seek redress. "I hoped the Institution would make a final effort to follow the ethical vision of the Emancipator and really become 'a living memorial sustained by a grateful people,'" he wrote. In the end, none of the dismissed professors received compensation or an apology from the school.[20]

Poststrike Stories

The people involved in the student strike of 1930 put their lives back together with varied degrees of success. Hervin U. Roop never again held a job in academia. "I am daily in receipt of threats & appeals from poor Roop," Hill informed C. P. Williams. The former president wanted his salary payments. but the university could not afford to pay him. Roop was pastor of the United Methodist Church in Christ at West Willow, Pennsylvania, from 1931 to 1937, and he later wrote a book on courtship and marriage that took a decidedly old-fashioned, Christian view of both subjects. Roop died in September 1955 at Annville, Pennsylvania.[21]

Judge Morison continued to live and work in Claiborne County until his friend, Cordell Hull, arranged for a federal judgeship in Fairbanks, Alaska, where the stern administrator served from 1934 to 1944. He returned to Tennessee and passed away in September 1952 at age eighty-seven.[22]

Little is known of the 155 students who voluntarily left Lincoln Memorial University as a result of the strike. Presumably, most of them transferred to other institutions. Paul Graham, for example, entered Emory and Henry College in Virginia in June 1930, only two months after the strike, and graduated in 1933 to become a public school teacher. But we can assume a certain percentage of the students who fled the campus to escape the turmoil of April 1930 never continued their college studies.[23]

Among the dismissed students, few were anxious to be reinstated. Most of them, however, wanted their credits transferred to other institutions. Ernest W. Fields completely turned around and strove to rehabilitate himself. He met privately with Hill and "confessed his transgressions," in Hill's words. The chancellor demanded that Fields divulge all he knew of the strike, and the student wrote a letter blaming Miller and Diller for starting it. "I see now where I made a mistake and was too hasty," Fields told a newspaper reporter. "The strike did no good and we should have used other means to express our disapproval." Elmer Heaberlin had a different view: "As far as being reinstated, I don't desire it. I fought for what I thought was right, honorable, and just." While the university reinstated dismissed students only if they demonstrated their renewed loyalty to the school, it was willing to transfer credits for anyone who did not owe money to the university. In the end, only 16 percent of the dismissed students eventually received a degree from Lincoln Memorial University.[24]

Soon after the strike, Clay McCarroll asked Seiberling for a job, but the industrialist did not trust him. McCarroll instead transferred to the University of Virginia and finished his undergraduate degree in June 1931. He went to Columbia University in the fall of that year and attended Teachers College for one year, studying to become a science teacher. He did not continue in his studies, however, and eventually moved to Birmingham, Alabama, where he founded and owned Buffalo Electric Company, an electrical supply store. He passed away in January 1974.[25]

Ernest W. Fields was reinstated and finished his degree at Lincoln Memorial University, then went to law school and worked for board member Ferdinand LaFrentz's organization, the United States Surety Company. He held no grudges against the university, writing to lawyer Ketron in 1957 upon the elderly man's retirement that he recalled the day when Ketron argued against him in the Claiborne County Court House and suggested that the university's charges should be pressed. "Incidentally, you were quite right," he assured Ketron. Board member William E. Schenck became Fields's boss, friend, and mentor at the United States Surety Company, where the young man worked for many decades. Fields was killed in an automobile accident while on his way to a university board meeting in 1999.[26]

Most of the professors who had been driven away landed safely on their feet. Lucia Danforth went to Iowa Wesleyan College and T. Edward Terrill to Bethany

College in West Virginia, while Elizabeth Harris received a teaching fellowship at Vanderbilt and Maude Smith began teaching in the public school at Athens, Tennessee. Danforth continued to worry about her "darling cabin" at Cumberland Gap and wished it were nearer Mount Pleasant, Iowa. Merlin G. Miller taught at Emporia State University but then became a full-time staff member for the consumer cooperative movement. He published an academic paper titled "Democratic Theory of Cooperation" in 1937 and worked to promote cooperative wholesale grocery stores. He passed away in Hays, Kansas, in 1976. Elliott Van Nostrand Diller finished his doctoral degree at Harvard University in 1934 but seems to have had no job when he was admitted to the American Philosophical Association later that year. Alfred R. W. deJonge worked for the *Detroit Tribune* for many years and passed away in Troy, Michigan, in 1974.[27]

Exit H. Robinson Shipherd

H. Robinson Shipherd left Lincoln Memorial University in the spring of 1931 after he had become bitter about his situation. When he told Morison that Lincoln Memorial University could never progress until Hill was dismissed, the judge replied that "he would see the institution become the home of bats and owls" before he would support such a move. Shipherd had good ideas about how to improve academic standards and boost the university's attempt to gain accreditation, and those ideas were shared by a handful of board members. But other board members, including Kincaid, Morison, and Hill, preferred higher teaching loads, lower salaries, and faculty who taught in multiple disciplines, even though those conditions militated against accreditation. Most board members were "interested primarily not in academic standards at all, but in saving money," Shipherd concluded. When the general manager of the *Knoxville Journal* inquired if an honorary degree could be awarded to a mutual acquaintance, Shipherd deferred the decision "to the gentleman who has for some years controlled the University and will continue so to do presumably until his final disposal."[28]

Initial efforts to replace Shipherd, surprisingly enough, centered on the American Association of University Professors. Seiberling and Hill took a liking to Joseph Mayer and nearly appointed him president. For unexplained reasons, the appointment was never made, and Lincoln Memorial University endured another year without a president. The rest of Shipherd's life and career lie in obscurity, except that he published a sermon, *Christianity at Stake,* which was delivered in North Amherst, Massachusetts, in April 1948. In it Shipherd argued that democracy and Christianity were "inseparably bound up together" and "Sovietism" was invariably hostile to them.[29]

Area Labor Strife

The student strike of April 1930 predated a labor strike in area coal mines by almost two years. Outside agencies such as the British-owned American Association still largely owned and operated local coal mines. While attempts to organize unions among the coal miners had taken place at Jellico and other regional towns since 1929, labor was quiet at Middlesboro, where coal operators had gained much influence in local government. Across southern Appalachia, from two-thirds to four-fifths of all coal miners lived in company housing and used company script to buy food at company stores. The system of housing students, giving them jobs, and keeping their earnings to pay debts at Lincoln Memorial University was quite similar.[30]

The Depression created so much unemployment that even Middlesboro became a hotbed of union activity. When the United Mine Workers of America could no longer provide relief for out-of-work miners, they began to turn to more radical organizations such as the International Workers of the World, or the National Miners' Union, both of which had ties to the Communist Party. Miners went on strike in Bell County, Kentucky, beginning January 1, 1932, which resulted in arrests, house bombings, and physical violence. Outsiders who tried to distribute food and literature in the county were beaten and refused entry. The strike weakened and ended by late March 1932 after affecting Claiborne and Campbell Counties in Tennessee and Harlan County in Kentucky. Kincaid's *Middlesboro Daily News* was a staunch defender of the power elite, while the *Knoxville News-Sentinel* was much more neutral. Ironically, only a year after the failed strike, Roosevelt's New Deal came to the miners' rescue with the National Industrial Recovery Act of May 1933, which offered encouragement to union organization. Within a short time, nearly every miner in Bell County had signed up with the United Mine Workers of America.[31]

Although an academic strike rather than a labor clash, the trouble at Lincoln Memorial University in 1930 foreshadowed the labor battle of 1932. Repressive policies, played out against a background of worsening economic conditions, led to a clash of competing visions. In both cases, the strikes were broken by an entrenched power structure that sought to retain absolute control at all costs, using the local law and overheated rhetoric about bolshevism as tools. The threat of anarchy existed in the form of dynamite planted in Duke Hall, a minor foreshadowing of bombings and burnings in the larger, more bitter labor agitation to come.

FUND RAISING AND PUBLICITY

Members of the board tried to find a successor to Shipherd by seeking "a good scholar who is also a business executive." But it was difficult to secure someone with those divergent qualities, and the office remained vacant during the academic year 1931–32. Miley filled in, doing triple duty as president, dean of faculty, and head of the Department of Physical Sciences, though he received only the salary of the last-named position.[32]

The first major fund-raising event following the strike occurred at the Mayflower Hotel in Washington, D.C., on February 12, 1931. An array of speakers, from Kincaid to the vice-president of the United States, gave talks to the dinner guests with Seiberling serving as toastmaster. President Herbert Hoover, the president of Czechoslovakia, and the Chinese minister of foreign affairs sent messages of support. Hill took the occasion to announce the most ambitious fund-raising campaign in the university's history, with an endowment of ten million dollars as the goal. He indicated a need for several new buildings, including a "Lincoln Library and Museum." Plans also included expansion of the liberal arts program to boost chances of accreditation. The Hancher Organization in Chicago was enlisted to manage the effort to raise millions even as the Depression was worsening. In the end the university failed in all the goals set in this all-too-ambitious "Expansion Program."[33]

On October 11, 1931, the university also dedicated a new farm as part of its efforts to expand the agricultural studies program and provide more jobs for students. The acreage lay south of preexisting university land, in a plot bordered by Highways 25E and 63. The university had purchased it two years before and paid it off due to the generosity of Frederick Kingsbury Curtis and his sister, Elizabeth Curtis, who wished to honor their brother, Francis Randolph Curtis. Francis had moved to Cumberland Gap to become part of the Gap Associates with Alexander Arthur. The Francis Randolph Curtis Demonstration Farm was meant to showcase "scientific and practical theories in agriculture." In addition

Lincoln Memorial University

A Living Memorial Sustained by a Grateful People
at
Cumberland Gap, Tennessee

CHANCELLOR'S OFFICE
MUNSEY BUILDING, WASHINGTON, D. C.

DR. JOHN WESLEY HILL
Chancellor

H. ARTIS MILEY, Ph.D., M.A.
Dean
Cumberland Gap, Tennessee

F. W. LAFRENTZ
Vice-President
New York City, N. Y.

F. A. SEIBERLING
Chairman of the Board
Akron, Ohio

HON. WADE H. ELLIS
General Counsel
Washington, D. C.

C. P. WILLIAMS
Treasurer
Cumberland Gap, Tenn.

"General Howard, you can trust the people in this section. I come from them and I know them. If you come out of this horror alive, and I pray God that you may, I want you to do something for the education of these mountain people who have been shut out of the world for all these years."

(President Lincoln to General O. O. Howard in 1863, as he was starting on his Tennessee campaign.)

Lincoln Memorial University is unique in its field, and numbers among its students young men and women who are struggling with the true Lincoln spirit to qualify themselves for a larger life. Theirs is an ambition that ennobles mankind—the ambition to be useful. In common with all other Americans I rejoice that an opportunity is afforded them that was denied to the youth of Lincoln's time. The entire country will be the beneficiary of the work that is going forward in the depths of the Cumberland mountains.

—Herbert Hoover

"I have every hope that the Lincoln Memorial University will so strongly appeal to national sentiment for Lincoln and for the fine mountain people of the Southern Appalachian area that the Institution may be placed upon the firm and assured basis upon which such a work should rest."

—Calvin Coolidge

"I have for a long time been genuinely interested in the welfare of Lincoln Memorial University."

—Woodrow Wilson

"There is no part of the world where education can do so much as in the region for which Lincoln Memorial furnishes the opportunity for advanced education."

—William Howard Taft

"There could be no finer memorial to Lincoln than this University placed just where you have it."

—Theodore Roosevelt

February 29th, 1932.

Dear Bob:

I am making steady progress. However, it will probably require at least two weeks treatment before I shall be able to resume my duties.

I am very anxious to see you at the earliest moment. I am anticipating the automobile tour, meeting old friends, and enjoying a little recreation, to say nothing of the inspiration of your companionship. I wish you would let me hear from you at the earliest moment.

I have just escaped from my prison cell of affliction, which accounts for the fact that I may have appeared to have been neglectful of your attentions. I assure you, however, that my appreciation of you is at one hundred per cent, and that when we have the visit in contemplation, it will be of great inspiration to me.

I am anticipating meeting you and your friends, and participating in the Address of which I was deprived by my illness.

With all good wishes,

Faithfully yours,

John Wesley Hill

Mr. Bob Poucher,
Dundee, Michigan.

John Wesley Hill letter, 1932. UA-LMU.

to this major addition, Henry Ford sold 186 acres of land to the university for one dollar. This deal had been in the making since 1927 and was consummated in February 1933. Ford hoped the university would grow goldenrod to see if it could be used as a substitute for rubber, but nothing of the kind seems to have been done with the land in subsequent years.[34]

The *Knoxville Journal* participated in a major effort to repair the university's image by printing a series of articles on February 12, 1932. Written by a variety of supporters and faculty members, the pieces sought to reestablish the university's image as a bulwark of American ideals. Kincaid wrote that "Lincoln graduates are pioneers" who serve "as an impregnable defense against the insidious forces which are creeping into our modern civilization, and threatening to destroy it." Alma Inman Parker more specifically referred to the strike two years earlier by noting that the campus community had become more tightly knit because the rebellion had been suppressed. The head of agricultural studies stressed the nine-hundred-acre university farm, one hundred acres of which were under cultivation, the herd of fifty dairy cows, and the five hundred chickens whose eggs graced the breakfast tables of the dorms.[35]

Stewart W. McClelland

The effort to find a new president centered on Monroe, Michigan, where Arthur Tagge, a prospective member of the board, suggested his pastor as a candidate. This appealed to Hill, for he called Lincoln Memorial University "God's work among His own people," an institution "permeated with the spirit of Jesus and that ministered in memory of the great Lincoln." Tagge was impressed by his pastor's warm personality and love of working with young people.[36]

Stewart Winning McClelland was born at Austenburg, Ohio, on March 10, 1891. He graduated from Denison University, attended the University of Chicago and McCormick Theological Seminary, and earned his doctor of divinity degree from Alma College. McClelland served as chaplain on board two battleships during World War I and taught English in public schools in Michigan and Pennsylvania before pastoring the Presbyterian congregation at Monroe for ten years before he was called to Harrogate.[37]

McClelland impressed everyone when he arrived on campus in August 1932. "He had a warm and attractive personality and drew people to him," a colleague recalled. Students remembered his unaffected manner and efforts to find jobs for them. "Many of the students became bonded to him because he would listen

Stewart W. McClelland, university president 1932–47. UA-LMU.

to their many problems," wrote Estle Evans. McClelland's initial term seemed hopeful, with a larger-than-expected enrollment in the fall of 1932 and smooth meetings with the Executive Committee. He also publicized the university in a new venue, the pages of the *Exchangite,* a publication of the Exchange Club that had a circulation of fifty thousand.[38]

Financial problems dominated McClelland's first years as president. The Depression made life difficult, in some cases impossible, for most of the nation's colleges. They experienced an 8 percent drop in enrollment from 1932 to 1934, and thirty-one out of seventeen hundred colleges and universities closed. An additional twenty-two merged with other institutions from 1934 to 1936. Private colleges and junior colleges were hardest hit. Overall, the institutions of higher education garnered only 60 percent of their 1930 income by 1934.[39]

Lincoln Memorial University survived these difficult years by cutting salaries drastically. Hill's pay dropped from nine thousand to seventy-two hundred dollars in 1934. McClelland did not receive a salary at all during his first year as president, and then received only four thousand dollars the second year. The number of faculty members decreased from twenty-one to seventeen by 1934, and nearly everyone who remained suffered large salary cuts.[40]

McClelland tried to find out how the university could garner more donations. Robert M. Lester, an official of the Carnegie Corporation of New York, frankly told him that "presidents came and went without imparting any degree of stability to the institution" and identified Hill as the chief source of this problem. McClelland confided in Lester that he was "having a hard time with Dr. Hill." Meanwhile, the situation became bad enough for the university to discontinue publishing the *Mountain Herald* in 1933, and by May 1934 the Executive Committee had learned that unpaid salaries amounted to nearly nine thousand dollars, which included a portion of Hill's salary.[41]

Hill continued his visits to campus and loved to impress the students. Gilbert Lycan found that he "had the most compelling personality I have ever known. When he spoke, the world seemed to pause and listen." But Lycan, a history major, also thought Hill "a desperately dyed-in-the-wool Republican. I heard him pompously describe his own role in defeating William Jennings Bryan and electing McKinley in 1896." Hill also retold the story of how he convinced Benjamin Duke to finance the construction of Duke Hall. While returning to Washington from one of his campus visits in January 1932, Hill "suffered a nervous breakdown," in his own words. He recuperated after eight months "of hope, and prayer and medical help."[42]

Hill continued to use strident personal appeals to raise money for the university. "The depression has reduced our resources to a hand to hand fight to provide food, fuel, books, work, scholarships and instructors," he informed a prospective donor. The money would "keep our flag floating over a Campus where nothing but pure Americanism is taught and the name of God is honored and revered." Nevertheless, Hill raised $216,353 from September 1, 1929, to April 1, 1931, "exclusive of endowment," for operating expenses. His pushy style rubbed some donors the wrong way. Edith Scott Magna of Holyoke, Massachusetts, was offended that the chancellor not only sent her half a dozen letters but also chastised her for not responding. "You seem to lack that heartiness of co-operation in the face of the peril confronting the University," he wrote. Magna could not donate at that time, and when she was able to contribute, she preferred, due to Hill's tone, to give her money directly to McClelland.[43]

The university's financial difficulties caused a great deal of trouble between McClelland and his faculty. Miley helped chart a retrenchment program to reduce salary budgets more than half by replacing several highly paid teachers with poorly qualified instructors. C. P. Cambiaire, a popular French teacher who held advanced degrees from prestigious universities, was eased out as part of this retrenchment effort in the spring of 1933. When he complained to the American Association of University Professors, McClelland explained that nothing more than money was involved, pointing out that the university had an operating budget of $269,000 in 1930 and was scheduled to run on a budget of only $100,000 in 1933–34. Affected faculty blamed C. P. Williams as well as McClelland, complaining that the president entrusted cost-cutting decisions to the financial manager. In fact, Education Department professor W. S. Woodward claimed that Williams bullied faculty in order to trim every penny he could from their departmental budgets.[44]

Hill soon became dissatisfied with McClelland, in part because he protested the president's policy of "hiring" new faculty members without pay, offering them only room and board. The chancellor thought this created expectations of a salary in the future, which the university could not afford.[45]

The McClelland-Williams-Miley program of retrenchment saved Lincoln Memorial University at a time when many colleges of its size and type folded. The number and quality of faculty declined, but some students continued to feel that they received a good education. The university accepted no aid from the federal government, even though Washington nearly doubled its meager assistance to higher education during the Depression. Lincoln Memorial University declined to participate in a federally funded work-study program to create on-campus jobs for students. This program was designed to keep students out of the larger job market at a time when unemployment still hovered around 12 percent nationwide. About one out of eight college students participated in this federal program, which lasted from 1934 to 1944. It is also possible that, if Lincoln Memorial University had applied to participate in the program, it might have found itself among the 234 colleges that did not qualify, due to its own campus-operated jobs program. The university continued offering scholarships as well, including many for descendants of Union and Confederate veterans of the Civil War.[46]

Student Life

The student strike had failed to loosen the restrictive social policies for women who lived on campus. They were required to sign out and sign in whenever they left and returned to the university. Library visits had to end by 9:00 p.m., and daily chapel attendance was required. When going to their physical education classes in the gymnasium, the girls had to wear skirts over their work-out shorts while walking across campus.[47]

Most students appreciated the opportunity to work. Bertha Masingo Goad thought her fellow students learned a stronger sense of responsibility because they had to pay their own way through college. "There were times when we resented work," admitted Paul E. Whiteside, "but we kept at it." The basic hourly rate remained twenty cents throughout the mid-1930s, similar to the average pay for unskilled agricultural workers in the southern states. The university catalog listed a set of "Labor Requirements" for students, including the need to take good care of tools and report beforehand if unable to meet their work schedule. The Labor Committee handled all job assignments and took jobs away from students if their grades dropped or they used tobacco or liquor. At the end of each academic year, student workers received a labor certificate if their grades averaged C or better and they had fulfilled their work duties promptly, cheerfully, and with "good moral conduct."[48]

As always, student workers kept the institution running. Bertha Masingo Goad "peeled potatoes, broke string beans," and did other duties in the kitchen of her dorm. Estle Evans worked on the university farm. Gilbert Lycan milked cows, something he had done since age eight, and then helped to lay a clay sewage pipe line across campus to replace the older, wooden one, which had rotted. Labor boss H. K. Ryder gave out candy bars to the boys at midafternoon to boost their flagging energies. Once Ryder chided a worker for slacking off, and the student retorted, "Right now my stomach is as empty as that piece of pipe." Ryder could not do anything about the scanty fare, but a woman who lived in a house nearby heard the conversation and offered the boys sandwiches and lemonade. "We accepted her gifts with gladness," recalled Lycan, "but we all felt abashed by the incident."[49]

Lycan also helped shovel coal to keep the university's power plants operating, but the job he enjoyed the most was working at the university's small limestone quarry. The university exploited a seam of limestone, located in the middle of a cow pasture, to crush gravel and sell it for profit to Tennessee's state highway department. In the quarry, a "perpendicular wall of stone eight to ten feet high extending about fifty feet," the boys drilled a line of holes four feet from the edge, some holding rods while others swung hammers. Dynamite inserted into the holes blew the rock apart, to the delight of the students, who then swarmed over the rubble to break up the larger rocks by hand so the fragments could be put into a mechanical crusher. Lycan marveled at the sight of "multitudinous crustaceous creatures whose small bodies went to form the stone," revealed for the first time in millions of years. The process produced dust that local farmers hauled away and used as fertilizer on their fields.[50] The university also operated a gas station in Harrogate, where student labor accounted for the second biggest operating expense, next to the cost of the gasoline itself.[51]

McClelland, the Southern Association, and Conflict

McClelland pursued admission to the Southern Association with patient determination, convinced that it was the key to the university's long-range success. This was a goal shared by nearly everyone on campus, especially the students, because it had an impact on the value of their course work in the larger academic world. The association, however, had no intention of admitting the university as long as Hill played a role in its administration, but it was willing to place Lincoln Memorial University on a nonmember list. This required that inspectors visit the campus regularly, and it allowed McClelland to attend the annual conference in December.[52]

Meanwhile, the university was approved by the Tennessee Department of Education, which allowed education graduates to teach in state schools or in states that had a reciprocal agreement with Tennessee. But Lincoln Memorial University's credits were not widely recognized outside the state. Since its creation in 1895, the Southern Association had become the most prestigious accreditation agency in the South. Its standards, which included the requirement that professors have at least two years of graduate study in the disciplines they taught and which recommended acceptable salary levels and teaching loads, set the pace for modernizing schools in the southeastern United States. The association also frowned on the too-liberal granting of honorary degrees and paid attention to the tone of public relations efforts. Association officials continued to advise McClelland, who they thought was "doing excellent work," to defer applying for full membership by citing "frequent shifts in administration" as the reason. They wanted McClelland to become firmly established and hoped Hill's influence would weaken.[53]

McClelland's problems lay not only with Hill but also with a group of recalcitrant faculty members who were allied with the chancellor. The board also took sides in the developing clash between president and chancellor, with Ferdinand LaFrentz and Kincaid supporting McClelland. Kincaid played a key role in diminishing the influence of Hill and his associates in university matters. The long struggle came to a climax at the June 1935 board meeting, at which Kincaid gave a long, impassioned speech to his associates, pleading for them to give McClelland a chance to function as a true president. The trigger for this plea was a report filed by board member Milton W. Harrison that included letters from faculty members critical of McClelland's leadership. Harrison recommended that the president and C. P. Williams be dismissed. Kincaid argued that this was the culmination of three years of plotting by a group of professors, including Miley and religion professor William Barnett Guerrant, who had worked against the president's efforts. McClelland lived "in an atmosphere of suspicion, doubt, distrust, and open hostility" because of this and was "subject to the inquisition of a cross-examination on many and paltry matters" by board members who sided with Hill.[54]

Kincaid also became a target because of his growing and open support for McClelland. The newspaper editor alleged that every time Hill visited the campus, he held furtive meetings with Miley and Guerrant. "We ARE making progress," Kincaid told the board, "despite what may be said to the contrary. . . . The name of Lincoln Memorial University is beginning to mean something more than a mere apology." He blamed "unwarranted selfishness" and jealousy for the "embroiled condition of disloyalty," which was now the chief stumbling block to progress, and he supported a resolution to dismiss Miley and Guerrant.[55]

Kincaid's plea had its effect. While McClelland had strong support from the Executive Committee, he needed a majority of votes on the full board to secure his position, and he received it. This was the turning point in the fate of the university. Miley, seeing the new direction of affairs, requested a leave of absence on half pay for the next academic year. The Executive Committee quickly approved, and it voted to discontinue Guerrant's position "because of our limited financial resources." The resignations of two other disgruntled faculty members were accepted as well, and the full board sanctioned all actions. Miley did not return to the university at the end of his sabbatical.[56]

McClelland's triumph involved important issues concerning Lincoln Memorial University's future. Those board members allied with Hill tended to be against membership in the Southern Association, doubting it was essential to the school's welfare and fearing it would take some degree of control from the hands of board members. Some of them even worried that the university was becoming like all other modern schools, producing "'half-baked brain trusters' chasing every rainbow of unsound economies, taxation and government, potential recruits for Radicalism and Bolshevism."[57]

Hill understood that his influence at Lincoln Memorial University had been dealt a final blow. According to Jesse H. Moore, the chancellor never visited the campus again after June 1935. McClelland was able to announce the next year that the university had a balanced budget for the first time in a decade, painfully overcoming the huge debt built up by the expansion of the late 1920s and the terrible impact of the Depression. Hill offered his resignation as chancellor to take effect May 31, 1936, after twenty years of service. "My years of devotion to Lincoln Memorial have been fraught with great pleasure and inspiration," he wrote. "I shall always recall them as a part of the happiest period of my life." He graciously declined the offer of a pension and the title chancellor emeritus, modestly claiming that he did not accomplish enough for the university to deserve the money and stating that he planned to remain active in his retirement. The post of chancellor was discontinued, and fund-raising efforts entrusted in the hands of the president.[58]

With Hill gone, discontented people came out of hiding. Lucia Danforth left Iowa Wesleyan and returned to the school and the log cabin she loved in time to teach during the fall term of 1936. She passed away in June 1944. Ernest W. Fields and Clay McCarroll became active in alumni affairs by 1938. Both men signed a circular letter to the graduates of 1930, drumming up seventy-five hundred dollars to finance the conversion of a room in Avery Hall for use as a student center in 1950. "Many of us have not done too much for L.M.U. since our days at school," the two wrote. "We owe it much and this is our chance to really do something for it."[59]

John Wesley Hill and his wife embarked on a three-month cruise after his resignation, and then he settled in New York city to pursue literary projects. His impact on Lincoln Memorial University was enormous, although controversial. His son, John Warren Hill, asserted with much truthfulness that the chancellor "took over when the University was bankrupt and on the threshold of defeat" to put it "on the map, nationally." The Methodist minister raised some two million dollars during his twenty years as chancellor. H. Robinson Shipherd had confessed to feeling "a little chilly around the spine when I realize how much our mere existence seems to depend on him." Hill's motivation was genuine. When Seiberling admonished him not to get too involved in university affairs after the strike, Hill told him that Lincoln Memorial University had grown "so completely into my life, that there are times when I am unable to distinguish between myself and it. . . . I somehow feel now more as a father to a child."[60]

Hill remained active after leaving the post of chancellor, writing letters to Alf Landon, the Republican candidate for president, chiding him for public statements that seemed to indicate he looked favorably on "Socialistic devices" once espoused by Teddy Roosevelt. He was deeply interested in Methodist missionary work in the Far East and endorsed Joseph Mayer as a speaker to the Democratic National Committee. Hill passed away due to a cerebral hemorrhage on

October 12, 1936. His son believed Hill had "lived for the University and undoubtedly over-worked and died in its service." Paris T. Houston, the staunch loyalist of the class of 1930, crafted a career for himself in law and government service before funding, in 1986, the John Wesley Hill Chair of Religion and Philosophy to honor the former chancellor.[61]

Hill's departure from Lincoln Memorial University cleared the final hurdle for admission to the Southern Association. McClelland applied for full membership in the fall of 1935 but was put off another year, pending the results of a full investigation by the association. The president and the new dean, Boyd A. Wise, attended the Southern Association's annual conference at Richmond in early December 1936 and telegraphed the news as soon as the organization voted to admit Lincoln Memorial University. This telegram arrived during the morning chapel service on December 4 and was announced at the end of the ceremony. The "students rose to their feet, some even standing in their seats, to cheer," reported the university's newspaper, the *Blue and Gray*. "A rain of hats, books, and paper filled the air, and even some of the faculty members raised their voices in lusty yells." The newspaper reported that "LMU is now standardized." It was a pivotal moment in its evolution from a backwoods school to a true university recognized outside the immediate region. As McClelland later put it, "We got over the position of being something of a junior college."[62]

Chapter 9
A New Day for Lincoln Memorial

Mr. Ochs visited our institution once and was deeply impressed with what we are doing. He said something which I have quoted many times: "You are boring with a gimlet when you should be using an auger."
—Robert L. Kincaid, November 17, 1937

We are just an ordinary set of folks who are trying to do the best job we can with over four hundred kids. We make lots of mistakes, and the youngsters are much on their own to work out their own destinies.
—Robert L. Kincaid, January 21, 1939

I have been thinking a great deal about L.M.U. lately. Once you go there, there is something that gets under your skin and stays there.
—Ray O. Welborn, May 29, 1939

Robert L. Kincaid became executive vice-president of Lincoln Memorial University at commencement time in 1937. His duties included fund raising and "assisting in other ways in the institution's development." In effect Kincaid replaced Hill to allow McClelland to devote more time to matters other than soliciting donations. "I am an alumnus of the college," Kincaid wrote, "and a mountain product myself. The institution has meant everything to me."[1]

One of Kincaid's early initiatives was to mend fences among the university's donors, and he did so by extolling Hill's accomplishments. In a speech given at the university's fortieth anniversary celebration on February 12, 1937, Kincaid called Hill "an inspiring personality." He sent a copy of the speech to disaffected donors who had sided with Hill during the stormy days of 1935 and asserted that Lincoln Memorial University "represents an imperishable monument to his ability, zeal, and devotion." In later years, Kincaid readily admitted Hill's faults, but he refused to ignore the chancellor's accomplishments, especially in gaining "national publicity" for the school.[2]

"It seems to me that we are on the threshold of a new day for Lincoln Memorial," wrote Stewart McClelland to a potential donor as the fall term began in 1937. Indeed, the picture for all American universities had brightened by this time. Enrollments increased, donations and income rose, and most institutions of higher learning were on an even keel financially. By 1941, the university's endowment had soared to $832,000. McClelland charted a conservative course, mindful of the fact that the institution had previously "attempted too many things and did too few well," as Kincaid put it. "We are now trying to do a quality job on a restricted scale."[3]

McClelland enhanced what he later called the "Lincoln story" as an important element in the university's image. He greatly increased the number of Lincoln books, artifacts, and manuscript material in the university's possession. McClelland created a Department of Lincolniana in the fall of 1937 and the Lincoln Diploma of Honor to award scholars in the field. The *Mountain Herald* had ceased publication in 1933 due to financial difficulties. McClelland resurrected it in October 1937 and changed its name to the *Lincoln Herald* in February 1938. Rather than deal with past and current stories about the university, the *Herald* now was devoted to Lincoln studies. The History Department also began to offer an upper-level elective course on Lincoln.[4]

Lincoln Room of Duke Hall, repository of the university's collection of Lincoln artifacts and documents from the late 1920s to 1977. UA-LMU.

While Hill and benefactor Thomas R. Madigan had accumulated a small number of Lincoln artifacts by the 1920s, displaying them in a special room on the upper floor of Duke Hall, little was made of this nucleus until McClelland sponsored an effort to enlarge it. He hired R. Gerald McMurtry to teach history courses and serve as head of the Department of Lincolniana in 1938. It surely was, as Kincaid expressed it, the only Lincoln library "south of the Mason-Dixon Line." McClelland's efforts to secure financial support from the Carnegie Corporation of New York failed because of the collection's specialized nature, but the university managed to acquire an impressive number of personal belongings and other artifacts associated with the sixteenth president, as well as some personal accounts by Civil War soldiers, a large assortment of Civil War song sheets, and thousands of rare books dealing with Lincoln and the Civil War in general. It was an astonishing achievement for this regional, independent college to create one of the three or four best collections of Lincoln material in the world.[5]

McMurtry also taught the Lincoln course, which was spread across three quarters of the academic term. The first quarter was "largely biographical," while the second dealt with "Lincoln in government," and the third covered "the influence of Lincoln's works and policies." As McClelland and Kincaid told people, it was "the only course on Abraham Lincoln given anywhere in the world."[6]

The university drew the attention of Ann Rutledge, the great grand niece of her namesake, the first love of Lincoln's life. The original Rutledge had died of typhoid fever before Lincoln's relationship with her could blossom into marriage. McClelland met the new Ann Rutledge, a direct descendant of the original's brother, while visiting Chicago in the summer of 1937, and he persuaded her to enroll at Lincoln Memorial University that fall. The auburn-haired Rutledge had attended the dedication of New Salem State Park in Illinois and had performed in a Federal Theatre play called *The Lonely Man,* which dealt with a "Lincolnian theme," in Chicago.[7]

Along with the Lincoln image came commemoration and study of the Civil War in general. An Iowa attorney named A. J. Walsmith was impressed that a university named after the Great Emancipator was located in a former Confederate state. Walsmith told McClelland that his father had served in the Thirty-sixth Illinois and his mother had seen and heard the Lincoln-Douglas debate at Ottawa, Illinois. McClelland assured him that there were a number of "Lincoln fans" on campus, some of whom had "gone off the deep end" about the sixteenth president. In 1938, a raging debate developed among students at the university as to whether the North had been justified to use force to reunite the country. While there were enough Confederate sympathizers to give the debate a heated tone, the only thing all could agree on was that the discussion was carried on without bitterness. McClelland was also not unmindful that the campus was located only a couple of miles from Cumberland Gap, the scene of two significant military confrontations during the war. In late 1937, he contracted with two local men to search the campus for Civil War relics, agreeing to split any proceeds with them, but the pair found nothing.[8]

The Hoover Commencement

The university managed its biggest public relations coup in convincing former president Herbert Hoover to give the commencement address to the graduating class of 1939. Former Ohio governor Myers Y. Cooper, who served on the Board of Directors, picked up Hoover at Asheville, North Carolina, where the Republican was visiting a friend, and drove him to Harrogate in his chauffeured car. Kincaid rode along as the university's representative, sitting "cramped under Governor Cooper's right wing, in order not to crowd Mr. Hoover." While Cooper asked questions, Hoover did most of the talking during the long, hot drive. Kincaid mostly remained quiet and listened intently, awed by the opportunity to rub elbows with a former president.[9]

Another celebrity attended that commencement ceremony. Actor Raymond Massey's portrayal of Lincoln in Robert Sherwood's play, *Abe Lincoln in Illinois,* was currently creating a stir. Born in Toronto, Ontario, the son of the man who owned the Massey-Ferguson Tractor Company, the actor, six feet one inch tall, had served in the Canadian artillery during World War I and had entertained American troops in Siberia near the end of the war. Sherwood's play was the most popular of the Lincoln biographical treatments on stage during the 1930s; it took the sixteenth president from his youth in New Salem to his departure from Springfield in 1861. The play premiered at the National Theatre in Washington, D.C., on October 3, 1938, and Massey began his role in this vehicle at the Plymouth Theatre in New York more than a week later.[10]

Up to ten thousand people gathered on the quiet campus of Lincoln Memorial University to see a former president, and an actor who played a president, on Sunday, June 4, 1939. Hoover gave his commencement to an audience of twenty-five hundred visitors (and fifty-one graduates) in the auditorium of Duke Hall. His half-hour talk was laced with criticism of New Deal policies without mentioning any names of the people responsible for creating them. NBC radio

Lunch at the Hoover commencement, June 4, 1939. UA-LMU.

broadcast the speech live, and Paramount filmed it for a newsreel. Thousands of visitors also listened to the talk by way of a public address system outside the building.[11]

Massey almost did not make it. Early that morning he flew from New York to Knoxville, where police escorted his car from the airport through town at twenty miles per hour. As a result, he arrived after Hoover's speech but in time to eat lunch, interrupted by many requests for autographs. Then he met Hoover for a photo opportunity in the Lincoln Room of Duke Hall. Hoover received an honorary doctor of humanities degree, while Massey and Sherwood received the university's Lincoln Diploma of Honor. Massey stayed in a hotel that night and flew back to New York the next morning so as not to miss a performance of the play. Hoover attended a reception for two hundred guests at the home of history professor Jane Lotspeich in Knoxville, where the former president again trumpeted his views on current politics.[12]

The presence of Hoover and Massey created what Kincaid called "the greatest Commencement in the history of the school," which garnered "much favorable publicity." The national exposure was unprecedented in the history of Lincoln Memorial University.[13]

The Southern Premiere of *Abe Lincoln in Illinois*

In July 1939, word arrived that Massey was to replicate his stage role in a movie version of *Abe Lincoln in Illinois.* Produced by Max Gordon Plays and Pictures Corporation and distributed by RKO Radio Pictures, it was directed by John Cromwell. Sherwood wrote the screenplay and Ruth Gordon played Mary Todd Lincoln, while Gene Lockhart performed as Stephen A. Douglas. The movie was previewed in Washington, D.C., on January 22, 1940, and released nationally on February 12. Lincoln Memorial University arranged to host the premiere of the film in the South, but Massey could not attend the event because he had resumed his role in Sherwood's play after filming the movie. Mary Howard, who played Ann Rutledge, attended the on-campus premiere.[14]

Unfortunately, bitter weather descended over the area to interrupt the festivities. The temperature dropped below zero as twelve inches of snow blanketed the campus and surrounding countryside. While Howard, Harry Goetz (a producer of the movie), and Governor Prentice Cooper of Tennessee managed to make it, along with the presidents of several regional colleges, most of the invited guests cancelled at the last minute. Howard enjoyed playing in the snow with the residents of the Grace Nettleton Home, and Roosevelt and Hoover sent the university telegrams of congratulation. After a dinner at Norton Hall, the movie was shown on the night of January 27, 1940. Despite the snow, everything went off as well as possible, and Kincaid was pleased. "I think our party was a great success," he declared. He expected the publicity would help not only the university but also the producers of the film. *Abe Lincoln in Illinois* did not make as much money as expected, but it garnered much favorable criticism, and the university's image was enhanced by associating itself with the project.[15]

Earl Hobson Smith

Speech professor Earl Hobson Smith was inspired to write a play about Lincoln in the late 1930s, adding his contribution to the university's Lincoln image. Born in western Kentucky, he had earned a degree at Lincoln Memorial University in 1919 and came back as a professor in 1926, after graduate studies at Columbia

University. Smith proved to be an inspirational teacher. He wrote about thirty plays on a variety of themes, including Daniel Boone, George Washington, Davy Crockett, and several that were set in an Appalachian environment. Smith got the most mileage out of his *Stephen Foster: Or, Weep No More My Lady,* which ran for many years at Bardstown, Kentucky.[16]

President Lincoln: A Two Hour Play in Three Acts with Three Scenes Each, which was published by the university in January 1940, was Smith's first attempt to depict the life of Lincoln on stage. It started with the president elect's departure from Springfield, taking over where Sherwood's play ended, and brought Lincoln to Ford's Theater in 1865. The play is typical of Earl Hobson Smith's work—earnest, wordy, turgid, and playing very loose with the facts. It pales in comparison to Sherwood's play and fails in Smith's stated purpose to portray Lincoln with historical authenticity, verve, and understanding. A New York agent considerately rejected the play, even for amateur productions, by telling Smith that it was too novel for the "masses." Apparently the play was produced only

Backstage at a production of *Lincoln Takes a Wife,* Earl Hobson Smith's effort to memorialize Lincoln on the stage, sometime after the play was written in 1952. UA-LMU.

on the campus of Lincoln Memorial University. Undaunted, Smith went on to write several more Lincoln scripts, including *Abe Lincoln's Other [Beloved] Mary* (ca. 1942), *Lincoln Takes a Wife* (1952), *Abraham Lincoln Goes to Washington* (1966), and *Abraham Lincoln's Love Affairs* (1976), all of them of similar quality as the first.[17]

University officials continued to commemorate the founders as they enhanced the school's Lincoln imagery. Two paintings of Howard graced the campus in the late 1930s, one hung in the Lee Reading Room, opposite the Confederate general's portrait, and the other hung close to Lincoln's portrait in McClelland's office. Howard's saddle, saddlebags, two bridles, a pair of leather leggings, and his wooden stirrups and saddle pad were donated to Lincoln Memorial University by Bowdoin College at the request of Harry S. Howard, who continued to take an interest in the welfare of the Harrogate school. Frederick B. Avery passed away in 1942 at his retirement home in Florida. At eighty-eight, he was the last member of the group that had created the idea for Lincoln Memorial University on the porch of the Harrow School in 1896.[18]

Although it was foreign to his nature, Kincaid proved to be an effective fund-raiser. He banked a great deal on his humble background, as well as the fact that he had graduated from Lincoln Memorial University, to convince donors that the school was fulfilling its mission. An attempt to persuade the U.S. Post Office to issue a stamp commemorating the university in time for its fortieth anniversary in 1937 failed to bring results, and McClelland's effort to win financial support from the Carnegie Corporation of New York also failed. Publicity efforts continued to stress that the university was "trying to cast new Lincolns from the old mold." Even as late as 1941, an article in the *Washington Sunday Star* portrayed the school as the only opportunity for native mountaineers, who had been bypassed by progress, to gain a college education.[19]

Student Life

By the late 1930s, tuition, room, and board cost each student $315 per year, and up to 90 percent of them worked to pay at least a portion of that amount. On average, each student brought only about $100 in cash when they entered the university at the start of the academic year, and they had to work off the rest. As Kincaid put it, the students willingly accepted "sweat and toil before they get their college diplomas."[20]

Female students worked in the laundry, using large washing machines and ironing by hand. They cleaned rooms in the dormitories or worked in the kitchens or serving tables in the basement dining room at Norton Hall. Each table accommodated ten students who helped themselves from large bowls of food, which the waitresses continually refilled. Faculty diners sat at a separate table. Breakfast consisted of "biscuits, scrambled eggs, . . . cream gravy and . . . coffee." Bonnie Masingo Page, who attended Lincoln Memorial University from 1937 to 1940, had inherited some credit from her sister and had received a scholarship, yet she worked throughout her days at the school, receiving from fifteen to twenty cents per hour. In the end, Bonnie had to pay only fifty dollars in cash over the course of three years, and she even left some credit for her younger sister, who entered the university after she graduated. "Money was scarce during the depression," Bonnie recalled years later. "A few classes I managed without a textbook because I couldn't afford to buy it."[21]

Male students worked on the farm, hauling hay from the fields or bringing loads of coal from local suppliers to campus. They fired the furnaces in each

Lincoln Memorial University's farm. The Seiberling dairy barn is on the right, and the faculty housing building constructed in 1928 is in the middle distance. Cumberland Mountain is visible in the left far distance. UA-LMU.

building, starting at 4:00 a.m., and checking the fires every two or three hours, banking the coal at 10:30 for the night. They worked as janitors, fed livestock, and cultivated the large university garden. Vergil Saine endured a hazing when he arrived on campus in August 1938. Accused of ogling girls, he was tried by a kangaroo court that night and punished with a spanking. Saine took it in good spirit, which won many friends for him during his stay at the university. He was the sixth member of his family from Manchester, Tennessee, to attend Lincoln Memorial University.[22]

World War II

On October 16, 1940, faculty members formed a committee to oversee campus registration for the first peace time draft in American history. They registered sixty-nine students, seven faculty members, five staff members, and two salesmen who happened to be passing through town. This was the beginning of a major effort by the members of the university community to support the country's role in World War II. The attack on Pearl Harbor on December 7, 1941, led to an immediate decrease in enrollment as young men entered the service. By June 1942 there were only 257 students on campus, compared to 656 in 1939, and the number dipped even lower in 1943. The enrollment problem became so acute that Kincaid admitted, "We look with fear upon the future." The number of graduating seniors dropped from a historic high of 58 in 1940 to only 17 in 1944.[23]

Nevertheless, the university strongly supported the war effort. McClelland "shifted the activities of the college to a war basis," reported Kincaid in a magazine article. Classes were cancelled for a half day as students collected more than twenty tons of scrap iron, with McClelland contributing two empty German gas shells he had owned as souvenirs since World War I. As in the first war, the campus became a basic training ground for military service. The War Department and Navy Department established requirements for courses designed to provide some degree of military training for all male students, and the U.S. Army Air Corps operated a unit of the Civilian Pilot Training Corps. Kincaid was proud to assert that university students who entered the service would "be true 'Lincoln men' carrying on the tradition of their patron saint."[24]

Many university students served, received awards for bravery, and died in the war. Casimir P. Williams's son, Pat McCamey Williams, lost his life when his fighter plane developed engine trouble during a flight across occupied Europe and crash landed near the small village of Moorsele, Belgium, on May 31, 1943.

Williams survived the crash but perished in the fire that engulfed his plane. With German permission, the local community buried him. The university held a memorial service for Pat on March 5, 1944, decorating the corridor of Duke Hall with his medals and the paintings he had made depicting landscapes and board member Ferdinand LaFrentz. Afflicted with illness, C. P. Williams was barely able to deal with his loss, and he sometimes interacted with his colleagues in disturbing ways; they tried very hard to understand his temper in view of his difficulties. In an effort spearheaded by local historian Lothair Vanoverbeke, Moorsele commemorated Williams's sacrifice in 2002 by erecting a monument to the Cumberland Gap native at the site of his crash.[25]

John R. Bumgarner earned his medical degree from the Medical College of Virginia in 1939, after attending Lincoln Memorial University, and was drafted into the army a year before Pearl Harbor. Bumgarner served in the Philippines and became a prisoner of war when the Japanese captured the islands in April 1942. He survived three and a half years of illness, malnutrition, and sometimes brutal treatment at the hands of prison guards. Bumgarner suffered severely from tuberculosis for many years as a result of his imprisonment, but managed to craft a fulfilling career in medicine after the war. He wrote a frank, unassuming book about his captivity, *The Parade of the Dead,* which was published in 1995. It is one of the most moving memoirs to come out of World War II.[26]

The university's most famous veteran was Ross Samuel Carter, who grew up at Duffield, Virginia. He attended the university just before the war broke out, milking cows and living in the Seiberling dairy barn. Carter thoroughly enjoyed his three-year stay at Lincoln Memorial University, graduating with a bachelor's degree in history in 1941. Carter served in the 504th Parachute Infantry Regiment of the Eighty-second Airborne Division. He participated in operations in North Africa and Italy, winning a Silver Star for heroism, and took part in the liberation of France. Wounded in the arm during the Battle of the Bulge on December 20, 1944, Carter rejoined his unit by late February, little more than two months before the war's end. Of the original forty men in his platoon, only Carter and two others survived the conflict.[27]

Carter's war stories were so vivid that his family encouraged him to write a book. He started in the summer of 1945, working entirely from memory, and finished that autumn. Carter set the manuscript aside and reenlisted in the paratroopers in November 1945. A few months later, a black mole on his back became inflamed and developed into cancer. Carter entrusted his manuscript to his brother, Boyd G. Carter, who edited and finished it for publication. Ross Carter died on April 18, 1947. His book was, as Boyd put it, Carter's "monument to his buddies," detailing the character and activities of himself and his comrades, although he gave everyone pseudonyms. Published in September 1951, *Those Devils in Baggy Pants* sold more than a million copies, became a Book of the Month Club selection, and was issued as a Reader's Digest Condensed Book. It was not only one of the first but also one of the truly great personal memoirs by a common soldier of World War II. After his brother's death, Boyd spearheaded the creation of the Ross S. Carter Prize for Original Writing at Lincoln Memorial University to stimulate literary creativity among students. The university remained proud of its World War II veterans, placing at least two plaques on campus to memorialize those who had lost their lives.[28]

The university rebounded from the strain of World War II quickly, helped by the Servicemen's Readjustment Act of 1944. It committed the federal government to a "long-term, direct, continuing program of student financial aid" for veterans. During its twelve years of existence, the GI bill helped more than four-

Students entering Lincoln Memorial University, probably in the late 1940s. The stone gateposts erected in 1915 now sport eagles instead of spheres. UA-LMU.

teen million former servicemen, and 16 percent of them used federal funds to pay for college expenses by 1950. By the fall of 1949, half of all college students in America were veterans. The bill also led to a sharp increase in the proportion of male college students and allowed "modest-income veterans" greater access to higher education. It cut across white class and income boundaries; while black veterans participated, the bill did not require colleges to change their racial policies. At Lincoln Memorial University, the GI bill contributed to a steady increase in enrollment. From a low of seventeen graduates in 1944, the university sent thirty-three graduates into the world the next year, fifty-six in 1947, and ninety-six by 1951. The tone of the student body had also changed because of the conflict. Former serviceman Martin Peters recalled the spirit on campus as "matchless." The former GIs "had a kind of live-and-let-live attitude. . . . They were responsible people, not afraid of hard work, able to laugh at adversity and grateful that the unpleasant war experience had now given them an opportunity to be somebody."[29]

McClelland Leaves

Stewart McClelland left Lincoln Memorial University under a mini-cloud of controversy. He quietly divorced his wife of twenty-four years in the summer of 1946 and then, when it became apparent that a relationship had developed between him and Ann Samonial, he offered his resignation in February 1947, to take effect at the next commencement. Samonial was twenty-six years younger than McClelland and had served as dean of women at the university for the past two years. She resigned that position and the couple married on August 2, 1947. The incident inflamed opinion on campus and in Middlesboro because McClelland seemed to abruptly abandon his much-admired first wife. "Stewart and the young woman in question knew but one thing," concluded board member Lester Schriver. "That was that they wanted each other. Everything that stood in the way of that had to go."[30]

Although lacking obvious credentials for a successful college president, McClelland nevertheless had broken John Wesley Hill's dominance in university affairs, gained accreditation by the Southern Association, developed the school's reputation in Lincoln studies, paid off it's debt, built the endowment to nearly a million dollars, and expanded the college's physical plant. McClelland spent the rest of his long life working as dean of instruction for the Dale Carnegie Institute, collecting Wedgwood pottery, and lecturing on a variety of topics. He developed complications from a head injury after slipping on the ice at his Indianapolis home and died at age eighty-six on February 9, 1977, survived by his wife Ann.[31]

Kincaid

Kincaid was a natural choice to succeed McClelland. The Board of Trustees offered him the presidency at their meeting on June 1, 1947. He accepted, telling the members that the university "had been a powerful influence in his life."[32]

For the unassuming man from northwest Georgia, the new job seemed a "quite considerable leap from that day when I came here as almost a penniless student." Many observers were impressed that the board had chosen a southerner and a graduate of the university. Kincaid made the obligatory contact with the Carnegie Corporation of New York to establish good relations, but he failed to secure commitments from the corporation for needed renovations of older campus buildings.[33]

Kincaid's background was reminiscent of Lincoln's. Born in a log cabin on May 17, 1893, near Blairsville, Georgia, his parents could barely provide for their

Robert L. Kincaid, university executive vice-president, 1937–47, and president 1947–58. UA-LMU.

seven sons on a rocky, two-hundred-acre farm in Union County. Robert disliked the hard, physical labor and preferred to read. Unlike his brothers, he was able to attend Bethlehem Public School and Blairsville Collegiate Institute. Kincaid began to write fictional stories based on local themes for the *Union County Banner,* a weekly newspaper, and learned the rudiments of journalism on the job. At age seventeen he left the Institute to teach one term at a rural, one-room school. He did a brief stint as editor of a county newspaper at Cairo, Georgia, the next year, then took advantage of an offer to go to Lincoln Memorial University for further studies. He had not solicited the offer; in fact, Kincaid had never heard of the school. Jim Nicholson, who had also been instrumental in admitting him to the Collegiate Institute, had contacted George A. Hubbell to pave the way for Kincaid's move to Cumberland Gap. The young man dropped everything and traveled to the university by train, arriving on January 15, 1912, to find the place covered with four inches of snow and with little more than fifteen dollars in his pocket.[34]

The move forever changed his life. Attending Lincoln Memorial University opened numerous doors along the path of Kincaid's personal development. In an obvious, exterior way, it put him under the tutelage of Hubbell, who met Kincaid on the boy's first night in Avery Hall and told him of the wonderful things Nicholson had written. "He probed deep into my heart and drew out my story," Kincaid recalled. Hubbell's support and friendship "were to sustain me in many hours of doubt and discouragement."[35]

In a less obvious way, the university opened Kincaid's mind and heart to Lincoln and the legacy of the founders. He had been named after Robert E. Lee, and one of his grandfathers had fought for the South, yet the young Georgian was impressed by the name and ideals of the university. "It was at my first chapel service I felt the touch of the tall man of the Western frontier which was to start a never-ending intellectual adventure," he recalled. Howard had passed away three years earlier, but Kincaid saw Arthur A. Myers and Robert F. Patterson as they visited campus to give talks. "I was drawn to him with partisan ardor," he wrote of Patterson, due to their connection with the Confederate army.[36]

Kincaid worked his way through Lincoln Memorial University by setting type in the print shop. He graduated in 1915, in the largest class thus far in the university's history. Nine of the thirteen graduates gave orations at commencement, Kincaid spoke about "The Price of Human Achievements," and his Jewish friend Ralph Hershon spoke of Lincoln. Frank A. Seiberling attended his first commencement at this time and asked to be introduced to Kincaid. The young

Georgian was munching on a piece of chicken when called to the rubber magnate's side, and he was so impressed by the "*big* man" that he "could hardly speak to him." The graduating class of 1915 donated two stone pillars to serve as a gate way to the main entrance of the campus; they graced the portal to the university for decades to come.[37]

Hubbell encouraged Kincaid to attend the University of Missouri's School of Journalism that fall. Financial difficulties forced Kincaid to return to Cumberland Gap, where Hubbell gave him a job as University Correspondent in the fall of 1916. He also became associate editor of the *Mountain Herald* and married Beulah Chance of Cumberland Gap in May 1917. Kincaid took a leave of absence from Lincoln Memorial University to serve in the army during World War I, teaching inductees how to be clerks. He resumed his position at the university when the war ended but resigned soon after Hubbell left in 1922. Kincaid realized his dream of running a newspaper by editing and publishing the *Middlesboro Daily News.* He joined Lincoln Memorial's Board of Directors in June 1930 but continued to edit the newspaper until named executive vice-president of the university in June 1937. The board also gave him an honorary doctor of laws degree.[38]

By the time Kincaid became president in 1947, he could truthfully write, "I have been actively identified with the institution in some capacity, either as a student, alumnus, member of the board, or as a staff officer." His commitment to the people of the university was deep and genuine. When a promising student named Ray Welborn had to drop out due to health reasons, Kincaid wrote him a long letter. "Every youth dreams," he mused. "He grows up, living dreams. I had them when I was a youngster." Helping worthy men and women of limited means drove Kincaid as a person. Deeply interested in history and biography, he learned how to become a good historian and published a landmark history of the Wilderness Road.[39]

Kincaid considered himself a kind of "Father Confessor to lots of young fellows," treating them much as he treated his own children. Tragically, his son Hugh died of a rare skin infection at age eighteen on November 10, 1941.[40]

Throughout the period of his eleven-year presidency, Kincaid tried to make sense of his life through the lens of Lincoln Memorial University and its ideals. He wrote *Boy Finds a College* as an autobiographical booklet to tell the story of his youth in Georgia and to detail how he came to be a student at Cumberland Gap. Kincaid often told donors, "What little I have accomplished I owe almost entirely to the institution and those devoted men and women who have built it." In *School Days at Bethlehem,* a booklet published by the university, he tried to understand how the individuals he encountered at each stage of his lower education prepared him to go to the university. In the article "Shadow of a Man," Kincaid portrayed himself as a symbol of reconciliation, retaining his deep southern roots while creating a devotion to the northern emancipator. Lincoln Memorial University shaped Kincaid's life deeply and broadly, and in ways that he could not fully understand until later in his life.[41]

Not surprisingly, Kincaid had a strong desire to write the history of the university as early as the 1930s. He gathered material and consulted the Oliver Otis Howard Papers at Bowdoin College; he also visited the Howard grave site at Burlington, Vermont. Howard was second only in importance to Lincoln in the spiritual life of the university, as far as Kincaid was concerned. "I have reveled in the stories which I have collected from various sources about the kindly, grey-haired, one-armed general who visited with the students, ate with them in the dining hall, talked to them in chapel, and rode on many missions into the surrounding hills," he wrote.[42]

While Kincaid never fulfilled his desire to write a history of the university, he provided the best short account of its creation as a chapter in his book *The*

Cumberland Gap from the Pinnacle on Cumberland Mountain. Poor Valley Ridge is to the left, with the university campus nestled close by on the other side. The town of Cumberland Gap is at the foot of the Pinnacle. UA-LMU.

Wilderness Road. Published in April 1947, just before he assumed the presidency, it became a classic history of the route that Daniel Boone pioneered and that made Cumberland Gap an important part of frontier history. Kincaid dedicated it to Hugh and wrote movingly of the many people who created and used the road. He has a good eye for human interest stories and a facility for relating them in an engaging style. In later editions, Kincaid personalized the introduction to describe his first thoughts upon arriving at Cumberland Gap. The book has gone through five editions; as the university librarian put it in 1969, the "demand for these books seems to increase with time."[43]

Chapter 10
The Lincoln Stamp

All about the campus and grounds are the scenes and evidences of General Howard's last work. . . . His service to humanity has been enlarged at Lincoln Memorial University and thereby has made more enduring the principles and philosophies of his commander-in-chief during the Civil War. These two great historical characters in American history are therefore inseparably linked at our institution.
—Robert L. Kincaid, February 7, 1951

We like to think that the students who come to us are potential Lincolns. They are of the same stuff. . . . Like Lincoln, these boys and girls dream and aspire to better things.
—Robert L. Kincaid, [1957]

The many people who contributed to the history of Lincoln Memorial University maintained a commitment to the school's Lincoln heritage and its original mission into the mid-twentieth century. Robert L. Kincaid played a sterling role in this historic trend. He understood the mission better than any president before or since because he was a living example of the kind of Appalachian youth the institution was designed to serve. He also developed a deep love for the Lincoln heritage and for the legacy of the founders. Kincaid became the most important keeper of the Lincoln-Howard flame at Lincoln Memorial University.

"Much has been done to project the life of Lincoln into our citizenship," Kincaid asserted just before he became president. "The career of the Sixteenth President has been held up constantly to the students as an inspiring example. His teachings have been incorporated into their thinking." He also asserted that the primary mission of the school was "to give educational opportunity to young people of limited means in the Southern mountains." Kincaid often used Howard's last conference with Lincoln to illustrate the university's mission to teach students "the principles of good citizenship and patriotic devotion to country exemplified in the life of Abraham Lincoln." The best way to fulfill the purpose of the founders was to produce students "with the Lincoln stamp upon them."[1]

Kincaid also described a ritual currently in vogue on campus during the 1950s wherein all entering freshmen were taken on a tour of the campus at the start of each fall semester. The most important stop was the Lincoln Room in Duke Hall, where "they sign a register, seated at a desk used by Lincoln when he was a member of the Illinois legislature." The purpose was to have "our young people walk with Lincoln . . . and think his thoughts, . . . catch the throb of his heart; and be enthralled by his matchless spirit." Kincaid hoped it would make "Lincoln a conscious and compelling part of the educational heritage" of the university's students, and constitute "a good beginning for their college careers." Lincoln Memorial University was unique among American colleges, even those half dozen or so named for the sixteenth president, in its incorporation of Lincoln studies into campus life. Even at a meeting of the Claiborne County Alumni chapter in 1954, 160 former students listened to a talk by Jesse Stuart extolling the Lincoln heritage of the school. After dinner, they watched "a Lincoln movie" in the Mary E. Mars Gymnasium.[2]

The university continued to serve primarily a local population while enjoying national stature as a college devoted to the Great Emancipator. Kincaid fully

Aerial view of Lincoln Memorial University, taken sometime between 1945 and 1952. Many historic buildings, Poor Valley Ridge, Cumberland Mountain, and the road system are documented in this photograph. UA-LMU.

understood this and discouraged Leonard Gardner, an alumnus who consulted with the South Koreans about setting up an effective government in 1948, about Gardner's idea to recruit students in that Asian land. "As you know, we are quite provincial here at L.M.U.," Kincaid wrote, "and foreigners might feel out of place." He recalled that a Chinese teacher had studied on campus two years before because "Abraham Lincoln had always been his ideal," but the president felt comfortable accepting foreign students only if they were bright and genuinely interested in the university's mission.[3]

Given its name, potential donors continued to assume that the institution recruited primarily African American students. Kincaid patiently explained to them the original intent of the founders: "Our college is for the training of the white boys and girls of the Southern mountains where there has been great need for educational opportunity beyond the high school." He found himself "constantly explaining the primary purpose of our institution as a worthy living memorial to the Great Emancipator for young people of his kind." Kincaid also defended religious diversity on campus, even though nearly everyone associated with the university was a member of some Protestant denomination. When a rabbi addressed the students in 1950 and a Knoxville friend of the university complained about it, the president told her, "We do not wish to emphasize religious intolerance of any kind."[4]

Kincaid's conservative political and social values led him to portray Lincoln Memorial University as a bulwark of Americanism during the Cold War. He blamed the nuclear threat and the "adoption of many socialistic schemes which would destroy the virility and independent will of our people" for the "strong undercurrent of fear" in the country as the Korean War raged along an indefinite course in 1951. "We have thrown away the spade of personal effort and have grabbed the spoon of government pap and subsidy," he complained. Reflecting on the effects of the New Deal, Kincaid noted, "We have started on the broad road that leads to destruction." It is no wonder that the president deeply admired Herbert Hoover for his "inspiring leadership and steadfast devotion to Lincolnian ideals and principles."[5]

Because his own life exemplified the type of student the founders sought, and the university had an extraordinary effect on his personal development, Kincaid used his life story as a promotional tool. Lincoln Memorial University provided Kincaid an opportunity to work his way toward a college degree and offered the springboard for developing his latent literary talent. He exemplified the spirit that education professor Mildred Shumate referred to when she positioned

Lincoln Memorial University as "a college begun for the common man, where labor has been respected as a means to culture."[6]

LINCOLN STATUES

The university acquired an outdoor statue of Lincoln for the first time in 1949, through the generosity of Cartaino S. Paolo, the Sicilian sculptor who had executed the bust of Benjamin Duke for Duke Hall. John Wesley Hill had initially suggested the idea in 1926, preferring a representation of the younger Lincoln. As a result, Paolo began working on a model of the future president as a lawyer, first in clay then in plaster. Paolo paid his first visit to the campus in 1930, expecting to receive a commission of ten thousand dollars for his work, but the Depression blasted all hopes of consummating the project.[7]

Ironically, this was not the first attempt to create an outdoor representation of a Civil War figure in the Cumberland Gap area. Residents of Middlesboro had suggested that equestrian statues of Grant and Lee be placed on the high point of Cumberland Mountain called the Pinnacle, immediately north of the gap. The city government made an initial appropriation, but the Depression stopped this project as decisively as it had stopped the on-campus Lincoln statue. Not long after, Norwegian sculptor Gutzon Borglum proposed the carving of "a gigantic head of Lincoln" on the limestone outcropping below the Pinnacle. This project elicited such protest that the plan was dropped, but not before another individual suggested something even more ambitious, a full-length statue of Lincoln, at least 150 feet tall, stretching up the limestone. Paolo liked this idea and planned out the details, with the statue's head nearly at the top and its feet at the level of the highway as it entered Cumberland Gap. A "wide rustic stairway" would lead farther down from there to a small Lincoln museum. Paolo was so excited that he offered to move to Cumberland Gap with his family in exchange for living expenses, but Hill did not like the idea. It was 1932, and the Depression was far from over. Nothing ever came of the project then, or four years later, when Paolo once again brought it up.[8]

In 1948, Paolo broke up his New York studio and destroyed some of his earlier models, but he kept the one he had made for *Lincoln the Lawyer.* He gave it to the university and Kincaid authorized a campaign to raise money for the cast, which was done at the Roman Bronze Works of Corona, New York. Paolo visited the campus in 1948 and agreed that a base of Tennessee pink marble would suit the work, which rose six feet, eight inches, including the base. Site prepara-

Cartaino Paolo's *Lincoln the Lawyer,* erected in 1949. "I made this work in love and prayer and I saved nothing in its execution," wrote Paolo. "I hope that it will serve as an inspiration to many young people and raise them to the highest ideals as Lincoln did." Paolo to Kincaid, August 6, 1948, Cartaino S. Paolo, Miscellaneous Papers, UA-LMU.

tion took place on the north edge of the quadrangle, near the Carnegie Library and directly opposite the front door of Duke Hall, with steps flanking the statue so that foot traffic toward the library would wend its way past the image.[9]

The statue is a magnificent representation of Lincoln as he makes a point with fervency at the bar. It expressed Paolo's deep admiration for the man. He admitted that his artistic values were "of the old school, which emphasizes form and a strict observance of nature." Paolo thought the statue had "strength, power, and at least it has part of that insight and spirituality that Lincoln undoubtedly had," and he sought to express Lincoln's "honesty, courage and understanding of human nature." The work was dedicated on February 11, 1949, with the great granddaughter of Lincoln's second vice-president, Andrew Johnson, in attendance. Paolo, unfortunately, could not be there due to developing health problems. But he sent his speech, after his son had helped him "put the English in good form," and Gerald McMurtry read it at the ceremony. *Lincoln the Lawyer* took its place among more than one hundred statues of Lincoln in the world at that time, and it was reportedly the first Lincoln statue to be erected in the South outside of Kentucky. The university garnered much publicity with its dedication, and Paolo suggested selling foot-tall replicas of the statue to raise money for the school. His widow donated two other plaster models of Lincoln to the university after he passed away in December 1955.[10]

Kincaid hoped to erect a "Lincoln Building" behind the statue to house the university's collection of artifacts and manuscripts. While that dream did not come to pass, the collection continued to grow through donations rather than through the regular budget of the school. Kincaid proudly reported that it was the third largest collection of Lincoln material in the world.[11]

HOWARD

In 1949, Kincaid assured Harry S. Howard that "the Howard spirit is still strong and purposeful" at Lincoln Memorial University. In fact, awareness of Howard's legacy was reinvigorated by contact with John A. Carpenter, a graduate student at Columbia University who was working on a biography of the general. From his office in Duke Hall, Kincaid gazed on a portrait of Howard and could look out of the window at *Lincoln the Lawyer.* "The spirit of these two men seem to be entwined with one noble purpose," he informed Harry, "and I am inspired by the memory of what [they] have meant in the growth and development of this institution of service."[12]

It was true, as Kincaid put it, that "the Howard stamp is dominant upon the life and purpose of Lincoln Memorial University," and some people in the area could still recall seeing and meeting the one-armed general during his visits to Cumberland Gap more than forty years before. Harry was "amused" that the W. C. Rice painting of Lincoln pointing to Cumberland Gap on a map had been destroyed when the old auditorium had burned down in 1924, for it erroneously depicted his father with two arms. Kincaid organized "a special Founder's Day Program" on November 4, 1953, "built around the life and achievement" of Howard so as to tell his story to those incoming students who knew little about him.[13]

Interior of university chapel, before 1924, showing painting by W. C. Rice of Lincoln's last meeting with Howard. Peace advocate, Lincoln enthusiast, and Union army veteran Jenkin Lloyd Jones stands at the podium during a visit to the university. Earl Hobson Smith Papers, UA-LMU.

STUDENTS

Student enrollment continued to rise steadily during the late 1940s and throughout the 1950s, although the Korean War caused a 15 percent decrease by June 1951, a year after the conflict broke out. After graduating ninety-six students that year, the number dropped to sixty-three in 1952 and did not begin to rise significantly until 1956. By that time, it was estimated that Lincoln Memorial University had awarded at least 1,522 bachelors degrees and had trained from fifteen thousand to twenty thousand other students who did not complete a four-year degree. The university continued to maintain its "student labor program," spending from sixty thousand to seventy-five thousand dollars on work grants to about half of the five hundred students on campus in 1955. Many of these students, and others who were not part of the work program, took advantage of the growing number of university-sponsored scholarships that were available. The college bulletin spelled out in detail what was expected of student workers and made it clear that work assignments would be changed or reduced if a student's grades suffered.[14]

Kincaid sponsored a careful survey of university students in the mid-1950s. Forty-three percent of them were from Tennessee, 11 percent from Virginia, and 9 percent from Kentucky. More than 40 percent of the students majored in education, and over 20 percent majored in business. He noted also that 80 percent of all public school teachers in Claiborne County were former students of the university. Over 60 percent of the university's graduates continued to live "in the immediate territory" rather than move to other parts of the country.[15]

KINCAID LEAVES AND A NEW ERA BEGINS

Kincaid worked hard as president, worrying over finances until he admitted "it is a man killing job and I do not know how long I will survive under it." Late in his term as president, Kincaid also admitted in a speech that the institution he loved had "shaped and, in a measure, controlled my life."[16]

He was ready to retire in 1958, partly due to his "physical condition" and in the belief that new leadership could more effectively manage a "long-range development program" the university had adopted. With the continued hope of writing a history of the university, Kincaid presided over his last commencement on June 2, 1958, and was voted the honorary title of president emeritus. Two years later, he entered the University Hospital at the University of Tennessee due to "some kind of inflammation or infection of his intestinal tract,"

Student workers, 1955. This view of workers in a dormitory kitchen is one of the few that documents the historic work-learn tradition of the university, which was phased out during the late 1950s and early 1960s. UA-LMU .

which caused so much difficulty in eating that Kincaid lost fifteen pounds in three weeks. He passed away on May 21, 1960. "His life was a study in simple example," concluded an editorial in his newspaper, the *Middlesboro Daily News*. "He quietly aided student and friend alike, believing that everyone must be responsible not only to ease the burdens of his friends but also those with whom he shares the earth."[17]

Provine-Rice-Livesay

Kincaid was succeeded by a string of capable administrators. Robert C. Provine, a native of Columbia, Tennessee, had earned his degrees at Vanderbilt, Harvard, and Brown University and had many years experience as a German and philosophy professor and president of small colleges in Nashville and Alabama. He served as president of Lincoln Memorial University from 1958 to 1963. H. LaMarr Rice, a native of Springfield, Ohio, held degrees from Denison University, Union College, and Columbia University. A professional college administrator, he served as president of Lincoln Memorial University from 1963 to 1967. Virginia-born Herbert Y. Livesay had been educated at Milligan College and the University of Tennessee. He taught in the state's public schools for eight years and acted as Lincoln Memorial University's chaplain before serving as president from 1967 to 1973.[18]

Demise of the Work Program

The most fundamental change of the Provine-Rice-Livesay period was to alter the historic work-learn program to take advantage of government-supported student aid. In the process, Lincoln Memorial University gave up an important part of its heritage to become an institution much more like other colleges in the United States. The involvement of the federal government in offering aid to college and university students began with the National Defense Education Act of 1958, which created a program offering student loans. The program's name was later changed to National Direct Student Loan, but its process remained the same: funneling government money to the university to administer to students. The government also created its College Work-Study Program in 1964, offering money for the creation of on-campus jobs for students. Educational Opportunity Grants, which started in 1965, offered government funds for a "program of nonrepayable grants."[19]

Lincoln Memorial University eased into this new system of government support in stages. The university began by filling out a form stating its current method of supporting students in May 1956. A total of 232 students worked in university-created jobs at a cost of $53,157 to the institution. Twenty-seven of them worked as teaching or research assistants for faculty members, 21 others combined service scholarships with other types of work, and 184 were employed in a variety of jobs without scholarship money. Forty-seven students were given loans ranging from less than $150 to $449. The university set limits on the amount freshmen could borrow (up to $250) and did not allow any student to borrow more than $500 in four years. It charged no interest on the loan while the borrower remained in school but set the rate at 6 percent after graduation, with the first payment due six months after leaving and the final payment due within two years. Former students paid more than seven thousand dollars against their loans during the academic year 1955–56, and nearly twenty-one thousand dollars was still outstanding.[20]

A year after becoming president, Provine worried because the university could not create more jobs for needy students. Harrogate, with a population of only three hundred residents, could not create more for them either. Moreover, Provine found that the university's work program was not administered well. He thought it and the scholarship program had been positioned mostly to recruit students, and that "in some cases, little or no work was really required."[21]

The independent status of the school was another compelling factor in the decision to take advantage of government support. "We are really independent," Provine told a prospective donor, "indeed, at times painfully so." He still wanted to teach students to rely on themselves, even as he began to incorporate government subsidies into the financial arrangements on campus. Administrators encouraged all students to apply for National Defense Student Loans and began to see these loans as "a base for the aid program." University funds were "used to supplement these loans" for those whose needs exceeded federal government limits or who failed to qualify for them. Provine insisted that on-campus jobs be allocated based on "the requirements of the University" as well as the student's "needs and willingness, his class load and grades, and his general sense of responsibility." A Student Aid Committee ruled on all issues relating to the award of scholarships, loans, and jobs.[22]

During the academic year 1961–62, the number of students taking government loans rose from 78 to 103, while the number of students depending on university scholarships dropped from 57 to 46. Although about 250 students had worked in non-scholarship jobs on campus in 1955, only 65 were doing so by May 1962. The number of university-created jobs continued to decline throughout the decade, while the university's participation in the Work Study Program offered by the federal government rose steadily. Lincoln Memorial University began its involvement in Work Study in the academic year 1965–66 with 42 students, increasing to 63 students the next year. The university continued to blend Work Study, loans, and scholarships in its student-support strategy while university-funded jobs disappeared. The nature of these Work Study jobs changed also. No longer were they oriented around the daily, fundamental needs of living on campus; rather, the student workers became administrative helpers, and basic jobs in the kitchen and on the farm were increasingly filled by hired, adult workers.[23]

Ironically, government-funded job creation led to student work that was far less vital to the life of the institution, becoming another form of grant aid to students rather than supporting a life-enriching experience that grew out of performing essential labor. Many alumni who had worked on campus before the end of the 1950s extolled the value of their labor experience. "It taught me to work," Paris Houston recalled more than forty years after leaving Lincoln Memorial University in the troubled class of 1930. "With that knowledge and a willingness to apply it one can make it almost anywhere."[24]

Only a handful of schools have retained their historic work-learn tradition. Berea College in Kentucky, Berry College in Georgia, and Warren Wilson College in North Carolina still maintain university-controlled work programs for students in Appalachia. In addition, Blackburn College in Illinois, College of the Ozarks in Missouri, Ecclesia College in Arkansas, and Sterling College in Vermont maintain such programs. These seven institutions make up the Work College Consortium. Most of them had work programs from their founding. The benefits of maintaining them include reduced funds spent on their labor force, because student workers receive less pay and fewer benefits than full-time employees. The programs aid in student retention as well. The weaknesses of maintaining these work programs include a work force with fewer skills and which experiences a high turnover rate. The institutions stress "the educational value of work, as opposed to the vocational value," and employers are usually impressed by students who have had experience in these programs. The conclusion of one study is "that 'earn-learn' plans are inexpensive ways to open higher education to impoverished rural populations," even in modern America.[25]

Athletics and Money

Provine tried to save money by trimming the university's commitment to intercollegiate sports. When rumors of this cutback circulated on campus, fueled by newspaper reports, many students protested by hanging the president in effigy, twice, on the evening of February 24, 1958, and the following morning as well. The reaction came in the wake of the basketball team's success in winning the

Volunteer State Athletic Conference Tournament. The Railsplitters had already won the Smoky Mountain Conference Championship.[26]

The president did not back down in the face of this opposition. One day after the incident, he told a meeting of the students that he wanted to stop intercollegiate sports altogether. Provine cited the comparatively large cost of maintaining the program, arguing that the university spent fifteen times more money on its sports teams than on the purchase of new books for the library. Moreover, it garnered no more than five hundred dollars per game in gate receipts. The university was suffering from a large deficit at the time and could not afford the cost, despite the basketball team's winning record. This announcement set off another round of protests as students burned one of the Provine effigies and cut down several trees to block the main road onto campus. They intensified their vandalism by breaking street lights and windows and turning over trash cans. In the end, the students vented their frustration and Provine relented insofar as he kept the teams in operation but cut all athletic scholarships. Intercollegiate sports languished at Lincoln Memorial University for the duration of the Provine presidency, but the athletic scholarships returned after he left in 1963.[27]

STUDENTS AND RACE

Enrollment at Lincoln Memorial University remained at historic levels well into the 1960s, at about 400 to 500 students each year. From 1956 to 1966, a total of 1,074 students received degrees at the university; 61 percent of them majored in education, continuing the school's heritage of training teachers for the mountains.[28]

The legal bar against admitting black students to Lincoln Memorial University was dropped when the Supreme Court case of *Brown v. Board of Education of Topeka* voided the Maryville law in 1954, ending fifty-three years of mandated segregation in Tennessee higher education. Kincaid continued to adhere to the university's traditional role as a school designed for whites. "We are not crusading in the present desegregation movement and thus far we have had no applications from Negroes," he wrote in 1956. "I am sure in time that will happen and we will meet the situation when it arises." Kincaid felt certain that racial integration would be "worked out" in the South and "solved gradually."[29]

The university still had not received any applications from black students when a group of African American teenagers visited the campus in 1961 to view the Lincoln Room in Duke Hall. Some university students apparently thought a black girl in the group acted in a "haughty" manner and were upset. The visit was sponsored by nuns at the Holy Cross Center in Big Stone Gap, Virginia, and Sister Mary Joseph wrote an apology and an explanation for the girl's behavior, believing she was merely tired after a long day on the road. "I honestly never thought we would run into such prejudice at an institute dedicated to the memory of Lincoln," Sister Mary Joseph admitted. She promised to "explain the situation" to future groups of black kids to avoid a repeat of the incident.[30]

A short while after Sister Mary Joseph wrote her letter, Lincoln Memorial University declined to participate in an attempt to integrate black and white high school students in the East Tennessee Regional Math Contest. Provine thought it was best not to risk this move until he had a chance to consult the Board of Trustees, which discussed the wider issue of recruiting black students to study at the Harrogate campus as well. The members voted to continue the school's tradition of service to whites in the area "for the time being." Provine decided not to invite blacks to participate in on-campus activities of any kind, for to do so "could cause acute embarrassment to them."[31]

Concerned donors from the North began to inquire if Lincoln Memorial University was open to admitting black students. H. LeMarr Rice responded by pointing out that the university's admission policy, as stated in its catalog, allowed students to attend without regard to race or religion, but no blacks had applied as of 1965.[32]

That situation began to change a year later, and to the credit of administrators and board members, Lincoln Memorial University readily accepted the change. While the university never required entering students to declare their race, the first documented instance of an African American attending classes occurred in 1966, when Mattie Babb took summer courses. Six black students attended classes in the summer of 1967, and one in the fall term that year. A dozen blacks applied for admission in the fall of 1968 and all were admitted, but only four of them enrolled in courses. "Those who are here are living happily," Herbert Y. Livesay reported. Another African American, Robert Lee Gordon, transferred to Lincoln Memorial University from Coahoma Junior College in Clarksdale, Mississippi, in the fall of 1969 and graduated two years later. The first African American to earn a degree fully at Lincoln Memorial University was Pearl Robinson Goins, who enrolled in the fall of 1968 and graduated in June 1972.[33]

A friend of the university, Marguerite T. Sundback of Meadville, Pennsylvania, wanted to know if student unrest had affected the institution. "What 'freedoms' are they requesting?" she asked about the students. "Have the radical organizers made any attempt to invade the campus? Has S.D.S. [Students for a Democratic Society] made any appearance?" Herbert Livesay replied that the campus "has not been touched by the surrounding upheaval." He indicated that recruitment policies were geared to entice those students who would be "conservatively oriented in behavior." Whether that was literally true, given the university's need for student income, is open to question. More accurately, Lincoln Memorial University drew most of its students from a regional population that was staunchly conservative in politics and social values. Livesay told Sundback that faculty and staff at the university were busy "educating young people in honesty, the free enterprise system, service to mankind, and love of country."[34]

FACULTY AND HOWARD'S LEGACY

Faculty salaries had been meager ever since the university's founding, and that trend continued into the mid-twentieth century. In 1959, the Committee on Faculty and Staff Relations reported to the board that salaries were "at the very minimum allowed to hold accreditation in the Southern Association of Colleges and Secondary Schools and we have been warned on this score." This situation continued because, as Provine put it, the university "both by choice and necessity lives within its income." Despite this frugal policy, both the administration and the faculty kept the institutional focus on students. "Since Lincoln Memorial University is definitely a teaching institution," Provine informed Marguerite Sundback, "there is no substitute for good instruction."[35]

Howard continued to be remembered as the chief founder of Lincoln Memorial University. Earl Hobson Smith authored a play commemorating the creation of the school that was performed on campus at the sixtieth anniversary celebration, on February 12, 1957. Rather like most of his historical plays, *The Genesis of Lincoln Memorial University* plays loose with the facts. For some reason, it is set in 1895 rather than 1896, and it involves Ulysses S. Grant as a major character even though Grant had passed away eleven years before the meeting on the Harrow School porch. He seems to be here mostly to goad Howard into kissing Ellen Myers as a reward for offering her inheritance as seed money for the university. The play also has long segments of spoken dialogue, offering innumerable details about the historic event rather than conveying the story through the flow of action and crisply written dialogue. Smith expanded on his original play so that the university could publish it in 1981 as an offering to potential donors.[36]

FRANK W. WELCH

The university's commitment to Lincoln remained strong in the 1970s as the new president, Frank W. Welch, asserted that the sixteenth president continued to be the central feature of life at Lincoln Memorial University. Livesay passed away in December 1972, and thereafter presidential duties were handled by Charles West, administrative assistant to Livesay, until Welch took over on June 1, 1973. With degrees from Lambuth College, Emory University, and Florida State University, Welch was only thirty-three years old when he became president. He spoke of the dignity of labor even though the college's work-learn program had long since disappeared. He also stressed that lessons involving democracy and a respect for the free enterprise system accompanied an education at the Harrogate campus.[37]

In the 1970s, there were attempts to resurrect old practices that seemed to have some value in the modern world. Eighty students grew vegetables on part of the university's farm to earn money for their college expenses in the summer of 1975. Welch considered the project a failure because the university spent "several thousand dollars" for very little gain. He blamed a drought and faulty marketing plans and never tried the experiment again. Welch reinstituted Lincoln Day, however, to remember the origins and purpose of the school, and the celebration has continued to the present under its new name, Founder's Day.[38]

Welch superintended a number of curricular innovations to keep the university current with modern trends. In 1973, the university adopted a four-point grading system, reorganized its many small academic departments into eight large divisions, and began to create associate degrees in several areas and a bachelor's degree in nursing. Welch also began to offer evening classes for nontraditional students, internships to gain off-campus work experience, and independent studies courses. The university hired its first African American faculty member in 1974 and began to offer courses at off-campus sites in the region by 1978.[39]

As part of an effort to maintain the finances of the university, Welch quietly dropped the faculty tenure system, which, in any case, had been short-lived. From the founding of the university until the early 1960s, all faculty members signed one year, renewable contracts, or up to three-year contracts if acceptable to the administration. The tenure system adopted in the 1960s included a probationary period of seven years before tenure was granted, but even then the tenure extended only for another seven years, subject to reevaluation by both the administration and the faculty member. Welch recommended that the Board of Trustees revert to the old tradition of relying on one-, three-, or five-year appointments with no tenure. The board approved his suggestion, after the faculty had voted their approval of the change, by 1977.[40]

Lincoln Memorial University had adopted tenure comparatively late, but it was part of a trend toward reducing tenure at colleges across the nation in the late twentieth century. While some of the larger universities had created tenure systems before the AAUP issued its Conference Statement on Academic Freedom and Tenure in 1925, most institutions did so during a ten-year period following the end of World War II, when college enrollment boomed. They modeled their tenure systems on the AAUP's 1940 Statement of Principles, which specified the details of how such systems should operate.[41]

Two factors worked to reduce the percentage of college-level faculty members who held tenure by the turn of the twenty-first century: a huge surge in the employment of part-time teachers and a smaller increase in the number of full-time but tenure-ineligible faculty positions. Institutions of higher education of all sizes and types experienced these two developments until less than a third of all college and university teachers were tenured, or held a tenure-track position, by 2005. Yet only small, struggling institutions tended to eliminate tenure altogether. Lincoln Memorial University was one of thirteen independent, four-year colleges that eliminated tenure systems from 1974 to 2000. According to one student of the phenomenon, "Most colleges without tenure are financially brittle institutions—small, unheralded places with limited resources and tight budgets." Out of nearly thirty-seven hundred institutions of higher education in the United States, eighty-eight operate completely in an oasis of short-term faculty contract. Most of those institutions have lower tuition, a lower percentage of full-time faculty with terminal degrees, lower faculty power in decision making, and presidents with almost unlimited ability to make decisions on campus. Lincoln Memorial University fit those characteristics in the 1970s.[42]

Abraham Lincoln Library and Museum

Welch was president when a historic dream, the erection of a separate building to house the important Lincoln and Civil War collection, was realized for the university. The artifacts and manuscripts had outgrown the confined space of the Lincoln Room in Duke Hall, and a modern museum was desperately needed. A major study of the university's library needs, conducted by the director of libraries at the University of Tennessee in 1965, suggested that the Lincoln collection could be housed in a separate wing of a new library building, but that new

Groundbreaking for Abraham Lincoln Library and Museum, 1975. Kentucky Fried Chicken king Harland Sanders donated funds for the construction of the university's museum. UA-LMU.

building never came to pass. Instead, Welch launched a major effort to drum up donations for a museum building to match the half a million dollars Kentucky Fried Chicken king Harland Sanders pledged to the effort. Sanders had started his business enterprise at Corbin, Kentucky, about fifty miles northwest of the university. Although he had never attended, his respect for the goals of the college led him to support its effort to properly house the Lincoln material.

Enough funds were gathered to initiate construction on June 1, 1975, and the building was finished and dedicated on June 4, 1977. Sanders and his wife were present for the dedication ceremony, and President Jimmy Carter sent a telegram of congratulations. Located near the old site of Norton Hall and the modern, main entrance of the campus, it is one of the first buildings one notices when approaching the university.[43]

BURCHETT-MILLER-BISHOP

Welch pointed the university in a number of different directions before he left the presidency in 1981, but the financial health of the institution suffered for the next twenty years as it tried to make progress in those directions. Gary J. Burchett succeeded Welch in the presidency. A native of Cumberland Gap and a graduate of Lincoln Memorial University, Burchett had taught on the elementary level and had worked for years as a college administrator at the University of Tennessee, Mountain Empire Community College, and Lincoln Memorial University. After ten years in office, he was succeeded by his executive vice-president, Scott D. Miller. Born in Edinboro, Pennsylvania, Miller held a bachelor's degree from West Virginia Wesleyan College and had served in administrative positions at several institutions before coming to Lincoln Memorial University in 1984. When Miller left the presidency in 1997, R. Martin Peters served as acting president for a year. A graduate of Lincoln Memorial, Peters had a good deal of experience as a staff member at the university before becoming dean of the graduate school at Tennessee Technological University. He returned to fill in at the president's office until Jerry C. Bishop was tapped to lead the Harrogate college in 1998. A native of Hawkins County, Tennessee, Bishop had graduated from Lincoln Memorial University in 1965 and went on to earn graduate degrees from the University of Virginia and the Virginia Polytechnic Institute and State University (Virginia Tech). He had been superintendent of schools in Lee County, Virginia, for many years.[44]

Progress was slow during the last twenty years of the century, despite steadily growing enrollments. A master of education program began in 1982 and the university created its own web site in 1995, but computers for faculty and staff, and for teaching in the classrooms, made their way slowly and uncertainly onto campus. The university resurrected its commitment to high school education by creating the J. Frank White Academy in September 1989, admitting local students in grades nine through twelve. The university had originated in an institution of lower education and had maintained the Lincoln Memorial Academy until 1930. After a hiatus of fifty-nine years, a new high school took its place on campus. Later the academy was expanded to include grades five to eight as well. White was an area lawyer deeply interested in education. When he died in 1927, he bequeathed money to support a private high school near Cumberland Gap, but it took the passage of forty-two years to realize his request.[45]

A Second Lincoln Statue

The second outdoor statue of Abraham Lincoln was erected at the main entrance to the university and dedicated on October 23, 1992. The work of sculptor Jack Witt, it is a full-length figure of Lincoln, depicting him as he looked during his presidency. Witt, who received his degrees from Virginia Military Institute and Virginia Commonwealth University, created a reliable image of the Great

Emancipator. While it lacks the immediacy and sense of restrained power evident in Paolo's earlier statue, it serves well as an icon of the university's namesake at the main campus entrance. Positioned on the median of the street, Witt's statue greets every visitor, faculty, staff, and student who drives by.[46]

Nancy B. Moody

The university entered a new phase in its history as it entered the twenty-first century by electing its first woman president. Having grown up in Middlesboro, Nancy B. Moody earned her bachelor's degree in nursing at Eastern Kentucky University and became a professor at Lincoln Memorial University in 1974. She earned graduate degrees in nursing and gained administrative experience at several other institutions before becoming president in 2002. Moody knew that women ran no more than 20 percent of the nation's colleges and universities, and she was keenly aware of the symbolism of her own election to a chair that previously had been occupied only by men. "Being selected as the first female president makes a statement about the institution and how times have changed," she commented. "It is proof that people can become whatever they desire if they work hard, set their goals high, don't allow stereotypes and other obstacles to get in their way, and above all demonstrate the qualities of honesty and integrity."[47]

More effective management of financial resources and the physical plant of the campus allowed the university to institute expansive programs during the first decade of the new century. By now Lincoln Memorial University had granted bachelor degrees to more than fifty-five hundred men and women. As of August 2007, fully 92 percent of its students took advantage of some type of financial aid to pay for their education. The university's off-campus offerings soared at the turn of the century. While enrollment on the Harrogate campus went from 952 students in 1998 to 1,253 in 2006, enrollment at ten off-campus sites increased from 849 students to 1,728 during the same time period. Off-campus students constituted 47.1 percent of the university's overall enrollment in 1998, but that percentage had increased to 57.9 percent by 2006.[48]

The nursing program drove much of this change, with course offerings at Corbin, Kentucky, in the Knoxville area, and at Madisonville, Tennessee. Courses in other programs, especially education, were offered at several locations in Tennessee and Georgia. The creation of the DeBusk College of Osteopathic Medicine charted a new path for the university in 2007. It trained doctors of osteopathy

Lincoln statue by Jack Witt, 1992. It is located at the modern, main entrance to the campus. Earl J. Hess.

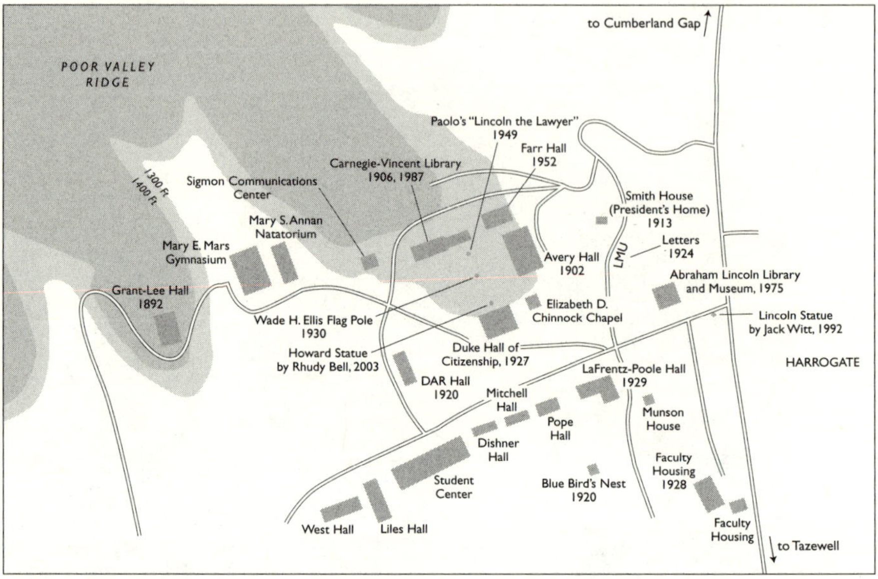

Old campus of Lincoln Memorial University, 2010.

in a new, state-of-the-art building on the one-thousand-acre campus at Harrogate. A doctor of education program also was created in 2009 as the university, for the first time in its history, crafted a role for itself as a research institution. While the number of baccalaureate students has risen steadily, the real change at the turn of the century was the explosive growth in postgraduate training for nurses, public school educators, medical personnel, and those in the field of business. As the most recent "branding" adopted by the administration indicates, Lincoln Memorial University now markets itself as a "career path university."[49]

The number of faculty grew with the continued growth of the university, and the advanced training they brought to the campus increased as well. On the eve of World War II, the university had thirty faculty members; a little more than one-fourth of them held a Ph.D. degree, and 60 percent held a master's degree, while 13 percent had only a bachelor's degree. Those statistics did not change too much until the late 1980s, when 34 percent of fifty-five faculty members held the Ph.D. About ten years later, at the turn of the twenty-first century, 42 percent of sixty-four faculty members held the advanced degree, half of the lot held a master's degree, and five held a bachelor's degree. The percentage of doctoral degree holders increased a bit, while the percentage of those holding a bachelor's degree declined, and the total number of faculty rose to seventy-three by 2005.[50]

REMEMBERING HOWARD

The university has continued its historic commitment to the founders and the man whose name has graced the institution since its founding. A bust of Howard now adorns the outdoor scene on the quadrangle. Executed by Rhudy Bell, a graduate of the class of 1952, it depicts the general as he looked during the Civil War. Dedicated on November 7, 2003, the statue occupies a spot in front of the main entrance to Duke Hall, facing *Lincoln the Lawyer* across the open space of the quadrangle. The flagpole, donated by board member Wade H. Ellis and dedicated in the immediate aftermath of the student strike of April 1930, still stands between the two statues.[51]

LINCOLN CURRICULUM

The university had been the first college to create a course specifically on Lincoln by 1939, divided across three-quarters of the academic year. Those courses were upper-level electives, and they supplemented an upper-level elective course on the Civil War that had been created in 1931. All of the courses appear to have been dropped by 1955 as part of a thorough modernization of the curriculum, but a one-term, upper-level elective course that combined the Civil War and Lincoln studies reappeared by 1971. "It is believed that Lincoln and the war are subjects that are particularly relevant to this region," states the course description. By 1978, this single course had been divided into a three-term sequence, only to be split between a one-term Civil War course and a one-term Lincoln's Life course in 1982.[52]

That split continues today, but an additional course on Lincoln was created during a thorough revision of the university's core curriculum in 2006. It is a one-hour survey of Lincoln's life and his impact on America in the Civil War era. Unlike the other classes, this 100-level course is required of all freshmen who enroll at Lincoln Memorial University. It is supplemented by a 300-level course that deals more specifically with Lincoln's impact on the ideals of American government from the Civil War to today, which is also required of all students who intend to complete a degree at the university.[53]

No other institution of higher education, not even those named for Lincoln, has incorporated the study of his life and career into their curriculum. Along with the Lincoln material, the Oliver Otis Howard Papers, the Howard artifacts in the Abraham Lincoln Library and Museum, the Oliver O. Howard Papers in the University Archives, the statues and paintings that constitute a store of icons, and the long-term spiritual commitment to the ideals that motivated the founders, Lincoln Memorial University has cherished its unique heritage to the present day.

Howard statue by Rhudy Bell, 2003. A Lincoln penny is placed on the arm of the statue near Howard's heart to symbolize the connection between the two men. Earl J. Hess.

Conclusion

More than 110 years of service allows us to gauge how well the founders of Lincoln Memorial University accomplished their goals and how well their successors followed through over time to sustain the original aims of the school. At least until the presidency of Robert L. Kincaid ended in 1958, university administrators were highly aware of the consistency evident in the school's mission and in the constancy with which their predecessors had dealt with the six major themes in the history of the institution. Even after 1958, several of those themes continued to be a vital part of the school's reason for existence.

Mountain Loyalists

The only idea behind the creation of Lincoln Memorial University that came directly from Abraham Lincoln was a desire to help those hardy mountaineers of East Tennessee who had remained loyal to the Union during the Civil War. Lincoln had planted this seed in Oliver Otis Howard's mind in 1863; the general extended aid to Christopher R. Robert's school on Lookout Mountain three years later, a project that lasted no more than a few years in its effort to offer educational opportunities to the children of mountain loyalists. Then the idea remained dormant for three decades until Arthur A. Myers offered an opportunity, and Cyrus Kehr reinforced it with an idea of his own to name a school after the sixteenth president. Howard saw Lincoln Memorial University as a chance to honor Lincoln, fulfill the president's last injunction to him, and use Lincoln's image as a publicity tool in fund raising among northern donors.

Even though Myers had used the mountain loyalty theme at least once in his promotional literature for the Harrow School, in the same year as the meeting on the porch, Howard remained the champion of this theme in promoting the new institution. Indeed, no one else took it up in any serious way. In part, this was due to Howard's personal experience with mountain loyalists during the Civil War, especially during the relief march to Knoxville. It was a cause that already had a place in his heart.

But the Robert school had been founded only one year after Appomattox, when the East Tennessee loyalists were dominant in state politics. By 1897, very few people, even in East Tennessee, seem to have remembered their wartime sacrifices. Public awareness of mountain loyalty weakened after the white conservative reaction to the fall of Reconstruction state governments in the South. When Howard passed away in 1909, the theme of mountain loyalty also died away in the promotional literature of the university.

Moreover, Lincoln Memorial University had been established in a place that was surprisingly strong in its Confederate sympathies. Although Claiborne County as a whole had voted against secession, a hard core of southern supporters lived on the very spot the university would later occupy as its campus. The county raised a company for the Twenty-ninth Tennessee and some troops for the Sixty-third Tennessee later in the war.

The theme of sectional reconciliation, which Howard publicized much more than that of mountain loyalty, came to overwhelm the theme that lay at the heart of Lincoln's last commission to the general. Reconciling sectional differences became a major effort, North and South, by the 1890s, and it had more power to attract attention to the university than did the needs of mountain loyalist families. In fact, the Cumberland Gap institution prominently symbolized sectional reconciliation through its choice of school colors, blue and gray, and the naming of its first building, Grant-Lee Hall. Robert Patterson, the former captain of Company C, Twenty-ninth Tennessee, served on the first Board of Directors. Robert Kincaid, student, staff member, director, vice-president, and president of the university, was the grandson of a Confederate veteran.

It should also be noted that the university never made a sustained effort to identify and recruit sons and daughters of Union veterans. Howard merely proclaimed that this was one part of the school's early mission and left it at that. In 1928, 1930, and 1932, college administrators offered scholarships to the descendants of Union soldiers and, apparently, Confederate soldiers. Of forty surviving student applications, twenty-four (60 percent) were by descendants of Union soldiers and six (15 percent) by descendants of Rebel soldiers. The other applicants could not specify for which side their ancestors had fought or they had ancestors who had worn the uniforms of both belligerents.[1]

Lincoln Memorial University barely fulfilled its early objective to reward the descendants of mountain loyalists with an opportunity to attend college. That aim had mostly symbolic rather than practical value by 1897, even though a great many sons and daughters of Union veterans would have been of college age by then. Time greatly lessened the awareness of students in the Harrogate area about mountain loyalty. In a survey of 129 members of the freshmen class of 2009, more than 60 percent thought that the residents of East Tennessee had mostly sided with the Confederacy.

DISADVANTAGED APPALACHIAN YOUTH

The university's appeal to disadvantaged Appalachian youth was distantly related to the mountain loyalty theme. It was shorn of any hint of sectional conflict and had deeper potency and longer legs than the idea of rewarding descendants of Unionist supporters. Howard stressed the theme to elicit sympathy for those mountain youth who were left behind by the march of progress. Stooksbury and Hubbell also pushed it, and Hill employed the message in a strident, even shrill, way for public relations effect. McClelland soft pedaled the idea and Kincaid tended to use his own life story to exemplify the theme. From Provine onward, the concept of disadvantaged Appalachian youth waned considerably as it was incorporated, in a sense, into federal government aid as a result of Lyndon Johnson's war on poverty in the mid-1960s.

Of course, there was a great deal of truth to the idea that Appalachian youth had fewer educational opportunities than those in other sections of the country, but it was only a matter of degree. It has been estimated that only about 4 percent of young Americans across the nation had earned a bachelor's degree at the start of the twentieth century. Enlarged opportunities to attend college occurred primarily for "a growing middle and upper-middle class of young white men," primarily in the North and West.[2]

It is also true that a college education was generally cheaper in the South than in the North. Brown University, in Providence, Rhode Island, charged at least $393 for tuition, incidental fees, room rent, board, and books in 1907–8. In contrast, Lincoln Memorial University charged $125 for roughly the same expenses in 1907–8.[3]

The turn of the century witnessed a developing retention problem on many college campuses. At Kentucky State College (currently the University of Kentucky), only 30 percent of those freshmen who entered in 1903 completed a bachelor's degree. At Amherst College in Amherst, Massachusetts, 75–90 percent of freshmen who entered in the time period from 1880 to 1900 completed a bachelor's degree; in 1905 to 1910, that ratio plummeted to 50–60 percent. The rate was only 10 percent at Transylvania University in Kentucky at about the same time. Lincoln Memorial University experienced a somewhat similar problem, but its freshman retention rate slowly improved with time. While 35.0 percent of the freshman class of 1908–9 returned to school the next academic year, the rate climbed to 44.8 percent by the mid-1930s and 57.1 percent by the mid-1950s. Today it stands at 74.2 percent, but this last statistic measures the number of freshmen who return in the spring semester of their freshman year, not the fall semester of their sophomore year. A further measure of retention lies in the percentage of freshmen who persist to complete a four-year degree. Among the freshman class of 1908–9, only four out of seventeen (23.5 percent) accomplished that goal at Lincoln Memorial University.[4]

Perhaps the real problem in educational opportunities for Appalachian youth was one of class, not region. It was difficult for all lower-class youth, black or white, to find a way to begin college study all across America in 1900, and it was also very difficult to sustain their college career for four years. Such opportunities were particularly limited in the southern states, and more intense than usual in Appalachia, but there was not such a clear, dramatic difference between the life of Appalachians and those of poorer elements in other regions of the country as missionaries and charity workers described in their speeches, articles, and books.

Nevertheless, the concept of disadvantaged Appalachian youth had great value to fund-raisers and they utilized it for decades to come. It was a concept developed by outsiders, not Appalachians themselves, and held its greatest potency among the wealthy who lived in northern cities. Thousands of dollars came to Lincoln Memorial University because a lot of good-hearted people believed in it.

This led to some degree of tension as a handful of outsiders came to Cumberland Gap, assuming the locals were backward. Oliver Otis Howard never adopted that attitude; he genuinely tried to understand mountain culture and respected the local inhabitants. New Englander John Hale Larry, however, was openly critical, as was the Belgian Alfred R. W. deJonge, and both men were resented by the students. John Wesley Hill seemed uninterested in Appalachian youth except insofar as he could use them as stereotypes of the deeply conservative political and social values he cherished. Most faculty and staff who came to Lincoln Memorial University from the world outside Appalachia accepted the mountain people for what they were and quietly did their jobs.

Interestingly, the local area around Cumberland Gap contributed relatively little in the way of funds to the university from 1897 to the mid-twentieth century. The comparative poverty of the region may be a sufficient explanation, but perhaps the appeal to help backward Americans catch up with the rest of the country failed to find a receptive audience there. As a result, for most of its history, Lincoln Memorial University has been sustained primarily by outside money. With the expansion of federal government aid in the 1960s, it continues to rely heavily on student tuitions subsidized by grants and loans offered by outsiders, even if it is money paid to the U.S. government in the form of taxes.

Outsiders defined the "problem" of Appalachia and contributed most of the people and the money to attack it on their own terms. Whether they acted with benign paternalism, as did Howard, or with sarcastic criticism, as did Larry, the wellspring of reform was located somewhere outside the mountains. Even some insiders, such as Stooksbury and Kincaid, went along with the northern-oriented program because they realized how important the benefits could be.

What did the students think about the idea that they were disadvantaged? Evidence can only be circumstantial. Stooksbury received dozens of letters from prospective students who pled poverty and asked for a chance to prove their worth by working their way through school. The numbers of young men and women who came to Lincoln Memorial University and participated in its work-learn program seems to confirm the idea that this was the only way they could afford a college education. When faculty expansion brought a number of inspirational teachers to campus in 1928–29, bringing with them training at famous schools outside Appalachia, some of the brighter students wanted to study at those schools too. This is indicative of an awareness that home-grown institutions were inadequate for at least a few of the mountain youth.

Clifford Lyons, the Berea man who spent an unhappy year at Lincoln Memorial University in the late 1920s, thought most students at Cumberland Gap resented John Wesley Hill's branding of mountain youth as backward and in need of special, outside help. Whether that was true is difficult to say. Most student memoirs assume a rosy view of the Lincoln Memorial University experience and do not refer to this topic.

But the idea that Appalachian youth have special problems that inhibit their ability to obtain a college education continues to persist in the Harrogate area. A survey of 129 entering freshmen in the fall of 2009 revealed that 34.8 percent believed regional young people faced problems in going to college not encountered by those who grow up outside the region. It is difficult to understand the persistence of this viewpoint when one notices that many students drive to campus in SUVs, open their personal laptops in class, and demonstrate that they know more about using power point in presentations than do old professors, but the responders often cited traditional family attitudes that discourage "book larning."

Work Program

For most of its history, the chief method by which Lincoln Memorial University offered opportunities for higher education to Appalachian youth was by creating on-campus jobs for them to earn their way through school. The work-learn program was the bedrock of the university's existence from 1897 to the 1950s. Not only would most of its students have been unable to pursue a college education without that program, but the university would not have been able to exist without it. The program offered advantages to both students and institution that were vital to the goals and aspirations of job giver and job taker alike. It made of Lincoln Memorial University a true "opportunity school," to use the phrase Hubbell coined and Hill employed in his fund-raising efforts, and it allowed the institution to save money by hiring fewer salaried employees.

Administrators managed the work program efficiently from the start, in contrast to other schools that often had difficulty ironing out the details. The chief problem was how to blend class and work schedules for students and faculty. While the Cumberland Gap institution arranged for a half day of classes and a half day of work from the start, Berea continued to schedule only short work periods of at least two hours, staggered throughout the course of the day. Berea administrators had found that one-hour work periods were inefficient, but they allowed for a half day of classes and a half day of work for those students who wanted it, without mandating the more efficient schedule for everyone. At Berea, the student work force was initially supervised by the treasurer, then the registrar, and then, in 1908, by a full-time dean of labor. At Lincoln Memorial University, a combination of staff and faculty members supervised the work force through committee. The university hired a full-time labor boss, assisted by trusted student foremen, to oversee the daily work.[5]

The work program administrator at Lees-McRae College in Banner Elk, North Carolina, also had difficulty ironing out student work schedules. Founded in 1900 in the mountains of North Carolina, Lees-McRae was still a junior college when the work administrator requested information about Lincoln Memorial University's handling of this problem in 1940. The Harrogate institution was viewed, in other words, as a model of efficiency in this regard.[6]

The work-learn program was closely tied to issues related to enrollment. On the surface at least, it seemed to govern how large the student body could grow. Presidents from Stooksbury to Provine lamented the fact that there was a limit to the number of jobs the university could create and, therefore, a limit to the number of students the school could admit. Provine and others also noted that the towns of Cumberland Gap and Harrogate were too small to offer more than a handful of jobs to students.

The university's enrollment often failed to reflect significant enrollment growth across the United States. In 1939–40, nationwide enrollment in colleges and universities had amounted to 1.5 million students; in 1949–50, the number rose to 2.7 million, 3.6 million by 1960, and 7.9 million by 1970. While the larger, state-supported universities garnered the lion's share of this expansion, small private colleges compensated for their higher tuition by guaranteeing financial support for all students they admitted as a way to share in the growth of student enrollment.[7]

Lincoln Memorial University also provided financial support for nearly every student it admitted, yet it failed to share proportionately in the great, postwar expansion of college students. While 462 students were enrolled in 1938–39, the number rose only to 543 in 1946–47 and was down to 526 in 1957–58. Ironically, even when the university gave up its historic work-learn program and switched to government subsidies for student expenses in the 1960s, the enrollment continued to remain at about the same level well into the 1970s.[8]

A possible explanation for why the school's enrollment failed to reflect national growth in college enrollments lies in the population levels of the five counties that remained the core recruiting area for the university. Claiborne County had a population of 20,696 in 1900. The number of people living in the county increased from 1900 to 1910, when the university was establishing itself, but remained stable from 1910 to 1950. A significant dip occurred in the 1960s, but the county's population was up to its 1950 level by 1980 and then experienced significant growth to 2008, when it reached 31,461. It could be concluded that the university's work-learn program provided a stabilizing influence on enrollment that helped to limit the school's distress in times of decreasing population, even if it failed to offer the university an opportunity to take advantage of the benefits of increasing population. When Lincoln Memorial University switched from its work-learn program to government support for student expenses, it could take advantage of increasing population more effectively because the number of students it could admit was no longer limited by the number of jobs. The work-learn program was a poor man's way of attending college, and it was a poor college's way of surviving even in bad times.[9]

Despite 110 years of operation, the percentage of residents who hold a bachelor's degree or more remains low in the five counties that still constitute the core recruitment area for Lincoln Memorial University. Among those residents who are twenty-five years or older, the percentage is only about half the statewide average in all five counties. Many factors account for why young men and women fail to attend college. The population of the five mountain counties remains rural and primarily working class, and the five counties rank lower than state averages in almost every economic indicator. The college has no control over family, cultural attitudes, or individual characteristics that could inhibit Appalachian youth from attending institutions of higher learning.[10]

The university gave up a distinctive aspect of its heritage when it phased out the work- learn program in the 1960s and became, in that sense, like most other colleges in America. But the program had served its purpose and was outdated and unnecessary. The university remained an independent, private college. Its reliance on government support is indirect, with money funneled to individual students and used by them to pay expenses at the time of enrollment. While nearly all students today take advantage of some kind of financial support, many seem willing to consider taking on tough campus jobs to help pay their way through school. When 129 entering freshmen were asked in the fall of 2009 if they had a serious interest in returning to something like the old work-learn program, 55 percent of them said yes.

Race

It is ironic that Howard and his colleagues planted a living memorial to the Great Emancipator in a formerly Confederate state, on land once owned by a man who possessed forty slaves. The irony, however, is appropriate, for race became a perennial source of controversy and tension at the university, infusing the history of Lincoln Memorial. School officials often had to explain to confused observers why the institution was not a black college.

The founders began the university with an agenda that did not include African Americans, and in a time and place inimical to racial inclusion into any aspects of white life. Blacks were off the radar screen when benefactors discussed the descendants of mountain loyalists. It is true that both slaves and free blacks in East Tennessee contributed to the Union war effort as laborers on the Federal fortifications at Knoxville and a regiment of black heavy artillerists was raised to garrison the city in 1864, but no one paid attention to black mountain loyalists either during the conflict or afterward.

African Americans also were off the radar screen when white philanthropists considered the plight of disadvantaged Appalachian youth. Most white charity and missionary work in the South shifted from blacks to whites after the collapse of Reconstruction in the 1870s. By 1897, a white conservative backlash against Reconstruction was settling in, characterized by extensive segregationist legislation, denial of black voting rights, and suppression of black economic opportunities. At least 122 African Americans were lynched in 1897, most of them in the South.[11]

In short, the turn of the twentieth century was not a time for a struggling college to mount a crusade for racial justice. The founders had no real alternative but to create a school for whites. Within the five counties around Cumberland Gap, the proportion of the population that was African American ranged from 2.44 percent (Hancock County, Tennessee) to 11.17 percent (Bell County, Kentucky) in 1900. In Claiborne County, Tennessee, it was 3.47 percent, and in Lee County, Virginia, it was 3.72 percent. The statewide proportions of African Americans were 23.7 percent (Tennessee), 13.2 percent (Kentucky), and 35.6 percent (Virginia) in 1900.[12]

The few blacks who lived in the area around Cumberland Gap, drawn there largely by jobs in the developing city of Middlesborough, Kentucky, had precious few opportunities even for primary and secondary education, much less education on the college level. There were no black students in the Harrow School, the feeder institution during the early days of the university, and Myers seemed to be uninterested in the problems of black education. There were no black public schools of any kind in Claiborne County and none in Bell County until the Middlesboro Colored Public School became operational in 1910. There were only five black high schools in the entire state of Tennessee in 1916, the nearest one located in Knoxville. Only 3.4 percent of blacks, aged fifteen to nineteen, were enrolled in a high school in Tennessee in 1910. It would have been difficult indeed to create an all-black college at Cumberland Gap with such an insecure system of black primary and secondary education to support it.[13]

If not an all-black college, what about a biracial college, as Frost suggested? That was equally impractical, in part because of the pro-Confederate sympathies of the immediate area around the school. More important, biracial higher education became illegal in Tennessee in 1901, only a year after college operations began on the Four Seasons property. The only feasible plan for the founders was an all-white school; to have attempted anything else would have been suicidal to the fledging institution. Berea's experiment in biracial education had been troubled even before it was rendered illegal by the Kentucky legislature in 1904.

The founders of Lincoln Memorial University accommodated the tenor of the times and focused on recruiting a white student population. The same thing happened all across the South at the turn of the twentieth century, through a combination of "institutional tradition and state law." It was not solely a southern phenomenon, for even in the Northeast it was "unusual" for a black student to enroll at a white college. "Racial exclusion in higher education was a national rather than a regional phenomenon," as historian John R. Thelin has put it.[14]

When the flow of events altered and legal barriers dropped, Lincoln Memorial University also accommodated the change. It refrained from soliciting black students but readily accepted them when they applied for admission. Ironically, when the university began admitting blacks in the late 1960s, the percentage of African Americans in the population of the five surrounding counties had plummeted compared to 1900. In 1967, only 1.6 percent of Claiborne County residents and only 3.6 percent of Bell County citizens were black. The proportion of Lee County residents who were black had dropped to only 0.6 percent by then. This was due to lack of black population growth to keep pace with white population growth during the last decades of the twentieth century. In the spring of 2009, only 1.7 percent of students at Lincoln Memorial University were African American.[15]

In another area, the university had always practiced gender-inclusive policies. It brooked the trend in the Northeast and Southeast, where gender exclusion tended to be more common than in the West and Midwest. The Harrow School was coeducational as well, and women made up 34.9 percent of the enrollment at Lincoln Memorial University, on average, from 1908 to 1958, even if the women tended to study domestic sciences or education for much of that time. With the great expansion of nursing programs, among other things, the percentage of women students at all teaching sites administered by Lincoln Memorial University amounted to 68.7 percent of the total enrollment by the spring of 2009.[16]

Abraham Lincoln

By far the most enduring theme in the history of the university has been the image of Abraham Lincoln. The sixteenth president links most of the other themes; he suggested the loyalist topic in his last meeting with Howard, represented disadvantaged but deserving youth as demonstrated by his life story, was the central figure in the destruction of slavery, and strongly promoted sectional reconciliation near the end of his life. The university's commitment to Lincoln as a symbol of its mission to Appalachia has been as strong as Howard's love for the Great Emancipator, and that commitment is unique among the half dozen colleges and universities named for Lincoln.

Like any good symbol, Lincoln has meant different things to different people. For Howard, he stood for loving-kindness to everyone regardless of class or race. For John Wesley Hill, he symbolized 100 percent Americanism in a world threatened by anti-capitalist dogmas. For the striking students of 1930, he symbolized reason and justice. For modern students, his most enduring legacy is as the savior of the Union and the Great Emancipator.

The university enshrines Lincoln's image in its current mission statement by proclaiming that one aim of the institution is to teach values associated with the Civil War president: "The University strives to give students a foundation for a more productive life by upholding the principles of Abraham Lincoln's life: a dedication to individual liberty, responsibility, and improvement; a respect for citizenship; recognition of the intrinsic value of high moral and ethical standards; and a belief in a personal God."[17]

Lincoln's image has so much potency and endurance largely because he has been viewed as a common man who succeeded to greatness. This had enormous appeal in a region struggling against endemic poverty, cultural isolation, and restricted opportunities in all areas of life, including higher education.

Modernization

Efforts to modernize Appalachia, to reshape its image and offer advantages to its young people to compensate for their being "left behind" in the march of progress, lay at the heart of Lincoln Memorial University's mission for most of its history. People associated with the university tended to agree with northern missionaries such as Ellen and Arthur Myers that Appalachian culture was a problem; the people and the region had to be homogenized, so to speak, with a modernizing America. Few reformers in the mountains agreed with John C. Campbell that an alternative concept was needed, one that blended useful aspects of Appalachian culture with scientific training in selected areas of modern economics. The only aspect of regional culture that seemed acceptable to the reformers was crafts. William L. Stooksbury began the effort to produce them on campus in a small way, but it was not institutionalized until the creation of the Nancy Hanks Department in the Matthews era. In contrast to Berea College, Lincoln Memorial University never made a success of this short-lived experiment. The Nancy Hanks Department actually had little to do with preservation of folkways, despite what was stated in its promotional literature; it really was an effort to mass produce and market folk crafts for profit and to create jobs for female students.

Howard and the other founders created an old fashioned institution to reshape Appalachian life. They stressed moral training, manual arts and crafts, and the need to instill a strong sense of civic responsibility. The academic curriculum in the early years was unimaginative, the teachers had little graduate training, and they taught in several different disciplines. Pupils in the "grades" far outnumbered the college students well into the Hubbell years, and those college students underwent a rigorous regimen within a restrictive, paternalistic campus environment where work, study, and prayer was the order of the day.

This kind of school was suited for the impoverished South in 1900, but it was badly outdated compared to developing trends evident elsewhere. The modern university was fast becoming a reality in the North and West, characterized in part by a professoriate with earned graduate degrees who taught only in one discipline. Universities offered graduate programs, encouraged scholarly research, and trained graduates for scientific and technical professions. They were not necessarily dependent on affiliated grammar or secondary schools as a source of students. It is no wonder that several observers scoffed at the notion that Howard's enterprise at Cumberland Gap had the temerity to call itself a university. Until the late 1930s, it was at best a junior college with greater aspirations than accomplishments.

Hubbell began the process of slowly wrenching the institution into modern educational concepts, but limited funds derailed his ambitious plans to create professional programs in law and other areas. The university took a large financial gamble by hiring appropriate faculty and improving its facilities in 1928–29, a gamble wrecked by Hervin U. Roop's irresponsible actions and the student strike that followed. The Depression set the university's modernization program back as much as John Wesley Hill's connection with the institution retarded its acceptance by the Southern Association. Only when Hill departed, and the administration kept the ship afloat financially, did the university reach an important turning point in its effort to modernize by securing membership in the Southern Association in 1936.

Sociologist David Riesman has written of what he calls the academic procession, the effort by institutions of higher learning to copy those schools that are acknowledged as national leaders. The head of the procession consists mostly of large, prominent universities in the North and West. The middle of the procession is filled with institutions eager to improve their standing and aware of the need to change according to latest trends. The tail of the procession consists of the rest, only indifferently drifting with the current. Riesman, writing in the late 1950s, thought the tail consisted mostly of small southern colleges, often denominational and as yet unaccredited by a major agency.[18]

For the most part, Lincoln Memorial University occupied a place in the tail of the academic procession. Some of the improvements it instituted were willingly copied from the example of leading institutions, an aspect characteristic of those schools in the middle of the procession. Hubbell copied basic improvements, such as the adoption of the elective system, from the academic leaders of his day, and did so voluntarily as a presidential initiative. But many other basic improvements took place only because the Southern Association required them for admission, which seems to be more characteristic of those institutions in the tail of the procession. Through a combination of internal desire, and a great deal of outside pressure, Lincoln Memorial University could be said to have made itself into a respectable member of the tail of the academic procession by the late 1930s.

By the latter part of the twentieth century, the institution had changed a great deal from what it had been in the Howard era. The changes were fostered not only by a desire to mimic models from outside Appalachia but also, increasingly, through efforts to adapt itself to the changing needs of the mountainous area that remained its home base. Lincoln Memorial University was shaped as much by Appalachia as its people tried to shape mountain youth. The paternalistic atmosphere on campus, in which students, faculty, and staff lived and worked together in a tightly knit community (which sometimes seemed an oppressive confinement), resembled Appalachian coal camps. This atmosphere contributed to the student strike of 1930 and to the massive coal strike in the area two years later. Restrictive social regulations, and what some could identify as exploitative reliance on cheaply paid student laborers, continued until at least the 1950s as aspects of the university that Howard probably would have approved. It was not until the mid-1920s that the number of college students roughly equaled that of the academy students, and both college and academy students mostly used the same facilities on campus. Old and new concepts coexisted on campus for over half its history.[19]

Lincoln Memorial University never developed into a trade school, despite Howard's emphasis on manual training, and it never developed into a primarily liberal arts college. From the start to the late twentieth century, its most important product has been a large corps of elementary and secondary teachers who staffed regional schools. This was a particularly important objective during the university's early years, an era of fledging public school education. It also was central to the original purpose of the university, given the Harrow School, the Ellen Myers School, the Lincoln Memorial Academy, and the J. Frank White Academy. The university has a rich history of teacher training within the context of a multipurpose university, which was a growing trend in the United States by 1900, as opposed to a normal school setting.[20]

Serving regional needs has always been the basic purpose of Lincoln Memorial University, but with the creation of the Appalachian College Association in 1990, the focus shifted to a heightened sense of institutional self-awareness as an Appalachian college. The tail of the academic procession has a new role model, one that exists inside Appalachia rather than outside the mountains.

Consisting of thirty small colleges and six major state universities, with 42,500 students, the Appalachian College Association sponsors yearly conferences and workshops to provide the faculty and staff of member institutions access to latest improvements in pedagogy and to allow them to share the fruits of current scholarship. The association provides much needed grant funding for improvements in teaching and the promotion of research opportunities. Technology initiatives have been a major emphasis of its work, and the association offers help to all faculty members across the disciplines. The role model for member colleges is now the peer institution, other private colleges in the mountains, not the large northern universities. The Appalachian College Association has helped foster modern development within a mountain setting, which helps member schools to do old jobs better (such as training public school teachers), and develop new approaches to regional problems that persist into the twenty-first century.[21]

On the threshold of the new century, the emphasis at Lincoln memorial University is shifting toward professional training, within a four-year college setting, for careers in a variety of areas. Vocational instruction leading to degrees in law, engineering, and medicine coexist with older vocational programs in teaching, nursing, and business. Liberal arts programs remain comparatively small as the university continues to provide practical education for working-class Appalachian men and women into the new era. In this way, the university's goals would seem consistent with much of Oliver O. Howard's vision for a living memorial to his beloved president.

Notes

Abbreviations

AAUP	American Association of University Professors
ALLM-LMU	Abraham Lincoln Library and Museum, Lincoln Memorial University
BEC	Special Collections and Archives, Berea College
BMC	Special Collections, Bryn Mawr College
BOC	Special Collections and Archives, Bowdoin College
CGNHP	Cumberland Gap National Historical Park
CU	Rare Book and Manuscript Library, Columbia University
DU	Rare Books, Manuscripts, and Special Collections, Duke University
FHS	Filson Historical Society
GWU	Special Collections and University Archives, George Washington University
LM	Lincoln Museum
LTS	Schaff Library, Lancaster Theological Seminary
MSU	Camden-Carroll Library, Morehead State University
NARA	National Archives and Records Administration
OHS	Archives/Manuscripts Division, Ohio Historical Society
OR	*The War of the Rebellion: A Compilation of the Official Records of the Union and Confederate Armies.* 70 vols. in 128. Washington, D.C.: Government Printing Office, 1880–1901
RU	Rockefeller Archives Center, Rockefeller University
SC-LMU	Special Collections, Lincoln Memorial University
SC-UTC	Special Collections, University of Tennessee, Chattanooga
SC-UTK	Special Collections, University of Tennessee, Knoxville
THF	Benson Ford Research Center, The Henry Ford
TU	Amistad Research Center, Tulane University
UA-LMU	University Archives, Lincoln Memorial University
UA-UTK	University Archives, University of Tennessee, Knoxville
UC	Special Collections Research Center, University of Chicago
UCB	Bancroft Library, University of California, Berkeley
UI	Special Collections Department, University of Iowa
UL	Special Collections, University of Louisville
UNC	Southern Historical Collection, University of North Carolina

PREFACE

1. Kincaid's *Wilderness Road,* published in 1947, was reprinted in 1955, 1966, 1973, 1992, and 1999; Avery to Cyrus Kehr, Sept. 8, 1934, Frederick B. Avery Papers, UA-LMU; "Passing of a Founder of Lincoln Memorial University," 2; Suppiger's *Phoenix of the Mountains,* published in 1977, was updated and reprinted in 1988 and 2001.

CHAPTER 1

A LARGER ENTERPRISE

Epigraph: Howard, "Personal Recollections of Abraham Lincoln," 877.

1. Kincaid, *Wilderness Road,* 340; Carpenter, "Architects and Builders," 10; *Harrow School of Cumberland Gap, Tennessee,* 1895–96, and Harrow School *Catalogue,* 1897–98, SC-LMU.

2. *National Cyclopaedia of American Biography* 30: 409; Carpenter, *Sword and Olive Branch,* 293; Howard, "Personal Recollections of Abraham Lincoln," 877.

3. Carpenter, "Architects and Builders," 10.

4. Donald, *Lincoln,* 21; Kincaid, "Crossing the Great Wilderness," 61.

5. Groce, *Mountain Rebels,* 1, 37, 39, 41; McKenzie, "Oh! Ours Is a Deplorable Condition," 203.

6. Coulter, "Parson Brownlow's Tour," 5, 8–27; Maynard's statement, enclosed in Maynard to Henry Halleck, Dec. 13, 1862, *OR* 20, pt. 2, 168–70; Johnson to Lincoln, May 29, 1863, in Graf and Haskins, *Papers of Andrew Johnson* 6: 233.

7. Lincoln to Buell, Jan. 6, 1862, and Buell to McClellan, Feb. 1, 1862, *OR* 7: 928, 931–32; Stanton to Halleck, June 30, 1862, and Lincoln to Halleck, June 30, 1862, *OR* 17, pt. 2, 52, 53; Lincoln memorandum, prior to Oct. 31, 1861, *OR* 52, pt. 1, 191–92; Johnson to Halleck, June 5, 1862, in Graf and Haskins, *Papers of Andrew Johnson* 5: 442; Johnson to Lincoln, Jan. 11, 1863, in Graf and Haskins, *Papers of Andrew Johnson* 6: 114.

8. Burnside to Johnson, Sept. 9, 1863, in Graf and Haskins, *Papers of Andrew Johnson* 6: 359; Lincoln to Williams and Taylor, Oct. 17, 1863, *OR* 30, pt. 4, 448; Halleck to Grant, Jan. 18, 1864, *OR* 32, pt. 2, 127; "Depositions in the case of Furney Jones vs. Burchfield et al.," Diaries and Pocket-Size Scrapbooks and Account Books, ALLM-LMU; McKenzie, "Oh! Ours Is a Deplorable Condition," 210.

9. Carpenter, *Sword and Olive Branch,* 1–3, 5–6, 11, 17–19; Howard, *Autobiography* 1: 29, 36, 40–41, 66, 69; Howard to John Otis, June 24, 1850, Box 1, Folder 1, Oliver Otis Howard Papers, ALLM-LMU; Howard speech, *Atlanta Constitution,* July 20, 1900.

10. Howard, *Autobiography* 1: 11, 14, 20.

11. Oliver Otis Howard, "Reminiscences of Lincoln: Address at Young Men's Republican Club, Montpelier, VT. Feb. 12, 1896," 1–4, O. O. Howard Papers, BOC.

12. Carpenter, *Sword and Olive Branch,* 23, 26, 30; Small, *Road to Richmond,* 9; Howard to wife, June 3, 1861, O. O. Howard Papers, BOC; Howard, *Autobiography* 1: 94–95.

13. Howard, "Personal Recollections of Abraham Lincoln," 873, 876; Howard, *Autobiography* 1: 137.

14. Howard, "Personal Recollections of Abraham Lincoln," 873–74; Oliver Otis Howard, "Some Reminiscences of Abraham Lincoln," Mar. 1, 1895, pp. 1–2, and Howard, "Reminiscences of Lincoln," 5, O. O. Howard Papers, BOC.

15. Carpenter, *Sword and Olive Branch,* 30, 32–34, 40–43; Howard, *Autobiography* 1: 245–51, 309, 349–50; Howard to Norvell, June 3, 1862, *OR* 11, pt. 1, 769–70; Oliver Otis Howard, "Fair Oaks Again," clipping from *National Tribune,* n.d., Scrapbook, Box 6, Oliver Otis Howard Papers, ALLM-LMU; Howard, "Some Reminiscences of Abraham Lincoln," Mar. 1, 1895, pp. 2–4, O. O. Howard Papers, BOC; Howard, "Personal Recollections of Abraham Lincoln," 875. Howard received a Congressional Medal of Honor in 1893 for his wounding at Fair Oaks. See Robert L. Kincaid, "General Oliver Otis Howard, Soldier in Peace and War," 12, Robert L. Kincaid Papers, UA-LMU.

16. Schurz, *Reminiscences* 2: 405, 432–33; Carpenter, *Sword and Olive Branch,* 44–49; Howard to Hooker, May 13, 1863, *OR* 25, pt. 1, 630; Howard, "Eleventh Corps at Chancellorsville," 196, 198, 200–201; Howard, *Autobiography* 1: 374–76, 378; Howard, "Some Reminiscences of Abraham Lincoln," Mar. 1, 1895, 4–5, and Howard to wife, May 12, 22, 1863, O. O. Howard Papers, BOC; Howard, "Personal Recollections of Abraham Lincoln," 876. Ironically, despite the trauma caused by the defeat at Chancellorsville, Howard named one of his sons Chancey because the child was born during the time of the campaign. See Howard, *Autobiography* 2: 546.

17. Howard, *Autobiography* 1: 410; Carpenter, *Sword and Olive Branch,* 52–54, 56–57; Howard to Meade, July 1, 1863, *OR* 27, pt. 1, 696–97; Howard, "Personal Recollections of Abraham Lincoln," 876; Howard to Lincoln, July 18, 1863, in Basler, *Collected Works of Abraham Lincoln* 6: 341n; Howard to wife, Aug. 29, 1863, O. O. Howard Papers, BOC.

18. Carpenter, *Sword and Olive Branch,* 58; Howard, *Autobiography* 1: 452–53; Howard, "Personal Recollections of Abraham Lincoln," 877; Howard to wife, Oct. 13, 1863, Howard, "Some Reminiscences of Abraham Lincoln," Mar. 1, 1895, 5–6, and Howard, "Reminiscences of Lincoln," 5, O. O. Howard Papers, BOC; untitled address on Lincoln, 17–18, Oliver Otis Howard Papers, ALLM-LMU. Howard repeated the story of his last meeting with Lincoln many times late in his life, often embellishing the details to suit his particular audience. He claimed that Lincoln asked him if he could march through Cumberland Gap in order to "seize" Knoxville, and Howard replied that he would have

to work within the framework of plans developed by Ulysses S. Grant and therefore could not commit to such an endeavor. These details could not be correct, for Ambrose E. Burnside had captured Knoxville three weeks earlier, as everyone in Washington knew, and Grant was not made commander of all Union forces in the West until October and thus as yet had no authority to direct plans at Chattanooga. Howard used the map Lincoln gave him at that last meeting throughout the Chattanooga campaign and the early phase of the Atlanta campaign. In January 1865, he donated it to the Colliaison Society at Kent's Hill Academy in Maine. It was still there as late as 1930. See "Lincoln's Map of Cumberland Gap Region," 18; McMurtry, "They Are Loyal There," 8–9; Harry S. Howard to editor of *Mountain Herald,* Jan. 16, 1930, Oliver O. Howard Papers, UA-LMU.

19. Howard, *Autobiography* 1: 462, 492; Howard to wife, Mar. 8, 1864, quoted in Holloway, *Laura C. Howard,* 113–14; Carpenter, *Sword and Olive Branch,* 61; Howard, "Folk of the Cumberland Gap," 506; Howard to Perkins, Dec. 28, 1863, *OR* 31, pt. 2, 352; Howard, "Personal Recollections of Abraham Lincoln," 877.

20. Howard, *Autobiography* 1: 481–82; Schurz, *Reminiscences* 3: 79–80; Sherman to Howard, Dec. 18, 1863, *OR* 31, pt. 3, 439–40.

21. Sherman to Ellen, July 26, 1864, in Simpson and Berlin, *Sherman's Civil War,* 672; Dawson, *Gen. John A. Logan,* 505–6; Herbert, *Fighting Joe Hooker,* 285; Hooker to Wilson, Dec. 8, 1864, *OR* 45, pt. 2, 110; Grant, *Personal Memoirs* 2: 638; Carpenter, *Sword and Olive Branch,* 70.

22. Sherman to Ellen, July 29, Aug. 2, 1864, and Sherman to Halleck, July 27, Sept. 4, 1864, in Simpson and Berlin, *Sherman's Civil War,* 673, 676, 681, 700; Howard to wife, July 29, 1864, and Howard, "Ezra Church," Oct. 4, 1894, 3, O. O. Howard Papers, BOC; Howard, *Autobiography* 1: 536–37.

23. Howard, "Struggle for Atlanta," 319–20; Howard to Dayton, Sept. 17, 1864, and General Field Orders No. 16, Headquarters, Department and Army of the Tennessee, Sept. 10, 1864, *OR* 38, pt. 3, 40–41, 50; Howard, *Autobiography* 2: 35; Carpenter, *Sword and Olive Branch,* 71–72.

24. Howard to Dayton, Sept. 17, 1864, *OR* 38, pt. 3, 47; Harwell and Racine, *Fiery Trail,* 98; Howard, "Sherman and the March to the Sea," Box 5, Folder 5b, Oliver Otis Howard Papers, ALLM-LMU.

25. Howard, *Autobiography* 2: 102, 124, 152; Howard to Sherman, Jan. 15, 1865, and Howard to Blair, Feb. 20, 1865, and General Field Orders No. 12, Headquarters, Department and Army of the Tennessee, Mar. 5, 1865, *OR* 47, pt. 2, 54, 505–6, 686; Harwell and Racine, *Fiery Trail,* 92–93, 100; Pepper, *Personal Recollections,* 502; Nichols, *Story of the Great March,* 141, 143; Carpenter, *Sword and Olive Branch,* 73, 84.

26. Howard, *Autobiography* 2: 159, 207–8; Howard to mother, Apr. 17, 1865, quoted in Carpenter, *Sword and Olive Branch,* 81; Sherman to Howard, quoted in Howard, *Autobiography* 2: 209.

27. Carpenter, *Sword and Olive Branch,* 87, 90–91, 111, 122, 157; Howard, *Autobiography* 2: 215, 218; Howard to editor of *Evening Bulletin,* July 16, 1870, quoted in Holloway, *Laura C. Howard,* 223; McFeely, *Yankee Stepfather,* 103–4, 110, 116; Howard to T. D. Eliot, Feb. 18, 1868, Box 3, Folder 21, Oliver Otis Howard Papers, ALLM-LMU.

28. Howard, *Autobiography* 2: 390, 396–401, 408–10, 413, 415–16, 452–53; Carpenter, *Sword and Olive Branch,* 180; Horace M. Bond to Robert Kincaid, Apr. 2, 1951, and Howard to Mrs. M. F. Armstrong, Sept. 10, 1873, quoted in letter by acting president of Hampton Institute to Robert Kincaid, May 1, 1951, Oliver O. Howard Papers, UA-LMU.

29. Abbott, "Mountain School," 70, 72–73; Howard to Grant, Feb. 20, 1868, Simon, *Papers of Ulysses S. Grant* 18: 514–15; Howard, *Autobiography* 2: 402–14.

30. Howard to James E. Rhoades, Oct. 9, 1865, Howard to Gen. Brown, Feb. 20, 1867, Howard diary, Jan. 10, 1871, and Howard letter, Dec. 7, 1883, quoted in Holloway, *Laura C. Howard,* 212, 215, 225, 229; Howard, *Autobiography* 2: 391, 394.

31. Carpenter, *Sword and Olive Branch,* 203–8, 229–35, 272; Hooker quoted in Carpenter, *Sword and Olive Branch,* 24–25; Howard, *Autobiography* 2: 455.

32. Howard, *Autobiography* 2: 416, 446, 460–61, 474–75; Carpenter, *Sword and Olive Branch,* 243, 246–65, 272, 277–81.

33. Howard to Osborn H. Oldroyd, Jan. 13, 1882, O. O. Howard Papers, BOC; Howard *Autobiography* 2: 552; Howard to Sherman, Dec. 30, 1884, quoted in Holloway, *Laura C. Howard,* 224, 231; Sherman to Mrs. Howard, Feb. 8, 1889, Box 3, Folder 16, Oliver Otis Howard Papers, ALLM-LMU; Dodge, *Personal Recollections,* 230.

34. Howard, *Autobiography* 1: 441–42 and 2: 473–74, 565, 575; Carpenter, *Sword and Olive Branch,* 283; "Grant and His Generals," Box 4, Folders 8 and 9, Oliver Otis Howard Papers, ALLM-LMU; Howard, "Some Reminiscences of Abraham Lincoln," Mar. 1, 1895, O. O. Howard Papers, BOC; publicity release about Harry S. Howard and Robert L. Kincaid to Harry S. Howard, July 6, 1949, Oliver O. Howard Papers, UA-LMU.

35. A. A. Myers to Harry S. Howard, June 9, 1896, Myers to Harry S. Howard, June 13, 1896, and Harry S. Howard to Oliver O. Howard, June 15, [1896], O. O. Howard Papers, BOC; Kincaid, *Wilderness Road,* 339–40; Carpenter, "Architects and Builders," 10.

36. Oliver O. Howard Engagement Book, Jan. 15, Mar. 8–Apr. 27, 1895, and June 1–20, 1896, Oliver Otis Howard Papers, ALLM-LMU. Years later Howard felt embarrassed by the thought that he had accepted money to talk to the audience at the

Harrow School. See Fairchild to Charles F. Eager, Apr. 18, 1920, Eugene P. Fairchild Papers, UA-LMU.

37. *National Cyclopaedia of American Biography* 23: 219; Clara M. Klippel to Kincaid, Jan. 29, 1940 [probably 1941], Robert L. Kincaid Papers, UA-LMU; Cornelia F. Avery to Robert L. Kincaid, Jan. 31, 1941, Frederick B. Avery Papers, UA-LMU.

38. Carolyn Myers Lundstrom, "A. A. Myers," 1, 3, and Lundstrom to Lee Ann Garland, May 5, 2004, Arthur A. Myers Papers, UA-LMU; *History of La Salle County, Illinois* 2: 656–57; Mrs. Vernon Denham to Kincaid, July 11, 1940, Robert L. Kincaid Papers, UA-LMU; Ernest G. Dodge to Kincaid, July 21, 1940, Robert L. Kincaid Collection, CGNHP; Kincaid, *Wilderness Road,* 332–33.

39. E. H. Fairchild, J. A. R. Rogers, and John G. Fee to Executive Committee, American Missionary Association, Feb. 6, 1878, and E. H. Fairchild to M. E. Strieby, May 15, 1878, American Missionary Association Archives, TU; Fairchild to Charles F. Eager, Apr. 18, 1920, Eugene P. Fairchild Papers, UA-LMU; Ernest G. Dodge to Kincaid, July 21, 1940, Robert L. Kincaid Collection, CGNHP.

40. Kincaid, *Wilderness Road,* 332–33; Suppiger, *Phoenix of the Mountains,* 6; Lundstrom, "A. A. Myers," 1–2, Arthur A. Myers Papers, UA-LMU; Mrs. Vernon Denham to Kincaid, July 11, 1940, and Clara M. Klippel to Kincaid, Jan. 29, 1940 [probably 1941], Robert L. Kincaid Papers, UA-LMU; Avery speech [1933], 7, Frederick B. Avery Papers, UA-LMU; Ernest G. Dodge to Kincaid, July 21, 1940, and Mrs. L. D. Denham, "Work of Rev. A. A. Myers At Williamsburg, KY.," Robert L. Kincaid Collection, CGNHP. When future Lincoln Memorial University president Robert L. Kincaid came to Cumberland Gap as a student in 1912, he saw "an old hand organ" on campus and later wondered if it had been the one used by the Myers in their missionary work. See Kincaid to Ernest G. Dodge, July 25, 1940, Robert L. Kincaid Papers, UA-LMU.

41. Shapiro, *Appalachia on Our Mind,* x, xiv, xvi.

42. Ibid., 64, 119–21.

43. Mrs. A. A. Myers, "Mountain White Work in Kentucky," 12–15.

44. Ibid., 14–16.

45. Kincaid, *Wilderness Road,* 99–105.

46. Kincaid, *Wilderness Road,* 298–99, 303–4, 312–13, 315–17, 319, 321–22, 324; Allen, "Through Cumberland Gap," 65–66; Warner, "Comments on Kentucky," 263–65; Arthur to G. W. Albrecht, Oct. 26, 1904, Alexander A. Arthur Family Papers, UA-LMU; Roberts, "Building of Middlesborough," 19; Eller, *Miners, Millhands, and Mountaineers,* 80–84; promotional booklet titled *Cumberland Gap: Its Geographical and Commercial Features and Importance as a Railroad Centre,* 7–14, 30–43, SC-UTK.

47. Kincaid, *Wilderness Road,* 326, 333–35, 338; Eller, *Miners, Millhands, and Mountaineers,* 84; Arthur to G. W. Albrecht, Oct. 26, 1904, Alexander A. Arthur Family Papers, UA-LMU; Charles Blanton Roberts, "A Notable Era in Kentucky History," 16–17, Charles Blanton Roberts Papers, FHS.

48. Kincaid, *Wilderness Road,* 313, 329; "Story of a Building," 15; *Harrogate, Tennessee,* 4, CGNHP; Suppiger, *Phoenix of the Mountains,* 5.

49. "Memorandum of Conversation with Mrs. Dora Harbison Thomas, 201 E. Chestnut St., Louisville, Ky., at the home of her son, Joe E. Thomas, 316 Cedar Street, Pineville, Ky., Oct. 2, 1940," and transcript of Robert F. Patterson to Mrs. A. A. Arthur, ca. 1898, and "Memorandum of conversation with Mrs. A. A. Arthur, Knoxville, Tenn., in 1938," Robert L. Kincaid Collection, CGNHP. Huff was the largest slave owner, and Patterson the second largest, in Claiborne County in 1860. Huff listed himself as a farmer born in Virginia, eighty years of age, with a wife and two children. His real estate was valued at $111,800, while his personal estate was valued at $32,775. Patterson had six children, was aged sixty-one, and had real estate valued at $32,000 and a personal estate valued at $29,135. See Kennedy, *Agriculture of the United States in 1860,* 238; Slave Schedule, Claiborne County, 1860, M653, Roll 1281, NARA; Population Schedules of the Eighth Census of the United States, 1860, M653, Roll 1244, NARA.

50. "Reminiscences of Middlesboro, Harrogate, and Cumberland Gap by Walter E. Bryson," 6, SC-UTK; Avery speech, [1933], 10, Frederick B. Avery Papers, UA-LMU; *Harrogate, Tennessee,* 7, CGNHP; Kincaid, *Wilderness Road,* 336; Suppiger, *Phoenix of the Mountains,* 8.

51. Kincaid, *Wilderness Road,* 336; *Harrogate, Tennessee,* 6, CGNHP; Suppiger, *Phoenix of the Mountains,* 8–9; "Story of a Building," 16.

52. Ella M. Hubbell to Kincaid, Sept. 3, 1947, Robert L. Kincaid Papers, UA-LMU; Kehr to Howard, Sept. 12, 1898, Cyrus Kehr Papers, UA-LMU; Kincaid, *Wilderness Road,* 337, 339; Suppiger, *Phoenix of the Mountains,* 9; Avery speech, [1933], 10, Frederick B. Avery Papers, UA-LMU. According to local reports, the physicians at the sanitarium quarreled over whether allopathic or homeopathic methods should be used. [Robert L. Kincaid], "Memo of conversation with Miss Manning," Robert L. Kincaid Papers, UA-LMU.

53. J. H. Rector to Avery, [ca. 1934], Frederick B. Avery Papers, UA-LMU; "Memorandum of Conversation with James H. Rector, Harrogate, Tenn., September 19, 1940, in the office of Lincoln Memorial University," Robert L. Kincaid Collection, CGNHP; Kincaid, *Wilderness Road,* 331–33, 337; [Charles F. Eager], "Lincoln Memorial University Outgrowth of Myers' School," essay serving as "Preface to Dr. F. B. Avery's History of Lincoln Memorial University," Frederick B. Avery Papers, UA-LMU; *Harrow School of Cumberland Gap, Tennessee,* 1895–96, 3, *Harrow School of Cumberland Gap, Tennessee,* 1896–97, 3–4, and Harrow School *Catalogue,* 1897–98, 2, SC-LMU.

54. Kincaid, *Wilderness Road,* 337; William H. Davis to Stanley McCordock, Nov. 4, 1942, Harrow Hall Folder, Buildings Papers, UA-LMU; [Eager], "Lincoln Memorial University Outgrowth of Myers' School," Frederick B. Avery Papers, UA-LMU; *Harrow School of Cumberland Gap, Tennessee,* 1895–96, 2, SC-LMU; "Harrow School Fathers Great Lincoln Memorial." Only the main, middle section of the casino became Harrow School, the two end sections were not built. See illustration in *Harrogate, Tennessee,* 5, CGNHP.

55. Kincaid, "Last of the Founders," 29; Clara M. Klippel to Kincaid, Jan. 29, 1940 [probably 1941], Robert K. Kincaid Papers, UA-LMU; Avery speech, [1933], 1–3, Avery to Charles F. Eager, May 3, 1920, and Avery to Mr. Mather, May 14, 1926, Frederick B. Avery Papers, UA-LMU.

56. Avery speech, [1933], 1, 3, 6, 9–10, and Cornelia F. Avery to Robert L. Kincaid, Jan. 31, 1941, Frederick B. Avery Papers, UA-LMU; Frederick B. Avery to Mr. Rector, May 8, 1935, Robert L. Kincaid Collection, CGNHP. Other efforts to create colleges around Cumberland Gap included Arthur College in nearby Arthur, Tennessee, which was organized by D. C. Webster in 1891 and destroyed by fire about 1914. Local people proposed the University of Cumberland Gap in 1891, but it never got off the ground. Cumberland Gap Baptist College operated for a short while in a bankrupt hotel in Shawanee, Tennessee, beginning in 1900. See transcripts of articles in *Middlesboro Daily News,* June 19, 1891, Sept. 2, 1899, *Baptist Evangelist,* Apr. 1900, and "Memorandum of conversation with Dan C. Webster, son of the founder of Arthur College, at Arthur, in December, 1939, in his office in Lexington, Ky.," Robert L. Kincaid Collection, CGNHP.

57. Harry S. Howard to Charles F. Eager, Apr. 15, 1921, Oliver O. Howard Papers, UA-LMU.

58. Ibid.; Howard, *Autobiography* 2: 568; Howard, "Folk of the Cumberland Gap," 506; Kincaid, *Wilderness Road,* 340–42. Kincaid believes that Howard told the story of his last meeting with Lincoln to the group assembled on the porch, but there is no evidence in the primary sources to support this assumption.

CHAPTER 2

A MONUMENT TO ABRAHAM LINCOLN

Epigraph: Copy of charter application, Charter Folder, UA-LMU.

1. Cornelia F. Avery to Robert L. Kincaid, Jan. 31, 1941, Frederick B. Avery Papers, UA-LMU; Howard to William E. Barton, Apr. 6, 1897, O. O. Howard Papers, BOC.

2. *National Cyclopaedia of American Biography* 30: 409; biographical sketch, Cyrus Kehr Papers, UA-LMU; Harry S. Howard to Charles F. Eager, Apr. 15, 1921, Oliver O. Howard Papers, UA-LMU; Oliver O. Howard Engagement Book, Apr. 16, 1895, Oliver Otis Howard Papers, ALLM-LMU.

3. Statement, Apr. 28, 1920, Cyrus Kehr Papers, UA-LMU; Howard to William E. Barton, Apr. 6, 1897, and Kehr to Howard, June 6, 1900, O. O. Howard Papers, BOC; Carpenter, "Architects and Builders," 10. Kehr asserted in 1920 that he had all along thought of Cumberland Gap as the place to erect the school named after Lincoln, based on a magazine article he had read about that region, but there is no evidence to support his contention. Walter Evans was born and lived his entire life in middle Kentucky, not in the mountains. He served as an officer in the Union army and held a seat in Kentucky's delegation to the U.S. House of Representatives from 1895 to 1899. Biographical Directory of the United States Congress, http://www.bioguide.congress.gov/.

4. Kehr to Howard, July 15, July 30, 1896, Jan. 23, 1898, O. O. Howard Papers, BOC; statement, Apr. 28, 1920, Cyrus Kehr Papers, UA-LMU; "The Saga of the Reverend and Mrs. A. A. Myers," Arthur A. Myers Papers, UA-LMU; Kincaid, *Wilderness Road,* 342–43.

5. Kehr to Howard, July 30, 1896, O. O. Howard Papers, BOC.

6. Ibid.

7. Howard to Kehr, Sept. 18, 1896, Jan. 4, 1897, O. O. Howard Papers, BOC; Howard, *Autobiography* 2: 569, 574; Carpenter, *Sword and Olive Branch,* 291–92.

8. Kehr to Eager, Oct. 10, 1896, and Kehr memo, Nov. 5, 1896, Cyrus Kehr Papers, UA-LMU; Harrow School *Catalogue,* 1896–97, SC-LMU; Myers to Eager, Oct. 24, 1896, Arthur A. Myers Papers, UA-LMU.

9. Reprint of editorial in the *Interior,* Jan. 20, 1898, attached to Kehr to Howard, Sept. 12, 1898, Cyrus Kehr Papers, UA-LMU.

10. Statement, Apr. 28, 1920, Cyrus Kehr Papers, UA-LMU; copy of charter application, and William S. Morgan to Charles F. Eager, Feb. 16, Mar. 4, 1897, Charter Folder, UA-LMU; Howard to James Bertram, Jan. 19, 1903, Oliver O. Howard Papers, UA-LMU; Kincaid, *Wilderness Road,* 343. The university changed the name of the "Board of Directors" to the "Board of Trustees" in 1940.

11. Copy of charter application, Charter Folder, UA-LMU; "Confederate Veteran's Tribute to Abraham Lincoln," obituary, and Robert F. Patterson, "Personal Recollections of Gen. Robt. E. Lee in Peace and in War," Robert F. Patterson, Board of Directors/Trustees Papers, UA-LMU; Seth Barton to Samuel Cooper, Jan. 1, 1863, and cards in Robert F. Patterson service record, 29th Tennessee, NARA; list of officers, Company C, 29th Tennessee, *Supplement to the Official Records,* pt. 2, vol. 67, 111; Seth M. Barton to

J. J. Reeve, Jan. 5, 1863, *OR* 17, pt. 1, 678; "Wonderful Ride," 28; Barton to Reeve, June 18, 1863, *OR* 24, pt. 2, 100; Robert F. Patterson service record, Compiled Service Records of Confederate General and Staff Officers, and Non-Regimental Enlisted Men, NARA.

12. Howard, "Folk of the Cumberland Gap," 507.

13. Directors' Minutes, Feb. 18, 1897, ALLM-LMU; copy of resolution to create Ellen M. Myers School, n.d., Board of Directors/Trustees Papers, UA-LMU; Carpenter, *Sword and Olive Branch,* 294; Lundstrom, "A. A. Myers," 1, and "Saga of the Reverend and Mrs. A. A. Myers," Arthur A. Myers Papers, UA-LMU; Kincaid, *Wilderness Road,* 344; Mrs. Charles Belden to Kincaid, Aug. 17, 1940, Robert L. Kincaid Papers, UA-LMU; Ernest G. Dodge to Kincaid, July 21, 1940, Robert L. Kincaid Collection, CGNHP.

14. Charles F. Eager, "Partial Statement to Managing Director of Receipts and Disbursements, from July 15, 1898 to April 1st, 1900," Box 43, Folder 55, and Cyrus Kehr to Howard, Jan. 23, 1898, O. O. Howard Papers, BOC; Directors' Minutes, Feb. 18, 1897, ALLM-LMU; Howard, "Folk of the Cumberland Gap," 507; Myers to Board of Directors, Dec. 13, 1897, Arthur A. Myers Papers, UA-LMU.

15. Drawing of Lincoln Memorial University flag, and Cyrus Kehr to Charles F. Eager, Mar. 1, 1897, Cyrus Kehr Papers, UA-LMU; Kincaid, *Wilderness Road,* 343; Robert L. Kincaid, "General Howard and Lincoln's Last Commission," Feb. 7, 1951, Robert L. Kincaid Papers, UA-LMU; Directors' Minutes, Feb. 18, 1897, UA-LMU; Lincoln Memorial University brochure, before Jan. 21, 1898, Appalachian Vertical Files, BEC.

16. Howard to John Wanamaker, Oct. 1, 1897, O. O. Howard Papers, BOC; Harry S. Howard to Charles F. Eager, Apr. 15, 1921, Oliver O. Howard Papers, UA-LMU.

17. Kehr to Eager, May 12, 1897, Cyrus Kehr Papers, UA-LMU; Fairchild to Eager, Apr. 18, 1920, Eugene P. Fairchild Papers, UA-LMU; G. W. Easton to Hughes, Dec. 6, 1897, Herman Y. Hughes Papers, UA-LMU; Kehr to Howard, Jan. 23, 1898, O. O. Howard Papers, BOC.

18. Kehr to Howard, May 7, 1898, and enclosed draft of letter to Board of Directors, O. O. Howard Papers, BOC; Howard to not stated, May 31, 1898, Box 3, Folder 1, Oliver Otis Howard Papers, ALLM-LMU.

19. Cyrus Kehr, "Report of the President of the University, May 24, 1898," Cyrus Kehr Papers, UA-LMU.

20. Ibid.; Jesse L. Rogers to Eager, Apr. 27, 1899, Charles F. Eager Papers, UA-LMU.

21. Howard to Eager, June 13, 1898, Oliver O. Howard Papers, UA-LMU; Directors' Minutes, July 15, 1898, ALLM-LMU.

22. Howard, *Autobiography* 2: 570–71; Carpenter, *Sword and Olive Branch,* 295; Kehr to Eager, Aug. 13, 1898, Cyrus Kehr Papers, UA-LMU; Fairchild to Eager, Aug. 12, 1898, Eugene P. Fairchild Papers, UA-LMU.

23. Howard to Kehr, Aug. 25, 1898, O. O. Howard Papers, BOC; Howard to Eager, Aug. 26, 1898, Oliver O. Howard Papers, UA-LMU.

24. Kehr to Howard, Sept. 12, 1898, and Howard to Attila Cox, Sept. 15, 1898, Oliver O. Howard Papers, UA-LMU.

25. Howard circular, Oct. 2, 1898, Oliver O. Howard Papers, UA-LMU; J. D. Gardiner to Eager, Nov. 6, 1898, Charles F. Eager Papers, UA-LMU; Howard to Myers, Aug. 22, 1898, O. O. Howard Papers, BOC. For letters regarding early donations to LMU, see Howard to Eager, Nov. 1, 1898, F. P. Stillman to Howard, Nov. 30, 1898, Miriam L. Woodbury to Howard, Dec. 8, 1898, and Edward W. Beach to Howard, Jan. 5, 1899, Oliver O. Howard Papers, UA-LMU; Fred Anderson to Eager, Nov. 30, 1898, and Bessie Howard to Eager, Dec. 12, 17, 19, 1898, Charles F. Eager Papers, UA-LMU.

26. Attila Cox to Howard, Jan. 18, 1899, Howard to Eager, Jan. 23, 25, 1899, Howard note to Eager written on D. K. Pearsons to Howard, Feb. 11, 1899, and Howard to Eager, Mar. 2, 1899, Oliver O. Howard Papers, UA-LMU; Eager to Howard, Nov. 29, 1898, Kehr to Howard, May 7, 1898, and Howard to D. K. Pearsons, Feb. 9, 1899, O. O. Howard Papers, BOC; Fairchild to Eager, Feb. 6, 9, 21, 24, 1899, Eugene P. Fairchild Papers, UA-LMU.

27. Howard to Eager, Feb. 25, 1899, and Howard to Eager, Mar. 17, 1899, Oliver O. Howard Papers, UA-LMU; Fairchild to Eager, Mar. 8, 1899, Eugene P. Fairchild Papers, UA-LMU.

28. Eager to Howard, Feb. 20, 1899, Charles F. Eager Papers, UA-LMU; Howard to Eager, Feb. 15, 1899, Oliver O. Howard Papers, UA-LMU; Fairchild to Eager, Feb. 24, 1899, Eugene P. Fairchild Papers, UA-LMU. The farm managers were, in turn, Meb Overton, Mr. Gee, James H. Rector, and Lon Harmon. "Memorandum of conversation with James H. Rector, Harrogate, Tenn., September 19, 1940," Robert L. Kincaid Collection, CGNHP.

29. Howard to Eager, written on D. K. Pearsons to Howard, Feb. 11, 1899, Oliver O. Howard Papers, UA-LMU; Edith M. Fairchild, Belle M. Blanchard, R. Laurence Baylor, and Smith S. Treat to Executive Committee of Harrow School, Mar. 6, 1899, and R. F. Patterson, M. F. Overton, and Charles F. Eager to G. W. Lawrence, n.d., Board of Directors/Trustees Papers, UA-LMU; Howard to Eager, Mar. 11, 1899, Oliver O. Howard Papers, UA-LMU.

30. Howard to Eager, Jan. 30, Mar. 11, 1899, Oliver O. Howard Papers, UA-LMU; Fairchild to Eager, Jan. 16, Feb. 21, 24, 1899, Eugene P. Fairchild Papers, UA-LMU.

31. Howard to Pearsons, Feb. 9, 1899, O. O. Howard Papers, BOC.

32. Howard to Attila Cox, Sept. 15, 1898, and Howard to Eager, Jan. 25, 1899, Oliver O. Howard Papers, UA-LMU.

33. Howard to Andrew Carnegie, Mar. 13, 1899, Series II, Reel 73, Carnegie Corporation of New York Records, CU; Howard to Mr. and Mrs. Russell Sage, Apr. 18, 1899, Box 83, Folder 785, Russell Sage Foundation Records, RU.

34. Howard to Eager, July 7, 25, Aug. 1, Sept. 12, 1899, Oliver O. Howard Papers, UA-LMU.

35. Howard to Eager, Mar. 3, 1899, with enclosed copy of *Lincoln University Herald,* Oliver O. Howard Papers, UA-LMU; Nwachuku, "Lincoln University," 1618–19; http://www.lincolnu.edu/.

36. Howard to editor of *Lincoln University Herald,* Mar. 3, 1899, Oliver O. Howard Papers, UA-LMU.

37. Howard to Eager, Mar. 3, 1899, Oliver O. Howard Papers, UA-LMU; Directors Minutes, May 17, 1899, ALLM-LMU; Eager to Howard, Mar. 8, 1899, O. O. Howard Papers, BOC; announcement of board meeting, Apr. 14, 1899, Charles F. Eager Papers, UA-LMU.

38. Lindstrom and Carruthers, *Lincoln,* 10, 13–14, 16; http://www.lincolncollege.edu/; http://www.lincolnu.edu/; Low, *Encyclopedia of Black America,* 506; *Lincoln College* pamphlet, and circular titled "An Appeal to Congregational Churches in Behalf of Lincoln College," American Missionary Association Archives, TU; *Kansas: A Cyclopedia of State History* 2: 887–89. Several higher educational institutions were created with Lincoln's name after 1897, including Lincoln University in San Francisco (1919), Lincoln Christian College and Seminary in Springfield, Illinois (1944), Abraham Lincoln University School of Law (a web-based school started in 1996), and Lincoln Tech, with branches in six states.

39. Howard to Eager, Jan. 25, 1899, Oliver O. Howard Papers, UA-LMU; "Our Past Presidents," 10; questionnaire, Jan. 23, 1906, John Hale Larry pension record, NARA; John Hale Larry service record, 8th Massachusetts (nine months), and 3rd Massachusetts Heavy Artillery, NARA; record of events, 3rd Massachusetts Heavy Artillery, and 8th Massachusetts (nine months), *Supplement to the Official Records,* pt. 2, vol. 27, 305, 319–21, 721–24.

40. "Our Past Presidents," 10; questionnaire, Jan. 23, 1906, and "Deaths Registered in the city of Providence, R. I.," Sept. 11, 1919, John Hale Larry pension record, NARA; "Memorandum of Robert L. Kincaid's Conversation with Mrs. John Hale Larry, Providence, Rhode Island, 1939," Robert L. Kincaid Collection, CGNHP; John Hale Larry to E. M. Cravath, Oct. 1, 1873, American Missionary Association Archives, TU.

41. Howard to Bessie, May 7, 1899, Box 1, Folder 59, Oliver Otis Howard Papers, ALLM-LMU; "Memorandum of Robert L. Kincaid's Conversation with Mrs. John Hale

Larry, Providence, Rhode Island, 1939," Robert L. Kincaid Collection, CGNHP; Larry to Eager, May 9, 27, 1899, and Larry to Howard, May 25, 1899, John Hale Larry Papers, UA-LMU; Howard to H. B. Frissell, May 15, 1899, Oliver O. Howard Papers, UA-LMU; Howard report, June 8, 1899, Box 43, Folder 55, O. O. Howard Papers, BOC.

42. Howard to Eager, July 11, 12, 1899, Oliver O. Howard Papers, UA-LMU; Larry to Eager, July 11, 28, Aug. 5, 14, 1899, John Hale Larry Papers, UA-LMU.

43. Kehr to Eager, May 22, June 30, 1899, Cyrus Kehr Papers, UA-LMU.

44. Kehr to Eager, Apr. 12, May 22, June 30, 1899, Cyrus Kehr Papers, UA-LMU.

45. Howard to Eager, July 7, 12, 1899, Oliver O. Howard Papers, UA-LMU; Kehr to Howard, Oct. 23, 1899, Cyrus Kehr Papers, UA-LMU.

46. Howard memorandum, Sept. 18, 1899, attached to Larry to Eager, Oct. 1, 1899, Larry to Eager, Sept. 14, 22, 26, Oct. 1, 1899, and "Proposition," n.d., John Hale Larry Papers, UA- LMU.

47. Larry to Eager, Sept. 22, 27, Oct. 1, 3, 1899, John Hale Larry Papers, UA-LMU.

48. Larry to Eager, Oct. 3, 5, 9, 1899, John Hale Larry Papers, UA-LMU.

49. Myers to Howard, July 25, 1899, Arthur A. Myers Papers, UA-LMU.

50. Kincaid, *Wilderness Road,* 345–46; Kehr to Howard, Oct. 23, 1899, Cyrus Kehr Papers, UA-LMU; Myers to Hughes, Oct. 30, Nov. 3, Dec. 20, 1899, Arthur A. Myers Papers, UA-LMU; "Memorandum of conversation with Mrs. A. A. Arthur, Knoxville, Tenn., in 1938" and *Charter and By-Laws of the Girls' Industrial Home and School, Grace Nettleton Memorial,* 12–13, Robert L. Kincaid Collection, CGNHP; Suppiger, *Phoenix of the Mountains,* 16.

51. Kehr to Howard, Oct. 23, 1899, Cyrus Kehr Papers, UA-LMU; Howard to Eager, July 28, 1899, Oliver O. Howard Papers, UA-LMU.

52. Howard, *Autobiography* 2: 475–76, 493, 572. Howard placed Guy's last words on a plaque that was displayed in the university's first chapel. The plaque was destroyed when the building burned in 1924. Kincaid, "Living Lincoln," 19.

53. Howard to Miss Chaumet, Feb. 5, 1900, O. O. Howard Papers, BOC; Eager to Howard, Oct. 24, 1899, Charles F. Eager Papers, UA-LMU; Howard note, Oct. 26, 1899, Oliver O. Howard Papers, UA-LMU.

54. Carpenter, *Sword and Olive Branch,* 296; Howard to John Jacob Astor, Nov. 23, 1899, Oliver O. Howard Papers, UA-LMU; Howard to Whitelaw Reid, Nov. 22, 1899, O. O. Howard Papers, BOC.

55. Henry H. Adams to Eager, July 8, 1899, Charles F. Eager Papers, UA-LMU; Howard to Eager, July 7, 1899, Oliver O. Howard Papers, UA-LMU; "Monthly Pall, L.M.U. Cumberland Gap, Tenn.," Box 43, Folder 55, Oliver O. Howard Papers, BOC.

56. Larry to Eager, Sept. 26, 1899, John Hale Larry Papers, UA-LMU; questionnaire, Jan. 23, 1906, and "Deaths Registered in the City of Providence, R. I.," Dec. 13, 1939, John Hale Larry pension record, NARA; "Lincoln Memorial's First President Dead," 9; Suppiger, *Phoenix of the Mountains,* 16, 18.

57. Larry to Howard, Nov. 2, 1899, John Hale Larry Papers, UA-LMU.

58. "General Howard's expenses incurred obtaining subscriptions for Lincoln Memorial University, credited as his subscription to the same," Dec. 13, 1899, Box 43, Folder 55, O. O. Howard Papers, BOC; Howard to Eager, Mar. 11, Dec. 12, 1899, Oliver O. Howard Papers, UA-LMU; speech, [1933], 10, Frederick B. Avery Papers, UA-LMU.

59. Eager, "Partial Statement to Managing Director of Receipts and Disbursements," O. O. Howard Papers, BOC.

Chapter 3

Young Lincolns

Epigraph: Mountain Herald, Dec. 1901, 14.

1. John S. Kendall to Kincaid, June 23, 1948, and Henry Bowe to Kincaid, Mar. 5, 1938, Robert L. Kincaid Papers, UA-LMU.

2. Herman Y. Hughes to Howard, Mar. 29, 1900, Box 83, Folder 785, Russell Sage Foundation Records, RU; Henry H. Adams to Eager, Aug. 28, 1899, Charles F. Eager Papers, UA-LMU; W. C. Thompson to LeRoy Johnson, Nov. 7, 1940, Student Papers, UA-LMU.

3. Lincoln Memorial University *Catalog,* 1900–1902, 6–7, and 1902–3, 6–7, SC-LMU; Herman Y. Hughes to Howard, Mar. 29, 1900, Box 83, Folder 785, Russell Sage Foundation Records, RU.

4. "Memo of conversation with Miss Manning," Robert L. Kincaid Papers, UA-LMU; Howard, "Folk of the Cumberland Gap," 507.

5. "Memo of conversation with Miss Manning," Robert L. Kincaid Papers, UA-LMU; R. E. Larry to W. I. Jones, Dec. 15, 1949, John Hale Larry Papers, UA-LMU.

6. Minutes of Executive Committee, Mar. 5, 1900, ALLM-LMU; Peck and Smith, *Berea's First 125 Years,* 110–11.

7. Lincoln Memorial University *Catalog,* 1900–1901, 13, and 1902–3, 12, SC-LMU; contract, June 1, 1901, Student Papers, UA-LMU.

8. Minutes of Executive Committee, Mar. 15, 1902, ALLM-LMU; J. H. Rector to Avery, [ca. 1934], Fredrick B. Avery Papers, UA-LMU; "Rector Continues Story of the Early Hardships of Lincoln Memorial U.," unidentified clipping, Oct. 23, 1940, Robert L. Kincaid Collection, CGNHP; Howard, "Folk of the Cumberland Gap," 507.

9. W. C. Thompson to LeRoy Johnson, Nov. 7, 1940, Student Papers, UA-LMU.

10. Wilson, *Berea College,* 53, 67;

11. Ibid., 20–21, 27, 33, 51–53, 63, 69–72, 75, 83; Nelson, "Experiment in Interracial Education," 17, 19–20; Peck and Smith, *Berea's First 125 Years,* 47–49, 63–74; Wilson, "Window on the Mountains," 384; Jacob D. Cox to Charles F. Cox, Dec. 3, 1898, William Goodell Frost Papers, BEC.

12. Wilson, "Lincoln's Sons and Daughters," 256–57; Roberts, "Lincoln Collection," 3; *Berea Quarterly* 12, no. 1 (Apr. 1908): 1, BEC; Wilson, *Berea College,* 98.

13. William Goodell Frost to Howard, Dec. 29, 1896, and Feb. 4, 1897, O. O. Howard Papers, BOC; Wilson, "Lincoln's Sons and Daughters," 258.

14. William E. Barton to Howard, Mar. 13, Nov. 13, 1897, and Howard to Barton, Apr. 6, 1897, O. O. Howard Papers, BOC.

15. Frost to Howard, May 5, 1900, in Minutes, Annual Meeting, May 15, 1900, Board of Directors/Trustees Papers, UA-LMU, and in Director's Minutes, May 15, 1900, ALLM-LMU.

16. Board of Directors to Frost, May 15, 1900, in Minutes, Annual Meeting, May 15, 1900, Board of Directors/Trustees Papers, UA-LMU, and in Director's Minutes, May 15, 1900, ALLM-LMU.

17. [Eugene P. Fairchild], "To 'The Church of Christ at Berea' and to any donors to Berea College, Berea, Ky.," and Fairchild to Eager, Apr. 9, Oct. 26, 1900, Eugene P. Fairchild Papers, UA-LMU; Kehr to Eager, May 22, 1899, Cyrus Kehr Papers, UA-LMU; Howard to Eager, Oct. 6, 1899, Box 3, Folder 2, Oliver Otis Howard Papers, ALLM-LMU; Howard to D. K. Pearsons, Feb. 9, 1899, O. O. Howard Papers, BOC.

18. Wilson, *Berea College,* 82–84, 87–89; Nelson, "Experiment in Interracial Education," 23–24; Frost, *For the Mountains,* 173–76; Peck and Smith, *Berea's First 125 Years,* 49–57; Jones, "Maryville College." The Kentucky legislature amended the Day law in 1950 to allow for integration on the college level, and Berea moved immediately to enroll black students. Wilson, *Berea College,* 147; Peck and Smith, *Berea's First 125 Years,* 60–62, 194.

19. Howard to Barton, Apr. 6, 1897, O. O. Howard Papers, BOC; Carpenter, *Sword and Olive Branch,* 287; Wilson, "Lincoln's Sons and Daughters," 256.

20. Wilson, "Lincoln's Sons and Daughters," 245, 248–51; Nelson, "Experiment in Interracial Education," 13–14, 16, 26–27; Washington speech, Nov. 8, 1900, in Harlan, *Booker T. Washington Papers* 5: 670; Washington to Frost, Feb. 12, 1903, William Goodell Frost Papers, BEC.

21. Klotter, "Black South and White Appalachia," 849; Wilson, "Lincoln's Sons and Daughters," 259.

22. Howard to Eager, Nov. 15, 1900, and Dec. 25, 1900, and Jan. 3, 1901, and Apr. 2, 1901, Oliver O. Howard Papers, UA-LMU; Howard to Bessie, Apr. 16, 1902, Oliver Otis Howard Papers, ALLM-LMU.

23. Howard, "Folk of the Cumberland Gap," 507; Rudolph, *American College and University,* 331–36.

24. Howard, "Folk of the Cumberland Gap," 506–7; Oliver O. Howard Engagement Book, Jan. 7, 1900, Oliver Otis Howard Papers, ALLM-LMU.

25. Howard, "Folk of the Cumberland Gap," 507; Board of Directors to Carnegie, Jan. 8, 1900, Howard to Carnegie, July 11, 1900, and Howard to Carnegie, Dec. 11, 1901, Series II, Correspondence as to Grants Promised and Made, Reel 73, Carnegie Corporation of New York Records, CU; Howard to E. S. Converse, Mar. 5, 1902, O. O. Howard Papers, BOC.

26. Herman Y. Hughes to Howard, Mar. 29, 1900, enclosed in Howard to Mrs. Russell Sage, Apr. 16, 1900, Box 83, Folder 785, Russell Sage Foundation Records, RU.

27. Howard to E. S. Converse, Mar. 5, 1902, and Howard statement, May 4, 1900, Box 43, Folder 55, O. O. Howard Papers, BOC; Howard to Bessie, Apr. 26, 1902, Box 2, Folder 20, Oliver Otis Howard Papers, ALLM-LMU.

28. Howard to Eager, Nov. 15, 1900, Oliver O. Howard Papers, UA-LMU; Oliver O. Howard Engagement Book, July 20, 1900, and Howard, "Abraham Lincoln: 'What would he have us do,'" 9, Oliver Otis Howard Papers, ALLM-LMU; "American Brotherhood Keynote to Camp Fire"; F. B. Avery, "Concerning Mr. Fairchild and L.M.U.," clipping of *Middlesboro Daily News,* Appalachian Vertical Files, BEC; Eckert, *John Brown Gordon,* 315, 317, 323, 328–29. Howard also told the Gordon story while introducing a speaker to the Bowdoin Club in May 1901, according to http://www.joshua.lurkeroo.com/ (last accessed Mar. 30, 1010).

29. "General Howard Talks of Battle of Atlanta"; Howard, *Autobiography* 2: 576; "Honor to Gen. W. H. T. Walker," 402.

30. Carpenter, *Sword and Olive Branch,* 298; Howard, *Autobiography* 2: 574; Howard, "Abraham Lincoln: 'What would he have us do,'" 9, Oliver Otis Howard Papers, ALLM-LMU.

31. Clemens to Howard, Jan. 8, [1901], O. O. Howard Papers, BOC; Howard to Clemens, Feb. 2, 1901, Mark Twain Papers, UCB; Ensor, "Lincoln, Mark Twain, and Lincoln Memorial University," 43–45; Ensor, "House United," 264; Achorn, *Oliver Otis Howard,* 21; Howard, *Autobiography* 2: 566.

32. Wall, *Henry Watterson,* 6, 21, 30–31, 35, 38, 84–87, 218; Fairchild to Eager, Jan. 9, 1900, Eugene P. Fairchild Papers, UA-LMU; Ensor, "House United," 261–63; Ensor, "Lincoln, Mark Twain, and Lincoln Memorial University," 45; Twain to Joseph Twichell, Jan. 23, 1901, in Paine, *Mark Twain's Letters* 2: 704.

33. Howard to Eager, Feb. 4, 1901, Oliver O. Howard Papers, UA-LMU; *New York Times,* Feb. 7, 1901; *New York Tribune Illustrated Supplement,* Feb. 3, 1901; *New York Mail and Express Illustrated Saturday Magazine,* Feb. 2, 1901, clipping attached to Howard to Clemens, Feb. 2, 1901, Mark Twain Papers, UCB; Howard to Eager, Jan. 11, 1901, Oliver O. Howard Papers, UA-LMU.

34. Howard to Eager, Jan. 3, 31, 1901, Oliver O. Howard Papers, UA-LMU; Clemens to Howard, Feb. 7, 1901, Mark Twain Papers, UCB.

35. *New York Daily Tribune,* Feb. 12, 1901; *New York Times,* Feb. 12, 1901; "On Lincoln's Birthday," in Paine, *Mark Twain's Speeches,* 228–31.

36. Howard to Clemens, n.d. [envelope marked Feb. 12, 1901], Mark Twain Papers, UCB; Clemens to Howard, Feb. 13, 1901, O. O. Howard Papers, BOC; Larry to Eager, Mar. 11, 1901, John Hale Larry Papers, UA-LMU; Carpenter, "Architects and Builders," 12.

37. Gates to Howard, Jan. 12, 1901, Box 74, Folder 528, Rockefeller Family Archives, RU.

38. *National Cyclopaedia of American Biography* 29: 3–5.

39. Fosdick, *Adventure in Giving,* vii, 13, 15–17; *National Cyclopaedia of American Biography* 22: 419 and 23: 250.

40. Howard to Gates, Feb. 26, Dec. 17, 1902, Box 74, Folder 528, Rockefeller Family Archives, RU.

41. *National Cyclopaedia of American Biography* 1: 157; Samuel P. Avery to Carnegie, Dec. 17, 1902, Series II, Correspondence as to Grants Promised and Made, Reel 73, Carnegie Corporation of New York Records, CU; "Memorandum of Robert L. Kincaid's Conversation with Mrs. John Hale Larry, Providence, Rhode Island, 1939," Robert L. Kincaid Collection, CGNHP; Frederick B. Avery speech, [1933], 9, Frederick B. Avery Papers, UA-LMU; Kincaid, "Story of Avery Hall," 6.

42. Kincaid, "Story of Avery Hall," 6; Frederick B. Avery speech, [1933], 9, Frederick B. Avery Papers, UA-LMU; "Reminiscences of Middlesboro, Harrogate,

and Cumberland Gap by Walter E. Bryson," 6, SC-UTK; W. C. Thompson to Leroy Johnson, Nov. 7, 1940, Student Papers, UA-LMU; "Memo of conversation with Miss Manning," Robert L. Kincaid Papers, UA-LMU; Howard to Bessie, Nov. 6, 1903, Box 2, Folder 31, Oliver Otis Howard Papers, ALLM-LMU.

43. Howard to Eager, Mar. 15, 20, Apr. 2, 1901, Oliver O. Howard Papers, UA-LMU; Larry to Eager, Mar. 11, 1901, John Hale Larry Papers, UA-LMU; Howard to Achorn, Apr. 26, 1901, O. O. Howard Papers, BOC.

44. Fairchild to Eager, Apr. 16, 1901, Eugene P. Fairchild Papers, UA-LMU; "Story of Robert W. Barnett, Middlesboro, Ky., as told to Dr. Robert L. Kincaid, Sept. 21, 1948," Robert L. Kincaid Collection, CGNHP; Howard to Larry, June 8, 1901, O. O. Howard Papers, BOC.

45. Howard to Eager, Apr. 2, 1901, Oliver O. Howard Papers, UA-LMU; Larry to Eager, Mar. 11, 1901, John Hale Larry Papers, UA-LMU.

46. Eager to Hughes, Apr. 30, [1901], Charles F. Eager Papers, UA-LMU; Avery to Howard, May 29, 1901, James to Howard, June 7, 1901, and Howard to Larry, June 8, 1901, O. O. Howard Papers, BOC.

47. F. B. Avery, "Concerning Mr. Fairchild and L.M.U.," clipping from *Middlesboro Daily News,* Appalachian Vertical Files, BEC; Avery, "Mr. Fairchild Helps Found University"; Eager to Hughes, Feb. 1, 1902, Charles F. Eager Papers, UA-LMU; Eager to Howard, Jan. 18, 1902, O. O. Howard Papers, BOC; Achorn to Hughes, Mar. 17, 1902, Edgar O. Achorn Papers, UA-LMU.

48. Howard to E. S. Converse, Mar. 5, 1902, O. O. Howard Papers, BOC; Howard to Gates, Feb. 26, 1902, and Howard to Rockefeller, Feb. 26, 1902, Box 74, Folder 528, Rockefeller Family Archives, RU; Achorn to Hughes, Mar. 17, 1902, Edgar O. Achorn Papers, UA-LMU.

49. Stooksbury to Hughes, Feb. 8, Mar. 22, 1902, Jan. 21, 1904, William L. Stooksbury Papers, UA-LMU; "Old Professor," 12; Trustee's Minutes, May 7, 1918, ALLM-LMU.

50. "Our Past Presidents," 4; Stooksbury to Hughes, Mar. 17, 1903, Jan. 21, 1904, May 10, 20, 1904, William L. Stooksbury Papers, UA-LMU.

51. J. F. Spence to Hughes, Mar. 16, 1904, and Stooksbury to Kincaid, Aug. 16, 1938, William L. Stooksbury Papers, UA-LMU.

52. Larry to Carnegie, Feb. 28, 1903, Series II, Correspondence as to Grants Promised and Made, Reel 73, Carnegie Corporation of New York Records, CU; Larry to Arthur, Feb. 6, 1904, Box 4, Alexander A. Arthur Family Papers, UA-LMU.

53. Achorn to Hughes, Aug. 5, 24, 1904, Edgar O. Achorn Papers, UA-LMU; Larry to Howard, Nov. 19, 1904, John Hale Larry Papers, UA-LMU; "Memorandum of

Robert L. Kincaid's Conversation with Mrs. John Hale Larry, Providence, Rhode Island, 1939," Robert L. Kincaid Collection, CGNHP; questionnaire, Jan. 23, 1906, and Declaration for Invalid Pension, Dec. 23, 1905, John Hale Larry pension record, NARA; "Our Past Presidents," 10; "Lincoln Memorial's First President Dead," 9.

54. Hughes to Eager, Apr. 26, 1900, Herman Y. Hughes Papers, UA-LMU; Kehr to Howard, June 6, 1900, and Howard to Eager, June 19, [1900], O. O. Howard Papers, BOC.

55. Kehr to Howard, Nov. 17, 1900, Cyrus Kehr Papers, UA-LMU; Howard to Eager, Nov. 15, 1900, and Howard to Kehr, Nov. 15, 1900, Oliver O. Howard Papers, UA-LMU; Kehr to H. A. Morgan, Aug. 8, 1919, Kehr to H. A. Morgan, Apr. 29, 1922, and Kehr to W. S. Shields, Mar. 20, 1928, Box 1, Folder 4, No. 1, Presidential Papers, UA-UTK; *National Cyclopaedia of American Biography* 30: 409; *Washington Post,* July 15, 1941.

56. Howard to Dr. Lansing, Dec. 27, 1900, and Howard to Eager, Jan. 3, 1901, Oliver O. Howard Papers, UA-LMU; Ernest G. Dodge to Kincaid, July 21, 1940, and "True Story of The Founding Lincoln Memorial University," unidentified clipping, Oct. 16, 1940, Robert L. Kincaid Collection, CGNHP.

57. Myers to Howard, Jan. 30, 1901, O. O. Howard Papers, BOC; Howard to Eager, Feb. 4, Mar. 22,1901, and Howard to Myers, Mar. 15, 1901, Oliver O. Howard Papers, UA-LMU; F. J. Lothrop to Eager, Mar. 4, 1901, Charles F. Eager Papers, UA-LMU; Larry to Eager, Mar. 11, 1901, John Hale Larry Papers, UA-LMU.

58. Fairchild to Eager, Mar. 4, 1901, Eugene P. Fairchild Papers, UA-LMU.

59. Howard to Eager, Apr. 2, 1901, and Howard to Hughes, May 19, 1901, Oliver O. Howard Papers, UA-LMU; "Memorandum of conversation with James H. Rector, Harrogate, Tenn., September 19, 1940," Robert L. Kincaid Collection, CGNHP.

60. Kincaid, *Wilderness Road,* 344; Kincaid to Ernest G. Dodge, Dec. 12, 1940, Robert L. Kincaid Papers, UA-LMU.

61. Myers to Hughes, May 10, 1904, and Lundstrom, "A. A. Myers," 1–4, Arthur A. Myers Papers, UA-LMU; *Middlesboro Daily News,* May 23, 1903; "True Story of the Founding Lincoln Memorial University," unidentified clipping, Oct. 16, 1940, "Rector Continues Story of the Early Hardships of Lincoln Memorial U.," unidentified clipping, Oct. 23, 1940, "Rev. A. A. Myers," transcript, and "Rev. A. A. Myers Died in Jackson," transcript of clipping, Robert L. Kincaid Collection, CGNHP; Matthews to Mrs. M. M. Wild, May 8, 1924, Robert O. Matthews Papers, UA-LMU; Kincaid, *Wilderness Road,* 345. Some residents of Cumberland Gap argued that Myers and Kehr had initiated the start of the university before calling Howard to visit Cumberland Gap. As J. H. S. Morison put it, "Howard and his following rooted Myers out." Morison boastfully proclaimed, "If there be any glory in the establishment of L.M.U., it is due to A. A. Myers, and not to O. O. Howard." Morison's account is full of errors and indicates the extent

to which Myers was able to spread his version of the truth among village residents. Another admirer of Myers, farm manager James H. Rector, bemoaned the fact that Arthur and Ellen Myers, "after doing so much to help the boys and girls of the Mountains should receive so little credit." Frederick B. Avery viewed the situation more accurately when he noted that Myers and Kehr organized the university but Howard took "the laboring oar" and "practically financed it." See Morison to Lincoln Memorial University, Aug. 20, 1940, J. H. S. Morison Papers, UA- LMU; Morison to Mae M. Wild, Oct. 13, 1935, Robert L. Kincaid Collection, CGNHP; Rector to Avery, [ca. 1934], James H. Rector Papers, UA-LMU; and Avery to Eager, May 3, 1920, Frederick B. Avery Papers, UA-LMU.

Chapter 4

Stooksbury's School

Epigraphs: Ola Good to Stooksbury, Apr. 19, 1906, Grover Day to Stooksbury, Jan. 19, 1909, and Stooksbury, "The Ideal University of the Future," William L. Stooksbury Papers, UA-LMU.

1. Stooksbury to Kincaid, Aug. 16, 1938, William L. Stooksbury Papers, UA-LMU; Howard to Arthur T. Abernethy, June 9, 1904, Oliver O. Howard Papers, UA-LMU; *New York Herald,* September 12, 1909; Jesse H. Moore, "J. H. Moore Reminiscences," Apr. 29, 1929, Jesse H. Moore Papers, UA-LMU.

2. Stooksbury to Hughes, July 30, 1904, William L. Stooksbury Papers, UA-LMU; Howard to Stooksbury, Sept. 19, 1904, Oliver O. Howard Papers, UA-LMU; entries of Oct. 24, 28, 1904, minutes of faculty meetings, Sept. 5, 1904–Mar. 27, 1922, 4–5, Faculty Papers, UA-LMU.

3. "Special Work Done by Lincoln Memorial University," William L. Stooksbury Papers, UA-LMU.

4. "Our Past Presidents," 4; Lincoln Memorial University *Catalog,* 1907–8, 19, SC-LMU; Clarence Ludlow Brownell essay, July 21, 1909, 8–9, William L. Stooksbury Papers, UA-LMU. Stooksbury also forbade the use of alcohol among the employees of the university. See Temperance Pledge, Dec. 24, 1908, William L. Stooksbury Papers, UA-LMU.

5. Form letter by Stooksbury, Sept. 11, 1907, and Stooksbury to W. A. McNiel, Jan. 18, 1910, William L. Stooksbury Papers, UA-LMU; George W. Morton Sr., quoted in *Knoxville News-Sentinel,* Feb. 12, 1958.

6. Lincoln Memorial University *Catalog,* 1905–6, 3–4, and 1910–11, 2–3, SC-LMU; Stooksbury to E. B. McKnight, Feb. 28, 1908, William L. Stooksbury Papers, UA-LMU.

7. Jesse H. Moore, "Observations and Experiences of His Life," 9, 45, 51–52, 54–55, and Moore, "J. H. Moore Reminiscences," Apr. 29, 1929, Jesse H. Moore Papers, UA-LMU.

8. "First LMU Graduate, G. W. Morton, Dies," 11–12; "Class Notes," 9; *Knoxville News-Sentinel,* Feb. 12, 1958; Mildred B. Shumate, "Our Story: Lincoln Memorial University," Dec. 1966, 14, Mildred B. Shumate, Faculty Papers, UA-LMU.

9. Ola Good to Stooksbury, Apr. 19, 1909, Lizzie Garrett to Stooksbury, Sept. 7, 1909, F. H. Hanson to Dear Sir, Sept. 9, 1909, Sam Suntotsky to Sir, Apr. 12, 1910, Grover Day to Stooksbury, Jan. 19, 1909, and Alexander Gambol to "Mr lincoln," Oct. 25, 1908, William L. Stooksbury Papers, UA-LMU.

10. Ray Dills to Principal of Harrogate College, Aug. 27, 1909, Stooksbury to Mrs. John Ingle, Aug. 27, 1909, Stooksbury to A. B. Lindsay, Aug. 26, 1909, Stooksbury to J. S. Smith, Aug. 26, 1909, Clarence Ludlow Brownell essay, July 21, 1909, 5–6, Stooksbury to F. H. Hanson, Sept. 11, 1909, and S. A. Lewis to G. W. Nichols, Feb. 10, 1910, William L. Stooksbury Papers, UA-LMU.

11. Clarence Ludlow Brownell essay, July 21, 1909, 9–10, and Carr Butcher to Frances W. Upham, Jan. 30, 1905, William L. Stooksbury Papers, UA-LMU; Erskine H. Cox to Howard, Jan. 28, 1905, Oliver O. Howard Papers, UA-LMU.

12. Mrs. John Engle to Stooksbury, Aug. 24, Sept. 2, 1909, Stooksbury to I. S. M. Day, Oct. 2, 1909, and Sarah Frost Hill to Stooksbury, Sept. 27, 1909, William L. Stooksbury Papers, UA-LMU.

13. Stooksbury, "Ideal University of the Future," William L. Stooksbury Papers, UA-LMU; *Mountain Herald* 9, no. 6 (1905–6): 15.

14. Lincoln Memorial University *Catalog,* 1907–8, 18, SC-LMU; Clarence Ludlow Brownell essay, July 21, 1909, 8, and Stooksbury to Theodore Chamberlin, Oct. 9, 1909, William L. Stooksbury Papers, UA-LMU; Braunhut, "Farm Labor Wage Rates," 195.

15. Laura Farris Sudderly to Stooksbury, Jan. 6, 1909, Stooksbury to O. B. Stark, Sept. 1, 1909, and "Lincoln Memorial University," William L. Stooksbury Papers, UA-LMU; Ezra T. DeBusk to Joseph Suppiger, Nov. 14, 1972, in Suppiger, *Phoenix of the Mountains,* 19–20; Time Book, September 7, 1907–April 23, 1910, UA-LMU.

16. "Lincoln Memorial University," and Stooksbury to A. Wilson, Jan. 13, 1910, William L. Stooksbury Papers, UA-LMU.

17. Stooksbury to Harry J. Myers, July 1, 1909, Stooksbury to Clarence Reynold, Aug. 26, 1909, Stooksbury to Hughes, May 1, 1905, Stooksbury to Wickliff Rose, Jan. 31, 1908, Stooksbury to John F. Spence, Sept. 10, 1909, Stooksbury to W. A. Wolfe, Jan. 15, 1910, and Stooksbury to Katherine Johnson, Jan. 15, 1910, William L. Stooksbury Papers, UA-LMU.

18. Stooksbury to L. I. Jencks, Nov. 10, 1909, Stooksbury to Isaac Hopkins, Sept. 10, 1908, Stooksbury to O. B. Stark, Sept. 29, 1909, and Stooksbury to W. A. Brock, Oct. 26, 1909, William L. Stooksbury Papers, UA-LMU.

19. Stooksbury to C. M. Stevens, July 1, 7, 1909, Stooksbury to Jerome Stevens, July 10, 1909, and statement by Jerome Allen Stevens, July 13, 1909, William L. Stooksbury Papers, UA-LMU.

20. Stooksbury to William Littrell, Feb. 18, 1910, William L. Stooksbury Papers, UA-LMU.

21. S. A. Lewis to Martha L. Patterson, Nov. 6, 1909, William L. Stooksbury Papers, UA-LMU.

22. F. H. Earle to Stooksbury, Jan. 29, 1909, Earle to Lewis, Jan. 15, 1909, and Lucretia Collingsworth to Stooksbury, Jan. 8, 1909, William L. Stooksbury Papers, UA-LMU.

23. Howard to Stooksbury, July 12, 1904, Apr. 24, 1905, and Howard to Eager, Apr. 2, 1901, Oliver O. Howard Papers, UA-LMU.

24. Howard to W. S. Witham, July 26, 1909, and Howard to Stooksbury, July 7, 1904, Oliver O. Howard Papers, UA-LMU; Avery to Stooksbury, n.d., Frederick B. Avery Papers, UA-LMU.

25. "Lincoln Centennial Endowment Fund," 4, William L. Stooksbury Papers, UA-LMU; "Confederate Veteran's Tribute to Abraham Lincoln," and "Personal Recollections of Gen. Robt. E. Lee in Peace and in War," Robert F. Patterson, Board of Directors/Trustees Papers, UA-LMU; Kincaid, "Confederate Veteran's Tribute," 20–24. Patterson became less active in university affairs due to declining health before passing away on May 2, 1915. *Knoxville Journal and Tribune,* May 4, 1915.

26. Clarence Ludlow Brownell essay, July 21, 1909, 11–12, John F. Spence to Stooksbury, Feb. 9, 1910, and Lewis to *Christian Work and Evangelist,* Dec. 16, 1908, William L. Stooksbury Papers, UA-LMU.

27. D. D. Walker to Thomas H. Hubbard, Nov. 27, 1909, and Robert Lee Dunn to Walker, Dec. 3, 1909, William L. Stooksbury Papers, UA-LMU.

28. Stooksbury, "Race that Will Predominate," 815–17.

29. Howard, "Negro as a Free Man," 206.

30. "Lincoln's People Not 'Pore Whites,' But Typical Mountaineers," William L. Stooksbury Papers, UA-LMU.

31. Washington to James R. B. Van Cleave, Feb. 9, 1909, in Harlan, *Booker T. Washington Papers* 10: 26; untitled lecture on Lincoln, 19, Oliver Otis Howard Papers, ALLM-LMU.

32. Howard to W. S. Witham, July 26, 1909, Witham to Howard, July 28, 1909, and Stooksbury to Howard, May 31, 1909, Oliver O. Howard Papers, UA-LMU.

33. Fairchild to Stooksbury, Apr. 14, 21, 1906, Eugene P. Fairchild Papers, UA-LMU.

34. Frost to R. A. Beard, Apr. 13, 1906, William Goodell Frost Papers, BEC.

35. R. A. Beard to Trustees of LMU, July 25, 1906, and Howard to Beard, July 27, 1906, Oliver O. Howard Papers, UA-LMU; *Mountain Herald,* 1905–6, 2.

36. Howard to R. A. Beard, July 27, 1906, Oliver O. Howard Papers, UA-LMU; Achorn to "Sir," July 27, 1906, Edgar O. Achorn Papers, UA-LMU; Fairchild to Stooksbury, Aug. 17, 1906, Eugene P. Fairchild Papers, UA-LMU.

37. Stooksbury to Hughes, May 1, 1907, William L. Stooksbury Papers, UA-LMU; *Mountain Herald,* June 1907, 2, and July 1910, 1.

38. Suppiger, *Phoenix of the Mountains,* 18; Eager to Stooksbury, Feb. 15, 1907, Charles F. Eager Papers, UA-LMU; Stooksbury to Charles R. Otis, Dec. 25, 1909, William L. Stooksbury Papers, UA-LMU; Howard to Stooksbury, Feb. 15, 1907, Oliver O. Howard Papers, UA-LMU; Howard to James Bertram, Feb. 16, 1907, Series II, Correspondence as to Grants Promised and Made, Reel 73, Carnegie Corporation of New York Records, CU.

39. "Brief History," Ellen Myers School, Buildings Papers, UA-LMU; Shumate, *Brief History,* 9–10; F. B. Avery, "Concerning Mr. Fairchild and L.M.U.," clipping from *Middlesboro Daily News,* Appalachian Vertical Files, BEC; Avery, "Mr. Fairchild Helps Found University."

40. Howard to Board of Directors, July 14, 1905, Oliver O. Howard Papers, UA-LMU; Orr, "History of Tennessee Medical College," 25, 34–35, 40–41, 44–45.

41. Howard to Henry R. Gibson, June 23, 1906, and Howard to Hughes, July 21, 1906, Oliver O. Howard Papers, UA-LMU; *Booklet of Information,* Oct. 1907, 15, Box 83, Folder 785, Russell Sage Foundation Records, RU; Orr, "History of Tennessee Medical College," 45.

42. Suppiger, *Phoenix of the Mountains,* 33, Manier, "On Going Back," 16; statement [ca. fall, 1909], William L. Stooksbury Papers, UA-LMU.

43. Stooksbury to Hughes, Jan. 3, 1907, and Stooksbury to Walter P. Brownlow, June 12, 1909, William L. Stooksbury Papers, UA-LMU.

44. Stooksbury to E. G. Hallock, Sept. 9, 1909, Stooksbury to Theodore Chamberlin, Oct. 9, 1909, Stooksbury to "My Dear Friend," Nov. 10, 1909, and "Lincoln Memorial University," [ca. fall 1909], William L. Stooksbury Papers, UA-LMU; Kincaid, *Wilderness Road,* 349–52.

45. Stooksbury to Emma B. Miles, Nov. 6, 1909, Stooksbury to Theodore Chamberlin, Oct. 9, 1909, Stooksbury to W. H. Merriman, Oct. 4, 1909, and Stooksbury to unknown, n.d., William L. Stooksbury Papers, UA-LMU; Shapiro, *Appalachia on Our Mind,* 130–31, 221.

46. Miles, *Spirit of the Mountains,* passim; Stooksbury to Emma Bell Miles, Nov. 6, 24, 1909, Jan. 20, 1910, William L. Stooksbury Papers, UA-LMU; Emma Bell Miles journal, Mar. 27, Apr. 10, 17, May 22, June 14, 18, 21–22, 1910, Jean Miles Catino Collection, UTC.

Chapter 5

Howard's Monument

Epigraphs: Howard, "Abraham Lincoln: 'What would he have us do,'" 13, ALLM-LMU; Howard, "Personal Recollections of Abraham Lincoln," 877.

1. Howard, "Lincoln's Monument in the Mountains," 299–303.

2. Howard, "Personal Recollections of Abraham Lincoln," 877; J. T. Turner to Howard, Nov. 21, 1908, Oliver O. Howard Papers, UA-LMU.

3. Howard to Stooksbury, Feb. 15, 1907, Oliver O. Howard Papers, UA-LMU; Howard, *Autobiography* 2: 575; Oliver O. Howard Engagement Book, Jan. 16, 1907; Oliver Otis Howard Papers, ALLM-LMU.

4. "Abraham Lincoln: 'What would he have us do,'" 1, 5–6, 8, 13, Oliver Otis Howard Papers, ALLM-LMU; "A Monument to the Mountain People," O. O. Howard Papers, BOC.

5. Howard to Stooksbury, Jan. 3, 1905, William L. Stooksbury Papers, UA-LMU; Howard, "Lincoln's Monument in the Mountains," 303–4.

6. Howard to Stooksbury, Apr. 13, 1905, Oliver O. Howard Papers, UA-LMU; Howard to John Gregson Jr., Feb. 7, 1906, Letters and Documents Collection, BMC; Howard to Edwin Ray Smith, June 25, Dec. 6, 1904, Rowland Bailey Howard Collection, BOC.

7. Howard to Stooksbury, Apr. 24, 1905, William L. Stooksbury Papers, UA-LMU; Carpenter, "Architects and Builders," 13; Howard, *Autobiography* 2: 574; "General Howard Remembered," 12; Shumate, *Brief History,* 9.

8. Howard, *Autobiography* 2: 568–69, 575; Carpenter, *Sword and Olive Branch,* 290. Howard also inserted the names of the "Officers and Directors of Lincoln Memorial University," on pages 586 and 587 of volume 2 of his autobiography, to thank them for their "hearty cooperation in the work" of the university.

9. Fairchild to Stooksbury, Sept. 14, 1905, Eugene P. Fairchild Papers, UA-LMU; Eager to Stooksbury, Feb. 8, 1907, and John A. Cass "Report for January, 1907," Charles F. Eager Papers, UA-LMU; Avery, "Mr. Fairchild Helps Found University."

10. Fairchild to Stooksbury, May 22, 1908, Eugene P. Fairchild Papers, UA-LMU; Howard, *Autobiography* 2: 575–76.

11. Howard, *Autobiography* 2: 574; Oliver O. Howard Engagement Book, May 15–19, 30, 1904, Oliver Otis Howard Papers, ALLM-LMU; Howard to Stooksbury, July 12, Sept. 19, 1904, Oliver O. Howard Papers, UA-LMU.

12. Howard to Stooksbury, Dec. 2, 5, 1904, Oliver O. Howard Papers, UA-LMU.

13. "Theodore Roosevelt Commends," 27; Wilbur P. Thirkield to John Wesley Hill, Dec. 14, 1927, and Roosevelt notes on two menu cards, Box 7, Roosevelt Folder, Hall of Holography Collection, ALLM-LMU.

14. Howard, *Autobiography* 2: 574; Howard to Theodore Roosevelt, Mar. 25, 1906, Charles Henry Howard Collection, BOC; Roosevelt to Howard, Oct. 16, 1908, Box 3, Folder 9, Oliver O. Howard Papers, ALLM-LMU; Carpenter, *Sword and Oliver Branch,* 298.

15. Fairchild to Stooksbury, Feb. 7, 1907, Eugene P. Fairchild Papers, UA-LMU; Howard to Mrs. Sage, Sept. 13, 1907, Box 83, Folder 785, Russell Sage Foundation Records, RU.

16. Howard to John D. Rockefeller, Mar. 24, 1905, Box 74, Folder 528, Rockefeller Family Archives, RU.

17. Frederick T. Gates to John D. Rockefeller, Mar. 30, 1905, Box 74, Folder 528, Rockefeller Family Archives, RU.

18. Ibid.

19. Howard to John D. Rockefeller, Apr. 26, 1905, Starr J. Murphy to Rockefeller, Apr. 28, 1905, Rockefeller to Murphy, Apr. 29, 1905, Frederick T. Gates to John D. Rockefeller, May 5, 1905, and Rockefeller to Gates, May 6, 1905, Box 74, Folder 528, Rockefeller Family Archives, RU.

20. Fairchild to Stooksbury, Oct. 5, 1905, Eugene P. Fairchild Papers, UA-LMU; Stooksbury to Gates, Jan. 30, 1908, William L. Stooksbury Papers, UA-LMU.

21. Howard to Rockefeller, Apr. 21, 1909, and John D. Rockefeller Jr. to Howard, Apr. 27, 1909, Box 74, Folder 528, Rockefeller Family Archives, RU.

22. *General Education Board: An Account of Its Activities,* 108–10, 119–20, 127.

23. Ibid., 109, 145, 157; *General Education Board: Report of the Secretary, 1915–1916,* 15–16; Stooksbury to Harry S. Howard, Dec. 27, 1909, William L. Stooksbury Papers, UA-LMU.

24. Stooksbury to Harry S. Howard, Dec. 27, 1909, William L. Stooksbury Papers, UA-LMU.

25. Howard to Herman Y. Hughes, Jan. 17, 1903, Jan. 20, 26, 1904, and Howard to James Bertram, Jan. 19, 1903, Oliver O. Howard Papers, UA-LMU; Howard to Carnegie, n.d. (but before Apr. 1, 1905), Apr. 13, 1903, Bertram to Howard, Dec. 28, 1904, Feb. 3, 1905, and Howard to Bertram, Jan. 20, Feb. 9, 1905, Series II, Correspondence as to Grants Promised and Made, Reel 38, Carnegie Corporation of New York Records, CU.

26. Undated petition of faculty and executive committee and application for library [1904], Bertram to Howard, Apr. 1, June 19, 1905, Howard to Bertram, Dec. 16, 1904, Apr. 4 [1905], Apr. 20, 21, 1905, Darwin R. James et al. to Carnegie, Apr. 11, 1905, Bertram to James, Apr. 18, 1905, and Howard to Carnegie, May 20, 1905, Series II, Correspondence as to Grants Promised and Made, Reel 38, Carnegie Corporation of New York Records, CU; Fairchild to Stooksbury, Mar. 31, 1905, Eugene P. Fairchild Papers, UA-LMU.

27. Howard to Carnegie, Aug. 22, 1906, Apr. 15, 1907, Stooksbury to Howard, Apr. 9, 1907, Bertram to Howard, Apr. 17, 1907, John A. Cass to Carnegie, Jan. 15, 1907, and Bertram to Cass, Jan. 18, 1907, Series II, Correspondence as to Grants Promised and Made, Reel 38, Carnegie Corporation of New York Records, CU.

28. Stooksbury to Carnegie, Dec. 16, 1907, Bertram endorsement, and Bertram to Stooksbury, Dec. 19, 1907, Howard to Carnegie, Apr. 22, 1908, and Howard to Bertram, Apr. 22, May 1, 1908, Series II, Correspondence as to Grants Promised and Made, Reel 38, Carnegie Corporation of New York Records, CU.

29. Fairchild to Stooksbury, Sept. 14, 1905, Eugene P. Fairchild Papers, UA-LMU; Carpenter, *Sword and Olive Branch,* 297; Howard to Edward Ray Smith, Dec. 3, 1908, Rowland Bailey Howard Collection, BOC; Howard to Mrs. Sage, Jan. 7, 1909, Box 83, Folder 785, Russell Sage Foundation Records, RU.

30. Howard to Samuel Clemens, Jan. 8, 1909, Mark Twain Papers, UCB.

31. Clemens to Howard, Jan. 12, 1909, Box 1, Authors Folder, Hall of Holography Collection, ALLM-LMU. This Twain letter is also printed in Paine, *Mark Twain's Letters* 2: 825–27.

32. Howard to Clemens, Jan. 14, 1909, Mark Twain Papers, UCB; Howard to Carnegie, Jan. 22, 1909, and Carnegie to Howard, Jan. 23, 1909, Series II, Correspondence as to Grants Promised and Made, Reel 38, Carnegie Corporation of New York Records, CU; *New York Times,* Feb. 7, 1909.

33. *New York Times,* Feb. 7, 10, 1909.

34. Howard to Bertram, Apr. 10, 13, 1909, Stooksbury to Bertram, Apr. 15, 1909, Stooksbury and Board Members to Carnegie, Apr. 12, 1909, Bertram to Howard,

Apr. 13, 1909, Carnegie to Buttrick, Apr. 21, 1909, Buttrick to Carnegie, Apr. 21, 1909, and Bertram to Howard, Apr. 23, 1909, Series II, Correspondence as to Grants Promised and Made, Reel 38, Carnegie Corporation of New York Records, CU.

35. Howard to Carnegie, Aug. 21, 1909, Series II, Correspondence as to Grants Promised and Made, Reel 38, Carnegie Corporation of New York Records, CU; Howard to John D. Rockefeller, Apr. 21, 1909, Box 74, Folder 528, Rockefeller Family Archives, RU; Stooksbury, "Ideal University of the Future," and Stooksbury to Le Roy Pope Walker, Sept. 18, [1909], and "Lincoln Centennial Endowment Fund," 6, William L. Stooksbury Papers, UA-LMU.

36. Howard to Carnegie, Aug. 21, 1909, Series II, Correspondence as to Grants Promised and Made, Reel 38, Carnegie Corporation of New York Records, CU; "Lincoln Centennial Endowment Committee" flyer, Box 83, Folder 785, Russell Sage Foundation Records, RU; postcards, William L. Stooksbury Papers, UA-LMU.

37. Copy of William H. Taft to Howard, June 24, 1909, copy of James S. Sherman to Howard, June 22, 1909, and copy of Theodore Roosevelt to Howard, n.d., Box 83, Folder 785, Russell Sage Foundation Records, RU; "The Lincoln Centennial Endowment Fund, Extracts from Newspaper Comments," and clipping titled "Lincoln University Endowment," William L. Stooksbury Papers, UA-LMU; *New York Herald,* Sept. 12, 1909.

38. Kincaid, *Wilderness Road,* 343–44; summary of financial statements, Lincoln Memorial University, 1906–9, William L. Stooksbury Papers, UA-LMU.

39. Oliver O. Howard Engagement Book, Oct. 1909, Oliver Otis Howard Papers, ALLM-LMU; Kincaid, "General Howard and Lincoln's Last Commission," 11–12, Robert L. Kincaid Papers, UA-LMU.

40. New York *Globe and Advertiser,* Oct. 27, 1909, quoted in Kincaid, *Wilderness Road,* 342.

41. Oliver O. Howard Engagement Book, Jan. 1910, Howard to Stooksbury, Oct. 26, 1909, Box 3, Folder 12, and Harry S. Howard to Bessie, Oct. 30, 1909, Box 2, Folder 62, Oliver Otis Howard Papers, ALLM-LMU; Harry S. Howard, "Last Days of General O. O. Howard," [1950], and Sue E. Howard recollections, enclosed in her letter to Kincaid, Oct. 14, 1950, Oliver O. Howard Papers, UA-LMU; Kincaid, *Wilderness Road,* 344–45.

42. Harry S. Howard, "Last Days of General O. O. Howard," [1950], Harry S. Howard to Kincaid, Oct. 13, 1950, and Report of Pension Committee of U.S. Senate, Apr. 10, 1910, Oliver O. Howard Papers, UA-LMU; Edsace Field Stark to Kincaid, Oct. 7, 1948, Robert L. Kincaid Papers, UA-LMU; Carpenter, *Sword and Olive Branch,* 299.

43. Carpenter, "Architects and Builders," 13.

44. Stooksbury's secretary to Sarah F. Hill, Oct. 30, 1909, William L. Stooksbury Papers, UA-LMU; Avery to Stooksbury, Jan. 14, 1910, Frederick B. Avery Papers, UA-LMU; Achorn to Stooksbury, n.d., Edgar O. Achorn Papers, UA-LMU.

45. Achorn to Stooksbury, n.d., Edgar O. Achorn Papers, UA-LMU; Stooksbury to Herman Y. Hughes, Nov. 13, 1909, and Stooksbury to P. P. Claxton, Dec. 16, [1909], William L. Stooksbury Papers, UA-LMU.

46. Stooksbury to Thomas H. Hubbard, Nov. 8, 1909, William L. Stooksbury Papers, UA-LMU; Achorn, *Oliver Otis Howard,* 4–5, 7–9, 10–13, 19, 25–26, 28, 30; Burrage, *Thomas Hamlin Hubbard,* 19, 23, 27, 29, 41, 45, 52.

47. Stooksbury to Thomas H. Hubbard, Nov. 8, 1909, "A Complete Monument to Abraham Lincoln," Stooksbury to "My Dear Friend," Nov. 10, 1909, Stooksbury to "My Dear Sir," n.d., and "An Appeal—In Lincoln's Name," William L. Stooksbury Papers, UA-LMU; *National Cyclopaedia of American Biography* 30: 554–55; Fred H. Wilson to Mrs. Sage, Nov. 9, 1909, and promotional literature, Box 83, Folder 785, Russell Sage Foundation Records, RU.

48. Moore, "Observations and Experiences of His Life," 55, Jesse H. Moore Papers, Faculty Papers, UA-LMU; "Memorandum of conversation with James H. Rector, Harrogate, Tenn., September 19, 1940," Robert L. Kincaid Collection, CGNHP; S. P. Lewis to Tip Fulkerson, Dec. 15, 1909, William L. Stooksbury Papers, UA-LMU.

49. "Memo of conversation with Miss Manning," Robert L. Kincaid Papers, UA-LMU; Stooksbury to Isabella Mitchell, Jan. 18, 1910, Stooksbury to Maggie Myers, Jan. 14, 1910, S. P. Lewis to Tip Fulkerson, Dec. 15, 1909, and Stooksbury to Miss L. R. Ward, Jan. 5, 1910, William L. Stooksbury Papers, UA-LMU; "Notes on Lincoln Herald," manuscript inserted into bound issues of *Mountain Herald,* 1910–14, SC-LMU.

50. "Memo of conversation with Miss Manning," Robert L. Kincaid Papers, UA-LMU; Stooksbury to Edgar O. Achorn, Jan. 22, 1910, William L. Stooksbury Papers, UA-LMU; Kincaid, "Story of Avery Hall," 6; Suppiger, *Phoenix of the Mountains,* 23.

51. Stooksbury to "My dear Friend," n.d., Stooksbury to Fred H. Wilson, Dec. 16, 1909, and Stooksbury to Hubbard, Dec. 16, 1909, William L. Stooksbury Papers, UA-LMU.

52. Stooksbury to Charles R. Otis, Dec. 25, 1909, Stooksbury to Mrs. S. P. Avery, Dec. 27, 1909, Stooksbury to Eager, Dec. 27, 1909, and Stooksbury to Achorn, Jan. 22, 1910, William L. Stooksbury Papers, UA-LMU.

53. Stooksbury to Isabella Mitchell, Jan. 18, 1910, Stooksbury to Hubbard, Feb. 22, 1910, Stooksbury to Pearsons, Jan. 26, 1910, and Stooksbury to Maggie Myers, Jan. 14, 1910, William L. Stooksbury Papers, UA-LMU.

54. Stooksbury to Mitchell, Jan. 18, 1910, Stooksbury to Pearsons, Jan. 26, 1910, petition to Pearsons, Feb. 8, 14, 1910, Stooksbury to Hubbard, Feb. 22, 1910, Stooksbury to Carnegie, Feb. 11, 1910, Stooksbury to Achorn, Jan. 22, 1910, Stooksbury to Bertram, Feb. 17, 1910, and Stooksbury to James, Jan. 5, 1910, William L. Stooksbury Papers, UA-LMU.

55. Stooksbury to Mitchell, Jan. 18, 1910, receipt for insurance payment, Feb. 28, 1910, Stooksbury to Hubbard, Feb. 22, 1910, "List of subscribers and contributors to the fund for rebuilding the boys dormitory at Lincoln Memorial University, Cumberland Gap, Tenn.," Apr. 10, 1910, and Stooksbury to Achorn, Jan. 22, 1910, William L. Stooksbury Papers, UA-LMU.

56. Howard to Stooksbury, Oct. 26, 1909, Box 3, Folder 12, Oliver Otis Howard Papers, ALLM-LMU; Stooksbury to James, Dec. 13, 1909, and Stooksbury to Achorn, Jan. 22, 1910, William L. Stooksbury Papers, UA-LMU; Orr, "History of Tennessee Medical College," 46–47.

57. Stooksbury to Avery, Feb. 22, 1910, and minutes of Executive Committee meeting, Mar. 9, 1910, William L. Stooksbury Papers, UA-LMU; Moore, "J. H. Moore Reminiscences," Apr. 29, 1929, Jesse H. Moore Papers, Faculty Papers, UA-LMU; Achorn to George Allen Hubbell, June 11, 1910, Edgar O. Achorn Papers, UA-LMU; Orr, "History of Tennessee Medical College," 49, 51–53.

58. *Knoxville Sentinel,* May 30, 1910; Achorn to Hubbell, June 11, 1910, Edgar O. Achorn Papers, UA-LMU.

59. Kincaid, *Boy Finds a Friend,* vi; Kincaid, "George Allen Hubbell," 4, 22; "Genealogy of the Gridley Family," and Willis Boughton letter of recommendation, May 15, 1899, George A. Hubbell Papers, UA-LMU.

60. Fairchild to Stooksbury, July 22, 1907, Eugene P. Fairchild Papers, UA-LMU; Suppiger, *Phoenix of the Mountains,* 24; Mrs. George A. Hubbell to Fred Brownlee, July 31, 1948, George A. Hubbell Papers, UA-LMU; Stooksbury to Hubbell, Jan. 26, 1910, William L. Stooksbury Papers, UA-LMU.

61. Stooksbury to Martha Cowgill, Jan. 31, 1910, William L. Stooksbury Papers, UA-LMU.

62. "Old Professor," 12–13; Brown Ayres to Stooksbury, Jan. 5, 1917, Stooksbury to Ayres, Jan. 16, 1917, and Stooksbury to H. A. Morgan, Oct. 31, 1922, Box 32, Folder 605, No. 2, Presidential Papers, UA-UTK.

CHAPTER 6

MODERNIZATION

Epigraphs: Hubbell to Osborn H. Oldroyd, Jan. 27, 1919, George A. Hubbell Papers, UA-LMU; Hill, *Story of Lincoln Memorial University,* 9; Hammond, "Lincoln Memorial University at Cumberland Gap Educates the Sturdy Mountain People."

1. Hubbell to Board of Directors, June 1, 1910, George A. Hubbell Papers, UA-LMU; Kincaid, "George Allen Hubbell," 22.

2. Kincaid, *Boy Finds a Friend,* 3; Suppiger, *Phoenix of the Mountains,* 25, 27, 33; Kincaid, "George Allen Hubbell," 5.

3. Stewart L. Woodford to Theodore P. Gilman, July 24, 1911, and W. S. White to Abraham Lincoln Memorial University, June 29, 1911, George A. Hubbell Papers, UA-LMU; Mrs. Van Rensselaer Adams to Mrs. Russell Sage, Oct. 5, 1910, and Robert Dunn to Mrs. Sage, Oct. 9, 1911, Box 83, Folder 785, Russell Sage Foundation Records, RU.

4. Kincaid, *Boy Finds a Friend,* 4; Dunn to Carnegie, May 4, 1911, Jan. 30, 1912, John S. Allen to Dunn, Jan. 18, 1912, and Bertram to Dunn, Jan. 31, 1912, Series II, Correspondence as to Grants Promised and Made, Reel 73, Carnegie Corporation of New York Records, CU.

5. "General Howard's Birthday" (1912), 1; Lawrence D. Tyson to Moore, Oct. 28, 1912, Jesse H. Moore Papers, Faculty Papers, UA-LMU; "General Howard's Birthday" (1917), 11–12; Harry S. Howard to Eager, Apr. 15, 1921, Oliver O. Howard Papers, UA-LMU.

6. Hubbell to Oldroyd, Jan. 17, 1919, Mar. 26, 1920, Nov. 5, 1921, Osborn H. Oldroyd Collection of Personal Correspondence and Autographs, UC.

7. "Story of a Building," 19; Kincaid, "George Allen Hubbell," 5; *Mountain Herald,* May 1914, 1.

8. Eugene P. Fairchild to Bertram, Mar. 10, 1913, Thomas H. Hubbard to Carnegie, Apr. 1, 1914, Fairchild to Carnegie, Apr. 9, 1914, and Bertram to Fairchild, Apr. 14, 1914, Series II, Correspondence as to Grants Promised and Made, Reel 73, Carnegie Corporation of New York Records, CU; Orr, "History of Tennessee Medical College," 63–64.

9. "Lincoln Memorial Hospital," 3, 5; Kincaid, "George Allen Hubbell," 5; Suppiger, *Phoenix of the Mountains,* 20; Brown Ayres to Morgan Smith, July 28, 1915, Box 29, Folder 526, Presidential Papers, UA-UTK; Orr, "History of Tennessee Medical College," 56–57, 62, 65–66.

10. "Another Important Worker Will Be Missed," 2; Kincaid, *Boy Finds a Friend,* 5–6; Isidor Loeb to Committee on Advanced Standing, Sept. 17, 1915, and [Brown Ayres] to Loeb, Oct. 12, 1915, Box 29, Folder 526, Presidential Papers, UA-UTK.

11. Kincaid, "Shadow of a Man," 45; Seiberling biographical sketch, *Alumnus* 1 (May 1945): 6.

12. Seiberling biographical sketch; frontispiece of *Mountain Herald,* Apr., Sept. 1917, Mar.–Apr. and May 1922; Suppiger, *Phoenix of the Mountains,* 28; S. A. Mitchell to S. Gale Lowrie, Aug. 2, 1930, AAUP Records, GWU.

13. Kincaid, "Shadow of a Man," 45; *Living Memorial to Lincoln,* 10–11, 13, 16–20, 21, 33, 36–37, 39, 41, 46, 49; Richard Lloyd Jones, "Lincoln's Best Monument," *Collier's,* Feb. 19, 1916, copy in Promotion and Publicity Papers, UA-LMU.

14. Extract from *Who's Who in America* 18 (1934–35), John Wesley Hill Papers, UA-LMU.

15. *New York Times,* Nov. 1, 1891, Dec. 13, 1908, Sept. 6, 1909, Dec. 24, 1910, and Oct. 2, 1915; *Dr. John Wesley Hill,* UI.

16. Hubbell to Hughes, Nov. 25, 1916, George A. Hubbell Papers, UA-LMU; *Lincoln Memorial University,* 1, brochure in Promotion and Publicity Papers, UA-LMU.

17. Hill, *Story of Lincoln Memorial University,* 9, 17.

18. Kincaid, *Boy Finds a Friend,* 8; Kincaid, "Lincoln Pilgrimage," 6–10; Kincaid, "Shadow of a Man," 45–47; Hill to Bertram, Jan. 16, 1917, Series II, Correspondence as to Grants Promised and Made, Reel 73, Carnegie Corporation of New York Records, CU; "Letter From Mr. Robert Todd Lincoln," 6–7.

19. Kincaid, "Lincoln Pilgrimage," 8–10, 12–13; Kincaid, "Shadow of a Man," 46; *Celebration of Lincoln's Birthday,* 8–28; *Knoxville Journal,* Feb. 12, 1917; *Claiborne Progress,* Oct. 14, 1936.

20. Kincaid, "Lincoln Pilgrimage," 14–15; *Knoxville Journal,* Feb. 12, 1917.

21. *Celebration of Lincoln's Birthday,* 1, 3–4, 6, 29–35, 37; Kincaid, "George Allen Hubbell," 5.

22. John C. Campbell to John Glenn, Apr. 17, 1917, Box 16, Folder 135, Russell Sage Foundation Records, RU; *Who Was Who in America* 1: 188; Shapiro, *Appalachia on Our Mind,* 195–96.

23. Olive Dame Campbell Diary 5: 29–30, John Charles Campbell and Olive Dame Campbell Papers, UNC; Campbell, *Southern Highlander,* 273–74.

24. Campbell to Glenn, Apr. 17, 19, 1917, Box 16, Folder 135, Russell Sage Foundation Records, RU; Shapiro, *Appalachia on Our Mind,* 217, 237–40; Campbell, *Southern Highlander,* 290, 292–95.

25. Campbell to Hubbell, Apr. 20, 1917, Box 16, Folder 135, Russell Sage Foundation Records, RU; *Who Was Who in America* 1: 188.

26. *New York Times,* Apr. 7, 1917; Hill, *"Democracy versus Autocracy,"* 7–32.

27. Kincaid, "George Allen Hubbell," 5; "Another Important Worker Will Be Missed," 2; "Enlistments from L.M.U.," 7.

28. Levine, *American College,* 27–28.

29. Kincaid, "George Allen Hubbell," 5; "The S.A.T.C.," George A. Hubbell Papers, UA-LMU; "Story of a Building," 20; Moore, "J. H. Moore Reminiscences," Apr. 29, 1929, Jesse H. Moore Papers, Faculty Papers, UA-LMU; Suppiger, *Phoenix of the Mountains,* 166n.

30. *Tech,* Jan. 13, 1920; Hill to Carnegie, Apr. 8, 1919, Seiberling to Mr. and Mrs. Carnegie, May 1, 1919, and Carnegie's secretary to Seiberling, May 6, June 3, 1919, Series II, Correspondence as to Grants Promised and Made, Reel 73, Carnegie Corporation of New York Records, CU.

31. Hubbell to H. A. Morgan, Sept. 3, 1920, and Morgan to Hubbell, Sept. 4, 1920, Box 29, Folder 526, Presidential Papers, UA-UTK; Kincaid, "George Allen Hubbell," 5.

32. Kincaid, "Story of Avery Hall," 6, 21; Kincaid, *Boy Finds a Friend,* 3.

33. Copy of Willie Lea and Evelyn Provins to Lincoln Memorial University, July 19, 1922, and Myrtle G. Thompson to Charles S. Prickett, July 19, 1922, Board of Directors/Trustees Papers, UA-LMU; Braunhut, "Farm Labor Wage Rates," 195; *Knoxville Sunday Journal,* Feb. 15, 1925.

34. John R. Bumgarner reminiscences, in Page and Stephenson, *Lincoln Memorial University,* 26–28; Carter, "Frame of the Picture," 8–9.

35. *Beautiful Claiborne County Tennessee,* not paginated.

36. "Registration up to 324 Inclusive Fall and Winter Terms, 1916–17," and *Items of Information,* not paginated, George A. Hubbell Papers, UA-LMU; "An Analysis of Our Students," 12; "Some Items in the Development of the University," 1–2.

37. M. C. James to H. A. Morgan, Apr. 1, 13, 1921, and Morgan to James, Apr. 2, 20, 1921, Box 29, Folder 526, Presidential Papers, UA-UTK.

38. Shumate, "Our Story: Lincoln Memorial University," 14, Mildred B. Shumate, Faculty Papers, UA-LMU; Suppiger, *Phoenix of the Mountains,* 32–33.

39. Avery speech, [1933], 12, Frederick B. Avery Papers, UA-LMU; Avery, "Mr. Fairchild Helps Found University"; Suppiger, *Phoenix of the Mountains,* 24.

40. Minutes of Executive Committee, Board of Directors, Mar. 9, 1922, ALLM-LMU.

41. "Our Motion Picture Meeting with Success," 3–4; scenario for "Taking Up Where Honest Left Off," Promotion and Publicity Papers, UA-LMU; Pyramid Film Company, on companies list, http://imdb.com/; Suppiger, *Phoenix of the Mountains,* 35.

42. Suppiger, *Phoenix of the Mountains,* 36; Kincaid, *Boy Finds a Friend,* 9; Moore, "J. H. Moore Reminiscences," Apr. 29, 1929, Jesse H. Moore Papers, Faculty Papers, UA-LMU.

43. Mrs. George A. Hubbell to Fred Brownlee, July 31, 1948, George A. Hubbell Papers, UA-LMU; Kincaid, *Boy Finds a Friend,* 9–10; *Middlesboro Daily News,* May 24, 1960.

44. Kincaid, *Boy Finds a Friend,* 10–13; Kincaid, "George Allen Hubbell," 22.

45. Suppiger, *Phoenix of the Mountains,* 36; "Robert Orville Matthews," 17; Hammond, "Lincoln Memorial University at Cumberland Gap Educates the Sturdy Mountain People."

46. Stewart W. McClelland to L. K. Sunderlin, Sept. 21, 1942, and "Nancy Hanks Articles," Nancy Hanks Memorial Association Papers, UA-LMU; "Wanted: An Opportunity for Girls," 7–8; Grannis, "Revival of Mountain Weaving," 4. The Nancy Hanks Department failed to fulfill the hopes of everyone concerned with it. Whatever profit and donations it generated dried up during the Depression and the department had become defunct by 1931. Many of its instructional functions were taken over by the Department of Domestic Sciences.

47. *Blue and Gray,* Mar. 15, 1924; Suppiger, *Phoenix of the Mountains,* 60.

48. Clarke, "Living Memorial to Abraham Lincoln," 20–21, 76, 78; Hammond, "Lincoln Memorial University at Cumberland Gap Educates the Sturdy Mountain People."

49. Dickson, *Lincoln Memorial University,* 12, 22, 34, 36–37.

50. "President Harding's Last Tribute to Lincoln Memorial University," 2–3; "President Coolidge's Letter," frontispiece of *Mountain Herald,* Nov. 1923.

51. Hill to Iris Grannis, Nov. 6, 1926, John Wesley Hill Papers, UA-LMU; Hill, *Lincoln the Inspired Leader,* 1–4; Hill, *If Lincoln Were Here,* passim; Hill, *Abraham Lincoln: Man of God,* inscription and 441.

52. Suppiger, *Phoenix of the Mountains,* 63; Barnes, "Barnes on L.M.U."; Moore, "J. H. Moore Reminiscences," Apr. 29, 1929, Jesse H. Moore Papers, Faculty Papers, UA-LMU; Lucia Danforth to J. Samuel Guy, July 6, 1930, and Merlin G. Miller to Joseph Mayer, Sept. 9, 1930, AAUP Records, GWU; "Robert Orville Matthews," 17.

53. Lincoln Memorial University *Catalog,* 1926–27, 8, SC-LMU; Memorandum of Interview, Jan. 3, 1924, Mar. 15, 17, 1926, Frederick P. Keppel to Hill, Apr. 9, 1925, Keppel to Henry T. Allen, Mar. 17, May 10, 1926, C. S. Thompson to Carnegie Corporation, July 25, 1928, and Robert M. Lester to Thompson, Oct. 11, 1928, Series IIIA, Grants, Box 203, Folder 14 (1924–52), Carnegie Corporation of New York Records, CU.

54. Suppiger, *Phoenix of the Mountains,* 33; "Mr. and Mrs. Henry Ford Entertain," 10–11; S. P. Ruddiman to C. P. Williams, Jan. 28, Feb. 1, 1927, Accession 557, Henry

Ford and Ford Family Papers, Ford Properties Subgroup, THF; *Nancy Hanks Memorial Association* brochure, Nancy Hanks Memorial Association Papers, UA-LMU.

55. Williams to Ruddiman, Feb. 18, 1927, Ruddiman to Williams, Mar. 21, 1927, and Specifications for Proposed Auditorium-Administration Building, July 1925, Accession 557, Henry Ford and Ford Family Papers, Ford Properties Subgroup, THF.

56. *Who Was Who in American Art* 3: 2514; "Dedication of the Bronze Statue," 9; "Paolo, Noted Lincoln Sculptor," 19; "Memorandum of Extract from letter of Cartaino S. Paolo, 2910 Mabel, Tucson, Arizona Dated March 2, 1953 Comment by Dr. Robert L. Kincaid," and Paolo letter, Mar. 2, 1953, Cartaino S. Paolo, Miscellaneous Papers, UA-LMU.

57. Ruddiman to Williams, Mar. 5, 1927, and Frank Campsall to Lincoln Memorial University, Feb. 10, 28, 1927, Henry Ford folder, Miscellaneous Papers, UA-LMU; *Laying of the Cornerstone of the B. N. Duke Hall of Citizenship, Lincoln Memorial University,* Box 142, Miscellaneous Printed Material Folder, Lincoln Memorial University, 1927–39, and "Contributions Mr. B. N. Duke 1892 to Inclusive" and "B. N. Duke Contributions," Box 112, Financial Papers—Charitable Contributions, 1892–1928 Folder, and honorary diploma awarded Duke, May 31, 1927, Oversized Cabinet, OC: II: 4, Benjamin Newton Duke Papers, DU; Suppiger, *Phoenix of the Mountains,* 63. About the time that Hill accomplished the Duke donation, a massive effort was afoot to raise ten million dollars for the proposed Abraham Lincoln University in Westchester County, New York, which must have offered some competition to his efforts and some confusion with Lincoln Memorial University. See *Statement of the Purpose and Plans of the Abraham Lincoln Foundation and the Abraham Lincoln University* (1929), in William Preston Few Papers, DU; and *New York Herald Tribune,* Apr. 13, 1930.

58. Levine, *American College,* 38–41; Montgomery, Folmsbee, and Greene, *To Foster Knowledge,* 184.

59. *Alumnus* 1 (Feb. 1945): 5, 7, 9.

60. Shumate, "Our Story: Lincoln Memorial University," 14, Mildred B. Shumate, Faculty Papers, UA-LMU; Peck and Smith, *Berea's First 125 Years,* 100; applications, Nov. 29, 1926, and Nov. 7, 1927, SACS Papers, UA-LMU; "Higher Rating Given Lincoln Memorial University," 7.

61. Charles D. Lewis to W. T. Semple, May 5, 1928, Semple to Lewis, May 17, 1928, and Lucia Danforth to J. Samuel Guy, July 6, 1930, AAUP Records, GWU; C. P. Williams to A. L. Garford, Apr. 17, 1930, Box 66, Lincoln Memorial University Folder, Frank A. Seiberling Papers, OHS.

62. Resolution, June 4, 1928, SACS Papers, UA-LMU; Lincoln Memorial University *Catalog,* 1915–16, 5–6, and 1920–21, 7–9, SC-LMU.

63. Application, Oct. 1, 1928, SACS Papers, UA-LMU.

64. W. D. Hooper to J. H. S. Morison, Apr. 12, 1930, SACS Papers, UA-LMU.

65. *Who Was Who in America* 3: 740–41; "Dr. Hervin U. Roop, Dean," 15; Hervin U. Roop books at http://www.amazon.com/.

66. Application form, Lebanon Valley College, Mar. 7, 1903, Roop to Carnegie, Jan. 27, 1904, Dec. 26, 28, 1904, Apr. 22, May 31, Oct. 27, 1905, Bertram to Roop, Aug. 19, Dec. 29, 1904, Dec. 11, 1906, [1905], and J. D. Gossard to Carnegie, Feb. 1, 1913, Series II, Correspondence as to Grants Promised and Made, Reel 38, Carnegie Corporation of New York Records, CU; Lebanon Valley College, http://www.wikipedia.org/.

67. Lincoln Memorial University *Catalog,* 1928–29, 9, SC-LMU; *Who Was Who in America* 3: 741; Roop, "Issue of Modernism," 6–7, 9, 11; Roberts, "Conservative Evangelicals," 298, 301.

68. W. D. Hooper to J. H. S. Morison, Apr. 12, 1930, SACS Papers, UA-LMU; Shumate, *Brief History,* 14–15; Suppiger, *Phoenix of the Mountains,* 65; *Mountain Herald* 31, no. 7 (Spring 1929): 7; Trustee's Minutes, November 20, 1917–December 10, 1967 (June 3, 1929): 161, ALLM-LMU.

69. Lincoln Memorial University *Catalog,* 1926–27, 8–11, 1927–28, 8–11, 1928–29, 9–12, and 1929–30, 8–11, SC-LMU; *Middlesboro Daily News,* Aug. 30, 1929.

70. [Iris Grannis] to Hill, Feb. 6, 1928, Aug. 14, 1929, and Hill to Grannis, Jan. 9, no year, John Wesley Hill Papers, UA-LMU; "Exhibit E," n.d. [probably 1928 or 1929], SACS Papers, UA-LMU.

71. Clifford P. Lyons to Arthur O. Lovejoy, May 14, 1930, AAUP Records, GWU.

72. Ibid.

73. Ibid.; Lucia Danforth to Dr. Mayer, Sept. 12, [1930], AAUP Records, GWU.

74. Hill to Iris Grannis, Aug. 12, 1929, John Wesley Hill Papers, UA-LMU; [Grannis] to Hill, Aug. 14, 1929, Iris Grannis, Staff Papers, UA-LMU. Lewis's *Myths After Lincoln,* which appeared in 1929, disputes a number of legends about the president. The book is based on poor scholarship but employs a vibrant, popular writing style. Lewis did, however, support several other myths about people associated with Lincoln that have no basis in fact. Lewis, *Myths After Lincoln,* 62–63, 264, 270, 299, 373.

Chapter 7

Strike

Epigraphs: Hazel Fulton to Frank T. Hines, Apr. 16, 1930, Seiberling to A. B. Harmon, Apr. 8, 1930, and Hill to Seiberling, Apr. 9, 1930, Box 66, Lincoln Memorial University Folder, Frank A. Seiberling Papers, OHS.

1. *Knoxville News-Sentinel,* Apr. 10, 1930. James W. Schenkenfelder has compiled newspaper coverage of the strike into several notebooks, copies of which have been deposited in Special Collections at Lincoln Memorial University.

2. [Iris Grannis] to John Wesley Hill, Aug. 14, Nov. 15, Dec. 6, 1929, Iris Grannis, Staff Papers, UA-LMU; Ezra L. Gillis Information Blank, Nov. 14, 1929, SACS Papers, UA-LMU.

3. W. D. Hooper to J. H. S. Morison, Apr. 12, 1930, and Hooper to H. Robinson Shipherd, May 1, 1930, SACS Papers, UA-LMU.

4. Hill to Roop, Dec. 13, 1929, John Wesley Hill Papers, UA-LMU; Roop to Hill, Dec. 19, 1929, and Roop to not stated, Dec. 11, 1929, Hervin U. Roop Papers, UA-LMU.

5. *"Statement of personal grievances* of *Merlin G. Miller* against *Lincoln Memorial University,"* Aug. 28, 1930, "Outline of Sequence of Events Leading Up to Present Conditions at Lincoln Memorial University," Aug. 7, 1930, and unsigned notes, AAUP Records, GWU; Seiberling to Hill, Jan. 27, Apr. 2, 1930, Box 66, Lincoln Memorial University Folder, Frank A. Seiberling Papers, OHS.

6. Lincoln Memorial University *Catalog,* 1928–29, 9, SC-LMU; Hill to Miller, Sept. 7, 1928, Merlin G. Miller, Faculty Papers, UA-LMU; Special Collections Research Center, University of Chicago, to author, e-mail, May 3, 2007; Merlin G. Miller on social Security Death Index, http://www.genealogy.com/.

7. *"Statement of personal grievances* of *Merlin G. Miller* against *Lincoln Memorial University,"* Aug. 28, 1930, "Outline of Sequence of Events Leading Up to Present Conditions at Lincoln Memorial University," Aug. 7, 1930, and unsigned notes, AAUP Records, GWU; Lincoln Memorial University *Catalog,* 1928–29, 9; Hill to Seiberling, Mar. 21, 1930, and Seiberling to Hill, Mar. 24, 1930, Box 66, Lincoln Memorial University Folder, Frank A. Seiberling Papers, OHS. Rumor had it that, when dismissing Lewis in 1928, Hill had packed the faculty meeting with "the farmer and plumber and gardener and office force and chicken man" to ensure his firing. Lucia Danforth to J. Samuel Guy, July 6, 1930, AAUP Records, GWU.

8. Copy of Roop to Diller, Mar. 22, 1930, J. Samuel Guy to H. W. Tyler, Apr. 18, 1931, copy of Roop to deJonge (constituting his contract), and unsigned notes, AAUP Records, GWU.

9. Lincoln Memorial University *Catalog,* 1928–29, 9, SC-LMU; Elliot Van N. Diller to Joseph Mayer, Sept. 3, 1930, Lucia Danforth to J. Samuel Guy, July 6, 1930, and "Thompson's Statement," AAUP Records, GWU; *Knoxville News-Sentinel,* Apr. 12, 1930; *Blue and Gray,* May 14, 1929; Jesse Stuart, "My Teachers of Lincoln Memorial University," 14–16, UL; Jocelyn K. Wilk, Columbia University Archives, to author, e-mail, Apr. 30, 2007. Roop apparently refused to allow Diller to use a different psychology text in the classroom but approved his request for copies of an up-to-date psychology

book for the library. See Book Order Form, Sept. 25, 1929, and Book Order Form, n.d., Casimir P. Williams Papers, UA-LMU.

10. Hill to Seiberling, Mar. 28, 31, 1930, Seiberling to Hill, Mar. 29, 1930, Hill to Roop, Mar. 29, 1930, and C. P. Williams to A. L. Garford, Apr. 17, 1930, Box 66, Lincoln Memorial University Folder, Frank A. Seiberling Papers, OHS.

11. Copy of Roop to deJonge (constituting contract), deJonge to Mayer, Sept. 5, 1930, and Danforth to Guy, July 6, 1930, AAUP Records, GWU; Alfred deJonge on passenger records, http://www.ellisislandrecords.org/; Lincoln Memorial University *Catalog,* 1929–30, 8, SC-LMU; *Louisville Courier-Journal,* Apr. 14, 1930; petition regarding deJonge by Fred Fennell, n.d., Alfred Robert Willy deJonge, Faculty Papers, UA-LMU; Jocelyn K. Wilk, Columbia University Archives, to author, e-mail, Apr. 30, 2007.

12. Lincoln Memorial University *Catalog,* 1928–29, 10, SC-LMU; Danforth to Guy, July 6, 1930, Danforth letter, n.d., and "Conference Between Chancellor Hill and Dr. Mayer at 26 Jackson Place, Washington, D.C., May 14, 1930," AAUP Records, GWU.

13. Roop to Maude Smith, Mar. 22, 1930, and Danforth to Guy, July 6, 1930, AAUP Records, GWU.

14. Gertrude B. Bartlett, "Meeting of Student Body, Mar. 27, 1930," AAUP Records, GWU; *Knoxville News-Sentinel,* Apr. 12, 1930.

15. Social Security Death Index search, http://www.genealogy.com/; *Knoxville News-Sentinel,* Apr. 13, 1930.

16. Opal Ann McDowell reminiscences, and diary, Mar. 28, 1930, copy in Student Papers, UA-LMU; Gertrude B. Bartlett, "Meeting of Student Body, March 27, 1930," AAUP Records, GWU.

17. Gertrude B. Bartlett, "Meeting of Student Body, March 27, 1930," AAUP Records, GWU; *Alumnus* 1 (1945): 14; W. C. Thompson to LeRoy Johnson, Nov. 7, 1940, Student Papers, UA-LMU; Mrs. George A. Hubbell to Fred Brownlee, July 31, 1948, George A. Hubbell Papers, UA-LMU.

18. *Knoxville News-Sentinel,* Apr. 11, 1930; *Middlesboro Daily News,* Mar. 31, 1930; Minutes of Executive Committee, Mar. 29, 1930, ALLM-LMU; Harry Bullock to Frank Seiberling, Apr. 1, 1930, AAUP Records, GWU.

19. *"Statement of personal grievances* of *Merlin G. Miller* against *Lincoln Memorial University,"* Aug. 28, 1930, AAUP Records, GWU; *Middlesboro Daily News,* Apr. 9, 1930.

20. Minutes of special meeting of board, Apr. 6, 1930, AAUP Records, GWU; Trustee's Minutes, November 20, 1917–December 10, 1967, 165–66, ALLM-LMU; *Louisville Courier-Journal,* Apr. 13, 1930; Frank T. Hines entry, http://www.politicalgraveyard.com/; A. L. Garford to D. A. Dollarhide et al., Apr. 16, 1930, Box 66, Lincoln Memorial University Folder, Frank A. Seiberling Papers, OHS.

21. Avery speech, [1933], 11, Frederick B. Avery Papers, UA-LMU; *Middlesboro Daily News,* Feb. 10, 1933, Sept. 30, 1952; J. H. S. Morison information in Faculty Papers, 1930, UA-LMU; Trustee's Minutes, November 20, 1917–December 10, 1967, 161, ALLM-LMU; Seiberling to A. B. Harmon, Apr. 8, 1930, Box 66, Lincoln Memorial University Folder, Frank A. Seiberling Papers, OHS.

22. [Iris Grannis] to John Wesley Hill, Apr. 5, 1930, and Grannis to Eugene P. Fairchild, Apr. 17, 1930, Iris Grannis, Staff Papers, UA-LMU.

23. Hill to Miley, Apr. 8, 1930, John Wesley Hill Papers, UA-LMU; *Knoxville News-Sentinel,* Apr. 11, 1930; *Middlesboro Daily News,* Apr. 9, 1930.

24. *Middlesboro Daily News,* Apr. 9, 1930; *"Statement of personal grievances* of *Merlin G. Miller* against *Lincoln Memorial University,"* Aug. 28, 1930, AAUP Records, GWU; *Knoxville News-Sentinel,* Apr. 9, 1930.

25. Opal Ann McDowell diary, Apr. 9, 1930, copy in Student Papers, UA-LMU; *Louisville Courier-Journal,* Apr. 9, 1930.

26. *Knoxville News-Sentinel,* Apr. 10, 11, 1930; *Middlesboro Daily News,* Apr. 10, 1930; *Bristol Herald-Courier,* Apr. 10, 14, 1930; *Knoxville Journal,* Apr. 10, 1930; deJonge to Mayer, Sept. 5, 1930, AAUP Records, GWU; *Lexington Herald,* Apr. 10, 1930.

27. *Bristol Herald-Courier,* Apr. 11, 1930; *Knoxville Journal,* Apr. 11, 1930; *Knoxville News-Sentinel,* Apr. 11, 1930; Opal Ann McDowell diary, Apr. 11, 1930, copy in Student Papers, UA-LMU.

28. *Middlesboro Daily News,* Apr. 11, 1930; *Knoxville News-Sentinel,* Apr. 11, 1930. Hooper made it clear to Morison that strong-arm tactics in dealing with the strike seriously hurt the university's reputation in the wider academic community. Hooper to Morison, Apr. 12, 1930, SACS Papers, UA-LMU.

29. *"Statement of personal grievances* of *Merlin G. Miller* against *Lincoln Memorial University,"* Aug. 28, 1930, AAUP Records, GWU; *Knoxville News-Sentinel,* Apr. 12, 1930.

30. *Knoxville News-Sentinel,* Apr. 12, 1930.

31. *Louisville Courier-Journal,* Apr. 12, 13, 1930; *Knoxville Journal,* Apr. 12, 1930; *Bristol Herald-Courier,* Apr. 13, 1930; *Chicago Daily Tribune,* Apr. 13, 1930; *Knoxville News-Sentinel,* Apr. 12, 1930; Hill to Seiberling, May 19, 1930, Box 66, Lincoln Memorial University Folder, Frank A. Seiberling Papers, OHS.

32. *Knoxville News-Sentinel,* Apr. 12, 13, 17, 1930; *Louisville Courier-Journal,* Apr. 13, 1930; *Middlesboro Daily News,* Apr. 12, 1930; *Nashville Banner,* Apr. 13, 1930. The social rules for women students who lived on campus were just as strict in 1958 (amounting to more than six single-spaced, typed pages) as they had been in 1930. See "Regulations and Information for Women Students, Fall 1958," Student Papers, UA-LMU.

33. *Middlesboro Daily News,* Apr. 12, 1930; Miller to Mayer, Aug. 28, 1930, *"Statement of personal grievances* of *Merlin G. Miller* against *Lincoln Memorial University,"* Aug. 28, 1930, copies of Roop to Miller, May 22 [Mar. 22], 1930, Morison to Miller, Apr. 12, 1930, and Morison to Diller, Apr. 12, 1930, AAUP Records, GWU; *Knoxville Journal,* Apr. 13, 1930; Hill to Seiberling, Apr. 9, 1930, Box 66, Lincoln Memorial University Folder, Frank A. Seiberling Papers, OHS.

34. "John R. Neal: An Extraordinary Law Professor," http://www.utk.edu/; Chandler, "Cleaning House," iv, 1–2, 39, 86–90; Montgomery, Folmsbee, and Greene, *To Foster Knowledge,* 186–88.

35. *Knoxville Journal,* Apr. 14, 15, 16, 1930; *Middlesboro Daily News,* Apr. 14, 1930; *Knoxville News-Sentinel,* Apr. 14, 16, 1930; *Chicago Daily Tribune,* Apr. 15, 1930; John R. Neal to Frank T. Hines, Apr. 15, 1930, Box 66, Lincoln Memorial University Folder, Frank A. Seiberling Papers, OHS.

36. *Knoxville News-Sentinel,* Apr. 15, 17, 1930; *Middlesboro Daily News,* Apr. 16, 1930; *Knoxville Journal,* Apr. 17, 1930; Harry Bullock to Seiberling, Apr. 17, 1930, Seiberling to Hill, Apr. 16, 1930, Seiberling to A. L. Garford, Apr. 19, 1930, Student Committee to Seiberling, Apr. 17, 1930, Hazel Fulton to Frank T. Hines, Apr. 16, 1930, D. A. Dollarhide et al. to Garford, Apr. 16, 1930, Garford to D. A. Dollarhide et al., Apr. 16, 1930, Seiberling to Committee of Nine Faculty, Apr. 16, 1930, Seiberling to C. P. Williams, Apr. 17, 1930, and Seiberling to Morison, Apr. 14, 1930, Box 66, Lincoln Memorial University Folder, Frank A. Seiberling Papers, OHS.

37. *Knoxville News-Sentinel,* Apr. 18, 19, 1930; *Knoxville Journal,* Apr. 18, 1930; *Middlesboro Daily News,* Apr. 18, 1930; *Louisville Courier-Journal,* Apr. 20, 1930; Robert L. Kincaid to Seiberling, Apr. 18, 1930, and Shipherd to Hill, Apr. 23, 1930, Box 66, Lincoln Memorial University Folder, Frank A. Seiberling Papers, OHS. Morison reported that 168 college students attended classes on April 18. Seiberling to A. L. Garford, Apr. 19, 1930, Box 66, Lincoln Memorial University Folder, Frank A. Seiberling Papers, OHS.

38. *Bristol Herald-Courier,* Apr. 20, 1930; "Conference Between Chancellor Hill and Dr. Mayer at 26 Jackson Place, Washington, D.C., May 14, 1930," AAUP Records, GWU.

39. *New York Times,* Apr. 14, 1930; *Saint Paul Pioneer Press,* Apr. 14, 1930; *Washington Post,* Apr. 15, 1930; *Knoxville News-Sentinel,* May 7, 1930; *Middlesboro Daily News,* Apr. 19, 1930.

40. Typed extract of *Who's Who in America* 18 (1934–35) in John Wesley Hill Papers, UA-LMU; *Washington Post,* Apr. 20, 1930.

41. *Knoxville News-Sentinel,* Apr. 13, 14, 19, 1930; *New Republic,* Apr. 30, 1930, 286.

42. *Knoxville News-Sentinel,* Apr. 20, 1930.

43. Ibid.; *Alumnus* 1 (Dec. 1945): 8.

44. *Knoxville News-Sentinel,* Apr. 20, 1930; *Alumnus* 1 (Aug. 1946): 10; *Railsplitter,* 1928, 31; alumni list, Apr. 1956, Alumni Association Papers, UA-LMU.

45. *Middlesboro Daily News,* Apr. 21, 1930; *Mountain Herald,* 1930–31, 2; *Knoxville News-Sentinel,* Apr. 8, 1931; Hill to Seiberling, Mar. 25, 1930, Seiberling to Morison, Apr. 16, 1930, and Seiberling to A. L. Garford, Apr. 19, 1930, Box 66, Lincoln Memorial University Folder, Frank A. Seiberling Papers, OHS.

46. *Knoxville News-Sentinel,* Apr. 20, 1930; *Middlesboro Daily News,* Apr. 21, 1930; Hill to Seiberling, Apr. 15, 1930, Seiberling to Morison, Apr. 16, 1930, and Seiberling to Hill, Apr. 16, 1930, Box 66, Lincoln Memorial University Folder, Frank A. Seiberling Papers, OHS.

47. Shipherd to Hill, Apr. 23, 1930, Shipherd to Seiberling, Apr. 18, May 10, 1930, and Hill to Seiberling, Apr. 29, 1930, Box 66, Lincoln Memorial University Folder, Frank A. Seiberling Papers, OHS.

48. *Knoxville News-Sentinel,* Apr. 27, 1930; *Middlesboro Daily News,* Apr. 26, 28, 1930.

49. Lincoln Memorial University *Catalog,* 1929–30, 9, SC-LMU; Roop to Daniel H. Higgins, Apr. 27, 1929, Ethel T. Higgins to Shipherd, May 17, 1930, Ethel T. Higgins statement, n.d., and Ethel T. Higgins to Hill, Aug. 29, 1930, Ethel T. Higgins, Faculty Papers, UA-LMU; "Northwestern University, Department of Geology and Geography," and Lucia Danforth to J. Samuel Guy, July 6, 1930, AAUP Records, GWU; *Knoxville Journal,* May 7, 1930; *Knoxville News-Sentinel,* May 7, 1930.

50. Ethel T. Higgins statement, n.d., Ethel T. Higgins, Faculty Papers, UA-LMU; Hill to Shipherd, May 7, 1930, John Wesley Hill Papers, UA-LMU.

51. Frank C. Grannis to A. G. A. Balz, May 29, 1930, and Lucia Danforth to J. Samuel Guy, July 6, 1930, AAUP Records, GWU; Shipherd memo, Oct. 23, 1930, SACS Papers, UA-LMU.

52. *Morristown Gazette and Mail,* Apr. 22, 1930; *Middlesboro Daily News,* Apr. 22, 23, 1930; *Knoxville News-Sentinel,* Apr. 21, 23, 24, 1930; *Bristol Herald-Courier,* Apr. 25, 1930; *Louisville Courier-Journal,* Apr. 24, 1930; *Lexington Herald,* Apr. 21, 1930; Iris Grannis to Eugene P. Fairchild, Apr. 17, 1930, Iris Grannis, Staff Papers, UA-LMU.

53. *Knoxville News-Sentinel,* Apr. 23, 24, 1930; *Middlesboro Daily News,* Oct. 1, 1931; *"Statement of personal grievances* of *Merlin G. Miller* against *Lincoln Memorial University,"* Aug. 28, 1930, AAUP Records, GWU.

54. Hill to Shipherd, May 3, 8, 1930, John Wesley Hill Papers, UA-LMU.

55. Hill to Seiberling, Apr. 24, 1930, Box 66, Lincoln Memorial University Folder, Frank A. Seiberling Papers, OHS; Hill to Warren, Louis A. Warren Papers, Apr. 19, 1930, LM.

56. "Departmental History," Classical Languages Department, Carleton College, http://www.carleton.edu/; *Middlesboro Daily News,* Apr. 22, 1930; Seiberling to Hill, Jan. 27, 1930, and Hill to Seiberling, Feb. 10, 17, Mar. 31, 1930, Box 66, Lincoln Memorial University Folder, Frank A. Seiberling Papers, OHS; "Memorandum of conversation with James H. Rector, Harrogate, Tenn., September 19, 1940," Robert L. Kincaid Collection, CGNHP. Rector served as postmaster of Harrogate from February 15 to December 6, 1921. See Frazier, *Tennessee Post Offices,* 222.

57. Danforth to Guy, July 6, 1930, and Danforth to Joseph Mayer, Sept. 12, [1930], AAUP Records, GWU; Roop, "What Is Education?" 281–86.

58. Daniel Dollarhide, H. M. Harshaw, T. Edward Terrill, and Giles Roberts Floyd to S. A. Mitchell, Apr. 13, 1930, H. W. Tyler to Mitchell, Apr. 17, 1930, [Tyler] to Merlin G. Miller, Apr. 23, 1930, W. D. Hooper to Mayer, Apr. 21, 1930, and Hooper to Tyler, Apr. 28, 1930, AAUP Records, GWU.

59. S. A. Mitchell to W. D. Hooper, May 9, 1930, "Causes leading to dismissals," n.d., "Outline of Sequence of Events Leading Up to Present Conditions at Lincoln Memorial University," Aug. 7, 1930, William Bennett Munro to Shipherd, Apr. 28, 1930, Shipherd to Munro, Apr. 28, 1930, Arthur O. Lovejoy to Tyler, May 5, 1930, Mayer to Mitchell, May 5, 1930, and Tyler to Hooper, May 2, 1930, AAUP Records, GWU; *Knoxville Journal,* Apr. 28, 1930; *Middlesboro Daily News,* May 2, 1930; *Knoxville News-Sentinel,* May 4, 1930; Shipherd to Seiberling, Apr. 28, 1930, Box 66, Lincoln Memorial University Folder, Frank A. Seiberling Papers, OHS.

60. Mitchell to Hooper, May 9, 1930, Mitchell to Clyde Furst, May 8, 1930, Mitchell to Guy, May 7, 1930, Lovejoy to Mayer, May 3, 1930, Clyde Furst to Mitchell, May 16, 1930, Mitchell to Mayer, May 5, 1930, Tyler to Mayer, May 8, 1930, and Mitchell to Tyler, May 3, 5, 1930, AAUP Records, GWU.

61. Carl E. Sherrick, "Frank A. Geldard, The University of Virginia," http://www.tactileresearch.org/; http://www.chemistry.emory.edu/; Lowrie, "Proper Function of the State Budget," 47–63; Hill to [Shipherd], May 7, 13, 1930, John Wesley Hill Papers, UA-LMU; Mayer to Guy, May 16, 1930, and Mayer to Lowrie, May 1, 1930, AAUP Records, GWU.

62. Shipherd to Hill, July 24, 1930, H. Robinson Shipherd Papers, UA-LMU; Balz to Tyler, Dec. 23, 1930, and Mitchell to Tyler, May 20, 1930, AAUP Records, GWU; Hill to Seiberling, May 19, 1930, Box 66, Lincoln Memorial University Folder, Frank A. Seiberling Papers, OHS.

63. Mitchell to Frederick P. Keppel, May 22, 1930, Series IIIA, Grants, Box 203, Folder 14 (1924–52), Carnegie Corporation of New York Records, CU; Mitchell to Tyler, May 20, 27, 1930, and Tyler to Mitchell, May 23, 1930, AAUP Records, GWU; Hill to Shipherd, May 20, 1930, John Wesley Hill Papers, UA-LMU.

64. Hill to [Shipherd], May 13, 20, 1930, John Wesley Hill Papers, UA-LMU; *Knoxville Journal,* May 29, June 3, 1930.

65. Danforth to Guy, July 6, 1930, and Clifford P. Lyons to Arthur O. Lovejoy, May 14, 1930, AAUP Records, GWU.

66. *Nashville Banner,* Apr. 14, 1930; *"Statement of personal grievances* of *Merlin G. Miller* against *Lincoln Memorial University,"* Aug. 28, 1930, AAUP Records, GWU.

67. Vada Holt, "History of the Class," 13–14; Kincaid to E. E. Patton, Apr. 3, 1947, Robert L. Kincaid Papers, UA-LMU; Suppiger, *Phoenix of the Mountains,* 65, 167n; Moore, "Observations and Experiences of His Life," 60–61, Jesse H. Moore Papers, Faculty Papers, UA-LMU; Ramsey, "Reminiscing," 2; Grace Moore to Cindy Whitt, [May] 24, 29, [2000], Student Papers, UA-LMU.

Chapter 8

Crisis and Survival

Epigraphs: Shipherd to Hill, July 23, 1930, H. Robinson Shipherd Papers, UA-LMU; Hill to Walter T. Shepard, Feb. 12, 1933, John Wesley Hill Papers, UA-LMU; J. Samuel Guy to S. A. Mitchell, July 21, 1930, AAUP Records, GWU.

1. Annual Report of President to Board of Directors, June 2, 1930, 4, appendix, and Treasurer's Annual Report, Aug. 31, 1930, 33, Board of Directors/Trustees Papers, UA-LMU; Shumate, "Our Story: Lincoln Memorial University," 14, Mildred B. Shumate, Faculty Papers, UA-LMU.

2. Annual Report of President to Board of Directors, June 2, 1930, 4, Board of Directors/Trustees Papers, UA-LMU; Shumate, *Brief History,* 10; "Brief History," Ellen Myers School Folder, Buildings Papers, UA-LMU; *Knoxville Journal,* June 3, 1930; Peck and Smith, *Berea's First 125 Years,* 83, 98.

3. Shipherd to Hill, July 23, Aug. 13, 1930, H. Robinson Shipherd Papers, UA-LMU; Hill to Shipherd, July 26, Aug. 2, 1930, John Wesley Hill Papers, UA-LMU; Annual Report of President to Board of Directors, June 2, 1930, 9, Board of Directors/Trustees Papers, UA-LMU; data on faculty, 1930, Faculty Papers, UA-LMU.

4. Kincaid to Seiberling, July 28, 1930, Robert L. Kincaid Papers, UA-LMU; C. P. [Williams] to Shipherd, n.d. [1930], Casimir P. Williams Papers, UA-LMU; Hill to Williams, July 4, 18, 1930, John Wesley Hill Papers, UA-LMU; Seiberling to Morison, July 16, 1930, Frank A. Seiberling, Board of Directors/Trustees Papers, UA-LMU; Morison to Shipherd, July 15, 1930, J. H. S. Morison Papers, UA-LMU; minutes of meeting of executive committee, July 19, 1930, Board of Directors/Trustees Papers, UA-LMU; Minutes of Executive Committee, July 19, 1930, ALLM-LMU; Shipherd to

Hill, July 23, 24, 1930, H. Robinson Shipherd Papers, UA-LMU; Seiberling to Shipherd, May 15, 1930, and Hill to Seiberling, Apr. 28, 29, 1930, Box 66, Lincoln Memorial University Folder, Frank A. Seiberling Papers, OHS .

5. Hill to nephew, May 13, 1930, Hill to Williams, July 18, [1930], and Hill to Shipherd, July 26, Aug. 21, 1930, John Wesley Hill Papers, UA-LMU; Seiberling to Morison, July 16, 1930, Frank A. Seiberling, Board of Directors/Trustees Papers, UA-LMU; Shipherd to Hill, Aug. 13, 1930, H. Robinson Shipherd Papers, UA-LMU; Hill to Seiberling, May 19, July 1, 10, 1930, Box 66, Lincoln Memorial University Folder, Frank A. Seiberling Papers, OHS.

6. Hill to nephew, May 13, 1930, Hill to Williams, July 18, [1930], and Hill to Shipherd, May 20, 1930, John Wesley Hill Papers, UA-LMU; Mayer to Guy, June 18, 1930, and Mitchell to Guy, July 5, 1930, AAUP Records, GWU; Morison to Seiberling, May 18, 1930, and Hill to Seiberling, June 5, July 10, 1930, Box 66, Lincoln Memorial University Folder, Frank A. Seiberling Papers, OHS.

7. Mitchell to Lowrie, July 25, 1930, Lowrie to Mitchell, July 31, 1930, Tyler to Mitchell, June 7, 1930, Mitchell to Tyler, June 3, 1930, Mitchell to Mayer, July 19, 1930, Guy to Mitchell, July 17, 21, 1930, and Guy to Hill, May 6, 1931, AAUP Records, GWU; Annual Report of President to Board of Directors, June 2, 1930, 4, Board of Directors/Trustees Papers, UA-LMU; Hill to Shipherd, July 26, 1930, John Wesley Hill Papers, UA-LMU; Wade H. Cooper to Seiberling, July 25, 1930, Box 66, Lincoln Memorial University Folder, Frank A. Seiberling Papers, OHS.

8. Tyler to Mayer, June 21, 1930, Tyler to Mitchell, June 10, July 25, 1930, Mitchell to Guy, July 23, 1930, "Meeting with Trustees of Lincoln Memorial University, July 31, 1930," "*Recommendations for the Improvement of Conditions* at Lincoln Memorial University, by the *American Association of University Professors,*" and Mitchell to Tyler, Jan. 30, 1931, AAUP Records, GWU.

9. Mitchell to Lowrie, Aug. 2, 1930, and Mayer to Miller, Aug. 18, 1930, AAUP Records, GWU; Hill to Shipherd, Aug. 2, 1930, John Wesley Hill Papers, UA-LMU; Shipherd to Hill, Aug. 13, 1930, H. Robinson Shipherd Papers, UA-LMU.

10. Copy of Guy to Hill, Aug. 4, 1930, Guy to Lowrie, Sept. 19, 1930, J. Samuel Guy's "President Shipherd," copy of H. A. Morgan to Guy, May 16, 1930, copy of Loye W. Miller to Guy, May 16, 1930, "Professor Mitchell's Summary of the *Main Charges Against Shipherd,*" unsigned memo, Sept. 9, 1930, excerpt of Guy to Hill, Oct. 5, 1930, and Guy to Tyler, Oct. 28, 1930, AAUP Records, GWU; Morison to Seiberling, May 18, 1930, Hill to Seiberling, May 19, 1930, and Shipherd to Executive Committee, Oct. 6, 1930, Box 66, Lincoln Memorial University Folder, Frank A. Seiberling Papers, OHS.

11. Hill to Seiberling, Aug. 19, 21, Sept. 20, Oct. 11, Nov. 6, 1930, and Seiberling to Hill, Oct. 10, 11, 1930, Box 66, Lincoln Memorial University Folder, Frank A. Seiberling Papers, OHS.

12. Shipherd to Hooper, Apr. 29, May 5, 1930, Hooper to Shipherd, May 1, 1930, application for membership, Aug. 30, 1930, and Shipherd to Guy S. Snavely, Oct. 9, 1930, SACS Papers, UA-LMU; Shipherd to Wade H. Cooper, Oct. 17, 1930, H. Robinson Shipherd Papers, UA-LMU; Hill to Seiberling, July 1, 1930, and Seiberling to Hill, Dec. 16, 1930, Box 66, Lincoln Memorial University Folder, Frank A. Seiberling Papers, OHS.

13. Cooper to Shipherd, Oct. 14, Nov. 1, 1930, Wade H. Cooper, Board of Directors/Trustees Papers, UA-LMU; Shipherd to Seiberling, Oct. 29, 1930, and Shipherd to Cooper, Oct. 17, Nov. 4, Dec. 12, 1930, H. Robinson Shipherd Papers, UA-LMU; Shipherd memo, Oct. 20, 23, 1930, SACS Papers, UA-LMU; Morison to Shipherd, Nov. 12, 1930, J. H. S. Morison Papers, UA-LMU; Hill to Seiberling, Nov. 6, 1930, Box 66, Lincoln Memorial University Folder, Frank A. Seiberling Papers, OHS; Minutes of Executive Committee, Jan. 24, Feb. 7, 21, 1930, ALLM-LMU.

14. Mayer to Guy, June 18, 1930, Mitchell to Mayer, Aug. 8, 1930, John M. Maguire to Mitchell, June 10, 1930, Balz to Tyler, Dec. 23, 1930, Guy to Mayer, Aug. 4, 11, 1930, Mitchell to Lowrie, Oct. 29, 1930, and Tyler to members of Committee A, Dec. 17, 1930, AAUP Records, GWU.

15. Galley proofs of special committee report, and Mitchell to Tyler, Mar. 6, 30, 1931, Maguire to Tyler, Mar. 10, 1931, Lowrie to Mitchell, Apr. 15, 1931, and Guy to Tyler, Apr. 18, 1931, AAUP Records, GWU.

16. "Memorandum on Conference with Colonel Wade H. Cooper and Dr. J. W. Hill on Lincoln Memorial University, Wednesday and Thursday, Feb. 25 and 26" [1931], Hill to Tyler, Mar. 20, Apr. 25, 1931, Mitchell to Guy, May 11, 1931, and Shipherd to Tyler, May 21, 1931, with attached statement, AAUP Records, GWU.

17. "Lincoln Memorial University," *Bulletin of the American Association of University Professors* 17, no. 5 (May 1931): 409–13, and 18, no. 1 (Jan. 1932): 29–31; Hooper to Guy, May 26, 1931, and Tyler to Lowrie, Mar. 16, 1931, AAUP Records, GWU; Slaughter, "Danger Zone," 55.

18. Miller to Mayer, Aug. 15, 1930, Mayer to Miller, Aug. 18, 1930, and Miller to Cooper, Aug. 15, 1930, AAUP Records, GWU.

19. Mayer to Miller, Aug. 20, 1930, "*Claims of Merlin G. Miller* against *Lincoln Memorial University* arising from the unwarranted dismissals of Apr. 12, 1930," Aug. 28, 1930, copy of John P. Davis to Miller, Aug. 18, 1930, Miller to Mayer, Aug. 28, 1930, "*Supplementary memorandum* for Dr. Joseph Mayer relative to Merlin G. Miller's statement of claims against Lincoln Memorial University, August 28, 1930," "*Statement of personal grievances* of *Merlin G. Miller* against *Lincoln Memorial University,*" Aug. 28, 1930, and Diller to Mayer, Sept. 3, 1930, Apr. 3, 1931, AAUP Records, GWU; Wade H. Cooper to Seiberling, Aug. 4, 1930, Box 66, Lincoln Memorial University Folder, Frank A. Seiberling Papers, OHS.

20. Mayer memo, Nov. 4, 1930, "Memorandum on Conference with the Attorneys for the Dismissed Professors at Lincoln Memorial University (Mr. Charles V. Imlay and His Partner), Feb. 26, 1931," Miller to Mayer, May 14, 1931, Miller to Tyler, June 11, 1931, and Diller to Mayer, Apr. 3, May 6, 1931, AAUP Records, GWU; Seiberling to Hines, Aug. 21, 1930, Seiberling to Wade H. Cooper, Aug. 6, 20, 1930, and Seiberling to Hill, Aug. 21, 1930, Box 66, Lincoln Memorial University Folder, Frank A. Seiberling Papers, OHS.

21. Hill to Williams, July 18, [1930], John Wesley Hill Papers, UA-LMU; Wilma I. Musser, *Village of West Willow, 1719–1974, Lancaster County, Pennsylvania,* LTS, accessed at http://www.horseshoe.cc/; *Who Was Who in America* 3: 741.

22. *Middlesboro Daily News,* Feb. 10, 1933, Sept. 30, 1952.

23. Paul Graham interview with James W. Schenkenfelder, May 7, 2003, Student Papers, UA-LMU.

24. *Knoxville Journal,* June 3, 1930; Shipherd to Seiberling, June 11, 1930, Morison to Seiberling, Nov. 11, 1930, and Hill to Seiberling, June 5, 1930, Box 66, Lincoln Memorial University Folder, Frank A. Seiberling Papers, OHS; list of graduates, supplied by Development Office, Lincoln Memorial University, 2007.

25. Seiberling to Shipherd, May 7, 15, June 16, 1930, Box 66, Lincoln Memorial University Folder, Frank A. Seiberling Papers, OHS; Margaret D. Hrabe, Special Collections, University of Virginia, to author, e-mail, Apr. 25, 2007; Jocelyn K. Wilk, Columbia University Archives, to author, e-mail, Apr. 23, 2007; Woodbridge, *Jesse Stuart,* xxi; Clay McCarroll on the Social Security Death Index, http://www.genealogy.com/; Nancy Banks, daughter of Clay McCarroll, to author, e-mail, Nov. 27, 2007.

26. Fields to J. R. Ketron, July 30, 1957, Ernest W. Fields folder, Board of Directors/Trustees Papers, UA-LMU; dedication plaque, Ernest W. Fields gallery, Abraham Lincoln Library and Museum, LMU; *New York Times,* Jan. 26, 1999.

27. Terrill to unknown, Apr. 13, 1933, and Danforth to Guy, July 6, 1930, AAUP Records, GWU; Danforth to Iris Grannis, Oct. 16, 1931, James Still Collection, MSU; Miller, "Democratic Theory of Cooperation," 31, 35, 37; *National Co-Op Radio Friend* 28 (Jan.–Dec. 1942), http://www.libs.uga.edu/; Merlin G. Miller and Alfred deJonge on the Social Security Death Index, http://www.genealogy.com/; Diller, "Concept of Feeling in the Religious Philosophy of Schleiermacher"; "Proceedings of the American Philosophical Association, 1934," 166.

28. Shipherd to Myers Y. Cooper, Mar. 30, 1931, Shipherd to Kincaid, Mar. 23, 1931, and Shipherd to R. H. Clagett, Apr. 23, 1931, H. Robinson Shipherd Papers, UA-LMU; Shipherd to M. C. Huntley, Apr. 27, 1931, SACS Papers, UA-LMU.

29. *Knoxville News-Sentinel,* Apr. 8, 1931; Guy to Tyler, Mar. 26, 1931, AAUP Records, GWU; Shipherd, *Christianity at Stake,* not paginated. Shipherd also published a book, *Story of a Bookman,* in 1955.

30. Gaventa, *Power and Powerlessness,* vi, xi, 74–75, 77, 81, 84–87, 89–90, 92, 94.

31. Ibid., 96, 98–106, 109–10, 116–17.

32. Frank T. Hines to Frederick P. Keppel, Sept. 23, 1930, Series III A, Grants, Box 203, Folder 14 (1924–52), Carnegie Corporation of New York Records, CU; Miley to McClelland, June 15, 1935, Henry Artis Miley, Faculty Papers, UA-LMU.

33. *Tributes and Testimony,* frontispiece, 7–10, 30–31; *Alumni Bulletin* 10, no. 1, (Mar. 27, 1931), Alumni Association Papers, UA-LMU; Seiberling to Hill, Dec. 31, 1930, Frank A. Seiberling Papers, Box 66, Lincoln Memorial University Folder, OHS.

34. *Francis Randolph Curtis Demonstration Farm,* 23–25; clipping, *New York Times,* ca. June 4, 1930, AAUP Records, GWU; Hill to Seiberling, Sept. 19, 1930, Box 66, Lincoln Memorial University Folder, Frank A. Seiberling Papers, OHS; Warranty Deed, Feb. 6, 1933, Accession 557, Henry Ford and Ford Family Papers, Ford Properties Subgroup, THF.

35. *Knoxville Journal,* Feb. 12, 1932.

36. Hill to Arthur Tagge, Dec. 11, 1931, John Wesley Hill Papers, UA-LMU; Tagge to C. P. Williams, July 1, 1932, Arthur C. Tagge folder, Board of Directors/Trustees Papers, UA-LMU.

37. McMurtry, "Dr. Stewart W. McClelland," 32; "Dr. Stewart W. McClelland, President," *Mountain Herald* [33, no. 12] (Dec. 1932): 3.

38. McMurtry, "Dr. Stewart W. McClelland," 33; Evans, *Autobiography,* 43; McClelland to Tagge, Aug. 24, Oct. 8, 1932, Stewart W. McClelland Papers, UA-LMU.

39. Levine, *American College,* 185–87.

40. "Lincoln Memorial University Salary List," attached to Kincaid to Seiberling, July 28, 1930, Robert L. Kincaid Papers, UA-LMU.

41. Memorandum of Interview, Jan. 28, 1933, May 1, 1934, by Robert M. Lester, Series III A, Grants, Box 203, Folder 14 (1924–52), Carnegie Corporation of New York Records, CU; Minutes of Executive Committee, December 13, 1897–December 3, 1941, 327–29, ALLM-LMU; "Notes on Lincoln Herald," manuscript inserted into bound issues of *Mountain Herald,* 1901–14, UA-LMU.

42. Lycan, *Mountaineers Are Free,* 22–24; Hill to Tagge, Oct. 11, 1932, John Wesley Hill Papers, UA-LMU.

43. Hill to Walter T. Shepard, Feb. 12, 1933, and Frederic N. Tower to Hill, Sept. 23, 1932, John Wesley Hill Papers, UA-LMU; copy of Hill to Mrs. Russell W. Magna, Dec. 14, 1934, and copy of Magna to McClelland, Jan. 8, 1935, Edith Scott Magna, Board of

Directors/Trustees Papers, UA-LMU; Trustee's Minutes, November 20, 1917–December 10, 1967, 187, ALLM-LMU.

44. Minutes of Executive Committee, December 13, 1897–December 3, 1941, 322, ALLM-LMU; Miley to McClelland, June 15, 1935, Henry Artis Miley, Faculty Papers, UA-LMU; C. P. Cambiaire to Mayer, Feb. 20, Apr. 15, 1933, McClelland to Tyler, Mar. 6, 1933, W. S. Woodward to Carl Wittke, Feb. 12, 1936, and Maguire to Tyler, Feb. 20, 1936, AAUP Records, GWU.

45. Hill to McClelland, Jan. 17, 21, 1935, John Wesley Hill Papers, UA-LMU.

46. Lincoln Memorial University *Catalog,* 1931 to 1938, SC-LMU; Lycan, *Mountaineers Are Free,* 17; Levine, *American College,* 196–201; Lala Keck to Williams, Aug. 29, 1930, and J. Carroll Simms to Scholarship Committee, May 21, 1932, Scholarships Papers, UA-LMU.

47. Bertha Masingo Goad reminiscences, in Page and Stephenson, *Lincoln Memorial University,* 64; Lincoln Memorial University *Catalog,* 1934–35, 24, SC-LMU.

48. Bertha Masingo Goad reminiscences, in Page and Stephenson, *Lincoln Memorial University,* 65; Whiteside, "What LMU Means to Me!" 11, 20; Lincoln Memorial University *Catalog,* 1934–35, 21–23, SC-LMU; Braunhut, "Farm Labor Wage Rates," 195.

49. Bertha Masingo Goad reminiscences, in Page and Stephenson, *Lincoln Memorial University,* 62; Evans, *Autobiography,* 42–43; Lycan, *Mountaineers Are Free,* 10–12.

50. Lycan, *Mountaineers Are Free,* 12–16.

51. General Ledger, Sept. 1, 1934–Aug. 31, 1937, 335–37, UA-LMU.

52. Hooper to McClelland, July 1, 1932, Miley to Guy E. Snavely, Oct. 4, 1932, and M. C. Huntley to McClelland, Apr. 10, 1933, SACS Papers, UA-LMU.

53. Holt, *Claiborne County,* 49; "Lincoln Memorial University and the Southern Association of Colleges," and copy of Huntley to Milton W. Harrison, Apr. 22, 1935, SACS Papers, UA-LMU.

54. Lafrentz to McClelland, Feb. 5, 1935, Ferdinand W. LaFrentz, Board of Directors/Trustees Papers, UA-LMU; Trustee's Minutes, November 20, 1917–December 10, 1967, 167, ALLM-LMU; Kincaid speech to LMU Board of Directors, June 1, 1935, Robert L. Kincaid Papers, UA-LMU; Lincoln Memorial University *Catalog,* 1933–34, 7, SC-LMU.

55. Kincaid speech to LMU Board of Directors, June 1, 1935, Robert L. Kincaid Papers, UA-LMU.

56. Miley to McClelland, June 15, 1935, and McClelland to Miley, June 20, 1935, Henry Artis Miley, Faculty Papers, UA-LMU; Executive Committee Record Book A, June 16, 1935, ALLM-LMU.

57. Dalyrymple to J. R. Ketron, July 20, 1935, Arthur V. Dalyrymple, Board of Directors/Trustees Papers, UA-LMU.

58. Moore, "Observations and Experiences of His Life," Jesse H. Moore Papers, Faculty Papers, UA-LMU; McClelland to Keppel, Apr. 9, 1936, Series IIIA, Grants, Box 203, Folder 14 (1924–52), Carnegie Corporation of New York Records, CU; Trustee's Minutes, November 20, 1917–December 10, 1967, 213, ALLM-LMU; Hill to Williams, June 11, 1936, John Wesley Hill Papers, UA-LMU.

59. *Claiborne Progress,* Oct. 14, 1936; *Alumnus* 1, no. 3 (Aug. 1944), 12; "Lincoln Memorial University Alumni and Friends in and Near New York City," [1938], and circular letter by Ernest W. Fields and Clay C. McCarroll and four others, Feb. 28, 1955, Alumni Association Papers, UA-LMU.

60. Morison to Seiberling, May 18, 1930, Shipherd to Seiberling, Aug. 5, 1930, and Hill to Seiberling, Dec. 11, 1930, Box 66, Lincoln Memorial University Folder, Frank A. Seiberling Papers, OHS; John Warren Hill to H. LeMarr Rice, June 1, 1966, John Wesley Hill Papers, UA-LMU.

61. Hill to Alf M. Landon, June 18, 1936, Roper to W. E. Hammaker, June 22, 1936, Hill to Roper, June 30, July 2, 1936, and Roper to Mrs. Hill, Oct. 13, 1936, Daniel C. Roper Papers, DU; *Claiborne Progress,* Oct. 14, 1936; John Warren Hill to H. LeMarr Rice, Aug. 29, 1966, John Wesley Hill Papers, UA-LMU; *Alumnus* (Spring 1986): 10.

62. McClelland to Keppel, Apr. 9, 1936, Series IIIA, Grants, Box 203, Folder 14 (1924–52), Carnegie Corporation of New York Records, CU; *Blue and Gray,* Dec. 4, 1936; *Middlesboro Daily News,* Dec. 4, 1936; McClelland quoted in Suppiger, *Phoenix of the Mountains,* 75.

Chapter 9

A New Day for Lincoln Memorial

Epigraphs: Kincaid to Mrs. Arthur Hays Sulzburger, Nov. 17, 1937, Kincaid to Ray Welborn, Jan. 21, 1939, and Welborn to Kincaid, May 29, 1939, Robert L. Kincaid Papers, UA-LMU.

1. Kincaid to Henry Hornblower, Nov. 5, 1937, Kincaid to Mrs. Arthur Hays Sulzberger, Nov. 17, 1937, and Kincaid to Wade H. Ellis, Nov. 20, 1937, Robert L. Kincaid Papers, UA-LMU.

2. Kincaid speech, Feb. 12, 1937, in McCordock, *Lincoln Memorial University,* 14; Kincaid to Hornblower, Nov. 5, 1937, and Kincaid to E. E. Patton, Apr. 3, 1947, Robert L. Kincaid Papers, UA-LMU.

3. McClelland to George W. Clapp, Sept. 1, 1937, Stewart W. McClelland Papers, UA-LMU; Levine, *American College,* 190; "Lincoln Memorial University," *Exchangite* (July 1941): 7; Kincaid to Iris Grannis, Sept. 10, 1942, Robert L. Kincaid Papers, UA-LMU.

4. McClelland interview, Oct. 19, 1972, in Suppiger, *Phoenix of the Mountains,* 74; Temple, "Lincoln Diploma to McClelland," 87–88; "Notes on Lincoln Herald," manuscript inserted into bound issues of *Mountain Herald,* 1910–14, SC-LMU; frontispiece, *Lincoln Herald,* Oct. 1943; Kincaid to Mary Milne, Dec. 31, 1938, Robert L. Kincaid Papers, UA-LMU.

5. Kincaid to Mary Milne, Dec. 31, 1938, Robert L. Kincaid Papers, UA-LMU; Record of Interview, Robert M. Lester and McClelland, July 1, 1942, Series IIIA, Grants, Box 203, Folder 14 (1924–52), Carnegie Corporation of New York Records, CU; McMurtry, *Department of Lincolniana,* 3; Petz, *In the Presence,* 9–10; Taylor, "Lincoln Collection," 27.

6. McMurtry, *Department of Lincolniana,* 5; "Lincoln Memorial University," *Exchangite* (July 1941): 7.

7. News release by Kincaid, Oct. 1, 1937, Robert L. Kincaid Papers, UA-LMU.

8. A. J. Walsmith to McClelland, Apr. 18, 1941, and McClelland to Walsmith, Apr. 26, 1941, Stewart W. McClelland Papers, UA-LMU; "No Civil War Bitterness at L.M.U.," 19; Minutes of Executive Committee, December 13, 1897–December 3, 1941, 379, ALLM-LMU. A later survey by professional archaeologists disclosed an assortment of Civil War artifacts found in the fall of 2005. Marcel, "Phase I Archaeological Survey of Lincoln Memorial University," iii–iv.

9. Kincaid, "Ride with Hoover," 12–13.

10. Raymond Hart Massey, biography, http://www.wikipedia.org/, and http://www.imdb.com/; Sherwood, *Abe Lincoln in Illinois,* vii.

11. "Significant Commencement," 2–3.

12. Ibid.; Robinson, "'Lincoln' Steals Show from 31st President"; "Massey at L.M.U.," 14–15; summary of Hoover speech, *Knoxville News-Sentinel,* June 5, 1939; Massey to McClelland, June 19, 1939, Raymond Massey Letters, Miscellaneous Manuscripts and Papers, Box 2, ALLM-LMU.

13. Kincaid to Ray O. Welborn, June 12, 1939, Robert L. Kincaid Papers, UA-LMU; "Significant Commencement," 2–3.

14. "Massey at L.M.U.," 15; *Abe Lincoln in Illinois,* http://www.imdb.com/; Gutman, "Three Outstanding 'Abes,'" 126; Massey to Committee of Governors, Jan. 6, 1940, Raymond Massey Letters, Miscellaneous Manuscripts and Papers, Box 2, ALLM-LMU; Mary Howard biography, http://www.imdb.com/.

15. Gutman, "Three Outstanding 'Abes,'" 126; "Our Distinguished Guests," 8; Robinson, "Abe Lincoln Film Premiere Draws Host of Notables"; Kincaid to Manny Strauss, Feb. 5, 1940, Robert L. Kincaid Papers, UA-LMU.

16. Smith, *Genesis of Lincoln Memorial University,* 63; Jesse Stuart, "My Teachers of Lincoln Memorial University," 23, UL; Lincoln Memorial University *Catalog,* 1926–27, 9, SC-LMU; Smith, *President Lincoln,* v–vii, 1, 6, 89; Bonnie Masingo Page reminiscences, in Page and Stephenson, *Lincoln Memorial University,* 78; see drafts of various plays, and Barrett H. Clark to Smith, Sept. 21, 1937, in Earl Hobson Smith Papers, UA-LMU.

17. See drafts of various plays in Earl Hobson Smith Papers, UA-LMU.

18. "General Howard Remembered," 12; Kincaid, "Last of the Founders," 27.

19. Kincaid to Mrs. Arthur Hays Sulzberger, Nov. 17, 1937, Robert L. Kincaid Papers, UA-LMU; Dalyrymple to McClelland, Jan. 12, 1937, Arthur V. Dalyrymple, Board of Directors/Trustees Papers, UA-LMU; Record of Interview, Robert M. Lester and McClelland, Jan. 26, 1937, July 1, 1942, and McClelland to Carnegie Corporation, Nov. 8, 1938, Series IIIA, Grants, Box 203, Folder 14 (1924–52), Carnegie Corporation of New York Records, CU; Haskin, "New Lincolns from the Old Mold."

20. Kincaid to Mary Milne, Dec. 31, 1938, Robert L. Kincaid Papers, UA-LMU; Kincaid, "Lincoln Fights Again for Liberty," 4.

21. Grace Pirkle Dollar reminiscences and Bonnie Masingo Page reminiscences, in Page and Stephenson, *Lincoln Memorial University,* 74, 76–77.

22. Vergil Saine reminiscences, in Page and Stephenson, *Lincoln Memorial University,* 88, 90.

23. *Lincoln Herald* 42, no. 5 (Oct. 1940): 21; June 7, 1942, Trustee's Minutes, November 20, 1917–December 10, 1967, 250, ALLM-LMU; Suppiger, *Phoenix of the Mountains,* 81; Kincaid to Iris Grannis, Sept. 10, 1942, Robert L. Kincaid Papers, UA-LMU; Shumate, "Our Story: Lincoln Memorial University," 14, Mildred B. Shumate, Faculty Papers, UA-LMU.

24. Kincaid, "Lincoln Fights Again for Liberty," 5.

25. Hess, "Belgians Remember Downed Pilot," 16–17; *Knoxville Journal,* Feb. 15, 1946; Williams to Ferdinand W. Lafrentz, Mar. 13, 1944, and Williams to Olga L. Lafrentz, Apr. 3, 1944, Casimir P. Williams Papers, UA-LMU; McClelland to commanding officer, Fort Benning, Georgia, Feb. 26, 1944, and McClelland to Newton C. Farr, June 8, 1946, Stewart W. McClelland Papers, UA-LMU; Kincaid to Newton C. Farr, Sept. 1, 1944, Robert L. Kincaid Papers, UA-LMU.

26. Bumgarner, *Parade of the Dead,* 5–6, 199.

27. Jeanne Barkley tribute, Carter to "Dear folks," [1940], and copy of "Award of the Silver Star," Ross S. Carter Papers, UA-LMU; Ross Carter letter in *Blue and Gray,* Nov. 26, 1942; Carter, *Those Devils in Baggy Pants,* 188–89.

28. Jeanne Barkley tribute, Boyd G. Carter to president of Lincoln Memorial University, Oct. 22, 1947, Boyd G. Carter to Kincaid, Oct. 29, 1947, Oct. 10, 1951, May 28, 1956, and "Suggestions Concerning the Annual Award of the Ross S. Carter Prize for Original Writing," Ross S. Carter Papers, UA-LMU; Carter, *Those Devils in Baggy Pants,* 190–91; Stallard, "'Those Devils in Baggy Pants' to Become Movie," 28. The two plaques today hang in the Tex Turner Room of the arena and in a corridor on the first floor of Duke Hall.

29. Godzicki, "History of Financial Aids," 19; Brubacher and Rudy, *Higher Education in Transition,* 230–31; Thelin, *History of American Higher Education,* 263, 267; Olson, *G. I. Bill,* 27, 43–44; Martin Peters to Suppiger, Nov. 16, 1972, in Suppiger, *Phoenix of the Mountains,* 84.

30. *Knoxville News-Sentinel,* Aug. 17, 1947; Kincaid to E. E. Patton, Apr. 3, 1947, Robert L. Kincaid Papers, UA-LMU; Lester O. Schriver to F. Lauriston Bullard, July 16, 1947, Lester O. Schriver, Board of Directors/Trustees Papers, UA-LMU.

31. McMurtry, "Dr. Stewart W. McClelland," 32–33.

32. Trustee's Minutes, November 20, 1917–December 10, 1967, 307, 311, ALLM-LMU.

33. Kincaid to Herbert Acuff, Dec. 5, 1947, and Kincaid to Don West, Nov. 4, 1947, Robert L. Kincaid Papers, UA-LMU; George W. Morton to W. I. Jones, Nov. 19, 1950, in "Greetings Received from G. W. Morton '06," 11; Ella M. Hubbell to Kincaid, Sept. 3, 1947, George A. Hubbell Papers, UA-LMU; West to Kincaid, Oct. 30, 1947, Don West Papers, UA-LMU; Record of Interview, Robert M. Lester and Kincaid, Feb. 11, 1947, Kincaid to Lester, Aug. 19, 1952, and Lester to Kincaid, Aug. 22, 1952, Series IIIA, Grants, Box 203, Folder 14 (1924–52), Carnegie Corporation of New York Records, CU.

34. Temple, "Robert Lee Kincaid," 166–67; Kincaid, *Boy Finds a College,* 2–4, 6–12, 14–18; Kincaid, "Shadow of a Man," 42.

35. Kincaid, *Boy Finds a College,* 18; Kincaid, *Boy Finds a Friend,* 1.

36. Kincaid, "Shadow of a Man," 42–43; Kincaid, "Living Lincoln," 19; Kincaid to E. G. Dodge, July 15, 1940, and Kincaid to Mrs. William D. Gray, May 16, 1950, Robert L. Kincaid Papers, UA-LMU.

37. Kincaid, *Boy Finds a Friend,* 2, 4–5; Kincaid, "Shadow of a Man," 45; "Stone Gate-Way Dedicated," 6.

38. Kincaid, *Boy Finds a Friend,* 5–6; Temple, "Robert Lee Kincaid," 167–68; [Kincaid] to William I. Jones, Apr. 4, 1916, Robert L. Kincaid Papers, UA-LMU.

39. Kincaid, "Lincoln Pilgrimage," 5; Kincaid to Ray Welborn, Jan. 21, 1939, Robert L. Kincaid Papers, UA-LMU.

40. Kincaid to Welborn, Jan. 21, 1939, Robert L. Kincaid Papers, UA-LMU; *Middlesboro Daily News,* Nov. 11, 1941.

41. Kincaid to Nora Cobb Spencer, Jan. 10, 1956, and Kincaid to Mrs. William D. Gray, July 3, 1953, Robert L. Kincaid Papers, UA-LMU; Kincaid, *School Days at Bethlehem,* 5, 17; Kincaid, "Shadow of a Man," 47.

42. Kincaid to William L. Stooksbury, Aug. 17, 1938, Kincaid to John Warren Hill, Feb. 22, 1939, Kincaid to Harry S. Howard, Dec. 12, 1940, Kincaid to John S. Kendall, June 18, 1948, Kincaid, "General Oliver Otis Howard, Soldier in Peace and War," 1, and Kincaid, "General Howard and Lincoln's Last Commission," 10, Robert L. Kincaid Papers, UA-LMU; Kincaid, "Living Lincoln," 19.

43. Kincaid, *Wilderness Road,* various editions; Kincaid to E. E. Patton, Apr. 3, 1947, Robert L. Kincaid Papers, UA-LMU; Rudy Clark to Herbert Y. Livesay, Mar. 12, 1969, Rudy Clark Papers, UA-LMU.

CHAPTER 10

THE LINCOLN STAMP

Epigraphs: Kincaid, "General Howard and Lincoln's Last Commission," 1, and Robert L. Kincaid, "The Open Door at Lincoln Memorial University," [1957], Robert L. Kincaid Papers, UA-LMU.

1. Kincaid, "Shadow of a Man," 41; Kincaid, "Lincoln Memorial University," 23, 25; Kincaid to A. A. Wentles, Feb. 7, 1956, Robert L. Kincaid Papers, UA-LMU; Kincaid, *Boy Finds a College,* v; Kincaid, "Lincoln Memorial University of the Future," 25.

2. Kincaid, "Living Lincoln," 19; Kincaid, *Ageless Lincoln,* not paginated; Peterson, *Lincoln in American Memory,* 197; "Clubs Report," 9; Kincaid, "Open Door at Lincoln Memorial University," and Kincaid to Lena G. Barrett, June 22, 1956, Robert L. Kincaid Papers, UA-LMU.

3. Leonard Gardner to Kincaid, Jan. 15, 1948, Leonard Gardner, Student Papers, UA-LMU; Kincaid to Gardner, Jan. 23, 1948, Robert L. Kincaid Papers, UA-LMU; "Leonard Gardner—Globe Trotter," 20; Kincaid, *Lincoln Heritage in the Cumberlands,* 5.

4. Kincaid to Mrs. W. H. Cathey, Jan. 18, 1950, Kincaid to Louise Chou, Nov. 12, 1956, and Kincaid to Lowell M. Greenlaw, Dec. 20, 1957, Robert L. Kincaid Papers, UA-LMU.

5. Kincaid, *Lincoln's Faith,* not paginated; Kincaid to Herbert Hoover, Aug. 10, 1956, Robert L. Kincaid Papers, UA-LMU. Many students imbibed the conservative values taught on campus. See, for example, Whiteside, "What LMU Means to Me!" 11.

6. Kincaid to Mrs. William A. Swaney, Apr. 26, 1956, Robert L. Kincaid Papers, UA-LMU; Shumate, "Our Story: Lincoln Memorial University," 1, Mildred B. Shumate, Faculty Papers, UA-LMU.

7. Paolo speech, 1, Box 8, C. S. Paolo Folder, Hall of Holography Collection, ALLM- LMU; "Dedication of the Bronze Statue," 8–10; "Paolo, Noted Lincoln Sculptor," 19.

8. Kincaid, *Wilderness Road,* 363–64; Paolo to Ferdinand W. LaFrentz, Feb. 3, 1936, and Paolo to Kincaid, Mar. 2, 1953, Cartaino S. Paolo, Miscellaneous Papers, UA-LMU.

9. "Dedication of the Bronze Statue," 2, 8–9.

10. Paolo speech, 1–2, Paolo to Kincaid, Feb. 3, 1949, and Paolo to McMurtry, Jan. 13, 1950, Box 8, C. S. Paolo Folder, Hall of Holography Collection, ALLM-LMU; Paolo to Kincaid, Aug. 6, 1948, Cartaino S. Paolo, Miscellaneous Papers, UA-LMU; "Paolo, Noted Lincoln Sculptor," 19; "Dedication of the Bronze Statue," 2, 10; Kincaid, "Living Lincoln," 14; Kincaid to McClelland, Feb. 15, 1949, Robert L. Kincaid Papers, UA-LMU; *New York Times,* Dec. 21, 1955.

11. Kincaid to John S. Kendall, June 18, 1948, and Kincaid to Mrs. William A. Swaney, Apr. 26, 1956, Robert L. Kincaid, UA-LMU.

12. Kincaid to Harry S. Howard, July 6, 1949, and Kincaid, "General Howard and Lincoln's Last Commission," and Kincaid to Sue E. Howard, May 17, 1950, Robert L. Kincaid Papers, UA-LMU; John A. Carpenter to Kincaid, Feb. 27, 1949, John A. Carpenter, Oliver O. Howard Papers, UA-LMU; Harry S. Howard, "Last Days of General O. O. Howard," [1950], Harry S. Howard, Oliver O. Howard Papers, UA-LMU.

13. Kincaid to Harry S. Howard, July 6, Aug. 5, 1949, Nov. 10, 1953, and Kincaid, "General Oliver Otis Howard, Soldier in Peace and War," 1–2, Robert L. Kincaid Papers, UA-LMU; Harry S. Howard to Kincaid, July 2, 1951, Harry S. Howard, Oliver O. Howard Papers, UA-LMU; Kincaid, "Shadow of a Man," 42; Kincaid, "Living Lincoln," 19.

14. Trustee's Minutes, November 20, 1917–December 10, 1967, 351, ALLM-LMU; Shumate, "Our Story: Lincoln Memorial University," 14, Mildred B. Shumate, Faculty Papers, UA-LMU; Kincaid, "Lincoln Memorial University," 24–25; Lincoln Memorial University *Bulletin* (Mar. 1958): 21–22, SC-LMU.

15. Kincaid, "Lincoln Memorial University," 26.

16. Kincaid to McClelland, Feb. 15, 1949, Robert L. Kincaid Papers, UA-LMU; Kincaid, "Lincoln Memorial University of the Future," 24.

17. Kincaid to Francis S. Hutchins, Jan. 24, 1958, Robert L. Kincaid Papers, UA-LMU; Henard, "Dr. R. C. Provine," 46; Provine to Arthur F. LaFrentz, Apr. 26, 1960, Robert C. Provine Papers, UA-LMU; Temple, "Robert Lee Kincaid," 166; *Middlesboro Daily News,* May 23, 24,1960.

18. Nuhrah, "Dr. & Mrs. Robert C. Provine," 40–41; "Dr. H. LaMarr Rice," 1; *Alumnus* 8, no. 1 (Oct. 1956): 2, 8.

19. Godzicki, "History of Financial Aids," 19–20; Brubacher and Rudy, *Higher Education in Transition,* 233; Donham and Stege, "Grants, Loans, and Scholarships," 70.

20. Student Financial Aids in Institutions of Higher Education, May 21, 1956, 3–4, 7–11, Robert L. Kincaid Papers, UA-LMU.

21. Provine to David Altman, Mar. 30, 1959, Robert C. Provine Papers, UA-LMU; Trustee's Minutes, November 20, 1917–December 10, 1967, 458–59, ALLM-LMU.

22. Provine to Altman, Mar. 1, 1961, and Provine to Mrs. William A. Swaney, July 1, 1961, Robert C. Provine Papers, UA-LMU; Livesay memo to Provine, May 22, 1961, Herbert Y. Livesay Papers, UA-LMU; Lincoln Memorial University *Bulletin* 41, no. 2 (Apr. 1960): 20, SC-LMU.

23. Provine to Arthur F. LaFrentz, May 15, 1962, Robert C. Provine Papers, UA-LMU; Suppiger, *Phoenix of the Mountains,* 114; Livesay to Jesse Stuart, June 29, 1972, Herbert Y. Livesay Papers, UA-LMU.

24. Paris T. Houston to Suppiger, Nov. 20, 1972, in Suppiger, *Phoenix of the Mountains,* 35.

25. Peck and Smith, *Berea's First 125 Years,* 205–16; Dickey and Mathis, *Berry College,* 169, 185–86; http://www.workcolleges.org/; Bass, "Study of Student Work Programs," 1–2, 15–17, 22–23; Longstreth, "Lamps in the Mountains," 314–15, 317–19, 321, 328.

26. *Middlesboro Daily News,* Feb. 25, 1958.

27. Ibid., Feb. 27, 1958.

28. Suppiger, *Phoenix of the Mountains,* 114; Provine to Mrs. G. Sundback, Apr. 2, 1962, and Provine to Arthur F. Lafrentz, Jan. 22, 1963, Robert C. Provine Papers, UA-LMU; "Dr. Rice Speaks to the Alumni," 1; Shumate, "Our Story: Lincoln Memorial University," table after p. 20, Mildred B. Shumate, Faculty Papers, UA-LMU.

29. Kincaid to Walter N. Eastburn, June 26, 1956, Robert L. Kincaid Papers, UA-LMU.

30. Provine to M. Louisa MacNair, July 6, 1959, Robert C. Provine Papers, UA-LMU; Sister Mary Joseph to Director of Lincoln Memorial University, July 3, 1961, Herbert Y. Livesay Papers, UA-LMU.

31. Alton L. Smith form letter, Nov. 8, 1961, and Matthews to Smith, Nov. 14, 1961, Herman G. Matthews, Faculty Papers, UA-LMU; Provine memo, Jan. 19, 1962, Robert C. Provine Papers, UA-LMU.

32. Provine to Arthur F. LaFrentz, Jan. 22, 1963, Provine Papers, UA-LMU; Rice to Benson Heale Harvey, Aug. 23, 1965, H. LaMarr Rice Papers, UA-LMU.

33. Livesay to S. Sterling McMillan, Oct. 4, 1967, and Livesay to Benson Heale Harvey, Nov. 2, 1968, Herbert Y. Livesay Papers, UA-LMU; Helen Bailey to Regina Burns, e-mail, Mar. 9, 2006, and Burns to author, e-mail, Mar. 9, 2006.

34. Marguerite T. Sundback to LMU, July 31, 1971, and Livesay to Sundback, Aug. 11, 1971, Herbert Y. Livesay Papers, UA-LMU.

35. Trustee's Minutes, November 20, 1917–December 10, 1967, 465, ALLM-LMU; Provine to David Altman, Mar. 1, 1960, and Provine to Marguerite Sundback, Apr. 2, 1962, Robert C. Provine Papers, UA-LMU.

36. Smith, *Genesis of Lincoln Memorial University,* 4, 7–28, 46–48, 62, 64; Taylor, "'And So History Repeats,'" 3–5. Earl Hobson Smith also wrote a play commemorating the founding of Middlesboro, *The Magic City,* about 1980, two years before his death.

37. Suppiger, *Phoenix of the Mountains,* 118; Welch, "Lincoln and Current American Higher Education," 65; *Alumnus* 91, no. 1 (Winter 1998): 25; Welch, "Why Does Any Private College Deserve Support?" 114, 156; "Former LMU President Passes Away," 25.

38. Executive Committee Minutes, Sept. 29, 1975, ALLM-LMU; Suppiger, *Phoenix of the Mountains,* 120.

39. Suppiger, *Phoenix of the Mountains,* 119; Lincoln Memorial University *Catalog,* 1974, 60, and 1978–80, 35, SC-LMU.

40. Board Minutes, June 4, 1961, Board of Directors/Trustees Papers, UA-LMU; Faculty Handbook, 1970–71, 10, and 1977–78, 12, SC-LMU.

41. Slaughter, "Danger Zone," 54, 56, 59; Hutcheson, *Professional Professoriate,* 9, 13.

42. Chait, "Why Tenure? Why Now?" 8, 19, 25; U.S. Department of Education statistics reported in "Tenure," http://www.wikipedia.org/; Baldwin and Chronister, *Teaching Without Tenure,* 3; Mallon, "Why Is Tenure One College's Problem and Another's Solution?" 257; Chait, "Does Faculty Governance Differ at Colleges with Tenure and Colleges Without Tenure?" 71, 77, 79, 80–82, 97.

43. William H. Jesse, "Report on a New Library Building for Lincoln Memorial University, Harrogate, Tennessee," 16, Buildings Papers, UA-LMU; *Lincoln Herald* 75, no. 2 (Summer 1973); Suppiger, *Phoenix of the Mountains,* 120; Suppiger, "Official Opening," 47–48, 50.

44. Partin, "Being President Won't Alter Burchett's Style!" 6–7; "Scott D. Miller: LMU's 16th President," 2; Suppiger, *Phoenix of the Mountains,* 145; "Bishop Named Vice President," 10.

45. Lincoln Memorial University *Catalog,* 2007–8, 12, SC-LMU; Suppiger, *Phoenix of the Mountains,* 124, 138–39, 141.

46. Planck, "Inspiration and the Inspired," 159; information about Jack Witt, http://www.eaglesnest.net/.

47. "LMU's New President," 4–5.

48. Suppiger, *Phoenix of the Mountains,* 23; "Enrollment Trends by Teaching Site Fall 1998–Fall 2006," http://www.lmunet.edu/.

49. Lincoln Memorial University *Catalog,* 2007–8, 10–11, 14, SC-LMU; Data Sheet, Majors, 1995–96, and 2008–9, http://www.lmunet.edu/.

50. Lincoln Memorial University *Catalog,* 1940–41, 7–9, 1988–89, 134–36, 2000–2002, 123–33, and 2005–6, 155–60, SC-LMU.

51. Dedication program, Nov. 7, 2003, Oliver O. Howard Papers, UA-LMU; "1929 Story," 19.

52. Lincoln Memorial University *Catalog,* June 1931, 51–52, Mar. 1939, 36–38, Apr. 1955, 74–76, Apr. 1956, 74–76, and Lincoln Memorial University *Bulletin,* 1971–72, 42, 1979–80, 61, 1982–83, 72, SC-LMU.

53. Lincoln Memorial University *Catalog,* 2006–7, 50, 144, SC-LMU.

Conclusion

1. Scholarship applications and Fate Payne to Scholarship Committee, May 6, 1932, in Scholarships Papers, UA-LMU.

2. Veysey, *Emergence of the American University,* 269; Thelin, *History of American Higher Education,* 171

3. Thelin, *History of American Higher Education,* 170; Lincoln Memorial University *Catalog,* 1907–8, 16, SC-LMU.

4. Thelin, *History of American Higher Education,* 175–76; Lincoln Memorial University *Catalog,* 1908–9, 54, 1909–10, 48, 1924–25, 85, 88, 1925–26, 89–90, 1933–34, 78, 1934–35, 70–76, 1952–53, 93–96, and 1953–54, 104–9, SC-LMU; Larry Thacker to author, e-mail, June 30, 2009.

5. Peck and Smith, *Berea's First 125 Years,* 123–24; Frost, *For the Mountains,* 234.

6. Elizabeth Chesnutt to Williams, July 5, 1940, Casimir P. Williams Papers, UA-LMU.

7. Thelin, *History of American Higher Education,* 261, 291–96.

8. Lincoln Memorial University *Catalog,* 1908–9, 54, 1909–10, 60, 1911–12, 68, 1919–20, 91–92, 1924–25, 85, 1925–26, 87, 1933–34, 78, 1934–35, 81, 1938–39, 85, 1946–47, 94, 1948–49, 90–99, 1952–53, 90–96, 1953–54, 115, and 1957–58, 100–109, SC-LMU.

9. Historic population option, http://www.census.gov/, and http://www.quickfacts.census.gov/.

10. http://www.quickfacts.census.gov/.

11. Campbell, *Year that Defined American Journalism,* 60.

12. Bureau of the Census, *Twelfth Census of the United States, Taken in the Year 1900: Population, Part 1,* cxii, 540, 556, 561.

13. Holt, *Claiborne County,* 41–55; state historical marker for Lincoln High School, in Middlesboro, Kentucky; Anderson, *Education of Blacks,* 190–91, 199.

14. Thelin, *History of American Higher Education,* 173, 233.

15. *County and City Data Book, 1967,* 132, 332, 392; Larry Thacker to author, e-mail, June 30, 2009.

16. Thelin, *History of American Higher Education,* 173; Lincoln Memorial University *Catalog,* 1908–9, 54–63, 1909–10, 48, 1911–12, 57–58, 1919–20, 91–92, 1924–25, 87–88, 1925–26, 89–90, 1933–34, 78, 1934–35, 81, 1938–39, 85, 1946–47, 94, 1948–49, 90–99, 1952–53, 90–96, 1953–54, 115, and 1957–58, 100–109, SC-LMU.

17. Lincoln Memorial University *Catalog,* 2007–8, 8, SC-LMU.

18. Riesman, *Constraint and Variety,* 35, 60–64; Veysey, *Emergence of the American University,* 264, 283.

19. Lincoln Memorial University *Catalog,* 1908–9, 54–63, 1909–10, 60, 1911–12, 68, 1919–20, 91–96, 1924–25, 85, 1925–26, 87, and 1928–29, 88, SC-LMU.

20. Ogren, *American State Normal School,* 19–20.

21. http://www.acaweb.org/.

Bibliography

Archives

Berea College, Special Collections and Archives, Berea, Kentucky

Appalachian Vertical Files

Berea Quarterly

William Goodell Frost Papers

Bowdoin College, Special Collections and Archives, Brunswick, Maine

Charles Henry Howard Collection

O. O. Howard Papers

Rowland Bailey Howard Collection

Bryn Mawr College, Special Collections, Bryn Mawr, Pennsylvania

Letters and Documents Collection

Columbia University, Rare Book and Manuscript Library, New York, New York

Carnegie Corporation of New York Records

Cumberland Gap National Historical Park, Middlesboro, Kentucky

Charter and By-Laws of the Girls' Industrial Home and School, Grace Nettleton Memorial. N.p., n.d.

Harrogate, Tennessee. Louisville, Ky.: Courier-Journal Job Printing, [1891]

Robert L. Kincaid Collection

Duke University, Rare Books, Manuscripts, and Special Collections, Durham, North Carolina

Benjamin Newton Duke Papers

William Preston Few Papers

Daniel C. Roper Papers

Filson Historical Society, Louisville, Kentucky

Charles Blanton Roberts Papers

George Washington University, Special Collections and University Archives, Washington, D.C.

American Association of University Professors Records

The Henry Ford, Benson Ford Research Center, Dearborn, Michigan

Henry Ford and Ford Family Papers, Ford Properties Subgroup

Lancaster Theological Seminary, Schaff Library, Lancaster, Pennsylvania

Wilma I. Musser, *Village of West Willow, 1719–1974, Lancaster County, Pennsylvania,* http://www.horseshoe.cc/

Lincoln Memorial University, Abraham Lincoln Library and Museum, Harrogate, Tennessee

"Depositions in the case of Furney Jones vs. Burchfield et al.," Diaries and Pocket-Size Scrapbooks and Account Books

Director's Minutes

Executive Committee Record Book A

Hall of Holography Collection

Oliver Otis Howard Papers

Raymond Massey Letters, Miscellaneous Manuscripts and Papers, Box 2

Minutes of Executive Committee, December 13, 1897–December 3, 1941

Trustee's Minutes, November 20, 1917–December 10, 1967

Lincoln Memorial University, Special Collections, Harrogate, Tennessee

Alumnus

Blue and Gray

Lincoln Memorial University *Bulletin*

Lincoln Memorial University *Catalog*

Harrow School *Catalogue*

Faculty Handbook

Harrow School of Cumberland Gap, Tennessee

James W. Schenkenfelder Notebooks

Lincoln Herald

Mountain Herald

"Notes on Lincoln Herald," manuscript inserted into bound issues of *Mountain Herald,* 1910–14

Railsplitter

Lincoln Memorial University, University Archives, Harrogate, Tennessee

Edgar O. Achorn Papers

Alumni Association Papers

Alexander A. Arthur Family Papers

Frederick B. Avery Papers

Board of Directors/Trustees Papers

Buildings Papers

Ross S. Carter Papers

Charter Folder

Rudy Clark Papers

Charles F. Eager Papers

Faculty Papers
Eugene P. Fairchild Papers
General Ledger, September 1, 1934–August 31, 1937
Iris Grannis, Staff Papers
John Wesley Hill Papers
Oliver O. Howard Papers
George A. Hubbell Papers
Herman Y. Hughes Papers
Cyrus Kehr Papers
Robert L. Kincaid Papers
John Hale Larry Papers
Herbert Y. Livesay Papers
Robert O. Matthews Papers
Stewart W. McClelland Papers
Minutes, Annual Meeting
Minutes of faculty meetings, Sept. 5, 1904–Mar. 27, 1922
Miscellaneous Papers
Jesse H. Moore Papers
J. H. S. Morison Papers
Arthur A. Myers Papers
Nancy Hanks Memorial Association Papers
Promotion and Publicity Papers
Robert C. Provine Papers
James H. Rector, Staff Papers
H. LaMarr Rice Papers
Hervin U. Roop Papers
SACS Papers
Scholarships Papers
H. Robinson Shipherd Papers
Mildred B. Shumate, Faculty Papers
Earl Hobson Smith Papers
William L. Stooksbury Papers
Student Papers
Time Book, September 7, 1907–April 23, 1910
Don West Papers
Casimir P. Williams Papers

Lincoln Museum, Fort Wayne, Indiana

Louis A. Warren Papers

Morehead State University, Camden-Carroll Library, Morehead, Kentucky

James Still Collection

National Archives and Records Administration, Washington, D.C.

John Hale Larry pension record

John Hale Larry service record, 8th Massachusetts (9 months) and 3rd Massachusetts Heavy Artillery

Robert F. Patterson service record, 29th Tennessee, Compiled Service Records of Confederate Soldiers Who Served in Organizations from the State of Tennessee, M268, Roll 240, RG 109

Robert F. Patterson service record, Compiled Service Records of Confederate General and Staff Officers, and Non-Regimental Enlisted Men, M331, Roll 194, RG 109

Population schedules of the *Eighth Census of the United States,* 1860, M653, Roll 1244

Slave schedules of the *Eighth Census of the United States,* 1860, M653, Roll 1281

Ohio Historical Society, Archives/Manuscripts Division, Columbus

Frank A. Seiberling Papers

Rockefeller University, Rockefeller Archives Center, New York, New York

Rockefeller Family Archives

Russell Sage Foundation Records

Tulane University, Amistad Research Center, New Orleans

American Missionary Association Archives

University of California, Bancroft Library, Berkeley

Mark Twain Papers

University of Chicago, Special Collections Research Center, Chicago

Osborn H. Oldroyd Collection of Personal Correspondence and Autographs

University of Iowa, Special Collections Department, Iowa City

Dr. John Wesley Hill, Redpath Lyceum Bureau Archives

University of Louisville, Special Collections, Louisville, Kentucky

Jesse Stuart, "My Teachers of Lincoln Memorial University"

University of North Carolina, Southern Historical Collection, Chapel Hill

John Charles Campbell and Olive Dame Campbell Papers

University of Tennessee, Special Collections, Chattanooga

Jean Miles Catino Collection

University of Tennessee, Special Collections, Knoxville

Cumberland Gap: Its Geographical and Commercial Features and Importance as a Railroad Centre. N.p., n.d.

"Reminiscences of Middlesboro, Harrogate, and Cumberland Gap by Walter E. Bryson"

University of Tennessee, University Archives, Knoxville

Presidential Papers

Magazines and Newspapers

Atlanta Constitution

Bristol Herald-Courier

Bulletin of the American Association of University Professors

Chicago Daily Tribune

Claiborne Progress

Knoxville Journal

Knoxville Journal and Tribune

Knoxville News-Sentinel

Knoxville Sentinel

Lexington Herald

Louisville Courier-Journal

Middlesboro Daily News

Morristown Gazette and Mail

Nashville Banner

National Co-Op Radio Friend

New Republic

New York Daily Tribune

New York Globe and Advertiser

New York Herald

New York Herald Tribune

New York Mail and Express Illustrated Sunday Magazine

New York Times

New York Tribune Illustrated Supplement

Saint Paul Pioneer Press

Tech

Washington Post
Washington Sunday Star

Web Sites

acaweb.org

amazon.com

bioguide.congress.gov

carleton.edu

census.gov

chemistry.emory.edu

eaglesnest.net

ellisislandrecords.org

genealogy.com

horseshoe.cc

imdb.com

Jones, James B., Jr. "Maryville College: An Early Leader in the Struggle for Biracial Education in Tennessee, 1819–1901." southernhistory.net

joshua.lurkeroo.com

libs.uga.edu

lincolncollege.edu

lincolnu.edu

lmunet.edu

politicalgraveyard.com

quickfacts.census.gov

tactileresearch.org

utk.edu

wikipedia.org

workcolleges.org

Articles, Books, Dissertations, Theses

"The 1929 Story." *Alumnus* 2, no. 10 (Dec.–Feb. 1951): 19.

Abbott, Martin, ed. "A Mountain School in Tennessee: Some Reconstruction Letters." *Tennessee Historical Quarterly* 17, no. 1 (Mar.1958): 70–73.

Achorn, Edgar O. *Major General Oliver Otis Howard.* N.p., n.d.

Allen, James Lane. "Through Cumberland Gap on Horseback." *Harper's New Monthly Magazine* 73 (June 1886): 50–66.

"American Brotherhood Keynote to Camp Fire." *Atlanta Constitution,* July 20, 1900.

"An Analysis of Our Students." *Mountain Herald* 23, no. 9 (Sept. 1919): 12.

Anderson, James D. *The Education of Blacks in the South, 1860–1935.* Chapel Hill: Univ. of North Carolina Press, 1988.

"Another Important Worker Will Be Missed." *Mountain Herald* 27, no. 1 (Jan. 1923): 2–3.

Avery, F. B. "Mr. Fairchild Helps Found University." *Blue and Gray,* Oct. 25, 1935.

Baldwin, Roger G., and Jay L. Chronister. *Teaching Without Tenure: Policies and Practices for a New Era.* Baltimore: Johns Hopkins Univ. Press, 2001.

Barnes, Harry Elmer. "Barnes on L.M.U." *Knoxville News-Sentinel,* Apr. 19, 1930.

Basler, Roy P, ed. *The Collected Works of Abraham Lincoln.* 8 vols. New Brunswick, N.J.: Rutgers Univ. Press, 1953.

Bass, Randall Vivrette. "A Study of Student Work Programs at Selected Colleges Traditionally Emphasizing Student Work." Ed.D. diss., Univ. of Georgia, 1984.

Beautiful Claiborne County Tennessee, Rich in History, Resources and Good Neighbors. New Tazewell, Tenn.: Claiborne County Kiwanis Club, 1946.

"Bishop Named Vice President." *Alumnus* 91, no. 1 (Winter 1998): 10.

Braunhut, Herman Jay. "Farm Labor Wage Rates in the South, 1909–1948." *Southern Economic Journal* 16, no. 2 (Oct. 1949): 189–96.

Brubacher, John S., and Willis Rudy. *Higher Education in Transition: A History of American Colleges and Universities, 1636–1976.* 3rd ed. New York: Harper and Row, 1976.

Bumgarner, John R. *Parade of the Dead: A U.S. Army Physician's Memoir of Imprisonment by the Japanese, 1942–1945.* Jefferson, N.C.: McFarland, 1995.

Burrage, Henry S. *Thomas Hamlin Hubbard: Bvt. Brigadier General U.S. Vols.* Portland, Maine: n.p., 1923.

Campbell, John C. *The Southern Highlander and His Homeland.* Lexington: Univ. Press of Kentucky, 1969.

Campbell, W. Joseph. *The Year that Defined American Journalism: 1897 and the Clash of Paradigms.* New York: Routledge, 2006.

Carpenter, John A. "Architects and Builders of a Living Memorial." *Lincoln Herald* 59, no. 1 (Spring 1957): 6–13.

———. *Sword and Olive Branch: Oliver Otis Howard.* Pittsburgh: Univ. of Pittsburgh Press, 1964.

Carter, Roland D. "The Frame of the Picture." *Alumnus* 2, no. 4 (Dec. 1948–Feb. 1949): 8–9.

Carter, Ross S. *Those Devils in Baggy Pants.* Cutchogue, N.Y.: Buccaneer Books, 1976.

Celebration of Lincoln's Birthday and of the Twentieth Anniversary of the Founding of Lincoln Memorial University, Cumberland Gap, Tennessee, February 10, 11, 12, 1917. N.p.: n.p., n.d.

Chait, Richard P. "Does Faculty Governance Differ at Colleges with Tenure and Colleges Without Tenure?" In *Questions of Tenure,* edited by Richard P. Chait, 69–100. Cambridge: Harvard Univ. Press, 2002.

———. "Why Tenure? Why Now?" In *Questions of Tenure,* edited by Richard P. Chait, 6–31. Cambridge: Harvard Univ. Press, 2002.

Chandler, Stephen D. "Cleaning House: The U.T. Faculty Firings of 1923." Master's thesis, Univ. of Tennessee, Knoxville, 1998.

Clarke, Ida Clyde. "The Living Memorial to Abraham Lincoln." *Pictorial Review* (Feb. 1923): 20–21, 76, 78.

"Class Notes." *Alumnus* 17, no. 1 (Nov. 1966): 9–11.

"The Clubs Report." *Alumnus* 5, no. 1 (Spring 1954): 9–10.

Coulter, E. Merton. "Parson Brownlow's Tour of the North During the Civil War." *East Tennessee Historical Society Papers* 7 (1935): 3–27.

County and City Data Book, 1967: A Statistical Abstract Supplement. Washington, D.C.: Government Printing Office, 1967.

Dawson, George Francis. *Life and Services of Gen. John A. Logan as Soldier and Statesman.* Chicago: Belford, Clarke, 1887.

"Dedication of the Bronze Statue 'Lincoln the Lawyer.'" *Lincoln Herald* 51, no. 2 (June 1949): 2–17.

Dickey, Ouida, and Doyle Mathis. *Berry College: A History.* Athens: Univ. of Georgia Press, 2005.

Dickson, John L, ed. *Lincoln Memorial University.* Harrogate, Tenn.: Lincoln Memorial Univ., 1928.

Diller, Elliott Van Nostrand. "Concept of Feeling in the Religious Philosophy of Schleiermacher." Ph.D. diss., Harvard Univ., 1934.

Dodge, Grenville M. *Personal Recollections of President Abraham Lincoln, General Ulysses S. Grant, and General William T. Sherman.* Denver: Sage Books, 1965.

Donald, David Herbert. *Lincoln.* New York: Simon and Schuster, 1995.

Donham, Dennis E., and Les E. Stege. "Grants, Loans, and Scholarships." In *Money, Marbles, or Chalk,* edited by Roland Keene, Frank C. Adams, and John E. King, 67–79. Carbondale: Southern Illinois Univ. Press, 1975.

"Dr. Hervin U. Roop, Dean." *Mountain Herald* 31, no. 5 (Autumn 1928): 15.

"Dr. H. Lamarr Rice, the President of L.M.U." *Alumnus* 15, no. 1 (Oct. 1964): 1.

"Dr. Rice Speaks to the Alumni." *Alumnus* 15, no. 1 (Oct. 1964): 1–2.

"Dr. Stewart W. McClelland, President." *Mountain Herald* [33, no. 12] (Dec. 1932): 3.

Eckert, Ralph Lowell. *John Brown Gordon: Soldier, Southerner, American.* Baton Rouge: Louisiana State Univ. Press, 1989.

Eller, Ronald D. *Miners, Millhands, and Mountaineers: Industrialization of the Appalachian South, 1880–1930.* Knoxville: Univ. of Tennessee Press, 1995.

"Enlistments from L.M.U." *Mountain Herald* 20, no. 9 (Sept. 1917): 5–7.

Ensor, Allison R. "The House United: Mark Twain and Henry Watterson Celebrate Lincoln's Birthday, 1901." *South Atlantic Quarterly* 74 (Spring 1975): 259–68.

———. "Lincoln, Mark Twain, and Lincoln Memorial University." *Lincoln Herald* 78, no. 2 (Summer 1976): 43–51.

Evans, Estle. *Autobiography of Estle Evans.* Jacksboro, Tenn.: Action Printing, 1990.

"First LMU Graduate, G. W. Morton, Dies." *Alumnus* 18, no. 3 (Spring 1968): 11–12.

"Former LMU President Passes Away." *Alumnus* 91, no. 1 (Winter 1998): 25.

Fosdick, Raymond B. *Adventure in Giving: The Story of the General Education Board.* New York: Harper and Row, 1962.

Francis Randolph Curtis Demonstration Farm, Lincoln Memorial University. N.p: n.p., n.d.

Frazier, D. R., comp. *Tennessee Post Offices and Post Master Appointments, 1789–1984.* N.p.: n.p., 1984.

Frost, William Goodell. *For the Mountains: An Autobiography.* New York: Fleming H. Revell, 1937.

Gaventa, John. *Power and Powerlessness: Quiescence and Rebellion in an Appalachian Valley.* Urbana: Univ. of Illinois Press, 1982.

The General Education Board: An Account of Its Activities, 1902–1914. New York: General Education Board, 1915.

General Education Board: Report of the Secretary, 1915–1916. New York: General Education Board, n.d.

"General Howard Remembered." *Lincoln Herald* 41, no. 7 (Oct. 1939): 12.

"General Howard's Birthday." *Mountain Herald* 15, no. 11 (Nov. 1912): 1.

"General Howard's Birthday." *Mountain Herald* 20, no. 11 (Nov. 1917): 11–12.

"General Howard Talks of Battle of Atlanta." *Atlanta Constitution,* July 22, 1902.

Godzicki, Ralph. "A History of Financial Aids in the United States." In *Money, Marbles, or Chalk,* edited by Roland Keene, Frank C. Adams, and John E. King, 14–21. Carbondale: Southern Illinois Univ. Press, 1975.

Graf, Leroy P., and Ralph W. Haskins, eds. *The Papers of Andrew Johnson.* 16 vols. Knoxville: Univ. of Tennessee Press, 1967–2001.

Grannis, Mrs. Frank. "Revival of Mountain Weaving." *Mountain Herald* 28, nos. 8–9 (Aug.–Sept. 1925): 4.

Grant, Ulysses S. *Personal Memoirs of U.S. Grant.* New York: Viking, 1990.

"Greetings Received from G. W. Morton, '06." *Alumnus* 2, no. 10 (Dec.–Feb. 1951): 11.

Groce, W. Todd. *Mountain Rebels: East Tennessee Confederates and the Civil War, 1860–1870.* Knoxville: Univ. of Tennessee Press, 1999.

Gutman, Richard J. S. "Three Outstanding 'Abes': Lincoln's Image in the Cinema, Part II, 1931–1977." *Lincoln Herald* 80, no. 3 (Fall 1978): 122–32.

Hammond, John Hays. "Lincoln Memorial University at Cumberland Gap Educates the Sturdy Mountain People from Whom Abraham Lincoln Sprang." *New York Times,* Feb. 21, 1926.

Harlan, Louis R., ed. *The Booker T. Washington Papers.* 14 vols. Urbana: Univ. of Illinois Press, 1972–89.

"Harrow School Fathers Great Lincoln Memorial." *Claiborne Progress,* July 20, 1932.

Harwell, Richard, and Philip N. Racine, eds. *The Fiery Trail: A Union Officer's Account of Sherman's Last Campaigns.* Knoxville: Univ. of Tennessee Press, 1986.

Haskin, Frederic J. "New Lincolns from the Old Mold." *Washington Sunday Star,* Sept. 28, 1941.

Henard, Martha. "Dr. R. C. Provine Assumes LMU Presidency." *Lincoln Herald* 60, no. 2 (Summer 1958): 46.

Herbert, Walter H. *Fighting Joe Hooker.* Indianapolis: Bobbs-Merrill, 1944.

Hess, Earl J. "Belgians Remember Downed Pilot from LMU." *Alumnus* 96, no. 2 (Summer–Fall 2002): 16–17.

"Higher Rating Given Lincoln Memorial University." *Mountain Herald* 30, no. 10 (Jan. 1928): 7.

Hill, John Wesley. *Abraham Lincoln: Man of God.* 2nd rev. and enl. ed. New York: G. P. Putnam's Sons, 1927.

———. *"Democracy versus Autocracy" and Other Patriotic Addresses.* Harrogate, Tenn.: Lincoln Memorial Univ., 1917.

———. *If Lincoln Were Here.* New York: G. P. Putnam's Sons, 1925.

———. *Lincoln the Inspired Leader.* Washington, D.C.: Lincoln League, n.d.

———. *The Story of Lincoln Memorial University.* Boston: Chapple Press, n.d.

History of LaSalle County, Illinois. 2 vols. Chicago: Inter-State Publishing, 1886.

Holloway, Laura C. *Howard: The Christian Hero.* New York: Funk and Wagnalls, 1885.

Holt, Edgar A. *Claiborne County.* Memphis, Tenn.: Memphis State Univ. Press, 1981.

Holt, Vada. "History of the Class." *Mountain Herald,* June 1933, 13–14.

"Honor to Gen. W. H. T. Walker." *Confederate Veteran* 10 (1902): 402–7.

Howard, Oliver Otis. *Autobiography.* 2 vols. New York: Baker and Taylor, 1907.

———. "The Character of Abraham Lincoln." *Lincoln Herald* 59, no. 4 (Winter 1957–58): 3–11.

———. "The Eleventh Corps at Chancellorsville." In *Battles and Leaders of the Civil War,* vol. 3, edited by Robert Underwood Johnson and Clarence Clough Buel, 189–202. New York: Thomas Yoseloff, 1956.

———. "The Folk of the Cumberland Gap." *Munsey's Magazine* 27 (July 1902): 506–8.

———. "Lincoln's Monument in the Mountains." *National Magazine* 22 (June 1905): 299–304.

———. "The Negro as a Free Man." *Alexander's Magazine* 6 (Sept. 15, 1908): 206.

———. "Personal Recollections of Abraham Lincoln." *Century* 75 (1908): 873–77.

———. "Some Reminiscences of Abraham Lincoln." *Lincoln Herald* 55, no. 3 (Fall 1953): 20–22.

———. "The Struggle for Atlanta." In *Battles and Leaders of the Civil War,* vol. 4, edited by Robert Underwood Johnson and Clarence Clough Buel, 293–325. New York: Thomas Yoseloff, 1956.

Hutcheson, Philo A. *A Professional Professoriate: Unionization, Bureaucratization, and the AAUP.* Nashville: Vanderbilt Univ. Press, 2000.

Kansas: A Cyclopedia of State History. 3 vols. Chicago: Standard Publishing, 1912.

Kennedy, Joseph C. G. *Agriculture of the United States in 1860.* Washington, D.C.: Government Printing Office, 1864.

Kincaid, Robert L. *Abraham Lincoln: Miracle of Democracy. Historical Bulletin* 18. N.p.: Lincoln Fellowship of Wisconsin, 1960.

———. *Abraham Lincoln: The Speaker.* N.p.: n.p, n.d.

———. *The Ageless Lincoln: Lincoln Day Address on "The Worth of Personal Effort."* Harrogate, Tenn.: Lincoln Memorial Univ., [1950].

———. *Boy Finds a College.* Harrogate, Tenn.: Robert L. Kincaid, 1955.

———. *Boy Finds a Friend.* Harrogate, Tenn.: Robert L. Kincaid, 1956.

———. "A Confederate Veteran's Tribute to Abraham Lincoln." *Lincoln Herald* 57, no. 3 (Fall 1955): 20–24.

———. "Crossing the Great Wilderness." *Lincoln Herald* 47, no. 2 (June 1945): 58–69.

———. "Distinguished Career of an Early L.M.U. Graduate." *Alumnus* 5, no. 1 (Spring 1954): 8–9.

———. "George Allen Hubbell." *Alumnus* 4, no. 1 (Winter 1953): 4–5, 22.

———. "Jesse Stuart Bares His Soul." *Lincoln Herald* 40, no. 3 (July 1938): 19–20.

———. "Last of the Founders." *Lincoln Herald* 44, no. 3–4 (Dec. 1942): 27–29.

———. "Lincoln Fights Again for Liberty." *Exchangite* 22, no. 2 (Mar. 1943): 4–5.

———. *The Lincoln Heritage in the Cumberlands.* Los Angeles: Institute Press, 1951.

———. "Lincoln Memorial University, Harrogate, Tennessee." In *Educational Opportunities in the Appalachian Mountains,* edited by W. D. Weatherford, 21–27. Berea, Ky.: Berea College, 1955.

———. "Lincoln Memorial University of the Future." *Lincoln Herald* 59, no. 1 (Spring 1957): 24–26.

———. "Lincoln Pilgrimage and Celebration." *Lincoln Herald* 52, no. 3 (Oct. 1950): 5–19, 43.

———. *Lincoln's Faith: The Hope of Our Time.* N.p.: n.p., 1951.

———. "A Living Lincoln." *Lincoln Herald* 57, no. 3 (Fall 1955): 12–19.

———. "Mountain Youths Trained for National Leadership." *Knoxville Journal,* Feb. 12, 1932.

———. "A Ride with Hoover." *Lincoln Herald* 41, no. 4 (July 1939): 12–13.

———. *School Days at Bethlehem.* Harrogate, Tenn.: Robert L. Kincaid, 1952.

———. "The Shadow of a Man." *Lincoln Herald* 47, no. 1 (Feb. 1945): 41–48.

———. "The Story of Avery Hall." *Alumnus* 4, no. 1 (Winter 1953): 6, 21.

———. *The Wilderness Road.* 5th ed. Middlesboro, Ky.: n.p., 1992.

Klotter, James C. "The Black South and White Appalachia." *Journal of American History* 66, no. 4 (Mar. 1980): 832–49.

"Leonard Gardner—Globe Trotter." *Alumnus* 2, no. 4 (Dec. 1948–Feb. 1949): 20–22.

"Letter from Mr. Robert Todd Lincoln." *Mountain Herald* 20, no. 3 (Mar. 1917): 6–7.

Levine, David O. *The American College and the Culture of Aspiration, 1915–1940.* Ithaca, N.Y.: Cornell Univ. Press, 1986.

Lewis, Lloyd. *Myths After Lincoln.* New York: Harcourt Brace, 1929.

"The Lincoln Memorial Hospital." *Mountain Herald* 20, no. 12 (Dec. 1917): 3, 5.

"Lincoln Memorial's First President Dead." *Mountain Herald* 23, no. 9 (Sept. 1919): 9–10.

"Lincoln Memorial University." *Bulletin of the American Association of University Professors* 17, no. 5 (May 1931): 409–13.

"Lincoln Memorial University." *Exchangite,* July 1941, 7.

"Lincoln's Map of Cumberland Gap Region." *Lincoln Herald* 59, no. 1 (Spring 1957): 18.

Lindstrom, Andrew, and Olive Carruthers. *Lincoln: The Namesake College.* Lincoln, Ill.: n.p., 1965.

The Living Memorial to Lincoln. N.p.: n.p., n.d.

"LMU's New President: The Challenge and the Charge." *Alumnus* 96, no. 1 (Winter 2002): 4–6.

Longstreth, William Stacy. "Lamps in the Mountains: American Liberal Arts Colleges with On-Campus Mandatory Work Programs." Ph.D. diss., Claremont Graduate School, 1990.

Low, W. Augustus, ed. *Encyclopedia of Black America.* New York: McGraw-Hill, 1981.

Lowrie, S. Gale. "The Proper Function of the State Budget." *Annals of the American Academy of Political and Social Science* 62, no. 1 (1915): 47–63.

Lycan, Gilbert L. *Mountaineers Are Free.* Stone Mountain, Ga.: Linton Day, 1994.

Mallon, William T. "Why Is Tenure One College's Problem and Another's Solution?" In *Questions of Tenure,* edited by Richard P. Chait, 246–72. Cambridge: Harvard Univ. Press, 2002.

Manier, Camilla. "On Going Back." *Alumnus* 2, no. 10 (Dec. 1950–Feb. 1951): 16.

Marcel, Daniel L. "Phase I Archaeological Survey of Lincoln Memorial University." Archaeological Research Laboratory, Univ. of Tennessee, Mar. 2006.

"Massey at L.M.U." *Lincoln Herald* 41, no. 4 (July 1939): 14–15.

McCordock, R. Stanley. *Lincoln Memorial University: A Brief History.* N.p.: n.p., n.d.

McFeely, William S. *Yankee Stepfather: General O. O. Howard and the Freedmen.* New Haven, Conn.: Yale Univ. Press, 1968.

McKenzie, Robert Tracy. "'Oh! Ours Is a Deplorable Condition': The Economic Impact of the Civil War in Upper East Tennessee." In *The Civil War in Appalachia: Collected Essays,* edited by Kenneth W. Noe and Shannon H. Wilson, 199–226. Knoxville: Univ. of Tennessee Press, 1997.

McMurtry, R. Gerald. *The Department of Lincolniana.* Harrogate, Tenn.: Lincoln Memorial Univ., 1939.

———. "Dr. Stewart W. McClelland, 1891–1977." *Lincoln Herald* 79, no. 1 (Spring 1977): 32–33.

———. "They Are Loyal There." *Lincoln Herald* 40, no. 2. (Feb. 1938): 7–9.

Miles, Emma Bell. *The Spirit of the Mountains.* Knoxville: Univ. of Tennessee Press, 1977.

Miller, Merlin G. "The Democratic Theory of Cooperation." *Annals of the American Academy of Political and Social Science* 191 (May 1937): 29–37.

Montgomery, James Riley, Stanley J. Folmsbee, and Lee Seifert Greene. *To Foster Knowledge: A History of the University of Tennessee, 1794–1970.* Knoxville: Univ. of Tennessee Press, 1984.

"Mr. and Mrs. Henry Ford Entertain." *Mountain Herald* 29, no. 10 (Dec. 1926): 10–11.

Myers, Mrs. A. A. "Mountain White Work in Kentucky." *American Missionary* 38, no. 1 (Jan.1884): 12–16.

National Cyclopaedia of American Biography. 63 vols. Clifton, N.J.: James T. White, 1967–84.

Nelson, Paul David. "Experiment in Inter-racial Education at Berea College, 1858–1908." *Journal of Negro History* 59, no. 1 (Jan. 1974): 13–27.

Nichols, George Ward. *The Story of the Great March.* New York: Harper and Brothers, 1865.

"No Civil War Bitterness at L.M.U." *Lincoln Herald* 40, no. 2 (Feb. 1938): 19.

Nuhrah, Arthur G. "Dr. & Mrs. Robert C. Provine: *In Memoriam.*" *Lincoln Herald* 69, no. 1 (Spring 1967): 40–41.

Nwachuku, Levi A. "Lincoln University." In *Encyclopedia of African-American Culture and History,* vol. 3, edited by Jack Salzman, David Lionel Smith, and Cornel West, 1618–20. New York: Simon and Schuster.

Ogren, Christine A. *The American State Normal School: "An Instrument of Great Good."* New York: Palgrave Macmillan, 2005.

"The Old Professor." *Lincoln Herald* 41, no. 3 (May 1939): 12–13.

Olson, Keith W. *The G. I. Bill, the Veterans, and the Colleges.* Lexington: Univ. Press of Kentucky, 1974.

Orr, Bill M. "A History of Tennessee Medical College, 1889–1914." Master's thesis, Univ. of Tennessee, 1960.

"Our Distinguished Guests." *Lincoln Herald* 42, no. 2 (Feb. 1940): 8–9.

"Our Motion Picture Meeting with Success." *Mountain Herald* 26, no. 6–7 (June–July 1922): 3–4.

"Our Past Presidents." *Alumnus* 2, no. 7 (Dec. 1949–Feb. 1950): 4, and 2, no. 8 (May 1950): 10.

Page, Bonnie, and Cindy Stephenson, eds. *Lincoln Memorial University (Memories and More).* N.p.: Printone, 2001.

Paine, Albert Bigelow, ed. *Mark Twain's Letters.* 2 vols. New York: Harper & Brothers, 1917.

———. *Mark Twain's Speeches.* New York: Harper & Brothers, 1923.

"Paolo, Noted Lincoln Sculptor." *Lincoln Herald* 58, no. 3 (Fall 1956): 19.

Parker, Alma Inman. "In Memory of Abraham Lincoln This Page Is Humbly Dedicated." *Knoxville Journal,* Feb. 12, 1932.

Partin, Kathy. "Being President Won't Alter Burchett's Style!" *Alumnus* 73, no. 2 (Summer 1982): 6–7.

"The Passing of a Founder of Lincoln Memorial University." *Mountain Herald* 27, no. 1 (Jan. 1923): 1–2.

Peck, Elisabeth S., and Emily Ann Smith. *Berea's First 125 Years, 1855–1980.* Lexington: Univ. Press of Kentucky, 1982.

Pepper, George W. *Personal Recollections of Sherman's Campaigns in Georgia and the Carolinas.* Zanesville, Ohio: Hugh Dunne, 1866.

Peterson, Merrill. *Lincoln in American Memory.* New York: Oxford Univ. Press, 1994.

Petz, Weldon. *In the Presence of Abraham Lincoln.* Harrogate, Tenn.: Lincoln Memorial Univ., 1973.

Planck, Gary R. "The Inspiration and the Inspired." *Lincoln Herald* 94, no. 4 (Winter 1992): 159.

"President Coolidge's Letter." *Mountain Herald* 27, no. 11 (Nov. 1923): frontispiece.

"President Harding's Last Tribute to Lincoln Memorial University." *Mountain Herald* 27, no. 9 (Sept. 1923): 2–3.

"Proceedings of the American Philosophical Association, 1934." *Philosophical Review* 44, no. 2 (Mar. 1935): 154–81.

Ramsey, Helen Anderson. "Reminiscing." *Alumnus,* Feb. 1958, 2.

Riesman, David. *Constraint and Variety in American Education.* Garden City, N.Y.: Doubleday Anchor Books, 1958.

"Robert Orville Matthews." *Alumnus* 2, no. 6 (Aug. 1949): 17.

Roberts, Charles Blanton. "The Building of Middlesborough—A Notable Epoch in Eastern Kentucky History." *Filson Club History Quarterly* 7, no. 1 (Jan. 1933): 18–33.

Roberts, Gerald F. "The Lincoln Collection of Berea College." *Lincoln Herald* 93, no. 1 (Spring 1991): 3–4.

Roberts, Jon H. "Conservative Evangelicals and Science Education in American Colleges and Universities, 1890–1940." *Journal of the Historical Society* 3 (Fall 2005): 297–329.

Robinson, Bonnie Tom. "Abe Lincoln Film Premiere Draws Host of Notables to Namesake University." *Knoxville News-Sentinel,* Jan. 28, 1940.

———. "'Lincoln' Steals Show from 31st President as They Meet First Time." *Knoxville News-Sentinel,* June 5, 1939.

Roop, Hervin U. "The Issue of Modernism in Colleges and Universities." *Christian Fundamentalist* 1 (Sept. 1927): 6–11.

———. "What Is Education?" *Education* 51, no. 5 (Jan. 1931): 281–86.

Rudolph, Frederick. *The American College and University: A History.* New York: Alfred A. Knopf, 1962.

Schurz, Carl. *The Reminiscences of Carl Schurz.* 2 vols. New York: McClure, 1907.

"Scott D. Miller: LMU's 16th President." *Alumnus* 83, no. 2 (Summer 1992): 2.

Shapiro, Henry D. *Appalachia on Our Mind: The Southern Mountains and Mountaineers in the American Consciousness, 1870–1920.* Chapel Hill: Univ. of North Carolina Press, 1978.

Sherwood, Robert Emmet. *Abe Lincoln in Illinois: A Play in Twelve Scenes.* New York: Charles Scribner's Sons, 1939.

Shipherd, H. Robinson. *Christianity at Stake.* Andover-Harvard Theological Pamphlet, vol. 378.

———. *A Story of a Bookman: A Biographical Essay.* New York: Exposition Press, 1955.

Shumate, Mildred. *A Brief History of Lincoln Memorial University.* Kingsport, Tenn.: Franklin, n.d.

"A Significant Commencement." *Lincoln Herald* 41, no. 4 (July 1939): 1–11.

Simon, John Y., ed. *The Papers of Ulysses S. Grant.* 31 vols. Carbondale: Southern Illinois Univ. Press, 1967–2009.

Simpson, Brooks D., and Jean V. Berlin, eds. *Sherman's Civil War: Selected Correspondence of William T. Sherman, 1860–1865.* Chapel Hill: Univ. of North Carolina Press, 1999.

Slaughter, Sheila. "The Danger Zone: Academic Freedom and Civil Liberties." *Annals of the American Academy of Political and Social Science* 448 (Mar. 1980): 46–61.

Small, Harold A., ed. *The Road to Richmond: The Civil War Memoirs of Major Abner R. Small of the Sixteenth Maine Volunteers.* New York: Fordham Univ. Press, 2000.

Smith, Earl Hobson. *The Genesis of Lincoln Memorial University: A Play in Two Acts.* Harrogate, Tenn.: Harrogate Press, 1981.

———. *President Lincoln: A Two Hour Play in Three Acts with Three Scenes Each.* Harrogate, Tenn.: Lincoln Book, 1940.

"Some Items in the Development of the University." *Mountain Herald* 26, nos. 6–7 (June–July 1922): 1–2.

Stallard, Bernard. "'Those Devils in Baggy Pants' to Become Movie." *Alumnus* 35, no. 4 (Spring 1985): 28.

"The Stone Gate-Way Dedicated." *Mountain Herald* 18, no. 5 (May 1915): 6.

Stooksbury, William L. "The Race that Will Predominate." *Treasury* 22, no. 11 (Mar. 1905): 815–17.

"Story of a Building." *Lincoln Herald* 42, no. 3 (Oct. 1940): 13–21.

Suppiger, Joseph E. "The Official Opening of the Abraham Lincoln Library and Museum." *Lincoln Herald* 79, no. 2 (Summer 1977): 47–52.

———. *Phoenix of the Mountains: The Story of Lincoln Memorial University.* 3rd ed. Harrogate, Tenn.: Lincoln Memorial Univ. Press, 2001.

Supplement to the Official Records of the Union and Confederate Armies. 100 vols. Wilmington, N.C.: Broadfoot, 1993–2000.

Taylor, William E. "And So History Repeats." *Lincoln Herald* 59, no. 1 (Spring 1957): 3–5.

———. "The Lincoln Collection." *Lincoln Herald* 59, no. 1 (Spring 1957): 27–31.

Temple, Wayne C. "Lincoln Diploma to McClelland." *Lincoln Herald* 66, no. 2 (Summer 1964): 87–88.

———. "Robert Lee Kincaid." *Lincoln Herald* 62, no. 4 (Winter 1960): 166–69.

Thelin, John R. *A History of American Higher Education.* Baltimore: Johns Hopkins Univ. Press, 2004.

"Theodore Roosevelt Commends." *Mountain Herald* 30, no. 11 (Feb. 1928): 27–29.

Tributes and Testimony to Abraham Lincoln and His Living Memorial on the Occasion of a Lincoln Day Dinner, February 12, 1931, Washington, D.C. Cumberland Gap, Tenn.: Lincoln Memorial Univ., 1931.

U.S. Bureau of the Census. *Twelfth Census of the United States, Taken in the Year 1900: Population, Part 1.* Washington, D.C.: United States Census Office, 1901.

Veysey, Laurence R. *The Emergence of the American University.* Chicago: Univ. of Chicago Press, 1965.

Wall, Joseph Frazier. *Henry Watterson: Reconstructed Rebel.* New York: Oxford Univ. Press, 1956.

"Wanted: An Opportunity for Girls." *Mountain Herald* 29, no. 7 (Aug.–Sept. 1926): 7–8.

Warner, Charles Dudley. "Comments on Kentucky." *Harpers New Monthly Magazine* 78, no. 464 (Jan. 1889): 255–71.

The War of the Rebellion: A Compilation of the Official Records of the Union and Confederate Armies. 70 vols. in 128. Washington, D.C.: Government Printing Office, 1880–1901.

Welch, Frank W. "Lincoln and Current American Higher Education." *Lincoln Herald* 75, no. 2 (Summer 1973): 65, 75.

———. "Why Does Any Private College Deserve Support?" *Lincoln Herald* 80, no. 3 (Fall 1978): 114, 156.

Whiteside, Paul E. "What LMU Means to Me!" *Alumnus* 1, no. 11 (Feb. 1947): 11, 20.

Who Was Who in America. 16 vols. Chicago: A. N. Marquis, 1943–2004.

Who Was Who in American Art, 1564–1975. 3 vols. Madison, Conn.: Sound View Press, 2001.

Wilson, Shannon H. *Berea College: An Illustrated History.* Lexington: Univ. Press of Kentucky, 2006.

———. "Lincoln's Sons and Daughters: Berea College, Lincoln Memorial University, and the Myth of Unionist Appalachia, 1866–1910." In *The Civil War in Appalachia: Collected Essays,* edited by Kenneth W. Noe and Shannon H. Wilson, 242–64. Knoxville: Univ. of Tennessee Press, 1997.

———. "Window on the Mountains: Berea's Appalachia, 1870–1930." *Filson Club History Quarterly* 64, no. 3 (July 1990): 384–400.

"A Wonderful Ride." *Confederate Veteran* 24 (1916): 28.

Woodbridge, Hensley C., comp. *Jesse Stuart: A Bibliography.* Harrogate, Tenn.: Lincoln Memorial Univ. Press, 1960.

Index